# ASIA'S COMPUTER CHALLENGE

# ASIA'S COMPUTER CHALLENGE

## Threat or Opportunity for the United States & the World?

Jason Dedrick
Kenneth L. Kraemer

New York · Oxford
Oxford University Press
1998

Oxford University Press

Oxford   New York
Athens   Auckland   Bangkok   Bogotá   Buenos Aires   Calcutta
Cape Town   Chennai   Dar es Salaam   Delhi   Florence   Hong Kong   Istanbul
Karachi   Kuala Lumpur   Madrid   Melbourne   Mexico City   Mumbai
Nairobi   Paris   São Paulo   Singapore   Taipei   Tokyo   Toronto   Warsaw

and associated companies in
Berlin   Ibadan

Published by Oxford University Press, Inc.
198 Madison Avenue, New York, New York 10016

Oxford is a registered trademark of Oxford University Press

Library of Congress Cataloging-in-Publication Data
Jason Dedrick.
Asia's computer challenge : threat or opportunity for the
United States and the world? / Jason Dedrick and Kenneth L. Kraemer.
p.   cm.
Includes bibliographical references and index.
ISBN 0-19-512201-1
1. Computer industry—East Asia.    2. Computer industry—Japan.
3. Computer industry—United States.    4. Competition, International.
I. Kraemer, Kenneth L.    II. Title.
HD9696.2.E182D43   1998
338.4'7004'095—dc21        98-19114

9 8 7 6 5 4 3 2 1
Printed in the United States of America
on acid-free paper

# Preface and Acknowledgments

This book examines the rapid rise of computer industries in the Asia-Pacific region, identifies the key factors explaining their different levels of success, and draws out the implications for the United States and Asia-Pacific countries as they compete in computers in the emerging network era. The book focuses on Japan's development of a computer industry beginning with mainframes in the seventies, and the development of PC-based computer industries in Hong Kong, Korea, Singapore, and Taiwan in the eighties. At a broader level, the book traces the evolution of the computer industry from a country- and company-based enterprise to a global industry involving complex, dynamic relationships between companies and countries.

The genesis of this book was the debate in the early nineties concerning the relative merits of plan versus market approaches to economic development. We were persuaded—by key works such as Chalmers Johnson's *MITI and the Japanese Miracle*, Alive Amsden's *Asia's New Giant* on Korea, Robert Wade's *Governing the Market* on East Asia industrialization, and Marie Anchordoguy's *Computers Inc.* on Japan's mainframe computer industry—that government policy played a critical role in East Asia's rapid economic growth. We also were intrigued, though less convinced, by the views of political economists who challenged these new views with neoclassical economic explanations for East Asia's postwar growth (World Bank, *The East Asian Miracle*). We felt that systematic comparison of the historical development of the computer industries in these five countries would provide a solid basis for examining the relative influence of government policy and market forces.

We discovered that the plan versus market, or country versus company, dichotomy was useful in focusing the analysis but provided insufficient explanation for the differences observed. We identified a new force that came to bear on developments in the computer industry during the PC era, a factor that was not incorporated in previous explanations. This new force was the emergence of a "global production network" that operated more or less independently of company or country boundaries and was based on a changing international division of labor. How well individual companies did in this context was determined by how well they were integrated into this global production network. How well different countries did was determined by the capabilities of their companies, the portfolio of companies in their computer industries, and the extent to which their governments acted to provide opportunities and remove barriers to domestic participation in the global production network. Together, these forces created path dependencies that influenced the development trajectory of individual companies and countries.

In explaining company and country success, we used Brian Arthur's concepts of increasing returns and path dependency as analytic tools. The concept of increasing returns is that higher levels of production could result in lower costs and higher returns to producers; this concept is significant because neoclassical economists had built their growth explanations in the postwar period on the notion that there must be diminishing returns to scale on the margin. The notion of path dependency is that in many market competitions there is a tendency for that which is ahead to get further ahead and that which is behind to get further behind. In applying these concepts to the computer industry, we found that diminishing returns apply to bulk processing of commodity products, mainly in the hardware segments such as components, peripherals, and systems. This explains the hypercompetition that is found among hardware companies in the industry, and among the hardware-dominant producer countries of East Asia. In contrast, we found that increasing returns are more likely in the knowledge-based segments of the industry like software, information, and services, where control of product architectures leads to winner-take-all outcomes, and where the United States leads. We show that this analysis applies equally to the network era of computing, and that the challenge facing East Asia is to make the move from diminishing returns hardware businesses to the increasing returns software and information businesses of the future. The challenge for the United States is to maintain its leadership in standards, design, marketing, and business innovation.

As with any research project extending over many years, we are indebted to a great many institutions and individuals for support and assistance. First, we acknowledge that this book supported by grants from the Computer, Information Systems, and Engineering (CISE) Division of the U.S. National Science Foundation; the Pacific Rim Research Program of the University of California; the IBM World Trade Corporation for Asia Pacific; the National University of Singapore; and the Sloan Foundation. We would not have been able to undertake such an ambitious research program or complete the extensive visits to countries and personal interviews without their generous support. However, neither these institutions nor the individuals we acknowledge here are responsible for any views, omissions, or commissions that might exist in this book.

Second, we thank particular individuals and institutions that provided the valuable data for systematic comparison among the five countries in the study and those in the broader Asia-Pacific region. We are especially grateful to Dr.

Donald Bellomy and Mr. Kevin Hause, International Data Corporation; Ms. Joanne Guiniven, McKinsey & Company; Ms. Cathy Legge, Computer Intelligence; Dr. David Kahaner, Asia Technology Information Program (ATIP) in Japan; Dr. T. C. Tu and Mr. Chin-Yeong Hwang, Market Intelligence Center, Institute for the Information Industry, Taiwan; Mr. Capers Jones; Mr. Loh Chee Meng, National Computer Board, Singapore; Mr. Frederick Ho, Hong Kong Census and Statistics Department; Electronic Industry Association of Korea; Japan Electronic Industry Development Association; and the Japan Information Processing Development Center.

Third, we are grateful to Professor David Yoffie, Harvard University; Mr. Paul Seever, Global Business Opportunities; Mr. Peter Schavoir, IBM retired; Mr. Joel West, University of California, Irvine; and the anonymous reviewers at Oxford University Press for their review and comment on the entire book manuscript. Also appreciated are the reviews of individual chapters by Dr. Tain-Jy Chen, Professor Franklin Fisher, Dr. Sung-Gul Hong, Dr. Kuk-Hwan Jeong, Mr. Barry Lennon, Ms. Yu-Ping Liu, Mr. James McKie, Mr. Charles Morris, Dr. Mirek Stevenson, Mr. Seong-Taek Park, and Dr. Dennis Tachiki.

Fourth, we wish to thank the more than 600 individuals whom we interviewed in conducting the research over the past seven years and from whom we gained important insights. Although we appreciate the assistance of everyone, we mention here those who participated in multiple and/or unusually extended interviews. In Hong Kong, we thank, from ABC Data and Telecom Limited, Mr. Anthony Au; from Asia IT Business Consultancy Ltd., Mr. Colin Greenfield; from Hong Kong Air Cargo Terminals Ltd., Mr. Kwok Keung Yeung; from Hong Kong Government Census & Statistics Department, Mr. Dominic Leung, Ms. Karen Chan, Mr. Joseph Wong, and Mr. Frederick Ho; from Hong Kong Government Industry Department, Mr. K. S. Chiang, and Ms. Annie Choi; from Hong Kong Industrial Technology Centre Corp., Mr. Vincent Wong, Mr. James Liu, and Dr. Peter T. C. Yeung; from IBM Greater China Group, Mr. Richmond Lo, Mr. Tony Tai, Ms. Chelsia Kwan, and Mr. Luis Rodriguez; from IDG Communications Ltd., Ms. Anna Foley; from Information Technology Services Department (DTIS), Hong Kong Government, Mr. K. H. Lau; from Intel Semiconductor Ltd., Asia Pacific, Mr. Stephen Chan and Mr. Eric Cheng; from Legend Holdings Ltd., Mr. Michael Ng; from Office of the Telecommunications Authority, Mr. Anthony S. K. Wong; from Rascoe Development Ltd., Mr. Glen Rasmussen; from *The Economist* Intelligence Unit, Mr. Simon Cartledge; and from The Hong Kong University of Science & Technology, Professor Kar Yan Tam.

In Japan, we thank, from Asian Technology Information Program, Dr. David Kahaner and Mr. Jesse Casman; from AT&T Japan Ltd., Mr. Glen Fukushima; from CAC, Inc., Mr. Scott Nash; from Center for Global Communications, Dr. Stephen Anderson and Mr. Izumi Aizu; from Computing Japan, Mr. William Auckerman; from the Embassy of the United States of America, Mr. Edward Lincoln; from Fujitsu Laboratories Ltd., Mr. Hiromu Hayashi, Dr. Kaneyuki Kurokawa, and Dr. Yukou Mochida; from Fujitsu Limited, Mr. Haruhiko Yonezu; from Fujitsu Research Institute, Dr. Masahiro

Kawahata; from Hitachi Ltd., Mr. Masayuki Kohama and Mr. Toshiaki Kata-yama; from IBM Asia Pacific Service Corporation, Mr. Hitobiashi Itoh; from IBM Japan, Ltd., Mr. Norikazu Yahagi and Mr. Takayasu Matsuzaki; from IBM World Trade Asia Corporation, Mr. Yoshiaki Kimura, Mr. Ken Richeson, Mr. Tim Sheehy, and Mr. Ed Fox; from Institute of International Manage-ment, Dr. Gene Gregory; from International University of Japan, Professor Shumpei Kumon; from IPR, Mr. Tsuruo Yanaka; from Japan Market Engi-neering, Mr. John Stern; from Keio University, Professor Youichi Ito, Dr. Sa-chio Semmoto, and Dr. Minoru Sugaya; from Merrill Lynch Tokyo, Mr. Jo-seph Osha; from Ministry of International Trade and Industry, Mr. Hirofumi Katase, Mr. Tomio Tsutsumi, and Mr. Koezuka; from Ministry of Posts and Telecommunications, Mr. Yoichi Ogasawara; from Morgan Stanley Japan Lim-ited, Dr. Scott Callon; from NEC Corporation, Dr. Yuko Mizuno, Mr. Taka-yuki Yanagawa, and Dr. Hiraku Sakuma; from Nomura Research Institute, Ltd., Mr. Yasuhiko Arai, Dr. Teruyasu Murakami, and Mr. Kiyohisa Ota; from Oracle Corporation Japan, Mr. Chikara Sano and Mr. Masaaki Shintaku; from Research Institute of Telecom-policies and Economics, Dr. Seisuke Komat-suzaki; from Sakura Institute of Research, Mr. Dennis Tachiki; from Semi-conductor Industry Association, Mr. Roger Mathus; from Soka University, Professor Yoshi Sekiguchi; from Tokyo Institute of Technology, Dr. Yoshinobu Kumata; from Toshiba Corporation, Mr. Kaoru Kubo; and from the University of Tokyo, Professor Tadao Saito, Professor Fumio Kodama, and Mr. Kenneth Pechter.

In Korea, we thank, beginning with Daewoo Telecom Limited, Mr. Jung-Tae Lee; from Hewlett-Packard Korea Ltd., Mr. Joon Keun Choi; from HG Asia Limited, Mr. Matt Cleary; from Hyundai Electronics Industries Co., Lim-ited, Mr. Y. S. Cho and Mr. Kim Young Hwan; from IBM Korea Inc., Mr. Jong Yull Kim; from International Data Corporation Korea, Mr. Byeong Je; from Jardine Fleming Securities Limited, Mr. Tony Jung; from Kookmin Uni-versity, Dr. Sung Gul Hong; from Korea Information Society Development Institute, Dr. Shin Cho, Dr. Myeong-Ho Lee, Dr. Yoo Yang, and Mr. Hee-Su Kim; from Korea Institute for Industrial Economics & Trade, Dr. Kyung Tae Lee and Dr. Seong-Taek Park; from Korea University, Professor Jae-Ho Yeom; from LG Electronics, Inc. Mr. Ki Soon Park and Dr. Kyu Chang Park; from Ministry of Communications, Mr. Chun-Koo Hahn; from Ministry of Trade, Industry & Energy, Mr. Man-Gi Paik, Dr. Yong-Won Kwon, Mr. Jae-Hyun Kim, and Mr. Young-Sick Lee; from National Computerization Agency, Dr. Kuk-Hwan Jeong, Dr. Seung Ho Lee, and Dr. Jong-Sung Sunwoo; from Na-tional Computerization Board, Dr. Eun-Ju Kim; from Samsung Data Systems Company, Ltd., Dr. Hye Keun Kwag; Samsung Electronics, Mr. D. S. Chang and Mr. Sunny Kim; from Samsung–Hewlett-Packard Co., Mr. John Toppel; from Science and Technology Policy Institute, Dr. Linsu Kim; from Texas Instruments—Korea Ltd., Mr. Thomas Sims; and from TriGem Computer, Inc., Mr. Gi Man Kim and Mr. Il Hwan Park.

In Singapore, we thank, from Apple Computer Limited, Mr. Peter Tan and Dr. Louis Woo; from *Business Times,* Dr. Kenneth James; from Compaq

Asia Pte. Ltd., Mr. K. Y. Wong; from IBM Singapore Pte. Ltd., Mr. Barry Lennon; from IPC Corporation Ltd., Mr. Patrick M. J. Ngiam; from Nanyang Technological University, Dr. Neo Boon Siong and Dr. Eddie C. Y. Kuo; from National Computer Board, Mr. Chee Meng Loh, Mr. Stephen Yeo, Mr. Swee Say Lim, Ms. Eileen S. Y. Lim, Mr. Ken Wye Saw, Mr. Chin Nam Tan, and Mr. Boon San Gan; from National Computer Systems Pte. Ltd, Mr. Kwok Cheong Lee; from National University of Singapore, Dr. K. S. Raman, Dr. Chee Sing Yap, Professor Poh-Kam Wong, and Mr. Bernard Tiong Gie Tan; from Seagate Technology International, Mr. Rod MacKinlay; from Singapore Network Services Pte. Ltd., Mr. Chan Kah Khuen; and from Western Digital, Mr. Russell Stern.

In Taiwan, we thank, from *Asia Computer Weekly*, Mr. Albert Leung; from Acer Incorporated, Mr. George Hsu; from Acer TWP Corporation, Mr. David Lee and Mr. Tze-Chen Tu; from Barings Securities Ltd., Mr. Peter Kurz and Mr. Derek Tien; from Century Development Corporation, Dr. C. N. Liu; from Chung-Hua Institution for Economic Research, Professor Tain-Jy Chen, Dr. Chin Chung, and Dr. Wen-Jeng Kuo; from Coopers and Lybrand Consultants, Mr. Hsiu-Hsian Chen and Mr. David Hoffman; from EDS Taiwan, China Management Systems Corporation, Mr. Andrew Au; from First International Computer, Inc., Mr. Ming Chien; from H&Q Taiwan Co., Ltd., Mr. Moun-Rong Lin; from IBM Taiwan Corporation, Mr. Caesar Luk; from IDC Taiwan Ltd., Mr. Arthur Tan; from Industrial Development and Investment Center, Ministry of Economic Affairs, Mr. Steven Wu; from Industrial Technology Research Institute, Dr. Yeo Lin, Dr. Fuyung Lai, and Dr. Yuan-Liang Su; from Information Service Industry Association of R.O.C., Mr. Arthur T. S. Hwa and Mr. Jessy Cheng; from Institute for Information Industry, Mr. C. J. Cherng, Mr. Chin-Yeong Hwang, Ms. Yu-Ping Liu, Mr. Michael Wang, Ms. Mina J. M. Wang, and Mr. Sam Shen; from Ministry of Economic Affairs, Dr. Ray Yang; from Mitac, Mr. C. S. Ho; from National Central University, Dr. Gee San; from Tatung Corporation, Mr. J. L. Tsay and Mr. W. S. Lin; and from The Executive Yuan, Ms. Cher-Jean Lee and Dr. Chuan-te Ho.

In the United States, we thank, from AST, Mr. Safi Qureshey and Mr. Y. S. Kim; from IDG, Mr. Saiman Hui; from JTS Corporation, Mr. David Mitchell; from Oxford University Press, Mr. Herb Addison, Lisa Stallings, and Tamara Destine; from Quantum Electronics Database Inc., Dr. Mirek Stevenson; from Toshiba America, Mr. Jerry Goetsch and Mr. Tom Scott; from University of California, Berkeley, Dr. Dieter Ernst and Dr. Michael Borrus; from University of California, San Diego, Professors Roger Bohn and Peter Gourevitch; and from the United Nations, Dr. Dae-won Choi.

Fifth, we thank the support staff at the Center for Research on Information Technology and Organizations at the University of California, Irvine, for their patience and professionalism. Dr. Deborah Dunkle organized and managed our data; Debra Stolinsky arranged the many interviews on our long trips abroad and patiently formatted the final manuscript, as did Natalie Matlock with earlier trips and earlier versions of chapters; Terri Pouliot, Sandy Wojciechowski, and Julie Takahashi provided excellent administration support; Casey Lyon painstakingly checked all the references and Ciny Hwee lent her artistry to our figures.

Finally, we thank our wives for their patience, love, and support during our long and seemingly frequent trips abroad. We dedicate this book to Yanela Dedrick and Norine Kraemer.

*Irvine, California*                                                                                        J. D.
*October 1997*                                                                                         K. K.

# Contents

# List of Figures

# List of Tables

# ASIA'S COMPUTER CHALLENGE

# Competing in Computers

In the tropical city state of Singapore, scores of factory buildings are emblazoned with the logos of American computer companies such as Apple, Compaq, Seagate, Western Digital, and Hewlett-Packard. Trucks roll away from loading docks carrying personal computers, monitors, printers, and disk drives bound for air cargo terminals at Changi International Airport and then to markets around the world. Meanwhile, other cargo planes are arriving filled with various components and subassemblies from Taiwan, Malaysia, and Thailand to supply the just-in-time production schedules of the same American companies.

In Scotts Valley, California, Seagate engineers are designing a new generation of hard disk drives. They make regular flights to Singapore to confer with process engineers at the plant where the first production models will be built. In turn, these engineers consult with the plant manager and engineers in Penang, Malaysia, and Bangkok, Thailand, where critical subassemblies will be manufactured.

Meanwhile, in Singapore's rival city-state of Hong Kong, AST Research announced in 1995 that it was shutting down the colony's last remaining PC assembly line. AST followed most of Hong Kong's electronics manufacturers to China, taking advantage of the mainland's lower wages while still managing its business from offices in Hong Kong.

In Taiwan's Hsinchu Science-based Industrial Park, a little-known company called Mitac is busy designing and building PCs for Compaq. Mitac ships the computers directly to Compaq's distributors in the United States and even provides support services to Compaq's customers. Other Taiwanese companies design and build computers for Apple, Compaq, Dell, NEC–Packard Bell, and most of the world's other leading PC makers.

Elsewhere, in Korea and Japan, billion-dollar factories produce memory chips and LCD screens that are stuffed into computers of every make, but few of those computers carry Japanese or Korean brand names. Companies that overwhelmed the U.S. consumer electronics industry in the 1970s and 1980s have barely made a dent so far in the personal computer industry. While electronics superstores are filled with televisions, VCRs, and camcorders carrying the brand names of Sony, Panasonic, Sharp, and Samsung, the computer departments of those stores have only a smattering of Canon and Epson printers and Toshiba notebook computers. In 1995, Taiwan's Acer outsold all the Japanese and Korean giants in the U.S. PC market.

In Santa Clara, California, Intel analysts pore over market forecasts as they make plans for shipping Pentium microprocessors to hundreds of PC makers and distributors around the world, and wonder where the chips sold to distributors will eventually end up. In Redmond, Washington, sheltered from the cutthroat price wars of the hardware industry, teams of developers are busy creating new versions of Microsoft Windows, Office, and other applications in the hope of extending Microsoft's dominance throughout the software industry. But the sudden explosion of the World Wide Web catches even Bill Gates by surprise and causes a furious revision of business plans in order to keep new products such as Netscape's Navigator and Sun's Java from becoming standards in the Internet market.

It is natural to wonder if there is any significance to these diverse stories, and what they tell us about competing in computers. Does it matter who designs a new system, who builds the hardware, whose brand name is on the outside, whose components are inside, or where the computer is built? Are there any profits left to be made in hardware, or is the real action in software and services? And is another revolution taking place in networked computing that will upend the industry as much as the PC revolution did in the 1980s?

The computer industry, which did not exist at the end of World War II, is now a nearly $500 billion industry whose products continue to change the way businesses compete and the way people live and work. The continuing changes in the industry itself have confounded expectations and challenged traditional concepts of competition among both companies and countries.

The notion of competition has stirred considerable debate among academics, government leaders, and business executives. Some economists, such as Paul Krugman,[1] argue that firms, not countries, compete and that the notion of national competitiveness leads governments to a "dangerous obsession" with a chimerical goal, leading to bad economic policies. By contrast, President Bill Clinton has compared a country to a big corporation competing in the global marketplace. The term "Japan, Inc." has been used in a similar vein, comparing the Japanese economic system to a military system guided by government bureaucrats to conquer global markets.

Government leaders around the world regularly focus on national competitiveness, partly as a way of answering the question, "How are we (their country) doing?"[2] In order to answer this question, one must first ask "Who is 'Us'?" This question was the title of an influential article written in 1991 by Harvard professor Robert Reich[3] (later President Clinton's Labor Secretary). Reich argued that in a global economy, the United States should not worry so much about the competitiveness of its companies, but should be concerned with creating jobs for its workers, regardless of the nationality of the employer. In other words, if a Japanese company built cars or computers in the United States, using American workers, that was good for the United States (and better in fact than if a U.S. company succeeded by moving its manufacturing offshore). Reich said that human capital is a nation's most important asset, since unlike money or goods, people do not easily move abroad. Consequently, developing human capital is the key to providing a sustainable national competitive advantage.

Laura Tyson, a University of California professor (and later a Clinton economic advisor), responded to Reich's argument with an article entitled, "They Are Not Us: Why American Ownership Still Matters."[4] Tyson argued that "the economic fate of nations is still tied closely to the success of their domestically based corporations." This is in part because of the importance of maintaining control over key technologies, in order to avoid technological dependence on foreign firms. For instance, U.S. dependence on Japanese suppliers of flat-panel displays and semiconductors has raised concern in the Pentagon and elsewhere in Washington. These concerns were only amplified when Japanese Diet member Shintaro Ishihara[5] crowed that the U.S. military victory in the Persian Gulf couldn't have been achieved without Japanese electronics technology. Tyson's arguments have an economic basis as well, since foreign companies (especially Japanese) are considered less likely to move high value activities such as research and development (R&D) offshore to the United States. Without strong domestic companies, the fear is that the United States could become little more than an assembler of Japanese components.

Through most of the postwar era, the rest of the world worried about competing with the United States. For instance, European countries have long been nervous about U.S. economic imperialism, represented by the pervasive presence of American multinationals in their domestic markets. This concern has been especially acute in the case of high technology industries and has led European governments to support national champions in the aerospace, computer, and telecommunications industries. The Japanese government likewise supported domestic computer and telecommunications companies and has tried to create a national aerospace industry as well.

The tables were turned on the United States during the 1980s, as Japanese companies eclipsed U.S. firms in automobiles and electronics, and bought up American companies, real estate, and other assets. Fears were expressed that Japan was buying control over the U.S. economy and that America's manufacturing base was being "hollowed out," as U.S. companies moved production offshore. By the 1990s, however, it was Japan that was under pressure; a rising yen was forcing Japanese companies to shift manufacturing offshore, and the Japanese economy entered a long recession. As the *New York Times* put it, "Companies like Sony and Toyota might well continue as fearsome competitors on the world stage, but Japan will enjoy fewer benefits of their success."[6] A continuing concern for Japan has been the dominance of U.S. companies such as IBM, Intel, and Microsoft over key technology standards in the Japanese computer industry.

While it is true that national competitiveness is often vaguely defined, and obsession with competitiveness can lead to poor policy choices, it is simply wrong to say it is irrelevant. Competitiveness matters very much to governments, which are concerned not just about their countries' absolute standards of living, but their position relative to other countries in terms of military, technological, and economic status. All three of these considerations come into play in the computer industry. Computer-related technologies have become critical to military security, as the Persian Gulf War illustrated to a worldwide television audience. Not only does computer technology guide smart missiles, but it can also be used to interpret satellite photos of enemy territory, navigate tanks and airplanes, and better forecast the weather in war zones.

Computer-related technologies are on the top of every major country's list of critical technologies for research and development leading to commercialization. Technological leadership in the computer industry enables a country's companies to reap the greatest profits from being first, to set the standards that others must follow, to collect a stream of royalties from intellectual property, and therefore to make risky investments in R&D, production infrastructure, and new product launches.

Economically, the computer industry is itself a huge industry that has sustained double digit growth rates for decades. It employs over five million workers directly worldwide, and many millions more in supporting industries. The U.S. Department of Commerce estimates that information technology industry shipments will total more than $500 billion in 1998, making it the largest manufacturing sector in the United States, as well as the fastest growing.[7] More important, spending on computers is seen by leading economists as a means of stimulating economic growth without generating inflation, because prices for computers have continually fallen over time while performance has increased dramatically. Thus, computer-led economic growth is now seen as a new instrument of macroeconomic policy for developed and developing economies alike.

The spillover effects of computer technologies throughout the economy are even greater. Computers are incorporated into products throughout many other industries, from telecommunications to consumer electronics to automobiles. For instance, Ford Motor Company has integrated into millions of automobiles microcontrollers based on Motorola's PowerPC chip, a technology developed for computer microprocessors. Software technologies are increasingly becoming critical to new product development in everything from wireless communications to vacuum cleaners. What this means is that computer technologies make up an increasing share of the value in many other industries in the economy.

Finally, even if the true measure of national economic success is productivity, as Krugman argues, computer production and use can both lead to productivity growth. First, in spite of previous skepticism, there is growing evidence that the use of computers improves productivity across virtually all economic sectors.[8] Second, there is evidence that investment in research and development has strong economic payoffs,[9] and the computer industry is a highly R&D-intensive industry. Third, there is also strong evidence that investments in education and training have a positive impact on productivity growth,[10] and computer production creates a strong demand for highly skilled engineers and computer professionals. This demand can pull more students into computer-related careers and upgrade the overall quality of a country's human resources.

While there is a convincing case to be made for the importance of national competitiveness in computers, actually defining competitiveness is a tricky question. The issue of company versus country competitiveness debated by Reich and Tyson is displayed vividly in the personal computer industry. The divergence of company and country interest has grown wider in the past fifteen years as the computer industry has evolved into a global production network that pays little heed to company or country boundaries. For instance, the U.S. company Seagate leads the disk drive industry in total revenues, but less than 20% of its employees are in the United States. Meanwhile, nearly half the world's disk drives are shipped from Singapore, which does not have any domestically owned disk drive companies but is the host to Seagate and a number of other U.S. disk drive makers.

It is this dominance held by multinational corporations (MNCs) such as Seagate in most segments of the computer industry that complicates the issue. As David Yoffie points out, if an MNC "is free to serve markets anywhere in the world from any production location it chooses, then the link between the home base and trade patterns can become rather tenuous."[11] The fact that U.S. computer companies have created a massive production network focused largely on East Asia is evidence of the divergence of company and country interests. It was the investment decisions of Seagate and other U.S. companies that turned Singapore into the disk drive capital of the world. Thus, as governments try to nurture their own computer industries, they must deal with these MNCs who control most of the industry's key resources, a fact well perceived by the Singapore government. The most successful countries are those that can align their own interests with those of both domestic and foreign MNCs, but this is not always a simple matter.

The rapid globalization of the computer industry and the complex relationship between company and country interests raises a number of questions for both companies and countries trying to compete in computers. These can be summed up as follows:

- How and why has the industry evolved into its present global structure?
- What determines competitiveness for companies, and what are the consequences of continuing changes in markets and technologies for companies in the computer industry?
- What determines competitiveness for countries, and what are the consequences for countries trying to reap the benefits of the explosive growth of the industry and avoid being left behind in the competition for jobs, exports, and technology?

- How do company and country interests correspond or diverge in a global production system?
- Why have some Asian countries succeeded more than others as participants in the global production network?

These questions are complex, as the foregoing discussion suggests. They require close analysis of the evolution of the industry and the strategies of both businesses and governments. This book looks specifically at the experiences of Japan, Korea, Taiwan, Singapore, and Hong Kong in the broader context of developments in the U.S. and global computer industry in order to answer some of these questions.

## Plan versus Market Explanations

In comparing the different strategies of these countries in developing their computer industries, we seek to shed light on a central question in development economics: how can companies and countries establish and maintain a viable competitive position in a highly globalized, technologically dynamic industry? The experiences of Japan, Korea, Taiwan, Singapore, and Hong Kong are especially interesting because, although each succeeded in carving out a place in the global computer industry, each started from different positions, followed different approaches, and achieved markedly different levels of success. How can their different levels of success be explained? Most explanations are based upon either market-directed theories of neoclassical economics or plan-directed, revisionist theories of political economy.

Neoclassical development economics argues that countries should pursue their comparative advantages (such as low wages), and ascribe a minimal industrial policy role for the state beyond providing a stable macroeconomic environment and investing in infrastructure development (such as human resources, R&D, and telecommunications). Rather than intervene in the market via industrial policies, governments should seek to minimize distortion in the market by getting the economic fundamentals right. The neoclassical approach explains differences in industrial performance between countries primarily in terms of differences in initial factor endowments, the soundness of macroeconomic management, and the level and effectiveness of public investment in infrastructure development.[12] In the neoclassical view, a country's success in a particular industry such as computers results from the actions of the private sector—companies—rather than from the targeted industrial policy of governments.

A recent version of this neoclassical approach is the World Bank's analysis of the economic growth of the East Asian economies.[13] While acknowledging that many of the East Asian economies intervened substantially and selectively in different industries, the World Bank analysis argued that these interventions had no demonstrable positive contributions to industrial performance, or that they had been market friendly, that is, led to the right market prices.

In contrast, revisionist political economics argues that the success of the East Asian countries is better explained in terms of selective state intervention in industry development.[14] This view argues that countries may succeed in achieving high overall performance by targeting strategic industries, such as the computer industry, for promotion. Strategic industries are chosen for their long-term growth potential and for their strategic linkages to other sectors of the economy. Revisionists claim that government intervention can overcome market failures and attract investment into risky new ventures. Targeted industrial promotion can also support the accumulation of assets and capabilities that will provide long-term competitive advantage vis-à-vis other countries.

Our view is that both market and plan perspectives offer important insights into the success of the East Asian countries in computers, but neither is sufficient. Much of the East Asian success has been the result of the actions of companies and entrepreneurs acting in a highly competitive environment with limited government intervention. By contrast, governments outside the region, such as Brazil and India, that tried to develop their own computer industries in isolation from global competition have failed. European governments were not much more successful with their promotion of "national champions" in the computer industry. These failures of industrial policy support the neoclassical argument for limited intervention.

On the other hand, the East Asian countries have employed aggressive industrial policies to develop their own computer industries, as the revisionists point out. The success of these countries has been clearly tied to investments in human resources, technology development and infrastructure, as well as strong incentives for investment (foreign and domestic) in computer production. In fact, with the exception of Hong Kong (which holds a unique position in the world due to its relationship to China), no country besides the United States has become an important player in the global computer industry without some level of government intervention. And even the United States achieved its early leadership position in large part because of government procurement and research funding.

How, then, do we reconcile these two apparently different points of view? The answer lies not in ideological arguments over free markets versus government planning. Rather, it lies in the details. Industrial policies have been effective in the computer industry when they move in concert with market forces, and when they are aimed at developing strong linkages with the global computer production system. Governments can do a great deal to develop the capabilities necessary to support computer production, and governments can tip investment decisions by multinationals in their favor by providing the right incentives. Such policies have been effective in developing national computer industries in Singapore and Taiwan.

In contrast, policies that go against the grain of market forces have been ineffective or even counterproductive in Japan and Korea. Trade and investment barriers aimed at protecting domestic firms serve only to isolate a country and prevent the creation of strong linkages to the global production network and global markets. They also raise prices and discourage use of computers in the local economy. The key issue, therefore, is not whether industrial policy is good or bad, but rather which industrial policies are effective and which are not.

Our approach explains differences in industrial performance between companies and countries primarily in terms of: (1) the structure of the global computer production system, (2) a country's industrial policy for computers, (3) the entrepreneurial innovation and structure of its national computer industry, (4) the path dependencies created by company and country capabilities, including their linkages and adaptation to the global production system, and (5) increasing versus decreasing returns in the computer industry. The first three factors are contained in the boxes in figure 1-1. The fourth factor, path dependency, adds a time element to the model by emphasizing the continuing evolution of the relationships illustrated in the figure. The fifth factor, increasing versus decreasing returns, provides a valuable criteria for segmenting the industry and viewing company and country performance.

*The Structure of the Global Computer Production System.*   Both the structure and the evolution of that system are important. This includes competition, alliances, and market transactions among companies at different levels of the production chain, from silicon to systems to software. It also includes the geographical structure of the global production network, that is, who makes what, and where.

*Government Industrial Policies.*   These are the policies that influence the development of national computer industries. In an industry whose geographical structure is largely determined by the business decisions of a few MNCs, but also affected by the choices of thousands of small companies, government policy can be an important factor influencing those decisions. These policies include tariffs and other trade barriers, incentives to attract foreign investment or encourage local investment in computer production, export promotion, training of computer professionals, investment in infrastructure and R&D, and promotion of domestic computer use. Industrial policies can either help or harm a country's competitiveness, and policies that are helpful at one time

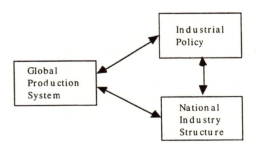

FIGURE 1-1. Framework for Analysis

can actually be counterproductive later on because of changes in the nature of the competitive environment.

*National Computer Industry Structures.*  Each country has its own industry structure, marked by several features. Some countries' industries are dominated by foreign multinationals, while others consist mostly of domestic companies. In some countries, a few large, diversified firms lead the industry, and smaller companies are generally part of the supply chain of one of these firms. In others, entrepreneurial smaller companies compete with each other and have only loose ties to each other and to larger firms. A given industry structure may be advantageous for competing in one product area, yet be detrimental in other markets. Equally important is a country's managerial culture, which may or may not be well suited to the fast-changing, highly competitive computer industry. A country will ultimately succeed in computers to the extent that its domestic companies succeed or it is able to attract investment from successful foreign multinationals.

*Path Dependencies.*  This refers to the development trajectories created by the acts of individual companies (or entrepreneurs) and countries, which become locked-in or amplified, leading to particular specialization patterns over time. A firm that has a first mover advantage, however small, may amplify that advantage into total market dominance. Similarly, a country that has a first mover advantage, however small, in attracting firms to engage in a particular computer sector, such as disk drive manufacturing, may become even more attractive to other firms engaged in similar or related activities (suppliers of materials, parts, subcomponents). Thus, the interactions in figure 1-1 must be seen as dynamic and evolving, rather than a fixed set of variables.

*Increasing versus Decreasing Returns.*  Closely related to the notion of path dependency is the concept of increasing and decreasing returns to scale. While the neoclassical models that have dominated economics for decades have assumed decreasing returns to scale (at least beyond some level of production), a number of scholars have argued in recent years that increasing returns not only exist, but are important drivers of economic growth.[15] In the case of standards-based competition, there is a tendency toward winner-take-all outcomes, as over time both users and creators of complementary assets such as software migrate to the standard that has the largest user base. However, while some segments of the industry, such as operating systems and microprocessors, are classic increasing-returns industries, much of the industry still operates under the traditional conditions of decreasing returns. This distinction is important in analyzing competition among both companies and countries.

## Evolution of the Computer Industry to a Global Production System

From the time of its invention in the 1940s until the late 1970s, a computer was a large, foreboding piece of equipment located in a glass house, maintained and operated by a team of specialists who spoke strange languages like FORTRAN and COBOL. This was the so-called central computing era in which the vast majority of computers were made in the United States, mostly by IBM. "Big Blue" stood astride the global computer industry like a colossus, controlling nearly half the world market for computers and producing virtually every key component and new technology in its own plants and laboratories. While companies and even governments launched expensive campaigns to unseat IBM from its position atop the computer industry, most competitors struggled to survive.

Although the U.S. government worried about IBM's near-monopoly position, the company's market dominance carried with it a corresponding national advantage for the United States. While IBM was an international company, with marketing, production, and even R&D operations around the world, most of its high-value activities remained in the United States. Much of the market not controlled by IBM was in the hands of other U.S. companies. This congruence of company and national interests was a latter day realization of Charles Wilson's (Chairman of GM in the 1940s) claim that "What's good for the country is good for General Motors, and vice versa." The issue of competing in computers was fairly simple when what was good for IBM was good for the United States. The world would not stay so simple for long, however.

In the late 1970s, a new machine was being created that would turn the world of computing on its head. Developed by hobbyists and tinkerers, the personal computer (PC) employed cheap microprocessors and off-the-shelf electronic components in a computer that sold for a few thousand dollars and could fit on an office desk or kitchen table. The mainstream computer companies scoffed at the PC as an underpowered toy for people who couldn't afford a real computer. However, when Apple Computer began selling PCs by the hundreds of thousands, Big Blue took notice. IBM moved quickly to develop its own PC, which gave the PC credibility as a business tool and created a mass market for it.

Rather than build its PC entirely in-house, IBM followed the lead of Apple, Commodore, and others by assembling components from outside suppliers. The de facto standards that allowed standardization of components were set when IBM introduced its PC in 1981 with an open architecture. Most important, IBM contracted with two upstarts, Microsoft and Intel, to develop the critical operating system and microprocessors for the IBM PC, and allowed them to license their technologies to other companies. IBM soon faced hundreds of competitors making IBM clones and selling them at cut rate prices, while Microsoft and Intel garnered the huge profit margins that IBM had been accustomed to in the mainframe business. While IBM had inadvertently given away control of its own creation, the open standards of the IBM PC architecture also lowered barriers to entry, allowing literally thousands of new companies to get into the computer business, making everything from keyboards to spreadsheets.

The PC revolution led to a huge expansion and a complete reshaping of the computer industry. From 1985 to 1995, sales of final systems rose from

$55 billion to $157 billion (figure 1-2). During the same time, PCs and workstations eclipsed mainframes and minicomputers in total sales. By 1995, PCs and workstations accounted for over 69% of computer system sales revenues, compared to just 29% in 1985.

Not only did large computers fall as a share of the market, but total sales of large and midrange computers also dropped from $55 billion in 1990 to $49 billion in 1995. Meanwhile, sales of workstations and PCs grew from $16 billion to $108 billion. The companies whose business depended on large computers suffered enormous losses during this period, while many PC companies prospered.

This remarkable shift in the computer market also led to a complete restructuring of the industry. The vertically integrated industry structure of the mainframe industry was replaced by a decentralized industry structure based on network economies. Different companies competed in each segment of the production chain, from components to systems to software. The disintegration of the industry into horizontal segments allowed the creation of a global production network, with different activities spread around the world. A Taiwanese entrepreneur could produce a cable or connector and sell it to any of the hundreds of PC makers in the world, and each of those PC makers could choose from hundreds of suppliers of cables and connectors. In such an environment, companies looked for the best or cheapest suppliers, subcontractors, or production sites, wherever they might be. The nature of competition changed and some companies and countries thrived while others struggled.

## Competing in Computers: Companies

The mainframe industry had been dominated by ten giants, including IBM, Burroughs, Honeywell, and Control Data in the United States, and ICL, Groupe Bull, and Nixdorf in Europe, which controlled 65% of the market in 1975 at the height of the central computing era, with another forty companies controlling 32% (table 1-1). The category "all others" accounted for just 3% of the market. By the 1990s, the industry was populated by thousands of firms, and many of the former giants had either gone bankrupt, been acquired, or were shadows of their former selves. IBM, which accounted for 37% of the world computer market in 1975, had only 14% by 1995. The "all others" category now accounted for 23% of the market, its growth mirroring IBM's declining market share. These "all others" included a large number of companies that were able to enter the computer industry because of the PC revolution. Membership in the top fifty had also changed significantly as well, because many newcomers from the PC industry had replaced older mainframe-oriented companies. Names such as Apple, Compaq, Dell, Microsoft, and Novell were now among the world leaders, replacing the likes of Wang, Prime, Data General, Cray, and CDC.

The shift from mainframes to PCs was so dramatic that IBM's stock plummeted from a high of more than $180 in the late 1980s to as low as $43 in

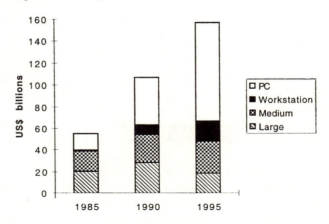

FIGURE 1-2. Computer Hardware Sales by Processor Type (systems only). *Source:* McKinsey & Company, *The 1996 Report on the Computer Industry*, (New York, NY: McKinsey & Company, 1996).

1993, and DEC's stock price dropped from more than $190 in 1987 to less than $40. In 1993, IBM reported losses of $7.5 billion, the second highest loss ever reported by a corporation. Contrasting with IBM's declining value was the growth of Intel and Microsoft, whose stock prices soared in the same period. By 1995 Microsoft and Intel each had a greater market valuation than IBM, even though the two companies' combined revenues were less than half of IBM's. Other big losers included centralized computing stalwarts DEC, Data General, and Amdahl, while big winners included PC-related companies such as Compaq, Dell, Adobe, Novell, and Lotus. Most symbolic of these changing fortunes, Compaq bought DEC in 1998. Among non-U.S. companies, some of the biggest success stories of the PC era were Japan's NEC and Toshiba; Taiwan's Acer, Mitac and FIC; and Singapore's Creative Technology. Losers included Japan's Fujitsu and Hitachi, and European companies such as ICL, Siemens, and Groupe Bull.

Company competitiveness can be measured in a number of ways, such as profitability, creation of shareholder wealth, growth, market share, and technology leadership. Each of these is important, but technology leadership and growth are critical in the computer industry. Leading in technology and controlling key standards enables a company to dominate the market and enjoy high margins that can be plowed back into further innovation. Growth further fuels the innovation cycle by ensuring there will be investors eager to underwrite expansion, talented employees willing to give their all, and a growing body of users waiting to adopt new products. Falling behind can be devastating, because product cycles are measured in months and most of the profits are made in the first few months. Slow-growth companies can cut costs and stay profitable for a while but eventually lose the confidence of customers, key employees, and stockholders if they cannot return to a strong growth rate.

TABLE 1-1. Worldwide Market Share (%)

|                | 1975 | 1985 | 1990 | 1995 |
|----------------|------|------|------|------|
| IBM            | 37   | 30   | 21   | 14   |
| Companies 2–10 | 28   | 29   | 28   | 32   |
| Companies 11–50| 32   | 29   | 28   | 31   |
| All others     | 3    | 18   | 23   | 23   |

*Source:* McKinsey & Company (1996).

Once those groups begin to abandon the company, the decline usually becomes irreversible.

One critical determinant of success is how effectively companies reach global markets and create linkages to the global production system. Companies that fail to grow beyond their domestic market cannot sustain high growth rates and achieve the sales volumes needed to lower production costs and recoup product development costs. Those that keep production in their home country and rely on domestic suppliers have failed to capitalize on the capabilities distributed throughout the global production system. The importance of global markets has been less apparent for some U.S. companies, which have sustained rapid growth by targeting the huge, fast-growing U.S. market; even those companies, however, are going global now as they realize that future growth will be fastest outside the United States.

## Competing in Computers: Countries

In the mainframe era, the United States enjoyed the lion's share of the computer market and was threatened only by Japan, despite the presence of European national champions. In the PC era, competition among countries has been much more vigorous and widespread. Not only did the PC create opportunities for new companies, but it also opened the door for new countries to participate in the industry. PC makers in the United States needed low-cost, reliable sources of components and peripherals; initially these companies turned to Japan, with its well-developed electronics and computer industries. The U.S. companies also wanted to move labor-intensive production activities to lower-wage locations, and they needed cheap sources of simple components that were becoming too expensive to source from Japan. Their search led them to Asia's newly industrializing economies (NIEs) of South Korea, Taiwan, Singapore, and Hong Kong, which were already making consumer electronics and electronic components. At the same time, those countries were looking to move into higher technology industries to sustain economic growth, and saw the emerging PC industry as providing just such an opportunity.

In the 1980s, three of the four countries (Hong Kong was the exception) enacted national strategies to promote the creation of personal computer industries and implemented the strategies with large sums of government spending for education and training, R&D, technology transfer, government computer use, and industry promotion. Even before they enacted these national computer plans, these countries had seen human resources as key to national competitiveness; the governments began upgrading the skills of existing technical professionals by engaging in long-term programs to produce more such professionals through education, both at home and abroad (table 1-2).

Between 1975 and 1992, Taiwan increased the number of bachelor degrees produced in natural science and engineering by eight times, Korea by nearly six times, and Singapore by 3.5 times (table 1-2). In 1992 the total baccalaureate students for all Asian countries exceeded those of Europe and the U.S. combined by 124,000. Their promotion of education abroad as a means of acquiring specialized skills and knowledge is even more impressive. For example, in 1991–92 there were about 81,300 Asian students enrolled in U.S. universities, which represents two-thirds of all foreign students enrolled in the United States.

Partly as a result of these investments in human resources, the East Asian countries had been successful in attracting multinational electronics companies to set up production in the 1960s and 1970s. The experience gained

TABLE 1-2. Bachelor's Degrees in Science and Engineering (Thousands)

| Country | Within Country Bachelor Degrees in Natural Science & Engineering | | Foreign Students in U.S. Universities: Natural Science & Engineering[a] |
|---|---|---|---|
| | 1975 | 1992 | 1991–1992 |
| Japan | 85.5 | 114.9 | n.a. |
| South Korea | 12.8 | 58.5 | n.a. |
| Taiwan | 8.7 | 16.9 | n.a. |
| Singapore | 0.7 | 2.5 | n.a. |
| Hong Kong | n.a. | n.a. | n.a. |
| East Asia 5 countries | 107.0 | 192.8 | n.a. |
| Asia total[b] | 221.1 | 527.7 | 107.8 |
| United States | 156.8 | 169.7 | n.a. |
| Europe | 105.2 | 239.6 | 14.4 |
| Latin America | n.a. | n.a. | 13.8 |
| Middle East | n.a. | n.a. | 15.2 |
| Africa | n.a. | n.a. | 8.1 |
| Total | | | 159.3 |

Sources: National Science Foundation (NSF), *Human Resources for Science & Technology: The Asian Region* (Washington, D.C.: NSF, 1993), Table A-3 p. 64; National Science Board, *Science & Engineering Indicators— 1996* (Washington, D.C.: U.S. Government Printing Office, 1996), Appendix Table 2-1; National Science Foundation, Human Resources for Science and Technology: The European Region (Arlington, VA: NSF, 1996).

[a]Applies to foreign students in all levels of U.S. higher education. Omitted regions are North America (Mexico, Canada) and Oceania, about 5% of total.

[b]Includes India and China.

producing electronic components and consumer electronics gave the East Asian countries an advantage in attracting PC companies to produce and source there in the 1980s.

The confluence of interests between U.S. companies looking for lower-cost production sites and the Asian countries seeking to develop their own computer industries led to a rapid growth in computer production in Asia. Between 1980 and 1995, U.S. companies developed a vast supply and manufacturing network throughout the region, with total production of computer hardware exceeding production in the United States. The shift in production to Japan, and then to the Asian newly industrialized economies (NIEs), is illustrated in figure 1-3.

This shift in production, especially to Japan, caused growing concern in the United States that American companies were weakening the U.S. computer industry. Japanese manufacturers had already used their control over key components and manufacturing technologies to drive their American competitors out of the market for most consumer electronics products. By the end of the 1980s, many analysts were predicting that Japan would use its control over memory chips and other components to eclipse the United States in computer hardware as well. For example, Clyde Prestowitz who was U.S. International Trade Representative in the Reagan Administration, predicted that the Japanese "are going to run away with the world computer market. It's going to be another TV industry."[16]

IBM was seen by many, including its own management, to be the last bastion against the Japanese onslaught. Japan's government and companies were investing in advanced R&D for supercomputers and new generation mainframes. In spite of large investments in production capacity and R&D, IBM was rapidly losing market share to its Japanese competitors in the mainframe market (table 1-3).

However, it turned out that the Japanese companies were winning the battle while losing the war in computers. Both IBM and the Japanese computer makers fell on hard times in the 1990s, as the PC revolution gained momentum and began to cut deeply into the market for big computers. The mainframe market dropped from $30 billion in 1989 to just $19 billion in 1995, pushing both IBM and the Japanese manufacturers into the red. Production of computer hardware in Japan dropped by more than 10% from 1991 to 1993 due to the effects of a domestic recession and the Japanese industry's dependence on the shrinking mainframe computer market.

While big Japanese computer makers such as Fujitsu and Hitachi struggled, the PC revolution was a boon for other companies. NEC and Toshiba became leading PC makers as well as major suppliers of components and peripherals. Companies such as Canon, Epson, Sharp, and Sony became leaders in printers, flat-panel displays, and monitors, while less well-known companies gained near-monopoly positions for many subcomponents and materials.

Japan's control of some key components has so far failed to translate into dominance in the PC industry, however. Computer makers in the United

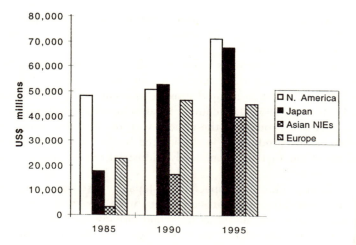

FIGURE 1-3. Computer Hardware Production by Region. *Source:* Reed, *Yearbook of World Electronics Data*, (Reed Electronics Research 1991, 1992 and 1996).

Total includes computer systems and peripherals, but not semiconductors. North America includes U.S. and Canada. Asian NIEs are Korea, Taiwan, Singapore and Hong Kong.

States avoided the fate of the U.S. consumer electronics industry partly by tapping the capabilities of the Asian NIEs to counter the manufacturing prowess of the Japanese. Taiwan, Korea, and Singapore moved rapidly upstream from simple assembly and production of cheap components to challenge Japan's leadership in large segments of the PC industry. Korea's Samsung became the world's leading producer of dynamic random access memory (DRAM) chips, while Taiwanese companies took the lead in motherboards, monitors, and other peripherals, and Singaporean companies controlled the world sound-card market. Japanese companies were struggling with high production costs due to the soaring yen, and were slow to take full advantage of Asia's production capabilities. Meanwhile, U.S. companies focused on their strengths in software, systems design, and marketing and leveraged the manufacturing capabilities of Asia to maintain their leadership of the global PC industry.

## Companies and Countries: Diverging Interests?

While American companies retained their leadership in the computer industry, the United States was losing both production share and employment in the computer industry to Asia. Hardware production in the United States declined as a share of global production between 1985 and 1990 by 22%. In 1995, U.S. companies accounted for about 65% of the global computer industry, but

TABLE 1-3. IBM versus Japan: Share of Global Large-scale Computer Market[a]

|  | 1985 | 1990 | 1995 |
|---|---|---|---|
| IBM | 49.0% | 40.6% | 32.4% |
| Japan (Fujitsu, NEC, Hitachi) | 17.0% | 32.6% | 47.2% |
| Total market | $21 bn | $28 bn | $19 bn |

*Sources:* McKinsey & Company, *The 1991 Report on the Computer Industry* and *The 1996 Report on the Computer Industry* (New York: McKinsey & Company, 1991, 1996).

[a]% of total industry revenue in mainframe, supercomputer, and mini-supercomputer processors.

only about 28% of total production took place on U.S. soil (figure 1-4). By contrast, Singapore has only a handful of successful domestic computer companies, but it produced more than $15 billion worth of computer hardware in 1995, putting it ahead of Germany, Britain, and France.

A good example of the divergence of company and national advantage is seen in the disk drive industry. While U.S. companies dominate the hard disk drive business, very few disk drives are actually manufactured in the United States. Singapore, without a major domestic disk drive company, accounts for nearly half of the worldwide output of disk drives, and most of the rest is located in Malaysia, Thailand, and the Philippines. Seagate is the leading merchant producer of disk drives in the world, and of its 58,000 employees worldwide in 1995, 48,000 were in Asia. The jobs remaining in the United States are mostly managerial, engineering, and software positions. The number of those jobs is relatively small, but they are precisely the kind of highly paid jobs that many U.S. workers aspire to. Seagate also supports a substantial supplier base in the United States of companies producing high value components for disk drives.

The issue of employment is very sensitive to national governments. Employment in the U.S. computer hardware industry has declined steadily since the mid-1980s, while employment in U.S. overseas affiliates has grown rapidly. As table 1-4 illustrates, employment in hardware production has been growing fastest in Asia, while the United States continues to see large gains in software and services. Even the software industry is now moving some production offshore to places like India and China, but the software and services industries need to be located close to users, and the United States is still the largest and most sophisticated computer market in the world.

The trend in hardware might begin reversing, however, as more Asian PC makers move production to the United States. As PCs become more consumer oriented and customized, there is a need to be close to the user to respond quickly to market changes. Also, there are cost advantages from maintaining a minimal inventory and assembling expensive components at the last possible moment. These forces are pushing final assembly back to the U.S. market, and production of some components might follow. The division of labor in the PC industry is likely to revolve less around labor versus capital intensity and

## World computer sales by location

## of vendor's headquarters

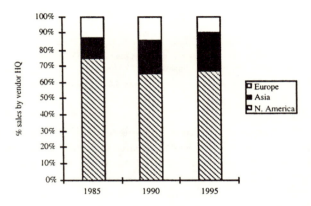

## World computer output by location of

## production

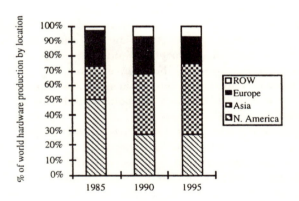

FIGURE 1-4. Company versus Country Position in the Computer Industry.
*Sources:* (Top) McKinsey & Company, 1996; (Bottom) Reed, *Yearbook of World Electronics Data*, Surrey, U.K.: Reed, Electronics Research, (various years).

more around the need to be close to the market. Simple assembly jobs will continue to follow low-cost labor, but other production will move closer to final markets in order to get the right product to market at the right time.

From a country's point of view, the key issue is getting the right kind of jobs to fit the capabilities of local workers and provide an acceptable standard of living for them. A poor country that needs to create large numbers of entry level jobs will likely be happy with low-wage assembly jobs. A newly industrializing country that hopes to create better paying jobs for engineers and other professionals might want smaller numbers of jobs that require higher skill levels. A wealthy country with low unemployment might favor higher paying jobs in management, R&D, product design, finance, and marketing.

Unfortunately, countries do not fall so neatly into such categories. The United States is a wealthy country that should be happy that it is creating many jobs for engineers and computer scientists. However, its education system fails to produce enough people with those skills, so it must rely on immigrants to fill those jobs. At the same time, there are many poor, unskilled workers who would like to have the assembly jobs that have moved to Asia. By contrast, India is a very poor country that needs many jobs for unskilled workers, but it also produces thousands of scientists and engineers who end up in the United States or other developed countries, because there are too few jobs for them in India. At the same time, Korea, Taiwan, and Singapore have created more jobs for engineers and managers than they can fill, and they now are turning to immigrants or moving production offshore. Finally, most European countries are seeing their computer industries stagnate even as they are faced with high unemployment levels.

There is no simple answer to the issue of employment. Immigration is only a partial solution for those with labor shortages, and it is seen as a "brain drain" for the sending countries. Overall, the computer industry continues to create so many jobs that all of the East Asian countries, as well as the United States, have benefited. But there are legitimate concerns about the match of skills to opportunities, and also about the ease with which jobs are destroyed as well as created in the industry (table 1-4).

A final concern raised by the shift of production offshore is the effect on trade. During the mainframe era, the global trade patterns of the computer industry reflected IBM's strategy of maintaining balanced trade in North America, Europe, and Japan. IBM's internal trade dominated the total trade in computers, so no region ran a major trade surplus or deficit, except the United States, which had a large surplus. As shown in Figure 1-5, this situation changed quickly in the PC era. The United States has run large trade deficits in computer hardware with Asia and surpluses with the rest of the world since the early PC era. Much of the deficit is accounted for by Japan, but an increasing share has been with other Asian countries. Korea and Taiwan are likewise concerned about their own growing trade deficits with Japan, and Japan itself now runs a deficit with China.

Trade in computers and components has grown rapidly as the Asian production network has developed, and the United States has seen its overall trade surplus in computer hardware turn into a deficit in the PC era. However, these data do not include microprocessors, which are included in semiconductors and where U.S. companies (mainly Intel) have more than 90% of the world market. Also, the hardware deficit is largely compensated for by a surplus in software and services. While there are no official data on imports and exports of software, the U.S. Department of Commerce estimates that U.S.

TABLE 1-4. Computer Industry Employment (Thousands)

| Region | 1985 | 1990 | 1995 |
|---|---|---|---|
| United States | | | |
| Hardware | 350 | 294 | 249 |
| Software and services | 600 | 800 | 1,100 |
| U.S. affiliates abroad | | | |
| Hardware | 198 | n.a. | 235 (1992) |
| Software and services | 12 | n.a. | 82 (1992) |
| Japan | | | |
| Hardware | 140 | 290 | 278 (1993) |
| Software and services | n.a. | 475 | n.a |
| Korea | | | |
| Hardware | n.a. | 19 | 27 (1993) |
| Software and services | n.a. | 39 | 50 |
| Taiwan | | | |
| Hardware | n.a. | 96 | 186 |
| Software and services | n.a. | n.a. | 22 |
| Singapore | | | |
| Hardware | n.a. | 43 | 43 |
| Software and services | n.a. | n.a. | 16 |
| Hong Kong | | | |
| Hardware | 12 | 24 | 11 |
| Software and services | n.a. | n.a. | 9 |
| Western Europe | | | |
| Hardware | n.a. | 282 | n.a. |

*Sources:* United Nations Industrial Development Organization (UNIDO), *International Yearbook of Industrial Statistics, 1996* (New York: UNIDO, 1996); McKinsey Global Institute, *Employment Performance* (Washington, D.C.: McKinsey & Company, 1994); Singapore Economic Development Board (EDB), *Singapore Electronics Trade Directory* (Singapore: EDB, 1996); U.S. Department of Commerce, *Global Trade Outlook 1995–2000* (Washington, D.C.: U.S. Department of Commerce, International Trade Administration, 1995); Hong Kong Census and Statistic Department (data provided to authors); Hong Kong Productivity Council, *Consultancy Study on Hong Kong's Software Industry* (Hong Kong: Industry Department, 1995); Organization for Economic Cooperation and Development (OECD), *Information Technology Outlook: 1995* (Paris: OECD, 1996); Institute for the Information Industry (III), *Taiwan Software Industry and Five-year Development Plan* (Taipei: III, 1995).

companies sell about $23 billion worth of software abroad, while foreign companies sell less than $4 billion worth in the United States. In computer services, the United States runs about a $3 billion surplus.[17]

The broad trade pattern that has emerged in the PC era shows the competitiveness of East Asia in hardware, the strength of the United States in software and microprocessors, and Europe's weakness in both hardware and software.

## Accounting for the Differences

The East Asian countries have not all been equally successful in computers, however. Japan has had mixed success at best and is only recently getting serious about the global PC market. Singapore and Taiwan have sustained

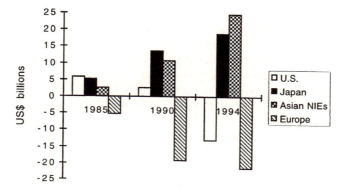

FIGURE 1-5. Trade Balances in Computer Hardware. *Sources:* Reed, *Yearbook of World Electronics Data,* various years.

Maryellen C. Costello and Benjamin Goures'-Casseres, *The Global Computer Industry,* case no. 9-792-072. Boston: Harvard Business School Press, 1992. Copyright 1992 by President and fellows of Harvard College. Reprinted by permission.

high growth rates in a variety of products, while Korea's success was limited to memory chips and monitors, which has more to do with its abilities in semiconductor and television manufacturing than its strength in computers. Hong Kong lost most of its manufacturing base, but retained its position in management, finance, distribution, and marketing for China's computer industry.

Why have some Asian countries succeeded more than others as participants in the global production network? It cannot be just a matter of who has the best domestic companies. Taiwan has many successful computer companies and Singapore has just a few, but both have been very successful as producers and have developed strong manufacturing and technical capabilities. Meanwhile, the Japanese and Korean giants that dominate much of the world's consumer electronics and the electronics components industries generally have struggled in the PC era.

Some would argue that government industrial policy is the key variable explaining the relative success of different countries. In fact, the governments of Japan, Korea, Taiwan, and Singapore have all developed national computer plans and have actively promoted domestic computer production through a variety of policy mechanisms. But, so did several European countries, with little success.

Ultimately, the key determinant of country success has been the ability to develop linkages to the global production system, and this ability is tied to both industrial policy and industry structure. Singapore and Taiwan have become tightly integrated into the global production network and have created strong national production capabilities for a variety of computer hardware products. Their success has been partly a result of their industrial structures, which have both corporate and personal ties to the global industry, and also to government policies that encouraged trade and investment. The large electronics conglomerates of Japan and Korea have been slower to develop tight linkages to the global production system because of their bureaucratic management styles and reliance on local suppliers. Both countries have also suffered from government policies that put up barriers to imports and foreign investment. Hong Kong's role in computers is based mainly on its position as the link between China and the outside world. Hong Kong's industrial structure is geared toward this role, as are its government policies. While the government does little to directly promote industries such as computers, it has invested heavily in developing an exceptional trade and communications infrastructure. It also maintains low tax rates and very liberal trade and investment rules to create a favorable environment for commerce and finance.

Overall, the evidence from the Asian countries clearly supports the argument that industrial policy makes a difference in national competitiveness. No country, including the United States, has competed successfully in computers without some government involvement. However, many governments have actively promoted computer production with little or no success.

Ultimately, the effectiveness of industrial policy depends on the details. The governments of Singapore and Taiwan have supported and facilitated their countries' integration into the global production system by promoting inward investment and technology transfer and by helping local companies develop specialized capabilities, identify export opportunities, and exploit them. They have also invested in developing the national capabilities necessary to participate in the global industry, particularly human resources, infrastructure, and R&D. By contrast, both Japan and Korea relied on domestic production and followed an export promotion strategy. This had worked well in electronics sectors, allowing companies to use the protected domestic market as a profit sanctuary to support exports. However, in PCs this had the effect of isolating the two countries from much of the dynamism of the global production network: from new technologies; from fast, responsive suppliers; and from sophisticated users. Also, both countries embarked on large R&D projects driven more by government fiat than as a response to market conditions or industry needs.

Similar efforts had paid off in some segments of the semiconductor industry, which requires huge investments in technology and capital, and where the target is more easily identifiable. In computers, however, both countries tried to catch up in large systems even as the market was moving to PCs.

Hong Kong is an interesting counterpoint to the other four countries, having generally eschewed industrial policy. Hong Kong has succeeded as a supplier of management and commercial services and as a link to China, but has not developed its own technological capabilities. This suggests that a laissez faire policy strategy might work in a unique case such as Hong Kong, with its position as a gateway to China, but it is unlikely to create the capabilities necessary to support a competitive computer industry in most countries.

Policy success also depends on policy coherence and coordination, because the different areas of state intervention closely interact; consequently, the effectiveness of any single policy intervention is often affected by whether it complements or conflicts with other policies—and with the actions of the private sector. Singapore and Taiwan had coherent policy interventions with regard to the computer industry, although each was guided by a different strategy. However, bureaucracies in Japan and Korea not only followed inappropriate policies from the past but also competed over policy turf, diverting their attention from the PC revolution. Thus, it is clear there has been no single set of computer industry policies, but rather a mix of effective and ineffective policies.

Industrial policy is not the whole story, however. A country's success or failure in computers depends equally on (1) the entrepreneurial innovation and focus of its individual companies wherein specialized capabilities are developed and continually upgraded, and (2) the diversity of its national computer industry wherein a deep and broad cluster of computer related capabilities is created. The PC industry has favored focused, fast, flexible companies and punished diversified, sluggish, bureaucratic organizations. Japan's and Korea's slow-moving, inward-looking industrial giants failed to seize opportunities, while Taiwan's entrepreneurial business culture, global network of human resources, and vast supply chain enabled it to respond rapidly to changing market demands. Singapore's SMEs quickly became preferred suppliers to the MNCs located there by offering specialized services and skills. Hong Kong's entrepreneurs were likewise quick to find new opportunities in China as high costs made manufacturing too expensive in Hong Kong.

We believe that it is the combination of the various interacting factors—industrial policy, national industry structures, and linkage to the global production system—that best explains the relative success of different countries of East Asia in the global computer industry. An example is provided by the interaction of these factors in Singapore's ascendancy to become the hard disk drive capital of the world. Singapore's 1980 national computer plan targeted the computer industry for development, and its Economic Development Board (EDB) actively promoted foreign direct investment. The EDB attracted Seagate in 1982 to move production to Singapore to take advantage of a skilled labor pool, quality infrastructure, and generous government subsidies. The success with Seagate led the EDB to more focused targeting of foreign investment around disk drive manufacturing. Singapore's initial advantages in hard disk drive manufacturing became amplified as the skills of its pool of engineers, managers, and technicians were upgraded through learning and experience. As a result, Singapore's leadership in hard disk drives continued to expand in the 1990s even as some companies moved lower-end assembly to Malaysia, Thailand, and China.

## Conclusions: Winners and Losers in a New Era of Computing

A revolution took place in the computer industry in the 1980s, driven by the relentless power of Moore's Law, which states that microprocessors will double in power every eighteen months. Like most revolutions, this one left some participants bloody and beaten while propelling others to fame, fortune, and power. Most of the business world was stunned to see corporate giants such as IBM being humbled by brash young entrepreneurs such as Steve Jobs and Bill Gates. Even more important, however, this revolution destroyed an industrial structure based on monolithic corporations and replaced it with a new structure built on networks of large, medium, and small companies mostly spread around the Pacific Rim.

This new production network was created largely through the investment and procurement of U.S. companies, but its creation has benefited some companies while hurting others. Those who have tapped the system effectively, such as Compaq, Seagate, and Hewlett Packard have benefited greatly, while more vertically integrated companies such as IBM and DEC suffered as their competitors outflanked them in the Asian production network as well as in the marketplace. Relative to their Japanese and European competitors, U.S. companies have gained a clear advantage from the growth of this network. For the United States, the effect of the PC revolution and the shift to Asia has been more mixed. It is clear that production and employment in the hardware industry have shifted offshore, but, at the same time, the software and services industries have grown rapidly and have recorded large gains in employment in the United States.

Likewise, the PC revolution and the shift to Asia have benefited some Asian countries more than others. Singapore and Taiwan have been clear winners, becoming far more important forces in the PC industry than could have been predicted, given their small markets and initial technological limitations. Japan's computer makers were slow to tap into Asia's capabilities and fell behind in the PC industry partly because of their preference for maintaining traditional Japanese supply networks. However, because of its strengths in manufacturing and key technologies, Japan has still succeeded in the PC industry as a supplier of components, peripherals and portable computers. Korea has likewise flourished as a producer of components, particularly memory chips, but it has had little success in developing a PC industry, either through its own companies or by attracting foreign multinationals to produce in Korea. Hong Kong has lost most of its manufacturing base in computers, but still remains a factor in the industry by managing production in South China.

The arguments about the twin roles of industry structure and industrial policy in creating national competitiveness help explain the success and failure of the East Asian countries, and in fact any other country that is not the market leader in the industry. But what about the United States, which is the leader and whose companies have created much of the global production system? It is clear that the U.S. success in PCs is driven mostly by U.S. companies, which invented the PC and have maintained their lead in the industry. However, there has been more government policy involved than many would suspect, starting with heavy military procurement and R&D during the Cold War and continuing with support for research at universities and national laboratories and the serendipitous decision to create the Internet.

More important than the relative weight of government or industry structure is the interaction of the two. Investment of the U.S. military in computers helped establish the country's leadership in the industry, and in turn, American strengths in electronics and computers encouraged the military to emphasize technology as a key strategic element in the Cold War. More directly, the interaction of government policy and business decisions helped Japan, Taiwan, Korea, and Singapore establish and enhance their competitive positions in computers and semiconductors.

Throughout this book we will look at the nature of the global production system and analyze how and why the companies and countries of the Pacific Rim have come to occupy their present positions in that system. In chapter 2, we review the evolution of the global industry from the centralized computing era to the personal computing era, focusing on the radical changes that took place in the global production structure between those two eras. In chapters 3–5, we look closely at the experiences of Japan, Korea, Taiwan, Singapore, and Hong Kong as participants in the computer industry. In chapters 6 and 7, we review our findings and draw conclusions about the successes and failures of those countries, and what they tell us about competing in computers.

Finally, in chapter 8, we look at the future of the global computer industry and what it means for companies' and countries' prospects. The emergence of the network era of computing is once again changing the nature of competition in computers, with important ramifications for companies and countries. The global production network is changing, too, as rising wages and emerging markets have led companies to shift production to places such as China, India, and Southeast Asia. We will look at what impact these changes will have on the United States, Japan, and the Asian NIEs, and what the prospects are for other countries trying to enter the industry.

# 2

# Globalization of the Computer Industry

During the 1980s, the computer industry changed from a company- and country-based production structure into a global production system with little regard for company or country boundaries. The agent of change was the introduction of the personal computer, which transformed the way computers were designed, built, sold, and used. No longer were computers primarily made by large, vertically integrated companies to their own proprietary standards using their own components, peripherals, and software. Instead, PCs were designed and assembled according to common standards using components, peripherals, and software made by thousands of suppliers. In this environment, anyone with a little capital and know-how could get into the computer business, and thousands of entrepreneurs did. As the industry grew and became more competitive, PC makers looked for cheaper sources of labor and components, and a global production system was born.

The globalization of the industry was made possible by the standardized architecture and decentralized structure of the personal computer industry; globalization was driven by the constant need to cut costs in a hypercompetitive industry. The global production system was not evenly distributed, however, but became concentrated in the East Asian region. Computer production had moved first to Japan in the mainframe era, and then Japan was joined by the Asian newly industrialized economies (NIEs) as the PC industry went global. To a large extent, the global production system for PCs was really a U.S./Asian network.

The reasons for Asia's prominent position are rooted partly in the earlier mainframe competition, in which only the Japanese survived intact against IBM. The causes are rooted even more deeply in the globalization of the electronics industry in the 1960s and 1970s. As U.S. electronics and semiconductor companies moved production to Asia, they helped create capabilities that formed the underpinnings for PC production. The U.S. computer makers located production throughout Asia to tap these capabilities, and also to avoid dependence on Japanese suppliers. The U.S. consumer electronics companies had become dependent on Japanese components and were ultimately driven from the market by low-cost Japanese producers who controlled their own supply of components. The U.S. computer industry feared the same fate, and diversified its supplier base beyond Japan to other parts of Asia.[1]

Why did so much of the computer industry end up in Asia? The answer boils down to a combination of effective industrial policies and national industry structures that were able to integrate effectively into the global production system. East Asian governments actively sought foreign investment, supported technology transfer, and promoted exports, thus facilitating the development of global linkages. They also maintained labor discipline, giving them an advantage over other places with cheap labor, and they achieved high levels of education, particularly in the critical technical and engineering fields.

The national industry structures of the East Asian countries were also well suited to competing in a global production network, partly due to the presence of leading multinational computer makers. In Japan, these were mostly domestic companies such as Fujitsu, NEC, and Toshiba, while in the Asian NIEs, they were mostly American companies. The MNCs provided technology, managerial skills, and access to global markets. Local companies were quick to seize opportunities in the new global production network, becoming original equipment manufacturers, subcontractors, suppliers, and in a few cases, multinational competitors themselves. In each country, industry clusters developed around one or more product areas, such as disk drives and PCs in Singapore and motherboards and peripherals in Taiwan. The East Asian countries developed capabilities and resources, from skilled workers to large supplier bases, that gave them a continuing source of competitive advantage even as rising costs forced them to move their own labor-intensive production offshore.

The rapid growth and technical progress of the computer industry in the United States shaped Asian perceptions of the industry's importance to economic and technological competitiveness. The evolution of the U.S. computer industry also provided the impetus for its Asian expansion, first to Japan, then to the East Asian NIEs, and still later throughout the Asia-Pacific region. The globalization process exploded along with the PC industry's growth in the 1980s, but it had important antecedents in the earlier stages of the industry's development.

## Stages of Development in the Computer Industry

Analysts such as Richard Nolan and David Yoffie of Harvard, and David Moschella of IDG,[2] characterize the computer industry as passing through three stages of development (figure 2-1). The first was the central computing era, which ran from the 1950s to the early 1980s, during which the mainframe

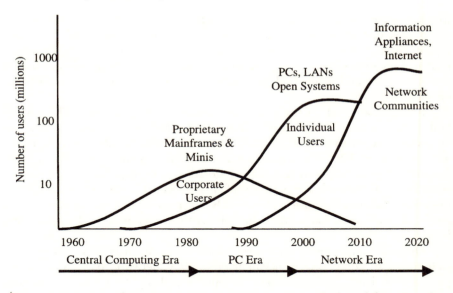

FIGURE 2-1. Stages of Computer Industry Growth. *Source:* Adapted from David C. Moschella, *Waves of Power: The Dynamics of Global Technology Leadership 1964–2010.* (New York: AMACOM, 1997). Excerpted by permission of the publisher. Copyright 1997 David C. Moschella. Published by AMACOM, a division of American Management Association. All rights reserved.

computer and its little brother, the minicomputer, reigned supreme. The second was the personal computer era, which ran from the early 1980s to the mid-1990s, with PC sales surpassing mainframe sales worldwide by 1985. The third is the network era, beginning in the mid-1990s and extending well into the twenty-first century, marked by the majority of computers being connected to networks within organizations and interconnected worldwide through the Internet.

The essential character of competition over time in the computer industry can be characterized as: (1) competition among firms in the central computing era, (2) competition among countries in response to U.S. dominance in the central computing era, and (3) competition among companies and countries within a global production network in the PC era. The nature of competition in the network era (chapter 8) is still evolving, but it appears to be moving toward a broader global production network that encompasses communications, entertainment, and consumer electronics companies. An increasing number of countries are participating, as the industry seeks new markets and lower cost production sites. Each competitive era can be characterized by different technologies, user markets, companies, and industry structures.

## Competition Between Firms: The Central Computing Era

The commercialization of computers began in the United States in the 1950s, led by IBM and Sperry Rand, and followed by several other U.S. firms. Throughout the 1960s, U.S. firms turned out increasingly sophisticated machines; by 1972, U.S. companies accounted for 92% of the world's installed computer base.[3]

The first computers were based on vacuum tube technology and were designed for specific government or defense industry customers. These early computers were expensive (running around $1.5–$2 million each) and required several years to build. Because initial government procurement and R&D funding was large, many firms rushed into the industry. IBM and Sperry Rand were already producing tabulating equipment, whereas most other entrants were large companies doing defense work, such as Control Data Corporation, General Electric, and Philco.

### Building Big Iron: The Mainframe

Originally developed as a tool for scientific and engineering calculation for military problems, the computer quickly gained use during the 1950s for business data processing, such as accounting, payroll, billing and inventory. The business data processing market was not limited to a particular country, but was global because all user industries shared a relatively common set of business applications. The global user markets for business data processing helped the computer companies support the large investments required for R&D and achieve economies of scale in production. IBM's marketing reach spanned the globe, a legacy of its tabulating equipment business, and it rapidly became the world's leading computer company.

The structure of the industry during the mainframe era was concentrated, with ten U.S. firms supplying most of the global market for computers. The key players during the 1960s were IBM plus the so-called "BUNCH" (Burroughs, the Univac division of Sperry Rand, NCR, Control Data Corporation, and Honeywell). A new set of non-U.S. competitors was also trying to challenge IBM in their home markets, most notably ICL, Siemens, and Groupe Bull in Europe, and Fujitsu, Hitachi, and NEC in Japan. The effects of that challenge would become increasingly important during the 1970s, when the Japanese companies in particular became serious competitors to IBM.

In the early stages of the central computing era, competition was mostly between vertically integrated firms. By making their own components, bundling the necessary equipment and software as a system, and using a "closed" proprietary architecture for their computers, firms were able to compete vigorously for market share and then concentrate on getting customers to upgrade with the firm's new technologies. This enabled the vendor to lock in a customer and lock out competitors due to the high costs of switching.

Individual firms within the industry were vertically integrated, with each performing its own R&D, production, distribution, marketing, sales, and support. Each firm had its own internal production network across all industry segments—from semiconductors to components to computer platform, peripherals, system software, and applications (figure 2-2). Initially, there was little outsourcing of business functions or of production for the different industry segments, except for parts, materials, or specialty items for the component segment. As the central computing era unfolded, however, competition broadened as many newcomers entered the market specializing in a particular segment such as software or peripherals.

IBM was the most successful company by far in implementing the proprietary strategy, using three key business practices to establish and maintain its market position. The first was to rent rather than sell its equipment. Customers were unwilling to install this new technology from an embryonic industry until they were shown how to make effective use of it; leasing rather than buying the equipment reduced their risk. The rental policy not only attracted new customers by lowering the risk of investment, but it also helped assure a steady revenue stream even in bad economic times when little new equipment was being installed.

The second practice was to build relationships with customers rather than merely selling equipment, as other vendors did.[4] Customers needed help in installing and maintaining the new equipment, adapting their business procedures to it, and training their employees. IBM's customer support became one of its most valuable hallmarks, creating strong customer loyalty—and generating scores of stories about how IBM sales and service people worked around the clock to keep customers' equipment running even when fire, flood, or other disasters occurred.

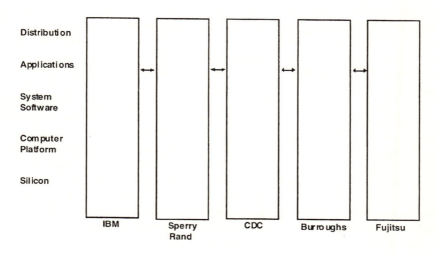

FIGURE 2-2.

The third practice was to "bundle" services, such as training, mainte-nance, and support in the price of the hardware.[5] Bundling allowed customers to pay one price and not be bothered with all sorts of additional costs after the initial sale or rental agreement was made. It also allowed IBM to avoid competing directly on the basis of price for each item on its menu of hardware, software, and services.

While IBM's effective implementation of these business practices helped it establish an early lead in the industry, there was also a bold technology gambit that propelled the company far ahead of its competitors. By the early 1960s, the nascent mainframe market was fragmented among a number of competing platforms, each of which was incompatible with the others. Com-puter users were stuck with one company's system and could not mix and match the best features of different vendors' hardware, software, and services. IBM itself was selling seven separate, incompatible lines of computers. The incompatibility created high costs for both customers and for IBM,[6] and led to a massive internal effort to design a family of computers that would run the same operating system and be completely modular and upgradable, both with respect to processors and peripherals. The result was the IBM System/360, introduced in 1964. The System/360 was so successful that a number of IBM's competitors were driven out of the market altogether while others strug-gled to hang on. By 1971, when IBM introduced the follow-on System/370, it had installed 35,000 System/360s.[7]

The advent of the IBM System/360, with its modularity and standardized interface features, enabled original equipment manufacturers (OEMs) to be-gin manufacturing peripherals that were plug-compatible with the System/360. The same peripheral could be used with any model of the 360 family; this minimized the number of models of a given peripheral device that needed to be designed. This resulted in two key benefits to IBM, and to manufacturers of IBM plug-compatible products: (1) reduction of development expenses, es-pecially those associated with developing the various models; (2) reduction of unit manufacturing costs, because higher production volumes for each prod-uct created economies of scale in production.

The benefits of plug compatibility have served as the basis for much of the competitive dynamism and technological improvements in the mainframe, minicomputer, and PC industries. The combination of economies of scale and reduced product development costs has supported the rapid price–perfor-mance improvements that have been a constant feature of the industry's de-velopment. Standardization and modularity also helped make possible the globalization of the industry by enabling foreign competitors to enter the mar-ket without huge start-up costs. It also allowed them to concentrate on making standardized products that could be sold throughout the world and compete on the basis of low-cost production.

The mainframe industry remained vertically integrated for the most part, with IBM and a few other large companies controlling a large share of the total market. But the development of a modular, standardized dominant plat-form along with the growth of plug-compatible systems and peripherals manufacturers and independent software developers foreshadowed the ultimate restructuring of the industry in the PC era.

IBM's decisions to open up parts of its vertically integrated production system were not just a result of market forces or company strategy, however. Rather, they were influenced for decades by the competition policies of the U.S. government. The Justice Department pursued antitrust actions against IBM, starting in the 1950s and running until 1982, when the Reagan administration abandoned the final case against IBM. In order to ward off the threat of a possible break-up of the company, IBM made several changes in its business model. In 1956, the company signed a consent decree that restricted a number of marketing practices. For instance, it agreed to limit its activities as a data processing services provider, an agreement that remained in force until 1995, when IBM was finally allowed to sell computer services under its own name.[8] This agreement created a market opportunity that was filled by the various service bureaus such as EDS and CSC.

Throughout the 1970s, the Justice Department continued to pursue antitrust action against IBM. Much of IBM's attention during those years was devoted to avoiding the appearance of anticompetitive practices, which included some of the very business strategies that had been responsible for IBM's success. In the words of Thomas Watson, Jr., CEO from 1956 to 1971:

> The government objected to virtually our entire way of doing business, from our total system sales—supplying customers with complete installations including hardware, software, engineering help, training, and maintenance—to the big discounts we gave universities.[9]

The effect of the U.S. government's antitrust pressure was probably not good for IBM, but it did help create a more dynamic industry in the United States and opened the door for many other companies who would also become strong global competitors. On the other hand, in the market directly targeted by the government—mainframe computers—the only successful challengers to IBM turned out to be Japanese companies, as we will see.

### The Minicomputer Challenge

While IBM and the other mainframe vendors were mainly building big computers for large corporations, several new companies focused on building new, smaller computers—dubbed minicomputers—beginning in the early 1960s.

The new technology of integrated circuits made minicomputers possible by decreasing manufacturing costs, increasing reliability, and enabling large improvements in price/performance. The early minicomputers were powerful but often stripped-down, in that they were sold without peripherals, software, or applications. The central processing unit (CPU) without peripherals cost from $80,000 to $90,000. In addition to its low purchase price, the minicomputer was especially attractive because it was easy to integrate with diverse types of special purpose equipment, such as scientific instruments and machine controls, and could also be connected remotely to a mainframe. It was also inexpensive enough to use just for one purpose. Peripherals could be bought from the minicomputer maker or from independent manufacturers. Independent software companies provided applications and were encouraged by the minicomputer makers to sell their applications under informal partnership arrangements where manufacturer and software vendors each provided information about the others' products to customers.

The new users for the minicomputer were scientists and engineers who had sufficient computer expertise to program, operate, and manage computers on their own for uses such as scientific computation, laboratory data acquisition, industrial process control, or computer research. SDS (Scientific Data Systems) started in 1961 by making high-performance hardware for real-time applications such as steam plant control, space vehicle launch control, and astronomical observation. However, as the business data processing community grew larger and more experienced, business users desired greater control over their own computing environments rather than depending on central data processing departments. In addition, there was a huge pent-up demand for applications that was not being met by central processing departments in many businesses. The minicomputer vendors saw this demand and marketed their machines to departmental users and smaller companies who had the funds or could clearly justify the equipment.

The minicomputer was a stepping stone from the mainframe to the PC era. It maintained the proprietary architecture of the mainframe but moved further toward the modularity and standard components of the PC. It also allowed a shift toward "distributed computing" in which tasks were distributed among a number of computers that were linked together in a network. In addition, the minicomputer greatly expanded the size of the independent software industry,[10] another step toward the PC era in which independent vendors would dominate in software.

In another foreshadowing of the PC industry, the first minicomputers were designed by the system vendor and powered by that firm's central processing unit (CPU) but assembled from parts, components, peripherals, and software made by other companies. Because these minicomputers were sold without support, they produced very high gross profit for the manufacturers, which could be plowed back into R&D and new product development to maintain technical leadership.

Initially, Digital Equipment Corporation (DEC) had made its own CPU but bought peripherals from outside suppliers; it then began making its own peripherals and finally its own complete systems. SDS similarly began making general purpose minicomputers by buying components and peripherals from the large array of original equipment and plug-compatible suppliers that had grown alongside the mainframe industry (table 2-1). Before long, SDS brought the manufacture of peripherals inside the company to achieve higher profit margins and competitive advantage from technology advances, greater complementary of CPU and peripherals, and better quality assurance.

DEC was singularly successful with its series of PDP minicomputers first introduced in the early 1960s. Whereas IBM computers were general purpose,

TABLE 2-1.  SDS outsourcing for components and peripherals

| Components | Sources |
|---|---|
| Transistors, resistors, and capacitors for CPUs and memory | Standard sources |
| Core memories | Fabri-Tek |
| | Ampex |
| | Magnetic Memories |
| Tape drives and controllers | Ampex |
| | Computer Products |
| | Potter Instruments |
| Printers and controllers | NCR |
| | Data Products |
| | California Computer Products |
| Card punches | Univac |
| Cathode ray tube terminals | Control Data |
| Standard teletype keyboards | Western Electric |
| Software | Digitek |
| | Programmatics |
| | Bonner & Moore |
| | Informatics |
| | Computer Usage Corporation |
| | Computer Science Corporation |
| | DatawareCII |
| | Scientific Resources |

Source: Franklin M. Fisher, James W. McKie, and Richard B. Mancke, IBM and the U.S. Data Processing Industry (New York: Praeger, 1983): 265.

ran many applications, and required an attendant staff of operators to handle the variety of software used, the DEC minicomputers were less expensive, special-purpose computers running one or two applications and operated without a 24-hour-a-day staff. These machines cost from $125,000 to $250,000 complete with necessary peripherals and software, substantially below large-scale computers.

DEC marketed most of its early machines to specialized users in science and engineering but soon began marketing more capable, easier to use machines to business users who wanted to perform applications in a decentralized way for greater control, responsiveness, and interactiveness. In addition, as much as 50% of DEC's minicomputers were sold on an OEM basis[11] to other manufacturers that incorporated the minicomputers into their systems. These vendors usually marketed turnkey systems—complete systems with all the hardware, peripherals, and software required for specific applications such as computer typesetting, geographic information systems, dispatching, business data processing, and library cataloging.

By 1980, DEC had grown to $1.8 billion in revenues from just $4.3 million in 1961 and $142.6 million in 1970, for a compound annual growth around 40%. DEC's remarkable success in minicomputers was due to its early entry into the market and its commitment to product development (8%–11% of revenue went to R&D) which led to superior price/performance. Market success was fueled by selling equipment to turnkey vendors and by DEC's extension of its product line into larger, general-purpose computers as its customers' needs grew. DEC minicomputers competed head-on with the lower end of IBM's product lines and frequently were chosen based on price/performance or the user's preference for decentralized computing. DEC expanded its customer support, marketing, and software and service offerings such that by 1980, it offered one of the broadest product lines in the industry and marketed to the whole spectrum of computing customers.

By 1970, the minicomputer industry consisted of a dozen medium-sized companies led by DEC, Data General, Prime, Wang, and Tandem. They were joined by IBM, NCR, Hewlett-Packard, and others, all responding to the rapidly growing demand for minicomputers. At their peak in 1985, minicomputers accounted for 34% of worldwide hardware revenues for all types of processors, nearly equaling mainframes (which accounted for 37%).[12] After growing at a stunning pace from the late 1960s until the mid-1980s, the minicomputer industry joined the mainframe in a slow decline starting in 1985, as the PC and workstation began to take its place in the business market.

The irony of the minicomputer industry is that it started out with a PC-like industry structure, then steadily consolidated itself towards the familiar vertically integrated structure of the mainframe industry. Systems makers such as DEC saw that much of the industry's revenues were in peripherals, software, and services and started providing more of those products and services themselves to expand their market. Unfortunately, by the 1980s they were fighting for a larger slice of a shrinking pie. DEC missed the PC revolution almost entirely, and by the 1990s was a shell of its former self, sustaining billions of dollars in losses and laying of tens of thousands of workers. The leading minicomputer platform, IBM's AS/400, has been redesigned to run on cheap PowerPC processors and has been repositioned as a network server. Other minicomputer makers such as Tandem, Data General, Wang, and Prime have either shifted their business strategies, been acquired, or gone out of business altogether.

During the 1970s, many countries saw the minicomputer as a great opportunity to enter the computer industry, since there was not one dominant company like IBM was in mainframes, and because the technological and financial barriers to entry were seen as being lower. Ironically, Germany's independent Nixdorf was quite successful in the minicomputer market while state-supported "national champions" such as ICL and Siemens struggled. Only the Japanese had any long-term success in minicomputers, as Fujitsu and NEC moved into third and fourth place in global sales by 1994. Outside of Japan's involvement, the industry remained mostly the domain of U.S. companies (table 2-2).

## Increasing Returns in the Central Computing Era

IBM's System/360 was not just a successful product, but also one that foreshadowed the future of the computer industry by creating the first increasing-returns franchise in the industry. Increasing returns means that under certain

TABLE 2-2. Top 10 Midrange Computer Companies[a] (percent share of industry revenue)

|  | 1985 | 100%= | $19B | 1995 | 100%= | $30B |
|---|---|---|---|---|---|---|
| 1. | DEC | | 14.4% | IBM | | 21.5% |
| 2. | IBM | | 10.5 | Hewlett-Packard | | 11.7 |
| 3. | Hewlett-Packard | | 5.6 | Compaq | | 9.4 |
| 4. | Wang | | 5.2 | Fujitsu | | 8.3 |
| 5. | Unisys | | 4.3 | DEC | | 5.5 |
| 6. | NCR | | 3.9 | NEC | | 5.1 |
| 7. | Data General | | 3.3 | AT&T/NCR | | 4.5 |
| 8. | Fijitsu | | 3.3 | Toshiba | | 4.0 |
| 9. | Siemens-Nixdorf | | 3.1 | Tandem | | 3.7 |
| 10. | Prime | | 2.7 | Siemens-Nixdorf | | 2.9 |
| Europe total | | | 3.1 | | | 2.9 |
| Japan total | | | 3.3 | | | 17.4 |

Source: McKinsey & Company, *The 1991 Report on the Computer Industry* and *The 1996 Report on the Computer Industry* (New York: McKinsey & Company, 1991, 1996).

[a]Midrange includes minicomputers, dedicated graphics servers, workstation servers, and PC servers. Data include processor revenues; excludes peripherals, software, and services.

conditions, higher levels of production can result in lower unit costs, and hence, increasing returns to scale for producers.

Arthur points to three conditions that account for increasing returns in high-tech industries. The first is up-front costs—such products have high R&D costs relative to their unit production costs, as is the case with a new drug, a new software application, or a new airplane design. The second is network effects—products are more valuable when they have a large number of users and when they have a large base of complementary assets. So as more people adopt a standard, and more third-party companies develop complementary assets (such as software or peripheral products), the value of adopting the standard increases to users. The third condition is customer groove-in, sometimes referred to as switching costs or lock-in. Here, customer training and organizational adaptation to a particular product makes it costly to switch to another (even superior) product.

In standards-based competition, increasing returns lead to a winner-take-all (or most) outcome, rather than the more balanced competitive equilibrium that would be expected in traditional industries. In the case of VCRs, one standard has come to achieve a monopoly position after competition between two technically similar standards. Once the VHS standard got ahead in the market, either due to chance or clever strategy, its lead was magnified as users and creators of complementary assets (videotapes) gravitated toward that standard.

The computer industry is the quintessential increasing returns industry, involving high up-front costs, customer groove-in, network effects, and winner-take-all standards competition; the IBM System/360 was the first product to achieve increasing returns status. It became a dominant standard in a winner-take-all competition, driving other platforms to the fringes of the market. Given the high cost of mainframe systems and the investment in software, peripherals, and user training, customers were truly locked in once they chose the IBM platform. The cliché that "no one was ever fired for buying IBM" was evidence of the strength of both the IBM brand name and the dominance of its technology standard.

The System/360 also created a standard platform for developing the complementary assets, including services, software, and peripherals, that created strong network effects for users. The first important complementary asset developed by independent vendors was the computer services business. Service bureaus such as Automatic Data Processing (ADP) and the McDonnell Automation Center grew rapidly by developing specialized business applications (such as payroll systems) and by selling information processing services to smaller businesses.[13] The service bureaus purchased IBM's hardware and then focused on a specialized set of services, doing a better job than the hardware vendors and filling a market niche (small businesses) ignored by those vendors. This was another pattern that would be repeated over and over in the industry; in time, many of those focused competitors would grow into large companies themselves.

Even more important was the growth of independent software vendors developing applications for the IBM platform. Perhaps the biggest decision by IBM in terms of energizing the whole computer industry was the decision to unbundle its software and hardware pricing in 1969. While the bundling strategy had worked well for decades and had helped IBM lock in its customers, external and internal conditions were making the strategy untenable by the late 1960s. At that time, IBM was facing a possible antitrust action by the U.S. government because of the company's huge share of the computer market. IBM was also having trouble keeping up with its software development costs and feared that those costs would continue to escalate.[14] There were already a number of independent software vendors developing applications for users, making it possible for IBM to retreat from its commitment to provide all the software its customers would need. In 1969, IBM announced it would unbundle its hardware and software pricing, a decision that would reshape the computer industry forever.

Once hardware and software were unbundled, independent software vendors could compete directly with IBM on price—now that customers saw the true cost of IBM's software. This helped lead to the rapid growth of an independent software industry in the United States, as software houses first offered custom programming services to users, then developed packaged business applications that could be sold to many users. The development of the independent software industry greatly increased the value of computer hardware, because users could purchase a wide array of software applications to meet their specific needs. It also changed the customers' thinking by making them put a value on software, rather than seeing it as just part of the whole system.

This change in attitude would not only make billionaires out of people like Microsoft's Bill Gates and Paul Allen and Oracle's Larry Ellison, but it would also propel the U.S. software industry into a position of enduring world leadership. To see the importance of unbundling, consider Japan, whose mainframe vendors have only recently begun to unbundle software from hardware. Japanese users have had a much narrower range of applications available, and have remained years behind U.S. companies in applying computer technologies to improve productivity. As a result, the Japanese software industry has remained small and lacked the dynamism of the U.S. industry.

IBM continued to thrive as a software producer in the new environment; it remains the world's largest software maker, mostly through sales of mainframe software. While IBM was unable to achieve similar success in PC software, other U.S. companies more than took up the slack, and U.S. companies accounted for over 75% of worldwide software revenues in 1995.[15]

## Competition Among Countries: Challenge from Europe and Japan

In a prescient warning to the U.S. computer industry in 1971, Mirek J. Stevenson, formerly with IBM, and then chairman of Quantum Electronics Database, wrote:

> Nothing can be more dangerous than discounting "foreign" competition and discounting the threat of Japanese companies and European companies. It was not long ago that "Made in Japan" was a slur. Soon it may be closer to a compliment. Consumer companies have found that if you can't beat them, you may as well join them. Even U.S. automakers are doing so. The computer industry is facing its worldwide challenge today and aggressive multinational posture is the road ahead.[16]

As it turned out, Stevenson was right. Competition did develop in Europe and Japan that limited the ability of U.S. companies other than IBM to penetrate these markets; these conditions gradually limited IBM as well.

### Europe's National Champions: Struggling Contenders

In the 1960s and 1970s the governments of Britain, France, Germany, and Italy became concerned about their weaknesses in computer technology and IBM's control of their domestic markets. IBM controlled more than 60% of the French and German computer markets, and more than 40% in the United Kingdom.[17] Each government chose a "national champion" strategy, whereby domestic computer makers were consolidated into one large company with the resources to compete with IBM. The national champions were ICL in Britain, Groupe Bull in France, and Siemens in Germany. Government agencies were required—and companies were encouraged—to buy from these local vendors. In addition, from the late 1960s through 1981, the three governments spent over US$3 billion for research on computer and microelectronics technologies.

Europe's efforts to create competitors to IBM turned out to be expensive failures for the most part. The various national champions never managed to gain significant market share outside their own domestic markets and remained second to IBM even in their home markets. Britain's ICL was eventually bought out by Japan's Fujitsu. France's Groupe Bull remained a consistent money loser supported by government subsidies and was reduced to reselling hardware made by Japan's NEC. Siemens is a major manufacturer of telecommunications equipment and other electronics products, but it never became internationally competitive in computers. Independent Nixdorf was more successful in the business computer market, with much less government help, but once it was bought by Siemens its share of the minicomputer market gradually declined. Even in the 1990s, IBM was by far the largest vendor in the European market.

Europe's computer industry would continue to struggle in the PC industry. In 1995, the five leading PC sellers in Europe were U.S. companies, and only two European companies were in the top ten.[18] Bull had merged its Zenith Data Systems PC division with Packard Bell, and both were effectively controlled by Japan's NEC. ICL's PC division was owned by Fujitsu, and in 1996 Italy's Olivetti put its PC division up for sale. The Europeans have nearly abandoned the computer industry, except as resellers of Japanese computers.

### Making a Winner: Japan Builds a Computer Industry

While Europe's computer industry floundered, Japan succeeded in creating a national computer industry capable of competing with IBM, at least in the domestic market, and eventually in developing products comparable in performance to IBM mainframes.[19] As a result of effective industrial policies and the efforts of the private sector, Japan's computer makers were able to grab 72.5% of the Japanese market by 1980; the same year, Fujitsu passed IBM into first place in the Japanese market for the first time. By the early 1990s, the combined global mainframe computer revenues of Fujitsu, Hitachi, and NEC surpassed those of IBM. As table 2-3 shows, IBM's share of the global mainframe market dropped from 49% in 1985 to 32% in 1995, while that of Japan's Fujitsu, Hitachi, and NEC rose from 17% to 47%.

In the early 1960s, Japan had no computer industry and lacked most technological capabilities needed to develop one. At that time, the Japanese government decided to target computers as a strategic sector for development. The Ministry of International Trade and Industry (MITI) and Nippon Telegraph and Telephone (NTT)[20] undertook a series of initiatives aimed at nurturing a national computer industry. The policies employed included erecting protective trade barriers, negotiating with IBM and other foreign companies for technology transfer on favorable terms, supporting public and private R&D, and stimulating domestic demand for Japanese computers. The Japanese government was simultaneously shaping the domestic industry structure,

TABLE 2-3. Top 10 Mainframe Computer Companies (rank and market share for large scale computers[a])

|  | 1975[b] | 1985 | (100%= $21B) | 1995 | (100%= $20B) |
|---|---|---|---|---|---|
| 1. | IBM | IBM | 49% | IBM | 32% |
| 2. | Burroughs | Unisys | 8 | Fijitsu | 25 |
| 3. | Honeywell | Fujitsu | 8 | Hitachi | 12 |
| 4. | Sperry Rand | NEC | 5 | NEC | 10 |
| 5. | Control Data | Hitachi | 4 | Siemens-Nixdorf | 4 |
| 6. | NCR | Control Data | 5 | Amdahl | 3 |
| 7. | Groupe Bull | Groupe Bull | 4 | Cray | 3 |
| 8. | DEC | Amdahl | 2 | Unisys | 3 |
| 9. | ICL | ICL | 3 | Groupe Bull | 2 |
| 10. | Nixdorf | Siemens-Nixdorf | n.a. | Comparex | 1 |
|  | Japanese total |  | 17% |  | 47%[c] |

Sources: Datamation, The Datamation 100 (June 1976); McKinsey & Company (1991, 1996).

[a]Includes mainframe, supercomputer, and minisupercomputer processor revenues; excludes peripherals, software and services.

[b]Market share not available for 1975, only estimates of rankings.

[c]Not including Amdahl, partly owned by Fujitsu.

investing in national capabilities and influencing the domestic market to favor domestic products.

MITI closely supervised IBM Japan's activities, limiting the number and types of computers it could sell in Japan. In return for access to the Japanese market, MITI required IBM to release its patents to Japanese companies at reduced royalty rates. IBM was also forced to develop local components suppliers and export a certain percentage of what it produced in Japan. MITI also promoted joint ventures between Japanese companies and foreign companies such as Sperry Univac as competitors to IBM. When IBM released the System/360 series in 1964, MITI delayed its introduction in Japan until 1966, by which time Fujitsu and NEC were able to develop similar, if still inferior, products.

In addition, the Japanese government raised tariffs on imported computers from 15% to 25% and put strong pressure on Japanese companies and government agencies to buy Japanese computers. While protecting the Japanese vendors from IBM, the Japanese government also held the threat of a flood of IBM computers over their heads to make them aware of the technological level they had to achieve to compete internationally. Protectionism bought them time, but it was always made clear that the protection was limited and the Japanese companies had to make good machines to survive. Also, unlike the Europeans who promoted "national champions" to compete with IBM, the Japanese encouraged competition among six major companies (although MITI did try unsuccessfully to get those six to merge into three larger firms to achieve economies of scale).

A critical challenge to the Japanese computer industry came in the early 1970s with IBM's introduction of the System/370, which drove U.S. competitors RCA, General Electric, and Xerox out of the mainframe business. The timing of the System/370 introduction corresponded with Japan's agreement, under heavy U.S. pressure, to open up its market to foreign computers. The still small Japanese vendors would face the full competitive might of IBM, or so it seemed. The Japanese government was not about to let its companies stand naked against IBM, however. It started by delaying liberalization until 1976; even after that, it maintained various unofficial trade barriers, especially in government procurement. The government also launched the New Series Project to help the Japanese vendors develop products to compete with the System/370 line. Fujitsu and Hitachi developed IBM-compatible M-Series mainframes,[21] while NEC worked on smaller Honeywell-compatible machines. Toshiba, Oki, and Mitsubishi concentrated on peripherals and components. Given time to respond, the Japanese vendors were able to protect their share of the domestic market while greatly improving their technological capabilities.

Even with protection, investment in computer production during this early period was a highly risky proposition for the Japanese companies, which had to compete with each other in the limited Japanese market. To encourage investment, the government used a variety of subsidies, low-interest loans, and tax benefits. One especially important initiative enabled the Japanese vendors to counter IBM's strategy of renting computers and providing complete services to users. The government created the Japan Electronic Computer Corporation (JECC), a public company owned by the government and seven companies. JECC bought Japanese computers and rented them to users. This enabled the vendors to get their money up front, while the users still had the benefit of renting rather than facing a large initial hardware investment. JECC borrowed from the Japan Development Bank at low interest rates and coordinated the prices of rentals, purchases, and repurchases of used computers to prevent price competition and allow the Japanese companies to make a profit. In time, the Japanese computer makers grew large enough to support their own rental programs, but the JECC was critical in the 1960s and early 1970s.

Along with MITI, NTT played a vital, if sometimes competing, role in the growth of the Japanese computer industry. It farmed out research on computers and data communications to its family of suppliers, particularly NEC, Fujitsu, and Oki. NTT also created a market for the domestic vendors, buying their products at higher than normal prices. While NTT did buy IBM products, it preferred to have domestic suppliers and avoid dependence on foreign products. One Fujitsu manager compared NTT's relationship with its family of suppliers to the relationship of the Pentagon and U.S. computer companies.

A final element in the government's efforts to develop the computer industry was the support of research and development. Over the years, a number of cooperative R&D projects were undertaken with the support of MITI and

NTT. The results of these projects have ranged from highly successful to complete failures. Table 2-4 presents a description of the nature and outcomes of the most important R&D projects from 1964 to 1981.

In general, the success or failure of R&D consortia seems to have been related to the degree to which their efforts focused on the commercial needs of industry. Projects aimed at leapfrogging ahead of IBM with new, untested technologies generally failed, while those aimed at catching up in existing commercial technologies were the most successful. The projects were plagued by competition among members of the research consortia, who were not anxious to share their own technology with Japanese competitors. There was also a good deal of competition between MITI and NTT, and many of their projects overlapped. Still, projects such as the DIPS-1 Project, the New Series Project, and the VLSI projects were very important in helping Japan catch up and become competitive in the computer industry.

The effectiveness of Japan's information technology policies in the 1960s and 1970s is seen clearly in the growth rates of the Japanese vendors and the extent to which they were able to displace IBM in the Japanese market (figure 2-3).

Japan's computer makers were domestically oriented, and there has never been much direct exporting of Japanese branded mainframes. Nonetheless, the Japanese companies were building up their international presence in other ways. Fujitsu bailed out struggling Amdahl (a company started by the designer of the IBM System/360, Gene Amdahl) in 1972, investing $54 million over four years in return for an equity stake and access to Amdahl's technology.[22] It soon began manufacturing some of Amdahl's mainframe computers as well as providing components and peripherals. Likewise, Japanese computer makers supplied hardware for European firms such as ICL, BASF, and Siemens and produced components for computer makers around the world. Computer hardware exports topped imports for the first time in 1981, and by 1983, exports surpassed imports by a 4:1 ratio.

Still, the Japanese vendors struggled to keep up with IBM's technology, especially in software. In 1982, an FBI sting operation caught Hitachi and Mitsubishi stealing IBM technology for mainframe operating systems. Hitachi settled with IBM by paying $45 million up front, plus $36 million to $54 million per year to continue using IBM's technology. Fujitsu had been able to get access to some IBM technology through its relationship with Amdahl, but after the Hitachi case it negotiated an agreement with IBM covering Fujitsu's use of the IBM-compatible software. In 1985, however IBM filed a complaint against Fujitsu for breaking this agreement. In 1987, arbitrators decided that Fujitsu could have access to IBM source codes for $833 million.

Why was Japan able to develop a domestic computer industry that was both profitable and technologically competitive with IBM during a period when U.S. companies were falling by the wayside and Europe's national champions were being steamrolled by the IBM juggernaut? The key factors were industry structure and industrial policy.

TABLE 2-4. Major Information Technology R&D Projects, 1964–1980

| R&D Projects | Sponsors/Participants | Cost | Objective | Outcome |
|---|---|---|---|---|
| FONTAC (1962–1966) | MITI/Fujitsu, Oki, NEC | $2 million | Increased speed and memory capacity of Japanese computers. | FONTAC computer did not work, but Fujitsu gained technology that it used in its FACOM computers. |
| Super High-Performance Computer Project (1966–1972) | MITI/Fujitsu, Hitachi, NEC, Oki, Toshiba, Mitsubishi | $33 million | Develop a prototype of a computer superior to the IBM 360. | Did not surpass IBM 360, but made important gains in hardware technology. Software side of project was a complete failure. |
| DIPS-1 (1968–1971) | NTT/Fujitsu, Hitachi, NEC | $83 million | Commercialize results of Super-High Performance Project. | Successful in creating a reliable mainframe system for NTT's network. |
| Pattern Information Processing System Project (1971–1980) | MITI/Fujitsu, Hitachi, NEC, Toshiba, Oki, Mitsubishi, Matsushita, Sanyo | $67 million | Develop technology for recognition of patterns, such as handwriting, characters, pictures, speech. | Few commercial applications were developed initially, but by mid-1980s, some technologies were being used in commercial products. |
| New Series (3.5 Generation) Project (1972–1976) | MITI/Fujitsu, Hitachi, NEC, Toshiba, Oki, Mitsubishi | $235 million | Develop a 3.5 generation computer based on IBM System/370 standards. | Helped Fujitsu and Hitachi develop M-Series computers and survive at a time when System/370 was driving other IBM competitors out of the market. |
| DIPs II (1973–1975) | NTT/Fujitsu, Hitachi, NEC | $15 million | Develop 3.5 generation computers for use in NTT networks. | Succeeded in developing computers compatible with DIPS I machines. |
| VLSI (1976–1979) | MITI/Fujitsu, Hitachi, NEC, Toshiba, Mitsubishi | $360 million | Develop very large scale integrated circuit (VLSI) technology, initially for 64K-bit RAMs. | Successful in key technologies for production of advanced memory chips. Members earned over 1,000 patents, although only 16% were jointly developed. |
| VLSI (1976–1980) | NTT/Fujitsu, Hitachi, NEC | $100 million | Develop VLSI technology for communication networks. | Complemented MITI's successful VLSI project. |

Sources: Compiled from various sources, including Marie Anchordoguy, *Computers Inc.: Japan's Challenge to IBM* (Cambridge: Harvard University Press, 1989); Martin Fransman, *The Market and Beyond: Cooperation and Competition in Information Technology in the Japanese System* (Cambridge: Cambridge University Press, 1990); Kenneth Flamm, *Targeting the Computer: Government Support and International Competition* (Washington, D.C.: Brookings Institution, 1987), and Japanese government documents.

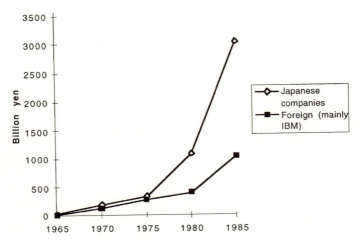

FIGURE 2-3.  Computer Sales in Japan (billion yen).
*Source:* Anchordoguy, 1989.

The industrial structure of the Japanese computer industry played an important role in its successful development. The major computer makers (NEC, Hitachi, Fujitsu, Oki, Mitsubishi, and Toshiba) are all part of different *keiretsu*, or families of companies headed by a bank and trading company. The *keiretsu* system helped the computer makers survive in several important ways. First, the presence of a friendly bank provided access to "patient" capital that would be available even through downturns in the market. Second, the *keiretsu* could organize production through vertical integration of the computer maker and numerous affiliated suppliers, to match IBM's tightly integrated production chain. This permitted development costs to be shared and avoided dependence on outside (particularly foreign) suppliers. The *keiretsu* system also provided built-in demand for computers, because other *keiretsu* members would be expected to buy the products of its own "family member." Finally, technology could be shared among *keiretsu* members, particularly the manufacturing process technologies that have provided the basis for much of Japan's industrial competitiveness. IBM's U.S. and European competitors did not have the advantages of the *keiretsu* system and were unable to match IBM's financial and technological capacities on their own.

The Japanese computer industry also benefited from strong competition among the six vendors, which had to fight each other for a share of the protected domestic market and could not count on government protection to guarantee the success of any individual company. While European countries each tried to promote one national champion to achieve economies of scale needed to compete with IBM, MITI and NTT consistently involved three to six domestic companies in their research projects, and MITI required IBM to broadly license technology to all Japanese makers. MITI persuaded the companies to specialize in different product and technology areas and to avoid "excessive" price competition, but it made subsidies available to all of the companies and did not prevent them from entering markets they felt were promising.

The key difference between Japan's and Europe's computer strategies was not simply the amount of money spent by the governments (as shown in table 2-5) or the level of protection of the domestic market. Among the European countries, the German government actually matched Japan in total spending, while France and the United Kingdom spent a proportional amount, given the size of their economies. The level of import protection was probably lower overall in Europe, especially in the 1960s, but each major country clearly created a substantial market for its national champion through government procurement.

The real difference between the computer industry policies of Japan and the European countries was in the nature of policies employed and the relationship between government and industry. First was the government's strategy for technology transfer. MITI's negotiations with IBM to require transfer of its patents at a low royalty rate at least gave the Japanese companies access to the formal technology base of the world's leading computer company.

The second difference was Japan's Darwinian industrial policy. The Japanese government gave extensive support to the computer industry, but it required that the industry perform in return. It did this partly by promoting competition in the domestic market rather than giving the whole protected market to one national champion. The government also limited the duration of market protection and would not continue to subsidize companies that did not keep up. For instance, after Oki failed to develop a commercially viable product based on its participation in the New Series Project, it was not included in MITI's ensuing VLSI project. In contrast, the British and French governments subsidized ICL and Groupe Bull for years even as they continued to lose money.

The third factor was Japan's ability to coordinate the efforts of government and the private sector to create a shared base of technology available to the major Japanese computer makers, who then developed their own commercial products. While the joint projects were often less cooperative than the "Japan, Inc." rhetoric would suggest, they did help to develop fundamental (or "precompetitive") technologies upon which commercial products would be based.

In more general terms, Japan's strategy was a flexible, pragmatic effort to create the technology base and domestic demand needed for private sector producers to compete against IBM. Combined with the energetic efforts of the private sector, the strategy was a remarkable success, especially in the light of the Europeans' failures.

The Japanese success story in computers did not come without a cost, however. Other Japanese industries and the Japanese government were saddled with inferior computers for the better part of two decades. In light of Japan's rapid growth during that time, it is difficult to argue that this disadvantage created much of a drag on the Japanese economy. However, it did

TABLE 2-5. Government Support for Computer-related R&D

| Country | Average Annual Government Expenditure (in US$ millions) |
|---|---|
| France | |
| 1967–1975 | 57 |
| 1976–1981 | 87 |
| West Germany | |
| 1971–1975 | 167 |
| 1976–1979 | 189 |
| United Kingdom | |
| 1969–1973 | 23 |
| 1974–1979 | 78–83 |
| Japan (MITI and NTT) | |
| 1970–1979 | 130 |

Source: Flamm (1987).

slow the diffusion of computers throughout the economy, lowering productivity in the service sector and retarding the learning-by-doing process that is critical to effective computer use.

The lack of sophisticated users has become a true disadvantage to the Japanese computer industry, especially in the software and services sectors, where close interaction between producers and users is a key to product development. As a result, Japan remains far behind the United States and even Europe in software, a gap that continues to plague the industry in Japan.

Ironically, perhaps the greatest cost was the effect of success on the attitudes of Japanese industry and government. The success of the 1970s was a result of an all-out "Beat IBM" strategy. If the significance of the PC revolution in the 1980s was underestimated by IBM, it was even less recognized in Japan. Japanese government policy and industry efforts focused on creating new generations of more powerful, more technologically advanced large computers, even as the market was undergoing a monumental shift away from such machines. The cost of this misplaced focus would become clear as Japan fell far behind in the PC industry.

### Globalization of Production in the Central Computing Era

The central computing era saw a gradual trend toward globalization, mostly through IBM's activities. International Business Machines, Inc., was aptly named, as it was international in focus even before the computer was invented. During the central computing era, IBM aggressively marketed its products around the world, getting into markets before either other U.S. companies could enter or domestic competitors could spring up. It was largely because of IBM's efforts that computer technology was adopted so widely around the world.

While it initially globalized its operations by setting up local sales and distribution operations, IBM also moved more gradually to globalize its production, design, and even R&D activities. The company set up factories, labs, and international procurement offices in Europe, Japan, and even in some developing countries. In 1972, IBM World Trade (representing non-U.S. operations) was active in 126 countries, with 22 manufacturing plants and 115,000 employees.[23] This was done partly to serve those markets better, partly to develop a better and cheaper supplier base, and partly to respond to government demands in many countries for local production and exports. Governments in Japan and Europe were concerned about trade deficits in computers, and IBM responded with a strategy aimed at balancing its own trade among the U.S., Japan, and Europe.

Outside of IBM, however, the mainframe and minicomputer industries were not very globally oriented. There were exceptions, such as DEC, which produced in Europe most of what it sold there. There were also many alliances across countries, such as Fujitsu with Amdahl and ICL, NEC with Honeywell and Groupe Bull, and Hitachi with Olivetti. Still, most companies kept the majority of their production in their home country and earned most of their revenues there as well.

Parallel with IBM's global distribution of its activities, a second engine driving the eventual globalization of production in the computer industry was the international investment of the broader electronics and semiconductor industries. The U.S. electronics industry started moving production offshore in the 1960s, with companies such as Motorola, General Electric, Texas Instruments, General Instruments, and Fairchild Semiconductor establishing production facilities in a number of Asian countries.

The Japanese electronics industry was likewise taking advantage of cheap labor, cheap land, and government incentives in Asian countries, although the Japanese companies were less inclined to move higher value added activities offshore than their American counterparts. Still, the Japanese played an important role in developing an electronics industry in Asia, particularly in Taiwan and several southeast Asian countries. European electronics companies such as Philips, Alcatel, and Siemens also were significant investors in Asia.

The spread of electronics production to Asia in the period 1960–1980 was a very important factor in East Asia becoming a major production hub in the PC industry. There were two reasons for this. First, East Asia developed the capabilities that would make it the logical place for PC companies to set up production, source components, and establish OEM relationships. These capabilities included large pools of experienced electronics engineers and other professionals, as well as production workers. There was also an established supply base of local companies able to produce everything from electronics components to plastic and metal parts.

Second, while the heroes of the U.S. PC industry were twenty-something hotshots who designed the hardware and software and were featured on magazine covers, most of the people in charge of manufacturing were veterans of the electronics industry who knew how to build and run factories. Many of them had spent time in Asia working for companies like Fairchild, Texas Instruments, General Instruments, and IBM, and they were familiar with the capabilities of the Asian companies and workers. This familiarity led U.S. companies to look across the Pacific, rather than to other parts of the world, as they globalized production in the PC era.

## Competition Among Global Production Networks: The PC Era

The computer industry was turned upside down in the 1980s by a product originally dismissed as a toy. That toy, the personal computer, turned out to be a David that would humble the mighty mainframe Goliath. Ironically, IBM—the company that created a mass market for PCs—was one of the biggest losers of the revolution it helped foment.

The PC industry would do more than remake the competitive landscape for companies. It also led to a globalization of the industry that went far beyond anything seen or even imagined in the previous era. Companies no longer globalized just to appease host country governments or to find cheap labor for simple assembly processes. Instead, with the encouragement and support of those governments, they built a production network in which all parts of the production process were located around the world (primarily around the Pacific Rim) to take advantage of local capabilities wherever they existed or could be created.

### Emergence of the PC

The PC revolution truly arrived with the IBM PC, but there were important antecedents. There were computer kits for hobbyists beginning in 1975 with the MITS Altair running a version of the BASIC programming language from Bill Gates and Paul Allen, and the Apple I from Steve Jobs and Steve Wozniak, who had written their own version of BASIC. Demand for these computers was so great that, only two years later, three important new machines entered the market: the Apple II, the Commodore Pet, and the Tandy TRS-80.[24] These were soon followed by the first portables—Osborne I in 1981, and the Kaypro and Radio Shack 100 in 1982. The Apple computers were initially very successful in the education market, but all of the computers quickly made inroads into business markets as professionals and analysts went for them in droves, attracted by simple but valuable applications like spreadsheets and word processing.

It was IBM's entry into the PC business that created a mass market for PCs, because it signaled that the PC was an important part of the total computing infrastructure and that users could be assured that these machines would be around in the future. The IBM PC that was first introduced on August 12, 1981, became the PC platform for the 1980s and 1990s. The original IBM PC was not technologically sophisticated, but it incorporated most of the features users wanted. It was a "system," not a single function appliance; it was an open box ready for expansion, reconfiguration, and continual upgrading.

The IBM PC came about through an extraordinary set of circumstances. As the early demand for PCs outstripped the ability of all producers to meet it, and as businesses began to adopt PCs, IBM executives realized that they were failing to capitalize on the developing business market for personal computers. They also realized that the rapid growth in demand made Apple and its competitors vulnerable to new entrants. So, in July 1980, IBM's Corporate Management Committee decided to get into the market for desktop computers and gave the executive in charge, William Lowe, a deadline of one year to market.

Lowe's response was to tell the Corporate Management Committee: "The only way to get into the PC business was to go out and buy part of a computer company or buy both the CPU and software from people like Apple or Atari— because we can't do this within the culture of IBM."[25] Because IBM did not want to put someone else's name on the computer, it gave Lowe a mandate to build the computer with complete autonomy from the IBM bureaucracy. This meant that the new PC division would operate like a start-up company with IBM serving as its venture capitalist. It would outsource wherever needed, thereby avoiding IBM's traditional dependence on internal sourcing. It would build the system from available proven technologies rather than invent new ones. And it would market the system through retail outlets (such as Sears and Computerland) rather than through expensive company sales agents.

Although there was no important technical advance in the IBM PC, there was a technical decision that had significant implications. IBM went from the 8-bit microprocessor, which had characterized the previous machines, to a 16-bit processor. It used the Intel 8088 microprocessor, which processed data internally in 16-bit words but used 8-bit external buses. This decision meant that the IBM PC could not use existing operating systems designed for 8-bit systems. Consistent with its other decisions about going to the market for the needed technology, IBM went to the market for its operating system. IBM first approached Digital Research, which was working on a 16-bit version of CP/M—the leading operating system for 8-bit computers—but the two firms could not come to terms. So, IBM turned to Microsoft.

IBM was already soliciting Microsoft to provide a new version of MBASIC and asked Bill Gates to develop an operating system for them. Rather than write a new system, Microsoft bought an operating system that had been created by a local Seattle software house, put the finishing touches on it, and sold it to IBM as PC-DOS. In what turned out to be a deadly mistake in an otherwise brilliant set of decisions and executions, IBM allowed Microsoft to license DOS to other computer makers as MS-DOS without sharing royalties with IBM. This helped to make DOS the de facto operating system for the

PC industry, but it was a double-edged sword. By allowing Microsoft to license its own version of DOS to other PC makers, IBM gave away control of the most important part of the PC architecture.

In order to keep costs low, the PC division outsourced all parts competitively. When internal IBM divisions complained, they were told to submit bids like everyone else. Some did, and they won contracts (keyboards and circuit boards), but the principal suppliers were outside of IBM. Tandon provided disk drives; Zenith made the power supplies; Japan's Epson made printers; SCI Systems stuffed the circuit boards; and China Picture Tube (part of the Taiwanese company Tatung) made the monitors as IBM sourced globally for components. The PC was assembled from these components on an automated assembly line in Boca Raton, Florida.

The IBM PC launched in 1981 was such a tremendous success that initial demand outstripped supply and there were enormous order backlogs. By the end of 1983, the IBM PC had captured 26 % of the market with about 750,000 shipments.

The success of the IBM PC brought forth a legion of application developers, producers of components and peripherals, and makers of IBM PC clones. Software developers were attracted to the PC because of its large and growing base of users. They quickly developed new applications, which stimulated further demand for the PC, and they fueled that demand by developing more applications and improving those that existed.

The rapid start-up of the PC industry had required sourcing from multiple suppliers, and soon there were many producers of components and peripherals that could be used to make complete PC systems. The large supply base of components and peripherals stimulated new companies to become clone makers by taking advantage of the PC's open architecture. These companies targeted IBM's high margins with aggressive pricing and filled the void created by IBM's inability to meet the huge demand for PCs.

IBM had tried to ward off the clone makers with two defenses. First, IBM expected that it would always be the low cost producer; because it was the largest-volume purchaser, it could exact the lowest prices from suppliers. Charles Ferguson and Charles Morris explain: "What happened instead was that IBM put its suppliers into the high-volume business and so bore their start-up and learning curve costs. The clone makers then rolled in behind IBM and bought suppliers' excess capacity, so their costs were usually *lower*."[26] This pattern was especially important in Asian countries such as Taiwan, where IBM helped a number of suppliers achieve high-volume production (e.g., Tatung in monitors).

IBM's second line of defense was the PC's BIOS software (basic input/output system), which translated signals from the operating system and other software for the PC's keyboard, display, and printer connections. It was copyrighted and not for sale; therefore, theoretically, no one could make a completely compatible IBM-PC without IBM's BIOS. Again, IBM turned out to be wrong. Compaq Computer of Houston, Texas reverse engineered the IBM BIOS. According to Ferguson and Morris, "A team of programmers who had never seen IBM BIOS specs took the thirty leading software applications and analyzed the signals each program sent to the PC hardware and the responses it needed to get back. They then wrote software that supplied all the right responses and it performed exactly like the IBM BIOS, but with completely different code, skirting any copyright issues."[27] IBM did win some copyright lawsuits against firms that directly copied its BIOS, but companies like Compaq that used a "clean room" approach were protected.

To clone the IBM-PC, Compaq and others then only needed to buy the 8088 microprocessors from Intel and MS-DOS from Microsoft. Bill Gates resisting licensing MS-DOS at first because he had been customizing the software for each vendor. However, Gates quickly caught on that the more clone makers used identical Microsoft software, the greater Microsoft's leverage in the industry. He therefore stopped a series of customizing projects and insisted from then on that every clone maker buy the identical DOS. This effectively removed the last proprietary hurdle to copying the original IBM-PC in its entirety and "the IBM-PC stood naked before the world."[28] Compaq's final insult was to hire away "Sparky" Sparks, who had set up IBM's PC distribution system. Since IBM's factories had not yet caught up with their orders, PC dealers jumped at the chance to buy Compaq's compatibles, which were cheaper and provided higher margins for dealers.

Compaq, Corona, and Eagle were among the first clone makers in the PC industry that had nearly 100 companies in the early 1980s. Compaq was one of the few that survived the industry shakeout of 1983–1984 as IBM caught up with its backlogs in demand and cut prices aggressively. Compaq survived by emphasizing quality, high-end PCs. In 1992, Compaq responded to another market downturn by changing its strategy to compete on price for individual PCs and target the higher margin market for PC servers, where it is now the market leader. In 1995, Compaq moved into first place in PC sales, capturing 13% of worldwide PC shipments.

## The Personal Computer Industry

The character of the computer industry changed dramatically during the PC era as thousands of new companies came into the industry. PC makers generally focused on design, distribution, marketing, and sales and many relied on lower cost foreign companies for production. The industry became very specialized, as components, peripherals, and sometimes whole systems were sourced from outside suppliers. Firms in the peripherals segment specialized in making disk drives, printers, or monitors. Other firms supplied the subassemblies that went into these peripherals. Still other firms supplied the parts, connectors, and cables used in the subassemblies. This segmentation was driven by new technologies and by the open architecture and standardized components of the IBM-PC. The result was the creation of new user markets, new forms of competition, and a new industry structure, as illustrated in table 2-6.

TABLE 2-6. PC Industry Compared to Mainframe and Minicomputer Industry

| Mainframes | Minicomputers | Personal Computers |
|---|---|---|
| **Technology** | | |
| Vacuum tube to transistors. | Integrated circuits. | Smaller, less expensive, more reliable integrated circuits. |
| **User markets** | | |
| Large business users globally. | Departmental users. | Individual users alone or in groups. Global markets because of common requirements. |
| **Key players** | | |
| First movers were U.S. firms: IBM, Honeywell, Sperry, Control Data. Followed in Europe by "national champions" ICL, Siemens, and Groupe Bull, and in Japan by Fujitsu, Hitachi, and NEC. | New players focused on minis: DEC, Hewlett-Packard, Prime, Wang, and Tandem in United States, Nixdorf in Europe. Later joined by mainframe makers IBM, Fujitsu, and NEC. | New companies and new countries: Intel, Microsoft, Compaq, Apple, Dell, Novell, et al. in United States; Toshiba, NEC, and Canon in Japan; Acer, FIC, and Mitac in Taiwan; Trigem and Samsung in Korea, Creative, IPC, and Aztech in Singapore. |
| **Business strategy** | | |
| Competition among companies using proprietary systems to lock in customers and lock out competitors. | Entry into niche markets not penetrated by mainframes, then moving up into large systems; competition among companies with proprietary systems. | Competition between platforms, then within victorious IBM/Wintel standard. Using features and functions to differentiate products. |
| **Application software** | | |
| Initially bundled with hardware, later developed by users and by independent vendors. | Initially developed by users, then sold by independent vendors. | Sold in "shrink wrap" by independent vendors through retail channels. |
| **Production system** | | |
| Company- and country-based production, with global distribution. Large, vertically integrated companies achieve internal economies of scale. | Company- and country-based production systems. Medium-sized vertically integrated companies make complete systems, but depend on third-party suppliers for many components and peripherals. | Horizontally segmented, global production network. Most R&D, design, and marketing done in United States, with manufacturing largely done in Asia. Reliance on outside suppliers to achieve external economies of scale and speed to market. |
| **Industry structure** | | |
| Concentrated oligopolistic industry with IBM dominating the market worldwide, except Japan. Others compete for niche markets or make plug-compatible systems. | Evenly distributed, competitive industry with many medium-sized companies. DEC, Hewlett-Packard, and IBM have large but not dominant shares. | Distributed, highly competitive industry divided among increasing and decreasing returns segments. Near-monopolies in increasing returns markets, oligopoly, or open competition in decreasing returns segments. |

*New Technology.*   The PC was made possible largely because of three technological changes. First was the introduction of new technologies that reduced both the cost and size of computers. New standardized semiconductors, introduced in the late 1970s, were smaller, less expensive, and more reliable than those that had been incorporated into traditional computers. The relentless force of Moore's law continued to double the number of transistors that could be packed into a microprocessor every eighteen months or so. Each doubling allowed the PC to perform a whole new range of functions that previously required larger computers.

The second technological innovation was the modularity of the PC, composed of standard components all the way from the semiconductors used for processing and memory, to the circuit boards, disk drives, power supplies, cables, and connectors that were embedded in a PC system. Moreover, peripherals such as printers, scanners, monitors, and keyboards were also modular products. The modularity of the PC meant that parts, subassemblies, components, and peripherals could be sourced in the open market from wherever the best price/performance could be garnered.

The third innovation was the change in the architecture of these systems. Mainframes and minicomputers had been proprietary "closed systems" whose architectures were incompatible with those of most other vendors. This meant that once a customer was committed to a particular vendor, it was very costly to switch to another vendor. The IBM PC brought about the rise of "open systems," which meant that standards for interconnection and interoperability were defined publicly so that third parties could design components and peripherals that smoothly connected and operated together as a system under the control of the central processor. The openness of the PC allowed various hardware and software firms to make and sell products that would be compatible with each other. The IBM PC was made from off-the-shelf components readily available in the market from a variety of firms, so anyone could imitate it, using the same or similar components. More important, the companies who controlled the key proprietary elements of the system, Microsoft and Intel, were not in competition with the PC vendors and were more than happy to sell or license their products to all comers.

It was this openness that made the IBM PC the winner against Apple's Macintosh computer in spite of the Mac's superior user interface and plug-and-play interoperability. Unlike Microsoft, Apple refused to license its operating system to other hardware companies until the mid-1990s. Consequently, the Mac never developed broad support within the industry and Apple had to bear most of the R&D costs for the Mac platform.[29] In contrast, the widespread support of the IBM PC and competition among clone makers and components suppliers led to widespread innovation and continually reduced costs, which brought prices down.

*New Users.*   The PC was revolutionary in its design, but an equally important revolution was in the concept for use behind the PC. In contrast to the mainframe, which was designed for "corporate users," and the minicomputer, which was designed for "departmental users," the PC had been designed—as its name suggests—as a personal tool, a tool for "individual users." The technology had been getting better, easier to use, and less expensive, so that it was now seen as a tool for everyone.

In the United States, advertising promised to make users more productive, empowered, and free from the tyranny of central computing. Users had become more knowledgeable and experienced with computers, and increasingly they wanted more from their computers. The introduction of the IBM PC therefore occurred at a unique juncture of the technology and the users' evolution. It brought widespread, immediate, and enthusiastic acceptance of the PC in markets that had not been tapped previously, including schools, homes, small businesses, and individual's desktops in larger businesses. This acceptance was unexpected and startling to most people in the industry, although it had been hoped for by many PC pioneers.

The PC found similar acceptance in other English-speaking countries, which could use IBM-compatible PCs with no modification. In other countries with Roman alphabets, the PC likewise caught on as soon as software was adapted or developed in local languages. In other countries, language was a bigger barrier. Most notable was Japan, whose computer makers had to modify MS-DOS to handle the Japanese language, leading to a fragmented hardware and software market and slow adoption of PCs.

As a result of its wide acceptance in most user markets, the PC transformed the structure of the computer industry dramatically. Around the world, new companies, aided in many cases by their national governments, sprung up rapidly to fill the growing user demand.

*New Competitors.* The PC industry was started primarily by firms that did not exist in the central computing era. These include well-known companies such as Apple Computer, Commodore, Compaq, Novell, and Microsoft, as well as companies that are no longer heard of, such as MITS, Kaypro, Osborne, Corona, Eagle, Digital Research, and VisiCorp. Most were new companies that were created specifically to produce PC hardware or software. Even large PC companies such as Apple, Compaq, and Microsoft were small compared to established firms in other sectors of the computer industry. These smaller, focused companies were able to compete successfully by bringing new innovative products to market faster, gaining higher margins initially, and then reducing prices to beat out latecomers and other competitors.

There were several hundred firms that made complete PC systems, but there were thousands of firms supporting them with components, peripherals, and applications. Many players that were in the market ten years ago are not even in the market today—they have gone out of business or been bought out by other companies—and many players that are in the market today were not there ten years ago.

Only a few companies have shown staying power in the highly competitive PC industry. Apple, Compaq, IBM, and Hewlett-Packard have remained in the top ten, but otherwise the market has continued to be in flux (table 2-7).

TABLE 2-7. Rank of Top 10 PC Makers in 1985, 1990, and 1995

| | 1985 | | 1990 | | 1995 | |
|---|---|---|---|---|---|---|
| Rank | Company | Market Share (%) | Company | Market Share (%) | Company | Market Share (%) |
| 1. | IBM | 25% | IBM | 13% | Compaq | 10% |
| 2. | Commodore[a] | 14 | Apple | 7 | IBM | 8 |
| 3. | Apple | 14 | NEC | 6 | Apple | 8 |
| 4. | Tandy[a] | 8 | Compaq | 4 | Packard Bell[b] | 7 |
| 5. | Compaq | 3 | Toshiba | 3 | NEC[b] | 4 |
| 6. | Atari[a] | 3 | Olivetti | 2 | Hewlett-Packard | 4 |
| 7. | Hewlett-Packard | 2 | ZDS | 2 | Dell[b] | 3 |
| 8. | ZDS[a] | 2 | Packard Bell | 2 | Acer[b] | 3 |
| 9. | DEC[a] | 1 | Hewlett-Packard | 1 | Fujitsu/ICL[b] | 3 |
| 10. | NCR[a] | 1 | Fujitsu | 1 | Toshiba[b] | 3 |
| Top 10 companies' share | | 73% | | 41% | | 53% |

*Source:* International Data Corporation: table provided to authors.

[a]Out of top ten since 1985.

[b]New of top ten since 1985.

IBM, which created the market for the PC, had 26% of world shipments at its peak in 1983 and has been slowly losing market share ever since (to 8% in 1995).

Some of the leading companies in the PC market are relatively recent newcomers such as Acer, Dell, Gateway 2000, and Packard Bell. Most of the leading PC vendors are still U.S. companies, with the exception of NEC, Toshiba (the world leader in portables), Fujitsu, and Acer. However, Packard Bell is now owned by NEC and AST has been taken over by Korea's Samsung. Also, many of the companies selling PC systems are essentially assembly manufacturers that provide design and marketing, but source components and peripherals (and sometimes entire systems) from outside suppliers, most of whom are in East Asia.

*New Industry Structure.*   It was the IBM PC with its modular, open architecture and global sourcing that changed the industry structure. During the central computing era, the industry involved a few large, vertically integrated companies and a fairly large number of specialized companies providing software, services, and plug-compatible processors and peripherals. Although the first minicomputer systems were assembled from components and peripherals readily available from outside suppliers, the leading minicomputer vendors quickly shifted to manufacturing these themselves like the mainframers before them. In contrast, the PC architecture was open from the very beginning and has stayed open.

The modular and open character of the PC meant that parts, subassemblies, and peripherals could be procured from any firm that had the needed manufacturing capabilities, and that these components in turn could be assembled into a system by any firm with the needed design capabilities and assembly facilities. Design was focused on the motherboard, whose arrangement of chips and circuits determined the system's speed and functions and how the PC's central processor interacted with the other components and peripherals; however, even the motherboards themselves could be assembled by specialized firms.

These specialized firms within horizontal segments (such as parts, subassemblies, peripherals, or software) were able to achieve economies of scale by specializing in that segment and supplying the many vendors who built complete systems. Firms building complete systems in turn realized network economies from the vast supply infrastructure that developed to meet the rapid growth in demand for PCs. Thus, the PC changed the structure of the industry from vertically integrated firms competing with one another across all segments to horizontally segmented firms competing with one another within segments and across "platforms" (figure 2-4).

Indeed, a key force bringing about the demise of the old model of the computer industry was the rise of independent vendors like Intel and Motorola in semiconductors; Microsoft and Lotus in software; Apple, Dell, and Compaq in personal computers; and Novell and Microsoft in PC networking. Rather than competing vertically across industry segments, these companies vied for market share within their horizontal segments and some of them such as Intel and Microsoft cooperated informally in an effort to set de facto industry standards.

The new industry structure of the PC era was much less concentrated than the structure of the central computing era (figure 2-2). There were hundreds of PC makers worldwide. Moreover, the predicted "shakeout" and concentration of the PC industry did not occur. Instead the industry was actually less concentrated in 1995 than it was in 1985, with the top 10 firms accounting for 73% of world shipments in 1985, and just 53% in 1995 (table 2-8). Only in 1996 and 1997 did some consolidation begin to take place, as Compaq, IBM, Bell and Hewlett-Packard increased their share of the market significantly.

Throughout the PC era, U.S. firms have held the greatest share of world shipments for PC systems. Among the top ten PC makers, U.S. firms held a 59% share of the world market in 1985 and still held 40% in 1995. However, while U.S. firms maintained a large share in final sales, many of the PCs they were selling were produced by Asian (particularly Taiwanese) companies, while U.S. vendors focused on design and marketing.

The shift from vertical integration to horizontal segmentation in the computer industry had a profound effect on the nature of competition in the industry. In the mainframe industry, IBM had achieved network externalities in the form of application software and plug-compatible peripherals that were available to anyone who bought an IBM or IBM-compatible computer. For IBM, mainframes were an increasing returns business, since the marginal cost for each system sold declined over the life cycle of each product family, and sales of applications, services, peripherals, and upgrades expanded as the user

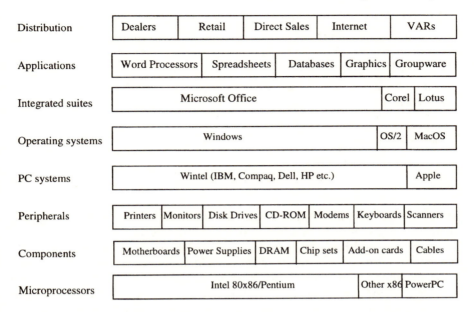

| Distribution | Dealers | Retail | Direct Sales | Internet | VARs |
|---|---|---|---|---|---|

| Applications | Word Processors | Spreadsheets | Databases | Graphics | Groupware |
|---|---|---|---|---|---|

| Integrated suites | Microsoft Office | | | Corel | Lotus |
|---|---|---|---|---|---|

| Operating systems | Windows | | | OS/2 | MacOS |
|---|---|---|---|---|---|

| PC systems | Wintel (IBM, Compaq, Dell, HP etc.) | | | | Apple |
|---|---|---|---|---|---|

| Peripherals | Printers | Monitors | Disk Drives | CD-ROM | Modems | Keyboards | Scanners |
|---|---|---|---|---|---|---|---|

| Components | Motherboards | Power Supplies | DRAM | Chip sets | Add-on cards | Cables |
|---|---|---|---|---|---|---|

| Microprocessors | Intel 80x86/Pentium | | | | Other x86 | PowerPC |
|---|---|---|---|---|---|---|

FIGURE 2-4. Structure of the PC Industry by Segment. *Source:* Adapted from Grove, 1996. Reprinted by permission.

base expanded. IBM also benefited from strong customer lock-in with users who had heavy investments in equipment, software, and training on IBM systems. And since IBM controlled all the key technologies that made up its systems architecture, other companies were relegated to the margins of the industry.

IBM's decision to outsource most of the components for the PC, and its loss of control over the microprocessor and operating system, created a new competitive environment altogether. The microprocessor and operating systems markets became new increasing returns businesses, with near-monopoly industry structures, while most of the hardware segments of the industry evolved into highly competitive decreasing returns businesses. A few segments (such as application software, printers, PC systems, and services) are hybrids that fall between purely increasing and decreasing returns markets.

The horizontal segmentation of the industry stimulated competition within the segments,[30] but the critical competition that distinctively marked the PC era focused on "hardware/software platforms." This was in marked contrast to the central computing era where competition had been between firms. The significant competing platforms in the PC era were two: the "Wintel" platform of Microsoft and Intel and the Mac platform of Apple and Motorola.

Strategic alliances were an important feature of the PC era and grew out of the competition and instability in the market. Alliances usually were formed by firms across segments, such as the Intel/Microsoft alliance on hardware/

TABLE 2-8.  Market Share of Top Ten PC Companies, Total and by Country

|                                   | 1985 | 1990 | 1995 |
|-----------------------------------|------|------|------|
| Top ten companies' share (total)  | 73   | 41   | 53   |
| Breakdown of total:               |      |      |      |
| U.S. companies                    | 59   | 29   | 40   |
| European companies                | 0    | 2    | 0    |
| Japanese companies                | 0    | 10   | 10   |
| Taiwanese companies               | 0    | 0    | 3    |

Source: Calculated from data in table 2-7.

software platforms and Adobe/Apple in desktop publishing technologies. Alliances were also formed in other parts of the industry, between manufacturers and suppliers and between manufacturers and large retail chains. These alliances were formed for a variety of reasons, including the sharing of costs and risks associated with research and new product development, the handling of distribution and marketing, and contract manufacturing. More critically, however, alliances were formed in an effort to set de facto standards for hardware, software, network, or other architectures. The aim of the standard-setters was to achieve a critical mass of customers and suppliers subscribing to the standards in order to capture market share for the alliance participants, and to grow the market for all industry participants.

The platform competition was won by Intel and Microsoft as Wintel became the worldwide de facto standard for PCs, initially because of IBM's market strength and eventually because it was an open system and attracted thousands of companies to produce hardware and software based on the standard. The victory of Wintel created near monopolies for Microsoft and Intel in the increasing returns businesses of operating systems and microprocessors. But the rest of the PC industry has been marked by brutal competition, with market structures ranging from oligopoly to free competition in different segments of the industry (table 2-9).

*Decreasing Returns Segments.*    Although there is a great deal of variety among the different segments of the hardware industry, most hardware companies operate on the basis of decreasing returns to scale. The differences among the various market segments are important, however, as they greatly influence what types of companies and countries are most competitive in each segment.

Some industries, such as those producing DRAMs and flat-panel displays, are very capital-intensive, high-volume industries that operate in commodity-like markets, with little differentiation among products and boom and bust price cycles. These industries require heavy R&D in both product and process technologies in order to stay competitive. They tend to favor large diversified companies that have the financial resources to make large investments in R&D and production facilities, and those that can weather temporary downturns in

TABLE 2-9. Competition in the Computer Industry, 1996 (% share of world market)

| 1. Micro-processors[a] | 2. Operating systems (1995)[b] | 3. PC Systems (1995)[b] | 4. Printers[b] | 5. Hard disk drives[a] | 6. DRAM[a] | 7. Floppy disk drives[b] | 8. CD-ROM drives[b] | 9. Monitors (1995)[b] |
|---|---|---|---|---|---|---|---|---|
| Intel 83.4 | Microsoft 80.1 | Compaq 10.0 | Hewlett Packard 49.4 | Seagate 26.8 | Samsung 16.4 | Mitsumi 18.6 | Matsushita 20.5 | Samsung 14.0 |
| IBM 8.5 | Apple 4.1 | IBM 8.2 | Canon 8.0 | IBM 24.4 | NEC 13.3 | Teac 17.5 | Mitsumi 14.0 | Acer 6.3 |
| AMD 6.7 | IBM | Apple 6.7 | Epson 7.8 | Quantum 15.2 | Hitachi 11.2 | Sony 14.3 | Toshiba 9.8 | Philips 6.2 |
| Motorola 1.9 | n.a. | Packard Bell 5.3 | Lexmark 5.3 | Western Digital 12.3 | Hyundai 9.2 | Matsushita 9.4 | Sony 9.4 | LG Electronics 6.1 |
| Texas Instruments 1.1 | n.a. | NEC 4.8 | Okidata 4.8 | Toshiba 5.7 | Toshiba 8.9 | Mitsubishi 7.7 | NEC 8.5 | ADI 4.8 |
| Top 3 92.5 | Top 5 95.0 | Top 5 35.8 | Top 5 79.0 | Top 5 84.4 | Top 5 59.0 | Top 5 67.5 | Top 5 62.2 | Top 5 37.4 |
| Increasing returns | | | Hybrid | | Decreasing returns | | | |

Sources: 1, Calculated from Electronic Buyers' News, "MPUs: MPU Makers Expect Lucrative Year," http://techweb.cmp.com/ebn/semicon/mpu.html; 2, International Data Corporation(IDC), "Worldwide Market Share of New PCs Shipped 1995," The Gray Sheet 30 (1995): 19–20; 3, IDC, 1997, data provided to authors; 4, U.S. shipments only, Computer Intelligence, 1997, data provided to authors; 5, Includes captive and noncaptive shipments. 1997 Disk/Trend Report: Rigid Disk Drives, Mountain View, CA: Disk/Trend, Inc.; 6, Calculated from Electronic Buyers' News, "DRAM: DRAM Leaders Gird for a Tough 1997," http://techweb.cmp.com/ebn/semicon/dram.html; 7, 1997 Disk/Trend Report: Removable Data Storage, Mountain View, CA: Disk/Trend, Inc.; 8, 1997 Disk/Trend Report: Optical Disk Drives, Mountain View, CA: Disk/Trend, Inc.; 9, MIC/III, "Taiwan's Major Monitor Producers," Asia IT Report, Special Edition: Taiwan 1995: 44.

aShare of revenues

bShare of unit shipments

the market. Not surprisingly, the DRAM and flat-panel industries are dominated by large Japanese and Korean electronics conglomerates such as Toshiba, NEC, Fujitsu, Samsung, Hyundai, and LG Electronics. The only large U.S. DRAM producers are IBM and Texas Instruments, both of which are large, diversified companies in their own right and independent Micron Technologies, a surprisingly resilient competitor. Given the high entry barriers and strong price competition, competition tends toward fairly stable oligopoly conditions with companies having little control over the price of their products.

Other segments of the hardware industry follow different rules, however. They do not require large investments or high levels of technology, and thus barriers to entry are relatively low. Some, such as motherboards, add-on cards, and a variety of peripherals and components are highly price sensitive and place a premium on speed-to-market of new product generations. They require flexibility rather than scale in production. These segments favor the many small-and medium-sized Taiwanese companies, which compete on the basis of speed, flexibility, the ability to squeeze costs to the bone, and close ties to the global production system via the overseas Chinese network. Now, virtually every major PC maker depends on Taiwanese suppliers in order to keep up with the rapid product cycles of the PC industry. There are also market segments based on more stable technologies in which price is the determining factor, such as monitors, floppy disk drives, CD-ROMs, keyboards, cables, and connectors. Most of these are made by Japanese, Korean, and Taiwanese companies, but production is often done in low-cost locations such as China or Southeast Asia.

While the various hardware segments have quite different industry structures and have favored different companies and countries, they all are marked by the characteristics of decreasing returns to scale. Competition is intense and margins are thin, and if one company starts to get ahead, it attracts even more aggressive attacks by its competitors. Even the Japanese giants who had driven most of their American competitors out of the DRAM industry in the 1980s were unable to enjoy the fruits of their victory because Korean companies soon entered the market with large-scale production.

*Increasing Returns Segments.*   The classic case of an increasing returns business is the operating systems market. Microsoft gained a critical first mover advantage when IBM chose MS-DOS as the operating system for the original IBM PC. IBM did much of the heavy lifting involved in making the IBM PC the dominant standard for PCs, and so Microsoft gained the corresponding dominant market share in operating systems. Eventually, Microsoft split with IBM when it abandoned its joint venture with IBM to develop OS/2 and instead put its energies behind Windows as the successor to DOS. Once Windows had defeated OS/2 in the marketplace, Microsoft had a virtual cash machine. Windows 3.1, Windows 95, and Windows NT cost millions of dollars each to develop, but the marginal cost of each new copy was just a few dollars. Meanwhile, as more users adopted Windows and more software developers wrote applications for Windows, the marginal value of each new copy of Windows actually grew, due to the external economies provided by a larger user base and a larger pool of complementary assets (third-party software, add-on hardware, distribution channels, user experience). So as more people adopted Windows, the incentives grew for others to follow, exemplifying the increasing-returns pattern that "things that get ahead tend to get further ahead." Or in the words of W. Brian Arthur, the tendency for "that which is ahead to get further ahead, for that which loses advantage to lose further advantage."[31]

Application software also functions as an increasing returns business, but with much greater competition in most market segments than is seen in the operating systems business. While the cost structure of application software is similar in terms of high up-front costs and low marginal costs, the customer lock-in effect is less pronounced. It is much easier to switch from WordPerfect to Word than it is to switch from Windows to Macintosh. However, Microsoft has been quite successful in extending its dominant market position in the critical office application market by bundling its software into the Microsoft Office suite. This application suite costs less than buying separate applications and offers some product integration among the component applications.

The other industry segment clearly characterized by increasing returns is the microprocessor market, where Intel has enjoyed a market share of more than 70% since IBM selected its processors for the original IBM PC. Microprocessors seem a less obvious increasing returns product. They are, after all, hardware products that require billion-dollar facilities to manufacture. But through its ability to control the hardware standards for the PC (and aggressive protection of its intellectual property), Intel has created a counterpart to the Windows franchise in operating systems. While it does have competitors in the x86 microprocessor market, Intel has actually been able to increase its share of that market over time, thanks in part to the huge profits garnered in this increasing returns market. Intel can thus afford to make heavy investments in R&D and production capacity in order to stay ahead of competitors technologically and achieve lower marginal production costs. It has also spent heavily on its "Intel Inside" campaign to create a franchise based on branding as well as architectural standards.

The world of increasing returns in the computer industry has been dominated by U.S. firms as far back as the original IBM mainframes. A few non-U.S. companies have found success in software applications, such as Germany's SAP, Canada's Corel, and Japan's Just Systems. But U.S. companies still control about 75% of the software industry overall, and they have virtually 100% of the operating system market. The vast majority of that software is still developed in the United States, although U.S. companies have turned to foreign countries in some cases for low-cost programmers or product localization. The story is similar in microprocessors, where Intel's competition, limited as it is, comes from U.S. companies such as AMD, Cyrix, Motorola, and IBM. And while the microprocessor industry is more globalized than the software industry in its production, most of the highest value design, engineering, and wafer fabrication activities still take place in the United States. While some of those activities have expanded to Europe and Asia, most offshore production involves low-value assembly and testing.

While Microsoft and Intel control the most important PC standards, other companies have succeeded by gaining control over other standards. These include Novell in network software, Hewlett-Packard in printer fonts, and Singapore's Creative Technology in sound cards. These standards are less critical and more open to competitive challenges, as in the case of Microsoft's attack on Novell with Windows NT. Other standards have been more enduring, such as Intuit's Quicken money management software.[32]

*Hybrid Segments.*   Some segments of the computer industry are not clearly in the increasing or decreasing returns world, but instead they show characteristics of both. These industries might start out as increasing returns businesses and mature into decreasing returns businesses—as happened with the original IBM PC, once other companies unlocked the secrets of cloning the IBM architecture. Others can start out in the decreasing returns business but be transformed into increasing returns by a change in the market or by management strategies that recast a company's role in the market. W. Brian Arthur (1996) illustrates the notion outside the computer industry with the example of McDonald's restaurants, which have gone beyond simply providing food service to create network externalities in the form of brand name recognition and customer loyalty.

Some examples of this effect also can be seen in information services. The information services business traditionally has been dominated by domestic companies in most countries. The need for close interaction with customers, local language skills, and intimate knowledge of local business culture has put even large companies such as EDS and Computer Sciences Corp. at a disadvantage outside North American and Europe. No matter how good they are in the United States, these companies must hire and train local people in each market and compete against local companies that have access to the same talent. The main advantage of U.S. companies is their size and ability to serve the global needs of large multinationals. However, there are very limited network externalities, because the business is based on providing custom solutions for each client's needs.

The situation changes, however, if the business can be changed from a decreasing returns basis (such as outsourcing, maintenance, or custom programming) to one of increasing returns by packaging services into a product that can be resold at a lower marginal cost. For example, a banking automation system developed for an individual bank can be sold as a package to banks around the world with minimal customization. In the case of ATMs, there is an incentive for all banks to standardize on a common platform to offer customers a wider range of locations to access their accounts. The marginal cost to each new customer goes down while the marginal benefit increases—a classic increasing returns market. In fact, even the kings of the increasing returns business, Microsoft and Intel, initially developed their key products for a single customer. Microsoft purchased and developed DOS for IBM, and Intel designed the original microprocessor as a custom product for a Japanese calculator company called Busicom.[33]

The hardware industry also has its hybrids. Among these are the PC systems and printer industries. PCs are seen by many to be the ultimate commodity product, with hundreds of producers all making nearly indistinguishable systems from the same array of components. Price competition is fierce and market share success is measured in 1% or 2% gains. Yet, the flip side to the commodity nature of PC hardware is the fact that success in the industry is now determined largely by factors from the knowledge-based world, namely branding, customer service, innovative distribution, and logistics. Companies such as Dell and Gateway 2000 have grown rapidly with a made-to-order sales mode that offers additional value to customers. And while volume matters in terms of getting the best prices on components, small local companies that build their own PC clones to order and provide specialized service to business users continue to hold their own against the industry's giants. By focusing on the knowledge side of the equation, these companies gain a competitive edge in what is primarily a decreasing returns business.

Printers are perhaps even a better example, since leading companies such as Hewlett-Packard (HP) and Canon not only take advantage of strong brand names, but they also control key technologies such as printer software, ink jets, and laser engines. The printer industry has been rapidly transformed from technology driven to market driven. HP in particular has leveraged its technology strengths and reorganized internally around market segments in order to provide a wide variety of printer configurations for different markets. While HP uses the global production network to reduce production costs and produce close to its users, it competes mainly on the basis of technology and marketing, both of which belong to the knowledge-based, increasing returns world.

The hard disk drive (HDD) industry is perhaps the most unusual of the hardware segments. HDD production requires constant improvement in basic technologies in order to pack more data onto a given area of storage media, and market success depends almost entirely on speed-to-market in order to hit the "sweet spot" in the product cycle. A company that is even a few months late to market with a new generation of hard drive can miss all the profits from that generation. The industry used to have low entry barriers, and more than 200 companies have come and gone from the market, but the past few years have seen a consolidation as costs of R&D and production facilities have risen. Now, four companies—Seagate, IBM, Quantum, and Western Digital—control more than 75% of the market. All of these are U.S. companies, but most of their production has been located in Singapore and elsewhere in Southeast Asia in order to tap low-cost labor and a well-developed supplier base. Japan's computer leaders NEC, Fujitsu, and Toshiba also make hard drives, but they mainly produce for their own captive use, because they have failed to keep up with the industry's short product cycles. The U.S. computer makers Hewlett-Packard and DEC were likewise unable to keep up and so decided to drop out of the disk drive industry altogether.

In such hybrid markets, U.S. companies have done well, maintaining some production in the United States even while using global production networks. This has occurred in the face of the general shift of hardware production to Asia, and the expectation of many that the United States could not compete in hardware against low-cost Asian producers. In fact, the low-cost Asian producers, particularly the Taiwanese, have taken over much of the decreasing returns side of the PC business by serving as original equipment manufacturers (OEMs) to U.S. and (increasingly) Japanese companies. In printers, the major producers have moved a good deal of production to places like Singapore and have sourced many components from Asia as well. But the knowledge-based parts of the business have remained mostly in the United States and Japan. The other Asian countries have not yet developed the key technologies or marketing capabilities to compete directly in the printer market.

### New Global Production System

Although IBM had been manufacturing and sourcing globally on a large scale by the 1970s,[34] the manufacturing and sourcing activities of most computer firms tended to be confined within their own firm (or *keiretsu*) and their own country's boundaries. The strategy of vertical integration was to optimize all the resources available within the firm. The confinement within country boundaries occurred by virtue of the firm's focus on its home market, its vertical integration, and the desire of governments in Europe and Japan for national self-sufficiency in the computer industry.

However, the modular and open nature of the PC and the intense competition among firms resulted in the PC industry becoming highly globalized. Now PC firms could locate wherever they needed to for overall optimization of the firm's interests. They could source components from whatever location within the global production system provided the best product at the best price. And they could focus their resources on their "core competencies" in design, marketing, and distribution of their own systems while sourcing the hardware from other manufacturers. This meant that firms no longer needed to be concerned about company or country self-sufficiency in order to be in business. Instead of optimizing resources within the firm, they could now optimize resources from wherever they were located globally. As long as there were multiple world-class suppliers available, firms could not be victimized by a supply cartel. This freed them to compete on design, features, speed to market, and brand image.

Globalization of the computer industry had two aspects: global sourcing and direct foreign investment. Global sourcing occurred because of demand and price competition. The large initial demand for PCs, fluctuations in demand, and the need for more than one supplier to ensure adequate quality

stimulated the use of sourcing from multiple suppliers so that the major vendors could meet quality standards and expand or contract rapidly in response
to changing market demand. Global sourcing also produced cost reduction,
which enabled vendors to take advantage of lower cost labor markets and to
ensure competition among suppliers. As a result, production of parts, subassemblies, components, and systems shifted from high-wage to low-wage countries and regions, particularly the NIEs of East Asia: Hong Kong, Korea, Singapore, and Taiwan. Firms in these countries had been developing technical,
manufacturing, and managerial capabilities in consumer electronics (appliances, radios, TVs, VCRs) for a decade or longer, and their governments targeted the computer industry for development just as the PC burst on the
scene. The results of that targeting is shown in table 2-10, which details the
extraordinary growth of computer and components production in Japan, Korea, Taiwan, and Singapore, each of which targeted those sectors.

As wages in the East Asian NIEs rose during the 1980s, both the multinational vendors and the NIE suppliers shifted production to still other low-
wage countries, primarily Thailand, Malaysia, Indonesia, and China. The result was the creation of a vast production network that extended from the
United States across the Pacific to East Asia, and from these countries
throughout much of the rest of Asia. It was mostly the established computer
companies, such as IBM, DEC, Hewlett-Packard, and Texas Instruments, that
helped create this global production system, but it was the PC industry newcomers such as Apple, Compaq, Dell, Packard Bell, and Gateway 2000 that
took greatest advantage of the system. The large multinational corporations
bore the early ramp-up and learning costs for the Asian suppliers, whereas the
newcomers followed behind the multinational giants to take up the excess
capacity in the production network. Some key results of these shifts in production were an increase in the foreign content (mainly Asian) of most PCs,[35]
a shift in manufacturing jobs to Asia, and an increase in U.S. trade deficits
for computer hardware with countries in Asia.[36]

TABLE 2-10. Production of Computers and Components, 1990 and 1995

| Country | Computers (US$ billions) | | Components (US$ billions) | | Computers/ Components as Percent of Total Electronics | |
|---|---|---|---|---|---|---|
| | 1990 | 1995 | 1990 | 1995 | 1990 | 1995 |
| United States | 48.6 | 65.1 | 34.2 | 54.6 | 40.9% | 48.0% |
| Japan | 53.2 | 63.5 | 46.9 | 67.6 | 54.3 | 60.2 |
| Korea | 3.2 | 5.8 | 8.1 | 15.1 | 48.9 | 57.8 |
| Taiwan | 4.9 | 12.7 | 3.5 | 4.9 | 59.7 | 76.6 |
| Singapore | 6.9 | 14.9 | 3.7 | 6.9 | 70.0 | 79.3 |
| Hong Kong | 1.8 | 2.3 | 1.2 | 1.5 | 36.8 | 41.5 |

Source: Reed, *Yearbook of World Electronics Data* (Oxford: Reed Electronics Research, 1995).

The globalization of the industry also was reflected in increased foreign investment by the major computer manufacturers. Computer makers increasingly located their own manufacturing, sales, and service abroad to take advantage of locations close to their suppliers. They also moved labor-intensive activities to low-wage countries, initially the East Asian NIEs, and more recently to China and Southeast Asia. As governments became aware of the opportunities presented by the PC industry, some began to require local production in exchange for access to the country's user markets, especially when the local market was large enough to justify such investments. These market entry requirements are illustrated most recently by China's demands on foreign multinationals, but similar conditions have occurred in nearly every major country in the world at one time or another, often with less than optimal results for the multinationals involved. However, by positioning themselves near foreign customers, firms have learned to improve product design, speed products to market, enhance customer services, and reduce transportation costs.

Foreign direct investment by computer companies is likely to continue expanding because of the need to participate in three types of markets. First are the leading markets, particularly the United States, which generally drive global technology trends. Companies must participate in the U.S. market to be close to the latest technology developments and interact with sophisticated users. This interaction is critical to product development and modification. Also, given the size of the U.S. market, garnering even a minor share of that market can help a company achieve the sales volumes necessary to achieve economies of scale. The trend toward increased foreign investment into the United States is illustrated by the recent decisions of NEC, Fujitsu, Hitachi, and Samsung to set up PC operations in California or to acquire U.S. PC companies.

The second type of foreign investment is targeted at large markets, either big emerging markets (such as China, India, Indonesia, and Brazil) or the unified European market.[37] The growth of the European market attracted investment to Ireland and Scotland, on the edges of the large European Community. Likewise, Hong Kong has retained a vital role in the computer industry through its position as the gateway to China.

The third major target of foreign investment remains low-cost production sites. Companies are not just looking for cheap unskilled labor to do simple assembly tasks, but are also looking for low-cost engineers and other professionals. The large pools of engineers in China, Russia, and Vietnam, and software professionals in India, are attracting increased multinational investment. In the case of China, the combination of a large potential market, cheap labor, and government requirements for local production is driving a steady flow of foreign investment, in spite of the often harsh business climate.

The globalization of the computer industry has not peaked by any means. In fact, some companies are just starting to understand the need to operate globally and to reorganize their operations accordingly. The continuing process of globalization has several implications for the organization of the global production system:

- Companies that had previously focused on the domestic market are quickly moving to target foreign markets. Some U.S. companies such as Compaq, Oracle, and Adobe have moved aggressively into Japan, Asia, and Latin America in order to maintain their high growth rates, while Japanese companies such as NEC and Fujitsu have recently targeted the U.S. market.
- Companies are establishing marketing and distribution centers to serve the major regional markets, for example: Singapore for Southeast Asia; Scotland and Ireland for Europe; Miami for Latin America; and California for the United States.
- Most companies have established product development operations in the United States. For instance, Fujitsu, NEC, and Hitachi have all set up PC subsidiaries in the United States to develop products specifically for the U.S. market.
- The bulk of research and development is still carried out in a company's home market. However, some technologies are now being developed abroad to serve specific local needs (such as Japanese and Chinese voice and character recognition).
- There is a continuing tension over the issue of vertical integration versus horizontal specialization. Companies such as Seagate, NEC, Acer, and Toshiba argue that their ability to produce many of their own components gives them an advantage in quality and control over their technological future. Others, such as Quantum, Western Digital, Dell, and Gateway 2000, outsource most or all of their components and production, choosing to focus on their core competencies in design or marketing. While it is possible that some companies will try to reintegrate vertically, it is highly unlikely that the PC industry will ever revert to the type of vertical structure of the previous mainframe and minicomputer eras despite Compaq's acquisition of DEC.

### Competition Within the Global Production System

The competitive character of the PC industry helps to position the computer industry of each country in the global production system and to explain how the unique features of the computer industries in the United States, Japan, and the East Asian NIEs have enabled each to find their own place in the industry.

United States firms lead the PC industry overall and also dominate many segments including microprocessors, complete systems, hard disk drives, operating systems, and packaged applications. Moreover, U.S. firms control high value-added segments of the industry like microprocessors, software, and laser printers where control over standards is critical. United States firms were able to set global standards because the United States was the lead market for PCs. However, their ability to maintain and expand their spheres of control is largely due to the business strategies of companies like Microsoft, Intel, Compaq, and Hewlett-Packard. On the hardware side, many U.S. firms rely heavily upon the production networks of Japan and East Asia for their supply of parts (resistors, capacitors, cables, connectors), subassemblies (memory chips, ceramic packaging), components (motherboards, power supplies, LCDs), peripherals (monitors, floppy disk drives, hard disk drives, scanners), and even whole systems (notebooks, desktops). Compaq sells PCs built in Taiwan. Seagate Technology assembles 80% of its disk drives at factories in Malaysia, Thailand, Singapore, Indonesia, the Philippines, and China.[38] IBM, Hewlett-Packard, DEC, Compaq, and Dell all have PC factories in Asia; AST has four of its six factories in Asia. In software, U.S. companies still develop and produce most products at home, with foreign activities mostly limited to localizing products for foreign markets and contracting out some programming.

Japan is a leading world supplier of critical components and peripherals such as memory chips, flat-panel displays, CD-ROMs, floppy disk drives, and laser printer engines. It is also a leading supplier of branded computers in its home market. Fujitsu, Hitachi, and NEC are players in all segments of the PC industry within Japan, and Toshiba is a leader in the laptop segment worldwide. Japan dominates key hardware segments by virtue of technical leadership and manufacturing capabilities. Japanese firms have been successful competing in oligopolistic markets where heavy investment, R&D, and process technology are critical to success. Japan also is unique among all countries for its control of upstream semiconductor production technologies such as manufacturing equipment (e.g., steppers), silicon wafers, and ceramic packaging.

Korea is a leading supplier of components, especially memory chips, flat-panel displays, and monitors. In addition, Korea's large electronics companies (Samsung, Hyundai, Daewoo, and LG Electronics) and independent Trigem produce full systems for the domestic market. Like Japan, Korea has been successful in oligopolistic markets that require heavy capital investment and process technology. But, the country's lack of R&D capabilities and upstream industries has made Korea heavily dependent upon Japan, the United States, and Taiwan for key technologies, components, and production equipment; this dependence has forced it to compete at the trailing edge of technology except in DRAMS, where it is a world leader.

Singapore is the leading production platform for the hard disk drive industry. Every major vendor has hard disk drive assembly or manufacturing in the country and is using Singapore as the business hub for coordinating supply networks in Malaysia, Thailand, Indonesia, the Philippines, and China. Singaporean firms are mainly suppliers to the multinational firms located there, but two of its firms, Creative and Aztech, lead the world in design and production of PC sound cards.

More than any country in Asia, Taiwan is the leading supplier of components, peripherals, and OEM systems to the world. Taiwan leads in production of motherboards, keyboards, power supplies, mice, and monitors. Acer ranked eighth in world PC sales in 1995. In addition, Acer, Mitac, Inventec, FIC, and a host of other companies assemble PCs or components for nearly all the major foreign multinationals. Taiwanese companies compete on the

TABLE 2-11.  Taiwan OEM Production for Worldwide PC Vendors

| Buyer | Taiwan Makers | 1995 Expenditure (US$ millions) |
|-------|---------------|-------------------------------|
| Apple | Tatung, Acer, Inventa, Delta | $300–400 |
| Compaq | ADI, Philips, TECO, Logitec, Primax, Inventec, Lite-on, Delta | $500 |
| DEC | Philips Taiwan, Lite-on, DEC Taiwan, Elite | n.a. |
| Dell | Lite-on, Royal, Inventa, GVC, Lung Hwa, FIC, Compeq, Lite-on | $450 |
| Gateway 2000 | Mag | n.a. |
| IBM | Sampo, Capertronic, GVC, Elite, Lung Hwa, Sun-Moon-Star, Delta, ASE | $450 |
| NEC | Tatung, Elite | n.a. |
| Packard Bell | Tatung, GVC, BTC | $500 |

Source: Market Intelligence Center/Institute for the Information Industry (MIC/III). Data provided to authors.

basis of low costs, high-quality engineering, speed, and responsiveness. As labor and other costs in Taiwan have risen during the 1980s, Taiwanese companies have begun moving lower-skill production offshore to Malaysia, Thailand, and China. Taiwan supplies PCs on an OEM basis to both the branded firms and clones all over the world to such an extent that it has been dubbed the "Krupps of the computer wars" referring to the legendary German company that supplied arms to all sides in World War I. The scope and scale of these Taiwanese firms can be seen in just a partial list of OEM arrangements between leading PC makers and Taiwanese suppliers (table 2-11).

Hong Kong serves as the link between the global production system and China. It is a conduit for investment and trade into and out of China, providing marketing, management, financial, and commercial services. In the past, it was also a major production platform for foreign multinationals and some domestic suppliers, but these have gone over the border since the late 1980s. Now Hong Kong's role is to provide value as an intermediary, rather than as a manufacturer.

What has emerged over the last fifteen years is a vast production system stretching throughout the Asia-Pacific region. Each focal country in Asia has established a unique place for itself based upon industry capabilities (technology leadership, commodity manufacturing, supply infrastructure, business hub); overall comparative advantage (large domestic market, low-cost labor and facilities, closeness to large market); and technology policy supporting industry or leveraging comparative advantage (table 2-12).

## Conclusions

The PC revolution changed the entire computer industry because it changed the structure of the industry and traditional boundaries within the industry. Historically the computer industry had clearly defined boundaries that were

TABLE 2-12. Country Roles in the Global Production System

| Country | Role in Global Production Systems |
|---|---|
| United States | Leading supplier of PCs, microprocessors, software<br>Lead market |
| Japan | Supplier of leading-edge components and peripherals<br>Leader in notebook PCs |
| Korea | Major supplier of DRAMs<br>Producer of trailing-edge monitors and flat-panel displays |
| Taiwan | Major producer of a wide variety of components and peripherals<br>OEM supplier to global industry |
| Hong Kong | Gateway to China; conduit for trade, technology, and capital flows<br>Business management for production operations in China |
| Singapore | Production platform for disk drive industry, large PC assembly operations, growing semiconductor industry<br>Regional business hub for MNCs |

set by vertically integrated firms like IBM, DEC, Fujitsu, and Hitachi. These firms produced full systems competing across all industry segments based on proprietary architecture for hardware, operating systems, and applications. Changing vendors was costly and risky for user organizations because of the different architectures; consequently, customers tended to stay with the same vendor for long periods. Since IBM was the market leader, some of the other mainframe vendors chose to imitate IBM's architecture and to make their hardware plug-compatible with IBM mainframes. This allowed them to participate in IBM markets with lower cost peripherals, central processors, and memory—and eventually, with complete mainframe systems. Thus, forces that would lead to disintegration in the computer industry were present in the central computing era in the form of plug-compatible systems and independent peripherals and software vendors, but they remained organized around the vertically integrated structures of the big system vendors.

It was the PC revolution, combined with globalization of production, that brought about the demise of the old industry structure. The development of faster, less expensive semiconductors and other components enabled entrepreneurs to enter the industry with visions of a new low-cost machine for the individual user. Although growing, the industry was small until the introduction of the IBM PC which "made" the industry. IBM established the PC as an open system, composed of modular components controlled by standard interfaces. IBM sourced globally for components and developed the capabilities of its suppliers who later supplied new clone-makers of the IBM PC. The huge demand for PCs brought still other new entrants, so that PC makers numbered in the hundreds and were supported by suppliers numbering in the thousands. As price competition increased among PC makers, they moved production abroad or sourced from abroad; new industry clusters sprung up in several countries of East Asia with low wages, skilled and disciplined labor, an entrepreneurial bent, and supportive government leadership. Thus a vast network evolved, spreading from the United States to the NIEs of East Asia and then throughout East Asia, especially in Malaysia, Thailand, and China.

As the price/performance of PCs has continued to improve, and more sophisticated PC software has been developed capable of managing large databases and networks, PC servers have been squeezing both minicomputer and mainframe makers. The demand for mainframe computers has rebounded somewhat after declining in the early 1990s, but mainframe revenues have stagnated as users have switched to networked PCs and client-server systems. Minicomputers have suffered the same fate though it was more delayed. These pressures were forcing the old vertically integrated computer vendors to shed more and more of their lines of business, products, and staff. The massive change that occurred started with IBM and DEC, but no traditional computer vendor has been spared the disintegration of their traditional computer business. The result is that the computer industry is highly segmented. Only IBM and the major Japanese vendors still offer a full line of hardware systems and peripherals.

IBM once dominated most sectors of the industry; today it is still a competitor in all sectors, but the leader in only a few. IBM still dominates the architecture of mainframes, but Intel sets the key hardware standards for personal computers and Microsoft controls the software architecture. Sun leads the workstation architecture although there is vigorous competition from others in this segment. Indeed, the changing structure of the computer industry increased competition in nearly all segments of the industry.

Similarly, the United States once dominated the computer industry; now its companies remain the industry leaders, but production has shifted dramatically to the Asia Pacific region. The United States accounted for 50% of hardware production in 1985, but it accounted for only 30% in 1995 (table 2-13). In contrast, the Asia-Pacific region has moved from 23% to 43% of global production. Moreover, the region took production away not only from the United States, but also from Western Europe. Japan's production increased from 19% to 28% and all of the NIEs, except Hong Kong, showed substantial production increases.

The essential consequence of the PC era was that it introduced complexity, instability, and blurring of boundaries into the production system for computers. Coordination of the production system moved from inside to outside the firm, creating tremendous dynamism, but also causing headaches for companies trying to manage those relationships. It is not only the PC industry that is shifting its boundaries; the entire computer industry has also become far more complex, unstable, and blurred than ever before. Whereas the mainframe and minicomputer industry had been driven by the internal scale economies of a few, large vertically integrated firms,[39] the PC industry has been driven by network economies among many small, specialized firms. This is an

TABLE 2-13. World Computer Hardware Production by Location of Production (%)

| Region | 1985 | 1990 | 1995 |
|---|---|---|---|
| United States/Canada | 50.0 | 28.8 | 29.7 |
| Asia-Pacific total | 22.6 | 39.5 | 43.4 |
|   Japan | 19.1 | 30.0 | 27.8 |
|   Singapore | 1.3 | 3.9 | 6.5 |
|   Taiwan | 1.0 | 2.8 | 5.5 |
|   Korea | 0.6 | 1.7 | 2.5 |
|   Hong Kong | 0.7 | 1.1 | 1.0 |
| Western Europe | 23.4 | 26.7 | 18.8 |
| Rest of World | 3.6 | 4.9 | 8.1 |

Source: Reed, *Yearbook of World Electronics Data* (Surrey: Research Electronics Research, various years).

entirely new model of industry organization. The new model is that of horizontal segments and organic growth. Many small-and medium-sized firms specialize in different segments of the industry and co-locate in regional clusters of industry customers and suppliers. Growth takes place through the creation of economic capabilities within this network of specialized firms whose major nexus of coordination is the market and the production systems of key multinationals.

The transformation of the computer industry from vertical integration to horizontal specialization was the key force behind the globalization of the industry. If there is one factor that explains the rise of East Asia as a competitor in the computer industry, it is the ability of the East Asian countries to develop strong linkages to the global production system that is coordinated mainly by U.S. firms. The ability of those countries to develop such linkages was due to three factors delineated in chapter 1. The first is the national industry structures of the countries, which had honed their skills as exporters in a variety of other industries and developed networks of social and business relationships. The second factor was the aggressive, outward-oriented industrial policies employed to develop national computer industries. The third factor was a path dependency created by the Asian countries' earlier experience in electronics production, which helped them gain important skills needed for computer production and familiarized U.S. managers with their capabilities.

While the East Asian countries as a group have become an important force in the computer industry, they have come to occupy very different positions in the global production system. Those differences are also explained by the same set of factors. For instance, while each of the countries had highly competitive private sectors, there were important differences among the countries in terms of industry structure, such as company size, interfirm relationships, entrepreneurship, and managerial cultures. Each of these structures was best suited to particular segments of the computer industry and led each country to play a different role in the global production system. Likewise, while four of the five countries promoted computer production, they did it with different policy mixes and different priorities. Some policies worked well, while others were unsuccessful or even counterproductive, leading countries to succeed in some areas but not in others. Finally, each country entered the computer industry under a different set of initial conditions and was affected by a different set of decisions and events; therefore, each nation followed its own path to its present position.

The next three chapters explore these differences in detail, starting with Japan, then Korea and Taiwan, and finally the two city-states of Singapore and Hong Kong. These case studies will show the critical role of linkages to the global production system and the roles of national industry structures, industrial policies, and path dependencies in each country.

# 3
# Japan and the PC Revolution

The personal computer revolution appeared to offer a tremendous opportunity for Japan. Combining their strengths in electronic components with their growing capabilities in computer technology, the Japanese computer makers appeared likely to become major competitors in the global PC industry. In fact, some in the United States expected that Japanese companies would eventually use their control over upstream components and technologies to dominate the industry. Former U.S. Trade Representative Clyde Prestowitz, predicted that the Japanese would run away with the world computer market.[1] Intel's Andrew Grove predicted that Japan would overtake the United States as the dominant world supplier of computer systems by 1992.[2] What few suspected was that the PC revolution would so change the nature of the computer industry that many of the presumed strengths of the Japanese companies would turn out to be liabilities in the PC industry.

Japanese companies did succeed in controlling the market for many PC components and peripherals, including DRAMs, flat-panel displays, and floppy disk drives, as well as many key subcomponents and materials. But for the most part they failed to build on those strengths to compete in the PC systems market. They were also unable to use their strength in DRAMs and other semiconductors as a base for challenging Intel's dominance in microprocessors and were locked almost entirely out of the PC software market. While Japan's computer hardware production grew rapidly, its companies were largely relegated to the decreasing returns segments of the industry.

Japanese companies are still world leaders in many components and peripherals, but their leadership has been challenged by aggressive competitors elsewhere in Asia. In 1996, a decade after driving Intel and other U.S. companies out of the DRAM business, Japan was passed by Korea as the leading producer of DRAMs. Korea's electronics companies were also gearing up for a challenge in flat-panel displays, another Japanese stronghold. Meanwhile, Taiwan had become so adept at producing PCs and components that Japan's computer makers were outsourcing production to Taiwanese OEMs to cut costs and get products to market more quickly.

Japan's problems were reflected in a steep decline in computer production in the early 1990s, reversing a decade of rapid growth (figure 3-1). Total output declined by 20% from 1991 to 1993, before rebounding slowly from 1994 to 1996. Most dramatic was the decline in mainframe production, as the shift from mainframes to PCs finally hit the Japanese market (figure 3-2).

Much of the short-term decline in production can be attributed to the stagnation of the Japanese economy in the aftermath of the "bubble" economy of the late 1980s. Economic growth hovered around 1% per year from 1992 to 1995, and the Japanese computer industry, heavily dependent on the domestic market, was especially hard hit. The domestic downturn also forced Japanese components manufacturers to reduce investment just as they were facing increased competition from U.S. and Asian competitors.

The problems of the computer industry went far beyond the temporary drop in domestic demand, however. The deeper problems involved Japan's industry structure and managerial culture, the fragmented development of its domestic PC market, and its weaknesses in software and associated "soft" skills. There was also a matter of strategic focus. Japanese computer makers remained obsessed with beating IBM, even as IBM was being pummeled by Microsoft, Intel, and Compaq. Ironically, IBM was equally worried about the Japanese challenge, having seen U.S. leaders in other industries humbled by Japanese competitors.[3] While the Japanese chased IBM, and IBM gazed in the rear view mirror at the Japanese, they both drove off the same cliff when the mainframe market collapsed, with each side suffering billions of dollars in losses (table 3-1).

While the corporate losses of the Japanese vendors did not match those of IBM, the impacts were greater than the numbers would suggest. For instance, Fujitsu showed a corporate profit of US$300 million in 1994, yet McKinsey & Company estimate that it lost US$583 million in the computer business that year. The decline in revenues and profits at Fujitu's U.S. mainframe subsidiary, Amdahl, was another warning sign to Fujitsu. Equally troubling for IBM and the big Japanese mainframe companies was the stagnation in revenues that occurred from 1991 to 1995, at a time when the computer industry as a whole was recording double-digit growth rates.

While mainframe and minicomputer companies around the world were victims of the PC revolution, in the United States their decline was compensated for by the rapid ascent of new PC-oriented companies such as Apple, Compaq, Dell, Microsoft, Novell, and Lotus. The problem for Japan was that its decline in computers was systemic. The handful of large companies that control most of Japan's computer industry all faced serious downturns in the 1990s, and there were few newcomers to take up the slack. And while IBM was able to reverse its fortunes through a painful restructuring and by shifting focus to emphasize its service and network businesses, the Japanese giants were hamstrung in their efforts to shift course by practices such as lifetime employment and seniority-based promotion. These practices—along with Ja-

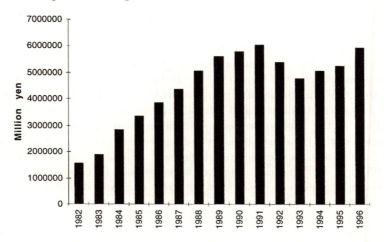

FIGURE 3-1. Japan's Computer Hardware Production, 1982–1996. *Sources:* Japan Information Processing Development Center (JIPDEC), *Informatization White Paper, 1996 Edition,* (Tokyo: JIPDEC, 1996); Reed, *Yearbook of World Electronics Data, 1997*, Reed Electronics Research, 1997.

pan's egalitarian educational system and emphasis on incremental improvement—were well suited to stable, decreasing returns manufacturing businesses, but they were liabilities in the unpredictable, rapidly changing increasing returns world of the PC industry.

## History of Japan's PC Industry

Japan's PC industry developed in parallel with the global industry, but for well over a decade did not converge with it.[4] The first 8-bit Japanese PCs were introduced in the mid-1970s soon after the first Altairs, Apples, and Commodores, and as in the United States, a variety of incompatible architectures competed in the market. But in the 1980s, while the United States and the rest of the world were standardizing on the IBM-PC architecture, with corresponding growth and competition in all segments of the industry, Japan remained a backwater of incompatible standards, high prices, and slow growth.

The fragmentation of the domestic market was due in part to the complexity of the Japanese written language.[5] Japanese PCs had to be able to input, store, display, and print around 6,000 *kanji* characters, compared to about 200 for European languages. This meant that IBM PC-compatible computers lacked the power to handle the complex Japanese language without special hardware until the 80486 generation of microprocessors became available in the late 1980s. In the meantime, Japanese PC makers had to develop

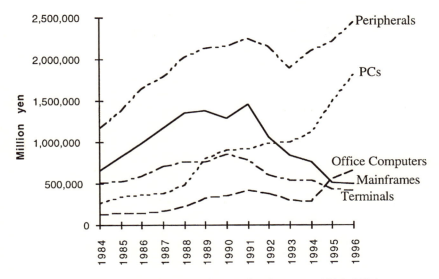

FIGURE 3-2. Hardware Production by Category, 1984–1996.
*Sources:* JIPDEC, 1996; Reed, 1997.

modifications of the IBM-PC platform to handle Japanese characters more efficiently.

NEC was the first Japanese company to develop 16-bit PCs based on Intel-design microprocessors and the DOS operating system, which it licensed from Microsoft. NEC developed its own adaptation of DOS, called JDOS, and it implemented the Japanese characters in hardware rather than software.[6] This helped deal with the demands of the Japanese language, but made NEC's PC-98 series incompatible with other DOS-based systems. Other Japanese vendors followed suit with their own 16-bit systems. The problem was that each major vendor developed its own adaptation of DOS, none of which was compatible with each other, or with the standard version of MS-DOS used in the rest of the world. Also, each vendor's hardware used nonstandard components that could not be sourced from the global production system.

NEC introduced the PC-98 series in 1982 and had nearly a year's lead in the 16-bit PC market in Japan. It capitalized on its first mover advantage and employed an aggressive marketing strategy to gain the lion's share of the Japanese market and establish the PC-98 as Japan's dominant PC standard. NEC mobilized a vast distribution network, including 7,000 retail outlets, to sell PCs. It also supported and trained the staff of its dealers and set up an information center for help calls. More important, NEC courted independent software developers to write applications for the PC-98, providing technical assistance, access to specifications for new products, and even free hardware. This helped NEC by 1993 create a software base of 15,000 titles from 3,300

TABLE 3-1. Revenues and Profits of IBM and Japanese Computer Makers In US$ millions. Losses in parentheses

|  | 1990 | 1991 | 1992 | 1993 | 1994 | 1995 |
|---|---|---|---|---|---|---|
| **IBM** | | | | | | |
| Revenues | 65,958 | 60,479 | 59,657 | 57,778 | 62,065 | 69,473 |
| Profits | 5,719 | (2,827) | (6,870) | (7,506) | 2,784 | 3,975 |
| **NEC** | | | | | | |
| Revenues—computer | 10,145 | 13,033 | 13,234 | 14,452 | 15,700 | 18,365 |
| Profits—corporate[a] | 580 | 370 | 120 | (375) | 70 | 700 |
| **Fujitsu** | | | | | | |
| Revenues—computer | 17,890 | 17,839 | 20,047 | 20,738 | 23,514 | 28,283 |
| Profits—computer | 440 | 338 | 21 | (92) | (583) | 911 |
| **Amdahl** | | | | | | |
| Revenues | 2,159 | 1,703 | 2,525 | 1,681 | 1,639 | 1,516 |
| Profits | 184 | 11 | (1) | (35) | 75 | 29 |
| **Hitachi** | | | | | | |
| Revenues—computer | 11,166 | 10,290 | 11,352 | 11,700 | 14,673 | 15,672 |
| Profits—corporate[a] | 1,703 | 1,091 | 666 | 634 | 1,280 | 1,337 |

Sources: McKinsey & Company, *The 1993 Report on the Computer Industry; The 1994 Report on the Computer Industry*; and *The 1996 Report on the Computer Industry* (New York: McKinsey & Company, 1993, 1994, and 1996); Datamation, *The Datamation 100* (June 15, 1996, and June 15, 1993); *Electronic Business Asia* (various issues).

[a]Separate computer industry net income data not available for NEC and Hitachi.

developers, far greater than any of its competitors.[7] The availability of complementary assets, in the form of a large software library, gave users a strong incentive to buy NEC. Software vendors were in turn attracted to write more programs for the PC-98 as its installed base grew.

NEC's strategy must be judged as a resounding success; the company was able to grab a dominant market share and create an increasing returns PC business for NEC in the Japanese market. Before the other Japanese vendors introduced their own DOS-based machines, NEC had more than 80% of the Japanese PC market, and its market share remained above 50% until the mid-1990s. Unlike IBM, which lost control over the PC standard it created, NEC was able to prevent cloning of the PC-98 (with the exception of Seiko Epson, which settled a lawsuit with NEC out of court for the right to produce PC-98 clones). As a result, NEC was able to keep its prices high and earn fat profit margins in the Japanese market. Other PC makers had the choice of offering their own proprietary solutions or trying to unite around a common standard to compete with NEC. While there were some efforts by smaller companies to unite around common standards, the major players—Fujitsu, Hitachi, IBM Japan, and Toshiba—chose to offer proprietary systems based on Intel processors and incompatible adaptations of DOS.

The fragmentation of Japan's PC market was partly due to the big vendors' mainframe orientation. Fujitsu, Hitachi, and even IBM Japan initially saw the PC as a front end to the mainframe or as an entry level computer. As a result, each developed incompatible PC standards to lock in their existing customers and were unwilling to unite around a common architecture to challenge NEC.

The major vendors also kept prices high to prevent cannibalization of their profitable larger systems. They were able to do so because of the lack of competition from either foreign vendors or smaller domestic companies. With the exception of IBM, which was well established in Japan, other foreign companies were kept out of the Japanese market by the high cost of developing distribution channels and the cost of modifying their products to handle Japanese software. There was also little competition from smaller domestic companies, which faced great difficulties raising capital, establishing distribution channels, and gaining acceptance from conservative customers, which were highly brand conscious.

The high cost of PCs kept demand low, and Japan's PC penetration level remained about one-third that of the United States well into the 1990s. The demand for PCs was also limited by the difficulty of using DOS-based Japanese PCs. Typing *kanji* characters on a keyboard requires multiple keystrokes and choices among different characters to represent the correct meaning among homonyms (which are very common in the Japanese spoken language). Rather than buy PCs, many users opted for specialized word processing machines designed to handle Japanese text more easily.

Several developments changed the face of the Japanese PC market in the 1990s, however. One was the availability of more powerful microprocessors capable of doing higher level tasks that previously were handled by mainframes, such as financial analysis and database management. These processors were also able to handle Japanese characters directly in the operating system more easily, making possible three major developments in the Japanese software market.

The first crucial development was IBM's 1991 introduction of the DOS/ V operating system, which handled Japanese characters entirely in software that could run on global-standard IBM-compatible PCs.[8] This opened the door to foreign PC makers by making thousands of DOS-based applications available on a standard Japanese operating system. IBM organized the PC Open Architecture Developers' Group, which was joined by U.S. and other foreign PC makers, as well as Toshiba and most of the smaller Japanese PC companies. DOS/V gained critical support in 1993 when Fujitsu announced a DOS/ V compatible version of its FM Towns multimedia computer. Even Seiko Epson announced in 1994 that it would shift from producing NEC clones to DOS/V machines. With the support of the major Japanese PC makers and IBM's efforts to court software developers, by 1994 there were over 5,000 software packages available to run on DOS/V.

In the second key development, Apple began to make great gains with a Japanese version of its Macintosh system, whose icon-based interface was much easier to use than the text-based DOS interface. Apple gained market share by aggressively expanding its distribution channels and developing agreements with Japanese partners such as Canon, Minolta, Fuji Xerox, and Sony, and Apple's market share grew from 1% in 1990 to 15.4% in 1994. The success of the Macintosh introduced Japanese users to the advantages of a graphical user interface and helped pave the way for the third key development in the Japanese operating system market.

That development was Microsoft's introduction in 1993 of a Japanese version of Windows 3.1 that could run on both NEC and DOS/V hardware. This effectively unified a majority of the packaged software market by allowing developers in Japan to write programs that would run on both hardware platforms. It also broke down the wall between Japan and the global market by allowing software packages and CD-ROMs developed for standard Wintel PCs to run on most Japanese PCs.[9] The spread of Windows 3.1 (J) extended Microsoft's dominance of the Japanese operating system market. By 1995, the introduction of Windows 95 in Japan was met by lines of PC users waiting to get a copy, just as in the United States.

The shift from DOS to Windows applications eliminated much of NEC's advantage in complementary assets by making its library of DOS-based applications obsolete. NEC was left to compete on the basis of price and features, and its competitors were already targeting its high margins with low-cost PCs that took advantage of cheap components sourced from the global production network.

Compaq was the first to shake up the cozy Japanese market in 1992, when it introduced PCs in Japan at half the price of equivalent NEC machines. IBM quickly followed suit, and other clone makers such as Dell and Acer entered the market with low-cost PCs. NEC initially responded to the so-called "Compaq shock" by stating it would not take part in a price war in Japan.[10] Rather it emphasized the large software library and nationwide service network available for the PC-98 series. NEC also appeared indignant that Compaq would break the unwritten rule against direct price competition in the Japanese market. Chairman Tadahiro Sekimoto complained, "I'm slightly angry at what happened, because what they did was demagoguery. . . . Compaq made an announcement of a PC with efficiency almost the same as existing Japanese models, but priced lower at 120,000 yen as opposed to 240,000. But Compaq's PC had only a single disk drive so that as a word processor . . . it was not able to operate efficiently. In order to have the ability to do word processing, you would have to add another floppy or hard-disk drive." Sekimoto failed to mention that Compaq simultaneously introduced a model with a 40 MB hard disk for 168,000 yen, still far below NEC's price.[11]

Even some elements of the Japanese press came to NEC's defense. An article in *Asahi Personal Computing* focusing on the PC-98 compared the increase of U.S. computer imports with the "Black Ships," the American fleet that in 1854 forced Japan to open its ports to foreign trade. It argued that NEC computers were as Japanese as rice and that "patriotic PC users" were delighted when NEC introduced a new product lineup.[12] Unfortunately for NEC, not only Compaq was invading its market. Other Japanese PC makers were cutting their own prices and turning to Taiwanese and other Asian companies to source components and contract out manufacturing. NEC was finally forced to defend its market share by cutting prices and sourcing more components offshore to lower its costs.[13]

Under the combined assault of Apple and U.S. vendors selling DOS/V machines, NEC's market share began to erode, from 52% in 1991 to 43% in 1994 (table 3-2). Fujitsu, Toshiba, and Seiko Epson also lost ground, while U.S. companies grabbed a 30% market share. The Japanese market had been cracked open by the efforts of IBM, Compaq, Apple, and Microsoft, which had done in computers what U.S. trade negotiators had struggled to accomplish in other sectors. However, the Japanese companies were not ready to capitulate in their home market, and in 1995 Fujitsu launched its own price war, leaving both NEC and the U.S. vendors reeling.

Compared to the tremor in the market caused by "Compaq shock," "Fujitsu shock" was a major earthquake. Fujitsu cut prices so low that many analysts claimed the company was losing hundreds of dollars on each PC it sold (a claim refuted by Fujitsu, which argued that those estimates included initial investments in marketing, distribution, and product development). And while Compaq was hindered by limited distribution channels and lack of brand name recognition, Fujitsu was able to mobilize its vast Japanese distribution system to challenge NEC. Fujitsu introduced a rash of new low-cost models, many of which were sourced from Taiwan to cut costs and quickly ramp up volume. The result was a leap in market share from just 9% in 1994 to 18% in 1995 and 22% in 1996. Some of Fujitsu's gains came at the expense of Apple, whose more general corporate problems were spilling over into Japan, but most of the gains came at the expense of NEC, whose market share dropped to 33% in 1996. By 1996, NEC announced that it would begin selling DOS/V machines in Japan via its Packard Bell/NEC subsidiary, in effect acknowledging that the PC-98's days were numbered.

The other impact of Fujitsu shock was a boom in PC sales. Interest in PCs was spurred by a multimedia fad in 1994 and Internet fever in 1995, and as prices fell, demand soared. Japan's PC market grew from 3.2 million units

TABLE 3-2.  Share of Japan's PC Market by Company, 1988–1996

| Company | 1988 | 1991 | 1992 | 1993 | 1994 | 1995 | 1996 |
|---|---|---|---|---|---|---|---|
| NEC | 51% | 52% | 52% | 49% | 43% | 40% | 33% |
| Fujitsu | 14 | 8 | 8 | 7 | 9 | 18 | 22 |
| Toshiba | 10 | 9 | 6 | 6 | 4 | 4 | 6 |
| Seiko Epson | 10 | 9 | 7 | 6 | 5 | 3 | n.a. |
| IBM | 7 | 7 | 8 | 7 | 10 | 10 | 11 |
| Apple | n.a. | 6 | 9 | 13 | 15 | 14 | 10 |
| Compaq | n.a. | n.a. | n.a. | 2 | 4 | 3 | 3 |
| Other | 8 | 9 | 10 | 12 | 10 | 10 | 10 |
| Total U.S. Companies | 8 | 13 | 18 | 23 | 30 | 28 | 26 |

Sources: IDC Japan, reported in Jon Choy, *Japan's Personal Computer Market: Awash in American Tsunami,* Japan Economic Institute (JEI) Report No. 6a (Washington, D.C.: JEI, 1994) [for 1988–1992]; Electronic Business Asia, "In Search of More OEM Partners" (April 1995): 15 [for 1933–1994]; "IDC Asia/Pacific and IDC Japan Announces PC Shipment Results for 1996," IDC press release (February 3, 1997) [for 1995–1996].

n.a., Not available

in 1994 to more than 8 million units in 1996, as Japanese businesses and households finally embraced the PC.

The revolution in Japan's PC market was largely instigated by U.S. companies, who unified the Japanese software market and introduced price competition, yet the consequences for those companies have been mixed. Microsoft has been the biggest winner, enjoying rapid growth in demand for its operating systems and applications, while Intel has likewise benefited from growth in demand for its microprocessors. For IBM and Compaq the results have been more ambiguous. Neither was able to make major inroads into the Japanese PC market, and their growth in sales volume was balanced by shrinking profit margins caused by Fujitsu's price war. More ominously, the challenge in their domestic market has led Japan's PC makers finally to become serious about competing in the global market where Compaq and IBM are the leaders.

Besides the role of U.S. companies in shaking up Japan's PC industry, the biggest story in recent years was Fujitsu Shock. Why did this stodgy mainframe vendor suddenly leap into the PC era with such an atypical strategy for a Japanese company? The most plausible answer, and one that is supported by discussions with a few Fujitsu managers, points to the decline in the mainframe business, which accounted for about 40% of Fujitsu's revenues in 1992.[14] Having gone into the red, and seeing its subsidiaries Amdahl and ICL in similar trouble, Fujitsu responded with an all-out price war to buy market share in the PC industry. The company felt that it could only compete by increasing its sales volume and gaining the economies of scale enjoyed by IBM, Compaq, and others. For the longer term, it targeted the export market, but initially it could get the biggest impact in the domestic market, where it could deploy existing production and distribution channels to rapidly increase its sales volume. By 1996, PC prices had begun to stabilize and Fujitsu had established itself as the major competitor to NEC in the Japanese market.

### Global Competitiveness

Rather than use their insulated home market as a profit sanctuary from which to invade foreign markets, Japan's leading computer makers—Fujitsu, Hitachi, and NEC—spent the first decade of the PC revolution fighting over the Japanese market. The only exception was Toshiba, which successfully targeted the global market with its line of portable PCs. However, Japan's PC makers might yet make their presence felt in the United States and other markets. Having driven the foreigners back from the ramparts of their domestic market, the Japanese vendors ventured into the U.S. market in 1996. Fujitsu and Hitachi established product development and assembly facilities in California to design and produce notebook PCs for the U.S. market. Consumer electronics leader Sony introduced multimedia PCs made by Intel for the U.S. market, hoping to position itself for the convergence of computers and consumer electronics. Toshiba began to move beyond its niche in notebook PCs by introducing a multimedia desktop PC for consumers in the United States in 1996 and followed with a line of desktops and servers for the business market in 1997. NEC went a step further and purchased a controlling interest in the U.S. PC maker Packard-Bell, which had used low-priced machines to take first place in the U.S. consumer market but had nearly gone bankrupt doing so. The Japanese vendors also abandoned many of their domestic suppliers and began tapping the global production system to cut production costs.

It is not clear yet how successful the Japanese companies will be in the U.S. and other foreign markets. The future of NEC–Packard Bell is cloudy at best, because Packard Bell has been losing market share since 1995. NEC faces enormous problems trying to consolidate two product lines based on incompatible standards and to manage two corporate cultures that could hardly be more different. Toshiba's initial consumer PC was a flop, and it faces a more crowded competitive field in desktops than it does in notebooks. Sony, Fujitsu, and Hitachi had limited success with their new product lines, although they promise to be in for the long haul.

Sony's strengths in the consumer electronics market may translate into success in the consumer PC market, but that market is the most competitive and least profitable of the entire industry. Sony's longer term goal is to position itself in the new consumer markets expected to be created by the convergence of computers, consumer electronics, and entertainment (where it already is a major force through its Sony Pictures and Sony Music divisions). So far, however, none of the Japanese vendors have been particularly innovative in product design, marketing, or distribution, relying instead on heavy advertising as a means to attract visibility in the market.

### Toshiba: Japan's Only Global PC Competitor

The only major global competitor in Japan's PC industry has been Toshiba, which has been the world leader in portable (laptop and notebook) PCs for more than a decade. Toshiba's success in portables came about in part because of its weakness in other computer markets. The company had no mainframe business to protect, and it was a latecomer to the PC industry, never garnering more than a small share of the Japanese market that was dominated by NEC. So Toshiba looked for a less-crowded market to enter. "By the time Toshiba was trying to get in, the PC market was mature enough that entry through the traditional desktop route was not going to cut it," said Tom Martin, former vice president of marketing for Toshiba America Information Systems.[15] Toshiba instead seized on the portable PC market that was emerging in the mid-1980s.

Toshiba's first portable was based on a Japanese word processor called the Rupo that sold tens of millions of units in the early 1980s. They developed a version of the Rupo based on the x86 architecture and made the first successful laptop: the 3100 model.[16] From the beginning, Toshiba's portables were aimed at the global market. The 3100 was sold in the United States and Europe even before it was introduced in Japan, and the lightweight T1000 line became the leader in the U.S. market after its introduction in 1985.

Not only did portables offer a new market niche to develop, but they also fit well with Toshiba's emphasis on products that were "small, light, thin and low power," and thus capitalized on the company's strengths in product miniaturization, engineering, and precision manufacturing. These capabilities are critical in producing very small systems that must be rugged enough to be carried around and must conserve energy when running on battery power. Toshiba also benefited from its leadership in key components such as flat-panel displays, small disk drives, and advanced batteries. Toshiba has invested heavily in a joint venture with IBM to produce flat-panel displays in Japan, and both companies' notebook divisions have benefited in times of supply shortages.

After leading the world in portables for several years, Toshiba was up-ended when it failed to anticipate the market shift from laptops to smaller notebook PCs in 1991. While Compaq, Dell, and others were introducing smaller, less expensive notebooks based on the latest generation of Intel processors, Toshiba was caught behind the accelerating product cycle. Its share of the U.S. portable market dropped from 43% in 1989 to 12.5% in 1992, when it fell into second place in the U.S. market.[17]

However, thanks to deep corporate pockets, Toshiba was able to weather the storm, and reclaim its position at the top of the notebook market. It strengthened its global marketing capabilities to keep closer tabs on market developments and also gave more operational authority to local managers, particularly in its U.S. subsidiaries. "There was a time when Tokyo took the initiative on product development," said Tetsuya Mizoguchi, head of PCs for Toshiba in Japan. "We have grown up since then."[18]

As a result of its changes in management style, Toshiba has become more aggressive in pricing and faster to introduce new products based on the latest processor generations. According to Atsutoshi Nishida, president of Toshiba America Information Systems Inc. in Irvine, California: "It used to take six months to a year for a new [generation of computers] to go from desktop to laptop. But from 1993 on, we've introduced a notebook product on the same day that Intel introduces a new chip."[19] Toshiba also has continued to improve its notebook technologies in areas such as power management, heat dispersion, and advanced displays. By 1996, Toshiba's share of the U.S. notebook market had risen to 24%.[20]

In 1996, Toshiba embarked on a new effort to enter the desktop and server markets in the United States. Corporate customers who prefer one-stop shopping for their PCs were buying notebooks from PC makers that offered a full line of products. Also, Toshiba wanted to position itself in the consumer multimedia market. Its first foray into the consumer desktop market turned out to be a disappointment, when it got caught with excess inventory of its multimedia PCs when the industry shifted to Intel's MMX processors.[21] But Toshiba's long-term commitment to the U.S. market contrasts with the sporadic attention paid by other Japanese PC makers, so it can be expected to continue its push into the desktop market even as it tries to protect its lead in notebooks.

## Software Failures

While the Japanese hardware industry has had mixed success in the PC era, the software industry has been an almost unqualified failure. The software and information services market is actually very large, totaling US$41.8 billion in 1995. However, packaged software accounted for only 23.6% of the Japanese software and services market, with users still relying largely on custom programs. In comparison, packaged applications accounted for more than 37% of U.S. software and services spending in 1995.[22] The balance is now shifting in Japan as PCs become more widely diffused, but the slow adoption of packaged software was detrimental to the Japanese software industry.

Packaged software can be commercialized and exported, while custom software is written to the specifications of a particular user. Producing packaged software is also an effective use of programmers' time. While a custom program will be written once and used by one customer, a packaged product will be written once and used by thousands or even millions of users.

So far, Japan has been unable to develop an internationally competitive software industry. In 1995, Japan ran a US$3.9 billion trade deficit in computer software (excluding games).[23] Japanese software makers are unable to compete effectively even in their domestic market. More than 60% of the packaged software sold in Japan is imported, mostly from the United States.[24] This is surprising because domestic producers should have an advantage in a local market, especially one with a unique language. Yet foreign producers have been able to adapt their programs to the Japanese language and market. Much of the PC software market is dominated by Microsoft, which not only controls over 80% of the operating systems market, but also has a majority of the office suite market with the Japanese version of Microsoft Office. Oracle also has made large inroads into the Japanese market, gaining more than 40% of the corporate database market in competition with proprietary products from Fujitsu and other Japanese vendors.

## Video Games

The only major exception to Japanese companies' lack of success in software has been in video games. Sega, Nintendo, and Sony established hardware and software architectures that became world standards and were able to tightly control the licensing of their technologies. Not only do Japanese vendors dominate the hardware market, but Japan is also the leading supplier of video game software. Japanese exports of video games totaled about US$750 million in 1994. Outside of video games, Japan's software exports were a meager $US40 million.[25]

Video game software is one industry in which Japanese companies can develop products for both the domestic and international market. Japanese teenagers are avid video game players, so the local market is big and there is a community of fanatics who often became programmers. Since games are mostly graphical and action-oriented, products developed in Japan appeal just as well to game players around the world. The success of Japanese video games is evidence that Japan's general software problems are due to its industry structure and domestic computer market more than a lack of creativity or skill on the part of Japanese programmers.

## Japan's Hardware Strengths

While Japan has struggled in PCs and software, it remains a world leader in a wide range of components and peripherals. Japanese companies are leading producers of DRAMs, flat-panel displays, floppy disk drives, CD-ROMs, laser printer engines, and cathode ray tubes for monitors. At the subcomponent level, Japanese companies have leading positions in everything from disk drive motors and heads to pure silicon wafers, ceramic packaging, and quartz parts.

Japan's strengths cover a wide range of technologies, including materials for silicon wafers, ceramic castings, read–write heads for various disk drives, and optoelectronics technologies for laser printers and semiconductor steppers. Most of these capabilities were developed initially in the consumer electronics industry. For instance, LCD technology developed for calculators and watches eventually led to Japanese dominance in flat-panel displays for notebook computers. Magnetic recording technologies developed for VCRs and camcorders were transferred to computer tape and disk drives. Optoelectronics technologies and manufacturing techniques developed for cameras were transferred to fax machines, copiers, and eventually laser printers and steppers. CRT technology for television sets was used in computer monitors. Finally, despite Korea's challenge in DRAMs and Intel's dominance in microprocessors, Japan remains a formidable competitor in the semiconductor industry. The inside of most PCs, printers, disk drives, and other computer products are still full of Japanese chips, and Japanese companies control important markets for advanced materials, components, and production equipment.

Some of the biggest Japanese beneficiaries of the PC revolution are not PC makers but specialized components makers. Sharp is the leading producer of flat-panel displays, Canon dominates in laser printer engines, and companies such as Kyocera, TDK, and Yamaha are leaders in various subcomponents markets. Japan's computer vendors such as Toshiba, NEC, and Fujitsu also have continued to benefit from the growth of the PC industry, but primarily as suppliers. What they cannot expect is that their PC business will get much benefit from their strength in components. While Toshiba used its strength in LCD screens to gain an advantage in notebook PCs, there is now an adequate supply of displays on the market and having a captive supply is probably not much of an advantage. In the present market, there are few components that cannot be bought from outside suppliers, and the benefits of having a captive supply during a shortage are neutralized by the costs of being stuck with that supply during a glut.

## Dependence on U.S. Standards

The inability of Japanese companies to control any of the major architectures for hardware or software has plagued the industry from the beginning. Mochio Umeda argues that while Japanese companies know *how* to manufacture, they lag behind American firms in knowing *what* to manufacture, allowing the United States to maintain its control over key standards.[26] For instance, Japanese mainframe makers had caught up with IBM in performance by the early 1980s but still depended on IBM standards and were forced to make large royalty payments to IBM. Japanese supercomputers had surpassed U.S. machines in some speed benchmarks by the late 1980s, but the large library of software available for Cray supercomputers allowed Cray to maintain its lead in the commercial market. The pattern repeated itself in the PC industry, where Japan's development of incompatible PC architectures left it isolated from international standards that were controlled by U.S. companies.

Dependence on U.S. standards has trapped the Japanese computer industry in the decreasing returns segments of the PC industry. While Japanese companies do hold near-monopoly positions in some profitable upstream technologies, they have been unable to break into the large increasing returns markets for software and microprocessors. Even NEC's proprietary PC-98 architecture was based on Intel chips and Microsoft's operating system. NEC was unable to protect its PC standard when IBM and Microsoft created open standards for the Japanese market.

Japan's dependence on Microsoft's software standards is not surprising, given its general weakness in software. Somewhat more surprising has been the failure of Japan's semiconductor industry to break Intel's control of the microprocessor market. Each of the major Japanese PC platforms was based on Intel processors, but there once appeared to be a good possibility that the Japanese could eventually challenge Intel's leadership. For instance, while NEC used Intel chips in the PC-98, it also developed its own version of the $80 \times 86$ chips, called the V-series. Intel sued NEC for patent infringement, but in 1989 a U.S. court ruled against Intel, opening the door for NEC to sell its V-series processors to any PC maker. At the time, many in the United States predicted that the Japanese, no longer blocked by legal challenges from Intel, would overwhelm the U.S. microprocessor industry. Japan's dominance of the DRAM industry was expected to give the Japanese chipmakers a critical advantage in achieving higher yields and lower production costs by applying process technologies developed for DRAM production. NEC was not the only likely challenger; Fujitsu, Hitachi, and Toshiba all had experience as second source producers of earlier Intel or Motorola processors and were licensing new RISC designs from U.S. companies.

When they tried to challenge Intel, however, Japan's chip makers came up against the power of increasing returns in the form of Intel's control of the x86 standard. NEC's V-series chips never caught on with PC makers, and by 1993 the company had stopped using them even in its own computers.

NEC then shifted to a RISC strategy with its VR-series of processors based on designs by the U.S. company, MIPS. But RISC processors never made it into the mainstream PC market, thanks in part to the huge library of x86-compatible software and also Intel's ability to squeeze more performance out of the x86 architecture than many had expected. NEC's PC division continued to use Intel chips for the PC-98, and the VR series was relegated to specialized markets such as workstations and microcontrollers. Fujitsu did somewhat better, becoming a major producer of Sun SPARC processors for the workstation market. But as a group, the Japanese companies failed to make even a dent in the mainstream PC microprocessor market. By the mid-1990s, most Japanese PCs carried the "Intel Inside" label, a small oval symbol of Japan's continuing dependence on standards set in the United States.

Rather than defining standards for the PC industry, Japanese computer makers have been forced to develop software and hardware based on architectures controlled by U.S. companies. The strategy of technological imitation that worked so well in other industries has kept the Japanese companies in the lower margin decreasing returns segments of the industry. And with Intel's control over hardware standards expanding (e.g., into chip sets, multimedia features, and networking functions), profit opportunities in the rest of the PC hardware industry continue to shrink.

### Summary

The preceding discussion considers the reasons for Japan's successes and failures in the PC era but leave some troubling questions. For instance, why were Japanese companies slow to recognize the importance of the PC, remaining fixated instead on the mainframe industry and IBM? Why didn't Japan produce a new wave of start-up companies to compete in the wide-open early days of the PC industry? Why has Japan been almost uniformly unable to develop an independent software industry? And why did most Japanese companies concentrate on the small Japanese PC market and make only half-hearted attempts to penetrate foreign markets?

The answers to these questions are complex, and they go to the heart of Japan's industry structure and corporate culture. The size, diversification, and vertical integration of Japan's computer makers are advantages in producing high-volume hardware products with stable technologies and long product cycles, but they are a liability in the PC industry, with its unpredictable market and technology shifts. Also, the hardware orientation of Japan's electronics industry has meant that software is not given the prominence it deserves, given its critical role in establishing technology standards. Finally, Japan's educational system has been very good at turning out a skilled manufacturing workforce, but it tends to stifle the kind of creativity and initiative that is needed in the innovation-driven segments of the industry.

A final question must be addressed. Why did the bureaucrats who had guided Japan's mainframe industry fail to come up with a successful strategy to help Japan compete in the PC era? This question becomes even more cogent when we look at the highly effective government policies employed in Singapore and Taiwan that helped those countries become important centers of PC production. To consider these issues in more detail, we look first at Japan's industry structure and business strategies, and then review the industrial policies employed by the Japanese government during the PC era.

## Industry Structure

Japan's industry structure and corporate culture made it difficult for Japanese companies to recognize and respond to the PC revolution. While Silicon Valley is marked by constant churning of people and companies, Japan is marked by stability. The same companies that created Japan's computer industry in the 1960s still dominate in the 1990s. Stability might be desirable in a mature industry such as automobiles or even mainframe computers, but in a dynamic environment like the PC industry, it can be synonymous with stagnation. It is not simply the size of Japan's computer giants that makes it difficult for them to compete in PCs, but their tendency toward vertical integration and bureaucratic decision-making. Worse yet is their ability to lock newcomers out of the domestic market, preventing the emergence of a new wave of entrepreneurial PC-oriented companies like those in the United States, Taiwan, and elsewhere.

### Vertical Integration

The vertically integrated structure of the Japanese electronics industry was a great advantage in high-volume standardized products such as TVs, VCRs, DRAMs, and flat-panel displays. Large, vertically integrated companies such as Fujitsu, Hitachi, NEC, and Mitsubishi had access to financial resources to make massive investments in manufacturing capacity and rapidly bring down production costs. As members of much larger *keiretsu* (industry groups) they had access to capital from the major banks affiliated with the *keiretsu* in addition to their own internal resources.

Low capital costs gave the Japanese giants a major advantage against American and European companies, and their manufacturing-led strategy crushed competitors in many sectors. They also used the members of their *keiretsu* as a captive market for products such as semiconductors and computers. However, in the 1990s the Japanese have faced difficulties in even their high-volume strongholds. The collapse of the Japanese stock market and instability of the banking system have made capital tight, and the Japanese manufacturers have had to cut back on R&D and overall investment. At the same time, Korean and Taiwanese companies are making big investments in high-volume products, particularly DRAMs and flat-panel displays, while newcomers from countries such as China are also trying to move into high-volume hardware production.

Vertical integration worked well for the Japanese in the mainframe computer industry, because that industry had been defined by IBM's vertically integrated structure. Competing with IBM required the ability not only to design and assemble the mainframe, but also to make most of the components as well. Vertical integration within the *keiretsu* allowed Japan's computer makers to have all the necessary capabilities under its control without having to provide lifetime employment for an excessive number of workers. The system maker did not have to build all of its own components; it could purchase from smaller suppliers in its vertical production chain. The computer makers also spun off companies to provide software and services to customers.

This structure turned out to be poorly suited for the PC industry, however. A vertical industry structure requires a great deal of control from the top, making it difficult to react quickly to changing market conditions or new technologies. By refusing to share their suppliers in order to maintain control, the big Japanese computer makers prevented those suppliers from gaining the economies of scale needed to lower costs. Also, the lack of competition in different industry segments was a barrier to rapid product development and cost reduction. For example, if NEC's disk drive division or one of its suppliers was slow to provide a necessary component, a new product introduction could be held up. In the United States, if Seagate was slow to bring a new generation of disk drive to the market, PC makers would gladly buy from Quantum, Western Digital, or Maxtor. The intense competition at each level of the production value chain gave the U.S. PC industry a dynamism that the Japanese industry could not match.

The vertically integrated structure of the Japanese computer makers and their associated supplier networks have been slow to respond to rapid changes in the market, in technology, and in the international production network. By relying on traditional domestic suppliers, the Japanese industry failed to take advantage of the capabilities of the horizontal, specialized structure of the PC industry. Only in the mid-1990s did the Japanese companies begin to move outside their vertical structures in a serious way, by using Asian suppliers and moving production offshore.

## Lack of Successful Newcomers

Japan has almost no equivalents to the independent start-ups that have come to dominate many market segments in the United States, including PCs, disk drives, and packaged software. There are also few equivalents to the highly responsive small-and medium-sized Taiwanese firms that have grown to become leaders in many segments of the PC industry. There are a few exceptions, such as software distributor and publisher Softbank and software maker Just Systems. There are also larger independent companies such as Canon and Seiko Epson in the printer and PC businesses. In general, however, the computer industry is dominated by large established companies like NEC, Fujitsu, Hitachi, Toshiba, and Mitsubishi.

Compare Japan's PC industry to the U.S. industry. Among the top six U.S. PC makers in 1995, four were start-up PC companies (Compaq, Apple, Packard Bell, and Dell); only IBM and Hewlett-Packard are pre-PC era companies. Of the top five Japanese (NEC, Fujitsu, Toshiba, Seiko Epson, and Hitachi), all except Seiko Epson are electronics conglomerates that have existed since before World War II. The situation is similar in other segments of the PC industry. For instance, the U.S. disk drive industry was led by IBM and four start-up companies—Seagate, Conner (now merged with Seagate), Quantum, and Western Digital—while Japan's top disk drive makers are the old familiar Hitachi, Fujitsu, NEC, and Toshiba.

Entrepreneurial newcomers are not the answer to competing in all segments of the computer industry, as illustrated by the fact that only Korean giants such as Samsung have been able to compete with the Japanese leaders in DRAMs and flat-panel displays. But in other industry segments such as PCs and software, the lack of entrepreneurial companies is very costly, especially when established companies have an older line of business that they are trying to protect. The one big international success in Japan's PC industry has been Toshiba, a company that gave up the mainframe business in the mid-1970s and had no installed customer base to protect. It is not so surprising that Fujitsu and Hitachi were reluctant to cannibalize their mainframe business with low-cost, low-margin PCs, at least in the 1980s when the mainframe market was still growing. The question for Japan is why new companies did not spring up to enter the PC industry when the giants were slow to move.

A number of standard answers are offered to these questions, generally falling into two categories. The first category explains the lack of entrepreneurship in cultural terms, that is, the belief that Japanese culture is inherently group oriented and that individual initiative is frowned upon (often expressed in the hoary maxim, "The nail that sticks up is pounded down"). The cultural explanations are challenged by Callon,[27] who points to a survey of U.S. and Japanese university students that shows similar numbers of students in each country preferring to start their own companies in the future. In fact, Callon argues that Japanese entrepreneurs establish new companies at a rate similar to the U.S. level. The difference is in the small number that actually grow into large companies in Japan. Still, it is difficult to ignore culture altogether. While Japan may have more aspiring entrepreneurs than is commonly believed, especially compared to the U.S. population as a whole, it simply does not have the entrepreneurial ethos that is pervasive in a high-tech enclave such as Silicon Valley.

The second category of explanations focuses on the dominance of the Japanese economy by the giant *keiretsu*, who control access to capital and distribution channels. This argument is supported by the example of NEC's use of an extensive distribution channel to dominate the PC market. However, this does not explain the absence of export-oriented start-ups, since international markets were not influenced by the *keiretsu's* distribution channels. Why were small Taiwanese companies able to develop linkages to the global production network, while small Japanese companies were left out? It is not surprising that existing small companies remained tied to their parent companies' domestic production chains, but why the lack of newcomers to test the international waters?

Several analysts argue that a key factor was the shortage of venture capital, which they blame largely on the Ministry of Finance (MOF) for limiting the number of initial public offerings (IPOs) by Japanese venture companies. Without the prospect of a big payoff from an IPO, venture capitalists have been unwilling to make risky investments. Also, Japanese companies cannot attract top workers with offers of stock options, as U.S. venture companies often do, since stock options have little value without the prospect of an IPO. The Finance Ministry squeezed IPOs to almost zero after the stock market crash in the early 1990s in order to prevent dilution of stock prices of existing companies and protect the banking system from a further meltdown of the stock market. The effect was to protect large companies, as well as investors, while starving small companies of capital.[28]

Japan's Fair Trade Commission also prevents venture capitalists from serving as board members on businesses in which they have a stake. This discourages investment—since investors have no influence over company management—and also robs the venture companies of a valuable source of managerial expertise. In the United States, venture capitalists help to guide new companies through the growth process until, and sometimes after, a successful IPO. Many U.S. venture capitalists point to this exclusion as a key reason for the shortage of venture capital in Japan.[29]

MITI has recently been pressuring MOF to loosen its restrictions on IPOs, and the number of IPOs did rebound after 1993. However, this might have been only a temporary phenomenon related to an upturn on the Tokyo exchange. Asking a bureaucracy (Japanese or otherwise) to give up regulatory powers is something akin to asking a person to cut off a body part. Even as it pressures other ministries to deregulate, MITI itself remains one of the leading propagators of regulation in Japan, and has not offered to reduce its own regulatory role. To create a truly dynamic venture business sector in Japan would probably require a radical change in bureaucratic mentality, as well as a willingness to shake up an industry structure that tends to block newcomers out of distribution channels and production networks. Such change is unlikely, but even some moderate changes in the regulatory and tax system could unleash quite a bit of entrepreneurial activity.

## Corporate Culture and Management Practices

The Japanese corporate culture is built around a number of time-honored practices that have been the object of much admiration among students of the Japanese economy. These include lifetime employment, seniority promotion, and on-the-job training. Lifetime employment and seniority promotion are believed to promote loyalty to the company and provide security for employees.[30] These practices ensure that the benefits of on-the-job training programs are retained by the employer (and not taken to a competitor) and provide continuing development of skills that match individual companies' requirements. Lifetime employment also helps companies build "tacit" knowledge, or "learning by doing," that is achieved through the experience of solving problems unique to a particular company.

Such practices have proven highly beneficial in established industries with predictable technology paths and market dynamics, such as steel, automobiles, most consumer electronics, and memory chips, where the Japanese have excelled. Under the new dynamics of the PC era, however, these practices have turned out to be liabilities. Lifetime employment makes it difficult for firms to cut costs or to make room for new employees with new skills needed in a new business. So while the companies have maintained the facade of job security by not imposing layoffs, they have resorted to other tactics to reduce their work forces, such as sending workers to subsidiaries in distant outposts or pressuring them to take early retirement.

Another measure taken to reduce head counts was hiring cutbacks. For instance, Toshiba announced it would reduce new hiring from 2,000 to just 1,000 workers in 1995.[31] The downside of this approach is that the most expensive senior employees (who were the least familiar with PC technologies) remained on the payroll, while fewer young, computer-savvy workers were brought in. Developing those new skills is critically important to Japanese companies as they shift into the PC and network computing world, but it is difficult to do from within. On-the-job training does not work when there is no one with the knowledge to do the training. And since Japanese corporate culture discourages companies from hiring workers away from competitors, it is not easy to accumulate the skill base needed to compete in new markets.

Large Japanese companies are also hampered by cumbersome, bureaucratic decision-making processes, making them slow to respond to changes in technology and markets. In an industry that moves as quickly as the PC industry, this can be a fatal flaw. The problems get worse as one gets further from headquarters and the decision-making chain gets even longer, adding to the problem of competing in international markets.

The industry is now well aware of the problems caused by its corporate culture, but that culture has been difficult to change. Workers expect their company, and the government, to take care of them in return for their loyalty to the system. According to one industrialist, "The end of lifetime employment would cause a social disaster, because Japanese people are not prepared to cope with unemployment." Even a limited change, such as tying compensation more closely to performance, is considered "very difficult, very [destabilizing]".[32] Japan's computer makers have made changes in their management practices in recent years, as exemplified by their creation of PC subsidiaries in the United States with more autonomy in design and marketing, but those changes tend to be gradual and cautious.

## International Orientation

Japanese companies have had great international success in industries such as automobiles and consumer electronics, producing hit products and developing strong brand recognition. Why have Japanese computer makers been slow to develop a similar strong presence abroad?

Japanese industry has traditionally followed a Japan-centric strategy toward product development for international markets. Foreign markets have been used to absorb excess production capacity and as new battlegrounds in the ongoing battle for market share among Japanese producers. Rather than compete directly in established markets, Japanese companies generally looked for new markets that they could develop. For instance, Japanese automakers entered the U.S. market with small economy cars and pickup trucks that filled a niche not well served by Detroit. Only later did the Japanese try to compete in the higher end of the market. Likewise, electronics makers such as Sony developed unique products such as the transistor radio and the Walkman to enter U.S. markets. They also took products developed by U.S. companies such as VCRs, camcorders, and microwave ovens and made them available at affordable prices. Only in a few cases, such as color TVs and DRAMs, did Japanese electronics companies compete directly against well-established U.S. competitors—and in those cases they were charged with dumping (selling below cost) to gain market share.

A key factor in Japan's export success was using the domestic market as a development platform for new products. Japanese consumers are sophisticated buyers of consumer electronics, who demand smaller, energy-efficient products suitable to their small living spaces and high energy costs. To meet this demand, Japanese electronics companies have emphasized products that are small and energy efficient. Just as small Japanese automobiles had become popular in the United States as gasoline prices rose, small electronics products, such as compact 35mm cameras and camcorders, were a hit in the United States and other markets. The success of the consumer electronics industry also created a new market in Japan for components, such as semiconductors, and supported the development of a components industry that was able to compete internationally. In each of these cases, the product developed for the domestic market was based on standard technologies and was suitable for export with little modification.

In mainframes and minicomputers, the Japanese computer makers focused on the domestic market, and did not seriously challenge IBM's dominance in the United States or Europe, although Fujitsu did compete in those markets through its investments in Amdahl and ICL. The PC seemed to offer an excellent opportunity for Japanese companies to compete in international markets, applying their manufacturing prowess to produce standardized, high-volume products. This did turn out to be the case in many components and peripherals, but the Japanese could not crack the global market for PC systems. The strategy of developing products for the domestic market and then exporting them was not viable in PCs due to differences in language and incompatible architectures.

The only exception to Japan's failure to penetrate international markets was Toshiba, which developed portable PCs based on international standards and became the world leader. As was the case with Honda and Sony, Toshiba's weakness in the Japanese market helped focus its attention on export markets, particularly the United States. Otherwise, Japanese companies were not able to develop products with features needed to compete in the international PC market. Only since 1992 have Japanese PC makers been able to standardize on one platform for domestic and international sales. With the rapid growth of the domestic market for both PCs and networking, Japanese vendors can finally hone their capabilities at home to compete abroad.

The problems faced by the Japanese companies in foreign markets have been exacerbated by their tendency to maintain tight control of foreign operations from Japan.[33] Foreign managers of Japanese affiliates were given little authority, and they often had to get permission from Tokyo even to change prices. They had little input into product development decisions and were often "out of the loop" in the decision-making process because of language—and because they were not part of the social circles in which real decisions are often made in Japan. This situation often frustrates foreign managers in Japanese companies and contributes to the companies' lack of flexibility and slowness to respond to changing market conditions. The situation is starting to change in companies such as Fujitsu and Hitachi, which have set up PC subsidiaries in California, but few Japanese companies give their foreign managers the kind of autonomy common to subsidiaries of American multinationals. Also, it is virtually unheard of for a foreign national to move into the highest management levels of a Japanese firm, reinforcing the Japan-centric view of top management. By contrast, major U.S. companies such as Apple, Compaq, and Intel have been run by foreign-born CEOs, and Silicon Valley is full of executives and engineers from various foreign countries.

Japan's relatively small presence in the U.S. PC market put Japanese companies at a serious disadvantage in product development. A strong presence in the United States would provide the ability to track market and technology developments, but the Japanese companies were slow to develop the close relationships with users that are critical to identifying market opportunities. Even Toshiba lost its initial lead in portables because it failed to respond to the market shift from laptops to notebooks. It only regained the lead when it upgraded its marketing operations in the United States and gave local managers more say over design and production decisions.[34]

Japanese companies also have been slow to take advantage of the opportunities provided by the Asian computer production network. While their competitors were sourcing around the world, Japanese PC makers stuck with their traditional domestic suppliers and failed to take full advantage of the manufacturing and engineering skills developing in Asia. Even when they produced offshore, Japanese manufacturers tended to buy components from back home (or persuaded their suppliers to move abroad with them) rather than developing supply networks in the countries in which they operated. Also, their hesitance to give much authority to local managers led to difficulties in attracting and retaining talented people.[35]

In contrast, U.S. computer companies sourced components and located production in Korea, Taiwan, Singapore, and elsewhere in Asia. As these countries gained experience, they also gained capabilities in engineering and manufacturing. The U.S. companies took advantage of those capabilities to outsource much of their production in order to focus on design and marketing, while Japanese companies continued to depend on their own manufacturing capabilities and those of their traditional suppliers.

The procurement patterns of the Japanese PC makers began changing in the mid-1990s. NEC opened an office in Hong Kong to manage production of low-cost PCs in China and source components throughout Asia. It plans to eventually use non-Japanese suppliers for up to 80% of its components. Fujitsu turned to Taiwanese manufacturers to produce low-cost desktop PCs; by 1996 it was procuring about 90% of the components for its FMV series computers from Asian countries. Hitachi, Seiko, and others have also contracted with Taiwanese companies to build PCs and peripherals for export and for the Japanese market. The shift to Asia was partly a result of the appreciation of the yen, which made production in Japan too expensive in times of falling prices. It was also an admission that Japanese manufacturers could not match the Taiwanese in production flexibility and speed to market with new products.

However, the Japanese computer makers remain uncomfortable managing a regional production network. While Asian components are less expensive (a motherboard from a Taiwanese OEM can cost 15%–30% less), the quality does not always come up to the standards expected by Japanese companies. The Japanese PC makers were unaccustomed to dealing with foreign suppliers, and in the words of Katsuya Yoshioka, of NCB Research Institute, "They weren't fully aware of some basic (non-Japanese) market facts: that high quality equates with high prices, and that the relationship between manufacturer and supplier is more-or-less equal."[36] As a result, some Japanese PC makers have reduced the scope of their foreign procurement, and some have moved production back to Japan.

### Software Industry Structure

The entire Japanese computer industry has been hobbled by its weakness in software, and the problem has been especially serious in the PC industry. While Japan's software industry is said to outperform its U.S. counterparts in some measures of programmer productivity and quality control, it has grown more slowly and is less innovative than the U.S. industry. Perhaps the most serious problem is that Japan has failed to develop a vibrant independent software industry able to produce a broad variety of commercial software packages for the PC. There are few Japanese equivalents to independent U.S. firms that dominate the global packaged software industry—and which now control more than half of the Japanese packaged software market. By contrast, most independent Japanese software firms are relatively small and sell only to the domestic market.

Some of Japan's software problems are the result of the evolution of the industry. Japan's computer makers originally sold software and services in conjunction with hardware sales, just as IBM had before it unbundled its software and hardware in 1969. The Japanese government required unbundling in 1977, but the practice of treating software as part of the hardware package remained common, hindering the growth of an independent software industry. Instead, most software was developed either by the hardware makers, their subsidiaries, or by users themselves. In each case, the focus was on custom software, either to lock in customers to the vendor's proprietary hardware or to offer users a perceived competitive advantage in their own industry by developing software tailored to their business processes.[37]

The custom approach created problems for the Japanese software industry. Custom programming is labor intensive and exacerbates the critical shortage of software personnel. If a Japanese programmer can produce more lines of code per hour than an American programmer, it would appear that the Japanese programmer is more productive. But this calculation is deceiving. If the Japanese program has only one user, while the American program is used by thousands, the American programmer has actually been thousands of times as productive in terms of the value of his or her output. Also, the claims that Japanese programmers deliver code with fewer errors[38] is misleading, since Japanese programmers are often making minor modifications on existing programs, while American programmers are more likely to be developing new products or major modifications of old programs.[39]

The custom software approach led to a rigid division of labor coordinated by hardware vendors and large users.[40] Initially, the vendors would assign personnel to the user site to develop custom programs and train the users' own information systems departments. Over time, both vendors and users began to spin-off their application developers into subsidiaries that now dominate the software and systems integration business in Japan. These include vendor spin-offs such as Fujitsu FIP, Hitachi Information Systems, Toshiba Information Systems, and NEC Software, and user spin-offs such as NTT Data Systems, Nomura Research Institute, and Nippon Steel Information Systems.

While hardware vendors keep operating system development in-house, the vendor and user spin-offs coordinate and develop most applications, contracting lower level activities to independent software houses, who subcontract work to even smaller firms. Software development is implemented through a top-down, centrally coordinated management system that bears a strong resemblance to Japan's manufacturing structure. Japanese companies treat software production as a factory operation, breaking development down into a linear progression of planning, design, system engineering, and coding. This process creates coordination problems and discourages creativity throughout the system.

Another problem is that custom programming is focused on the mainframe and minicomputer markets, and the skills required to develop and market custom programs do not translate easily to the rapidly growing PC software market. Packaged software requires a focus on creating products that are valuable to a large number of users, which is contrary to the idea of developing customized solutions to a specific user's needs. The inability of older software companies to make the switch to the PC market would not be a problem if new independent software houses were able to meet the demand for packaged software.[41] But while many software vendors did spring up to develop PC applications, their growth was stunted by barriers related to Japan's industry structure. These include lack of access to capital and barriers to distribution channels.

The shortage of venture capital is especially acute in the software industry. Japan's capital markets lack the knowledge and experience needed to evaluate software makers, whose assets are intellectual and intangible, and whose future profitability is difficult to predict. In the United States, there are venture capitalists who specialize in software companies and have the experience to judge their prospects more accurately. The Japanese venture capital market consists mostly of firms affiliated with banks and securities firms, who tend to invest in more traditional industries. In 1989, only 0.04% of total investment by venture capitalists in Japan went to the software industry, compared to 11% in the United States.[42]

There has been some effort by the government and banks to increase venture capital investment in software. The government has offered grants and loans to software companies with innovative products, although many argue that these are little more than bailouts to small subcontractors who have been squeezed by the recession. Also, software distributor Softbank has offered to help private banks screen software companies for investment. Softbank is one of the few big entrepreneurial success stories in the Japanese computer industry, but it remains to be seen if it has good instincts in the venture capital market.

The software industry also suffers from shortages and poor deployment of human resources. Most computer science graduates end up in large hardware firms. Software firms therefore are usually left hiring people with no training in computer science, whom they then must train as programmers. The small independent companies at the bottom of the software production chain are given such specialized tasks to perform that their staff is unlikely ever to gain the breadth of experience needed to take on more complex tasks. These companies find it difficult to hire or develop the skilled people that they would need to move into development of packaged programs. The training and personnel management in Japanese software companies tends to stifle creativity as well. New hires are all trained in identical programs, regardless of their previous education or experience, and the practice of seniority-based promotion does not reward a programmer's productivity or creativity.

Finally, software is simply not highly respected as a product in Japan. The tradition of bundling hardware and software caused both vendors and users to undervalue software, since it was not paid for separately. As a result, software professionals do not receive the respect given to hardware specialists. They generally do not receive top salaries, nor are they likely to rise to top management positions in major corporations. This discourages bright students from studying for careers in software. Likewise, Japan's highly regimented software industry has not produced any equivalent to Microsoft, Adobe, Novell, or other successful software start-ups in the United States. With few exceptions, the best-known companies and recognizable individuals in Japan are on the hardware side. As one software professional put it, "Software is not respected. It is not a good job to have because software people cannot be promoted to the top."[43]

Such factors have been obstacles to the development of Japan's software industry. Most important, these factors have severely stunted the growth of independent software companies producing packaged software. The weakness of Japanese packaged software is most vividly illustrated by the fact that over 60% of the packaged software market consists of imported programs. Add to that the large amount of pirated software in use, most of which is undoubtedly foreign in origin, and it is clear that very little of the software running on Japanese PCs originated in Japan. Software and information services are the fastest growing segments of the IT industry, and will become even more important as national and global information infrastructures are developed.

It does appear that the software market is changing in Japan, with packaged software finally gaining importance. However, the big beneficiaries of the shift to PCs and packaged software have been U.S. companies. Microsoft dominates the market for PC applications and Oracle is now the number one seller of database packages in Japan, competing against the proprietary products from Fujitsu and Hitachi. Developers of packaged software for the PC-98 platform now find their DOS-based applications obsolete and they must compete with giants like Microsoft in the Windows market. And while the big U.S. vendors have the resources to develop Japanese-language versions of their products, few Japanese firms can develop and market products for international markets. The best hope for the Japanese software industry is probably to focus on niche markets in Japan (and elsewhere in Asia) that could be profitable but are not large enough to attract competition from the large multinational software companies.

### Domestic Market: Slow Adoption of Information Technology

Japan has been slow to adopt computers, especially in comparison with the United States and leading European countries such as Sweden and the United Kingdom. A few numbers help illustrate Japan's low level of IT use compared to the United States (table 3-3). One reason has been language; major computer languages are based on English, making it harder for a country with a non-Roman written language to use the technology. Another is a cultural emphasis on face-to-face communication. But the most important reason has been cost. By protecting the domestic computer industry, the Japanese gov-

TABLE 3-3. Computer Use in the United States and Japan

| | United States | Japan |
|---|---|---|
| Computers in use (1995) | 74,400,000 | 18,300,000 |
| Computers/1,000 people | 287 | 146 |
| PCs installed/1,000 workers | 551 | 147 |
| Percent of PCs connected to LANs | 66 | 17 |
| Internet hosts (1996) | 10,110,908 | 734,406 |

*Sources:* Karen Petska-Juliussen and Egil Juliussen, *The 8th Annual Computer Industry Almanac* (Glenbrook, Nev.: Computer Industry Almanac, 1996); Network Wizard (1997; www.nw.com/); Japan Information Processing Development Center (JIPDEC), *Informatization White Paper* (Tokyo: JIPDEC, 1995).

ernment minimized price competition. Throughout the 1980s, Japan imported only about 10% of its computer purchases, while the U.S. figure rose from 10% in 1980 to nearly 40% in 1990. The Japanese figure reflects a number of factors, including government policy, but a major reason is the "locked-in" relationship between users and vendors, due to the proprietary, customized nature of Japanese hardware and software.

Japan is an advanced user of some technologies, such as on-line banking systems, but it is far behind in implementing client-server computing, local area networks (about one-fourth the U.S. level), and the Internet (one-tenth the U.S. level). Internet mania finally arrived in 1995, but the high cost of telecommunications and access services limited the diffusion of Internet use in Japan. The greatest benefits from PCs come when they are connected together in a network, creating "network economies" that can only be achieved when a significant number of computers are linked together.[44] Japan has been slow to realize these benefits.

The Japanese market has been conservative, lagging behind the United States in shifting from mainframes to PCs and adopting the Internet. This is partly because computer vendors did not encourage users to give up their expensive proprietary mainframes for cheap PCs. It is also due to the conservative nature of user organizations. Big companies were accustomed to centralized computing systems, and there was no ground swell from individuals or departments demanding PCs on their desktops. The PC was seen by users as a tool for secretaries, not managers, and communications systems such as e-mail were seen as impersonal and difficult to use with Japanese characters.

The conservative use of computers in Japan has limited the country's ability to achieve productivity gains by applying information technology. The muted competition in the PC market before 1992 also put the computer makers at a competitive disadvantage internationally. Japanese PC companies were not able to use the domestic market as a base for developing competitive products as they had in other industries, such as consumer electronics and automobiles. With the Japanese PC market fragmented among different standards and limited by high prices, no one could achieve economies of scale. Nor could they export the products they sold in Japan, since they were not built to international standards. Rather than an asset, the domestic market became a distraction that kept the Japanese industry from focusing on the U.S. market, where technology trends and standards were being set. The protected, profitable domestic market was big enough to support a few PC companies, reducing the imperative to do battle in more competitive global markets. This contrasts with Taiwanese companies such as Acer, which could not survive off the domestic market and so were forced to think globally.

The costs of a backward domestic market were even greater for the software and services industries. Close interaction between producers and sophisticated users is critical in the software development process. For instance, the alpha and beta testing of new software generations provides invaluable feedback to software developers on the features desired by users and helps eliminate bugs before the program is commercialized.[45] Sophisticated users also find new applications for programs that help expand the market for a product. In the rapidly growing systems integration industry, interaction between providers and users is vital to improving the knowledge and capabilities of both parties.

A good example of the importance of user feedback in product development is seen at Microsoft. Microsoft has a history of introducing technically weak products and steadily improving them until they become commercial successes. It is often said that Version 3.0 of any Microsoft product will be the first commercial success. Only a few Japanese software companies have achieved usage levels high enough to support continued product development and to survive against foreign software makers. The most successful is Just Systems, which makes the Ichitaro word processing program that was the most widely used program in Japan for more than a decade. For Just Systems, language is an advantage, because it was successful early on in developing a program to handle Japanese characters, and it has maintained a strong position against Microsoft Word and WordPerfect. But most Japanese software companies had a difficult time developing a large enough user base to support continual product improvement, a problem that was only exacerbated by high levels of software piracy (which is finally declining in recent years).

The PC boom of the mid-1990s is bringing Japan closer to international levels of computer use. With PCs, networking, and Internet use becoming more widespread, Japan is finally moving into the mainstream of the global computer market. This change should help Japan reap productivity gains in industry and government. The unification of much of the Japanese PC industry around the Wintel standard should make it more competitive internationally in hardware, but the prospects for the software industry are less promising.

### Human Resources

Japan has a large, high-quality pool of engineers to support its electronics and semiconductor industries, with particular strength in process engineering. Japanese universities granted 81,355 bachelor's degrees in engineering in 1990, compared to 64,705 for the United States.[46] Japan also produced 1,370 doctoral degrees in engineering, compared to 5,696 in the United States. Hardware skills such as electronics engineering have long been in high demand by the big electronics firms, which offer good salaries, job security, and prestige. This has lured top students into such fields, and the flow of top students into such companies has reinforced their competitive edge.

On the other hand, Japan has a serious shortage of computer professionals. While the number of software professionals as a share of total population in Japan is comparable to the United States, there is a much lower level of university-trained computer specialists. The number of graduates with bachelor's degrees in math and computer science was just 3,125 in 1990, compared to 42,369 in the United States. It is estimated that only 20% to 30% of the courses offered in Japanese computer science programs are comparable to courses in the U.S. standard ACM curriculum.[47] The situation is worse in advanced degrees. Japan has never produced more than 88 doctoral degrees in math and computer science in a single year, while the United States produced 2,024 in 1993 alone.[48] Japan has also sent far fewer students to the United States for graduate degrees in science and engineering than have other Asian countries such as China, Korea, and Taiwan.

Most of the small number of computer science graduates ends up working for major hardware vendors or large software firms, leaving the rest of the industry to get by with university graduates from other majors and graduates of vocational schools, two-year colleges, technical schools, and high schools. User organizations likewise have a limited pool of professionals to draw upon. Most computer skills are developed through on-the-job training, and few companies provide workers with systematic outside training in computer skills.

The lack of job mobility between Japanese companies often makes it difficult for companies to get experienced workers and limits the dissemination of skills throughout the industry. Also, the job status and compensation offered by the larger companies can not be matched by small companies, making it difficult for more dynamic small companies to get the skills they need to succeed. Strict limits on immigration into Japan shut off a supply of skilled foreign workers that has been very important to the U.S. industry.

The shortage and poor deployment of human resources is an obstacle to Japan's ability to compete in computer systems, develop an independent software industry, and effectively apply computers throughout the economy. Not only does Japan need more computer professionals, it also needs to increase the computer literacy of its entire workforce, from top management to the shop floor.

## Summary

The combination of industry structure, domestic market, and national capabilities (especially human resources) explains why Japanese companies thrived as producers of high-volume hardware and became competitive in the mainframe business, yet struggled in PCs and software. The closely integrated *keiretsu* industry structure provided ready capital, reliable supply chains, and captive customers. The domestic market also served as a proving ground for both consumer electronics and electronics components that could be exported in high volumes. However, both producers and users were slow to react to the PC revolution. Vertical integration left Japan partly isolated from the dynamic global production system for PC hardware. Software factories were of no use in creating packaged software. Entrepreneurial start-ups were starved for capital and access to distribution channels. And engineers, programmers, and other professionals were trained to be average, and they were lured into large organizations that offered prestige but discouraged innovation. Only in the 1990s, faced with a slump in the entire electronics industry, did Japanese companies begin to make changes in their corporate cultures and practices, and these changes have been incremental at best.

These facts return us to the question raised earlier concerning the ineffectiveness of Japan's industrial policies in the PC era. The concept of the capitalist development state rests on the notion of enlightened industrial policy guided by an economic "pilot agency" and carried out through close cooperation between government and industry. The prototype for this model was Japan's Ministry of International Trade and Industry, which has been credited for engineering the Japanese economic miracle, in particular by targeting key industries and successfully "making winners" in those industries. As we have seen in chapter 2, this appeared to be exactly the case in the development of Japan's mainframe computer industry. Why then, was MITI unable to help the Japanese computer industry make the adjustments necessary to compete in the PC era?

## Industrial Policy

By the 1980s, Japanese industries were reaching the limits of a strategy that depended on acquiring and applying technology developed elsewhere. Japan had caught up in many technologies, and foreign competitors were becoming more protective of their own technology. As a rich nation, Japan also was coming under international pressure to contribute its share to the creation of new knowledge.

Meanwhile, MITI had become a victim of its own success in helping create Japan's manufacturing and export powerhouse and was casting about for a new role. There was no longer a need for outright protection or subsidies for most industries. Japan was lowering formal trade barriers under continued pressure from the United States and Europe. Other barriers to trade and foreign investment were embedded in the Japanese industrial structure—in the form of closed distribution systems, bid-rigging in government procurement, and the "old boy network" of university alumni—and so MITI's protection was no longer needed. Also, Japanese corporations had gained confidence in their own capabilities and were less willing to seek or follow MITI's guidance.

The Ministry's role was therefore being reduced to the restructuring of declining industries and promoting imports to ease trade tensions—not a very appealing prospect for the oft-proclaimed architects of the Japanese miracle.[49] It was also facing new competition from the Ministry of Posts and Telecommunications (MPT), which hoped to use its regulatory power over the telecommunications industry as a basis for expanding its role in the newly evolving information industries. MITI saw more attractive possibilities in the realm of technology promotion, and it began to shift its emphasis from industrial policy to technology policy.

### R&D Consortia

In the field of computers, MITI was concerned about Japan's continued vulnerability to IBM's control over key standards and architectures in the mainframe industry. One way to escape this threat would be to develop a new architecture that would be superior to IBM's. In essence MITI was looking to leapfrog IBM by creating a new generation of computers incorporating artificial intelligence and parallel processing. To accomplish this, MITI employed a strategy that it had used in its efforts to catch up in mainframes and semiconductors—the R&D consortium. MITI initiated R&D projects aimed at moving Japan to the technological frontiers of hardware performance and developing a new generation of computer architectures. In addition, MITI supported consortia to develop non-IBM software standards for PCs and workstations. The four major projects undertaken in the 1980s were the Fifth Generation Computer Systems Project, the Supercomputer Project, the TRON Project, and the Sigma Project.

*Fifth Generation Computer Systems (FGCS) Project.* The Fifth Generation Project was funded by MITI and the Science and Technology Agency (STA), receiving 54 billion yen (US$356 million) over eleven years. Eight computer vendors and NTT participated, but all refused to provide funding, feeling the project's goals were too vague and noncommercial. The goal was the development of computers based on parallel and inference processing architecture, rather than conventional Von Neumann architecture. The goal was to develop computers that would mimic some aspects of human thinking, achieving so-called "artificial intelligence."

The project initially drew a great deal of attention, because it offered the promise of a new generation of computers based on Japanese technology. Joel West notes that the project was used to manufacture hysteria in the United States, particularly by proponents of a more active industrial policy.[50] However, as the project progressed, it failed to live up to expectations and was labeled a major disappointment, especially by U.S. opponents of industrial targeting, who were anxious to pounce on such a failure. But while the project did not propel Japan to the forefront of computer technology, its backers claim that it accomplished quite a bit. In 1992, the Institute for New Generation Computer Technology (ICOT), which is the home of the project, exhibited prototypes of five types of fifth-generation computers produced by Fujitsu,

Hitachi, Mitsubishi, Toshiba, and Oki. It also demonstrated more than twenty types of new software and released, free of charge, seventy-one software applications developed by the project[51] in the hope that research institutes and companies would develop commercial products.

Supporters of the project claim that the project allowed risky and future-oriented R&D to be conducted, something that would not be carried out by the private sector. Still, there is no question that the project failed to come near its initial goals of creating a new computing paradigm in which Japan would be a leader.

*Supercomputer Project.*   The Supercomputer Project, which ran from 1981 to 1989, targeted development of massively parallel processing (MPP) supercomputers. Parallel processing offers the possibility of tremendous performance gains over existing supercomputers, and the technology has potential applications in areas such as telecommunications. The technology was still in the early research stages and was too risky for the private sector to make major investments. So the project was funded completely by the government at a level of US$104 million over the life of the project.

Major areas explored were high-speed chip technology, Josephson junctions (high-speed switching using superconductivity), high-speed parallel processing, and control software. The six major computer makers were involved, with work divided up among the companies. NTT also conducted its own supercomputing research in cooperation with Fujitsu, Hitachi, and NEC. The Supercomputer Project was marked by a lack of cooperation among the participants that bordered on outright hostility. The work was done in-house and the companies were reluctant to share results with their competitors. The companies developed their own supercomputers with performance equivalent to American machines, but they were based on conventional technologies, not parallel processing.

*Sigma Project.*   The Sigma Project, conducted from 1985 to 1990, was aimed at improving software development productivity by providing developers with the latest technologies and tools. Another goal was to create UNIX-based software as an alternative to software based on IBM's proprietary operating systems. All the major Japanese hardware and software companies were involved and the 22 billion yen (US$ 147 million) cost was split evenly between the government and the companies.[52] A national company called the Sigma Center was created to build a workstation for software development and to house a database containing software development tools. A national network was established to give developers access to the Sigma Center databases. The project resulted in the development of just sixty programs, whose yearly sales are only 30 million yen, while the Sigma System, a company established to commercialize products from the project, lost 260 million yen.[53]

The failure of the Sigma Project has been blamed on rigid planning and inflexibility in a very fluid technology. The software selected for Sigma's software development program was obsolete after being on the market only five years,[54] and Japanese companies have failed to make inroads into the market for UNIX-based software.

*TRON Project.*    The Real Time Operating System Nucleus (TRON) project was an attempt to develop a purely Japanese computer architecture with a common operating system that could run on a wide range of information appliances. The originator of the TRON project was Professor Ken Sakamura of the University of Tokyo. Sakamura envisioned TRON as a series of intelligent objects that would be incorporated into buildings, appliances, and other everyday items, linked together into integrated wireless networks.

The project was initiated in 1984; the first goal was to develop a personal computer for use in Japanese schools as a way of introducing TRON technology and software into the market. The government planned to require that all schools buy TRON machines for the classroom, and telecommunications giant NTT had announced plans to implement TRON technology in its communications networks. The U.S. government saw TRON as an attempt to lock U.S. companies out of the Japanese PC market and pressured the Japanese government not to require schools to use TRON computers. The Japanese government dropped its plans to use TRON in the schools, and it never caught on in the commercial marketplace.

Ironically, it was NEC who had tried to stall the TRON project, since it dominated Japan's PC market and stood to lose the most from the development of a new standard. The intervention of the U.S. government saved NEC without the company having to look like it was putting its own profits ahead of the national interest.[55]

*Comments on R&D Initiatives of the 1980s.*    The four projects have not come close to achieving the ambitious objectives set for them. Japan is not a world leader in supercomputers and lags behind the United States in development of massively parallel supercomputers. The Sigma Project was nearly a total failure, and the TRON project failed to develop a commercially viable Japanese computing architecture. The Fifth Generation Project did not produce any commercial hardware or software in spite of some impressive accomplishments in artificial intelligence.

Each of the R&D projects involved attempts to end Japan's dependence on standards and architectures controlled by U.S. companies and to address Japan's fundamental weaknesses in software and innovation. While some successes have been claimed for each project, the combined effort did not move Japan any closer to controlling any key standards in the computer industry.

The poor performance of the R&D consortia was largely due to the lack of enthusiasm displayed by the participating companies. They went along with such projects in order to keep tabs on each other and maintain favor with the bureaucrats, but they were not willing to share their own independently developed technologies with their partners. Callon details the high level of tension among the participants in the supercomputer project. Fujitsu, which was in charge of the CPU subsystem, refused to allow engineers from NEC and Hitachi even to see the computer for which they were developing subsystems. NEC and Hitachi engineers were not allowed to ride a bus or eat with Fujitsu engineers for fear that they would overhear Fujitsu secrets. Most of the research in the R&D consortia was actually conducted in company labs, and joint labs produced only a few of the patents that came out of the consortia.[56]

Historically, Japan's R&D consortia have had their share of success and failure. In general, projects have worked best when the business community has had a leading role in selecting and implementing them, and when the projects had clear and specific goals.[57] This was not the case in the R&D consortia of the 1980s. Rather than responding to immediate needs of industry, the projects were designed by government committees[58] and had vague, long-term goals. The fact that the companies refused to invest their own money in the Fifth Generation project is evidence of their lack of confidence.

The projects were also too long-term in their planning and too inflexible in implementation. While Japan is often praised for its long-term strategic planning, computer technology changes too quickly for ten-year plans. Any government technology policy must be responsive to changes in technology and markets if it is to succeed. In the old era of catching up to IBM, it was more reasonable to undertake large-scale efforts targeting specific technologies with confidence that those technologies would still be relevant several years later. In the PC era, there are numerous targets to aim for, and they keep moving.

A fundamental problem with joint government-industry R&D consortia is the tug of competing interests among the participants. The government's interest is in improving the technology base of the nation as a whole, while the individual firms are more interested in improving their own position relative to their competitors, with whom they are expected to collaborate in such projects. The closer the research is to commercial development, the less cooperation is likely. However, as the focus moves toward more basic research, the question must be raised whether industrial consortia are really an effective mechanism for technology development.

## Targeting Software

MITI looks at the electronics and computer industries as a food chain, from silicon to software, and targets areas where Japan is weak. Software is clearly Japan's weakest link in the chain. MITI is trying to strengthen the software industry by providing tax incentives to the private sector, and by encouraging a realistic pricing structure that unbundles software and services from hardware so that their true value is reflected in prices. It is also working with the Ministry of Education (MOE) to increase the number of university courses in computer science and establishing curricula for students and workers to upgrade their IT skills in private schools. MITI says that the MOE is open to such changes but lacks the human and financial resources to implement them quickly.[59]

MITI made various efforts over the years to subsidize R&D by independent software companies, including providing funds to the Information Technology Promotion Agency (ITPA) during the 1970s to provide R&D subsidies and help software firms obtain more than US$450 million in loans. In 1979, the ITPA enacted tax breaks to software houses, exempting 50% of licensing revenues from taxes for five years.[60] MITI also offers grants and low-interest loans to software companies with promising products, but it is not clear that MITI has the ability to judge the promise of software products.

The government has not settled for simply trying to support Japan's software companies, however. It has also engaged in a series of efforts to weaken intellectual property protection to help Japanese companies decompile and reverse engineer software developed by U.S. companies.[61] This means the original program is decompiled to deduce much of its source code and develop an imitation of a program for a fraction of the cost of developing the original.

Japan's computer industry was split on the issue of decompilation during a 1993–1994 debate over copyright revision. Hardware companies and the custom software vendors supported decompilation as a means of catching up with the United States in software and increasing demand for Japanese hardware. For instance, Fujitsu announced in 1993 that it would not renew its license for compatibility data from IBM's mainframe operating system; it argued in favor of legalized decompilation to allow it to develop products compatible with the IBM standard without paying licensing fees to IBM. The fledgling packaged software industry was opposed to decompilation, since vendors were anxious to protect their own intellectual property, both in Japan and elsewhere in Asia. The issue grew into a dispute pitting leading U.S. software vendors and the U.S. government against the Japanese computer industry and a few sympathetic U.S. companies.

The Japanese government ultimately settled for issuing a series of options, rather than recommendations. As of 1997, the issue remained dormant in Japan, but was under consideration in Australia, the Philippines, and Hong Kong, with Fujitsu and other Japanese companies favoring decompilation.

In another trade dispute, the Japanese government announced in 1995 that it would require software makers to meet a variant of ISO 9000 quality standards to sell software in Japan. Most U.S. software makers saw this as a potential trade barrier, because Japan would have its own unique standards for software. It was also seen as a possible attempt to steal trade secrets by subjecting software code to inspection by Japanese auditors. The U.S. software industry appealed to the U.S. Trade Representative, and a private agreement was reached in the summer of 1995 between the U.S. and Japanese standards organizations, ANSI and JAB. However, in the fall of 1995, *Computing Japan* reported that the two sides' interpretations of the agreement were very different, and it appeared that the issue was not quite solved. Finally, under pressure from the United States, the Japanese government decided to drop the issue.

Each of the issues were examples of the ongoing effort of the Japanese government to challenge U.S. software hegemony by weakening intellectual property rights (IPR). Weak IPR protection might be justified, at least domestically, if it helped Japan's software industry catch up to the United States. However, lack of protection is just as likely to damage innovative Japanese software companies by making it difficult for them to earn a decent return on their investment in product development. It would mainly benefit imitative companies that want to produce "me-too" products, or companies that want to avoid licensing fees for existing software.[62] On a more positive note, protection of intellectual property has actually improved in recent years, with software piracy rates dropping from 66% in 1994 to 41% in 1996, possibly reflecting a change in attitudes toward IPR on the part of government and industry.

### Policy Initiatives in the 1990s

The government initiated several new IT projects in the 1990s. They include R&D projects such as the Real World Computing Program and the Micro Machine Project, and some efforts to promote small business and independent software firms. The major focus has been on developing a National Information Infrastructure (NII), an initiative that has fallen victim to the bureaucratic competition so prevalent in recent years.

*New R&D Consortia.*    Two new projects have been undertaken to develop new frontiers of computer technology. The first is the Real World Computing Program, which was announced in 1992 as a follow-up to the Fifth Generation project. The project applies neural computing, a concept based on creating computers that imitate the neural networks of the human brain. The goal is to develop applications that can rapidly process large volumes of incomplete data and allow management of large diverse networks, which are not always logically consistent. The implementation and direction of the project is more flexible and less centralized than in previous projects, and efforts are made to encourage sharing of findings. The Micro Machine Project is studying and developing component technologies and searching for principles unique to the micro world.[63]

The new R&D projects are being carried out by consortia of Japanese and foreign enterprises and institutes, a trend that started with the projects of the 1980s. The inclusion of foreign partners is part of what one MITI official referred to as a policy of "MITI for the world," rather than "MITI for Japan." Including foreign companies offers Japan opportunities to benefit from their expertise, as well as providing evidence to Japan's increasingly demanding trading partners of Japan's willingness to open itself to the world.

*Small Business Promotion.*    MITI has established a fund of 1 trillion yen (about US$10 billion) to support R&D by small companies. Funding is based on a competitive proposal process, with support given to companies that have good technology ideas. There is no targeting of particular industries; rather projects are evaluated on the basis of potential market demand and job creation. Support is in the form of R&D subsidies, loans, loan guarantees, and direct investment. MITI studied the venture capital system and over-the-counter stock market in the United States, and tried to create a similar "cradle to adult" system of support for start-ups. There are three stages in the program: (1) seed money for the start-up process; (2) enterprise development for product commercialization; and (3) over-the-counter stock listing. Pure start-ups will be favored over spin-offs, which might be supported in another program.[64] MITI has also been pressuring MOF to revise many of the regulations that are seen as hampering venture businesses.

### Policy Coordination: Bureaucratic Competition and the NII

Industrial policy in Japan was guided by MITI throughout most of the postwar era. MITI's preeminent position as an economic "pilot agency" was explicitly linked to Japan's economic miracle in 1982 by Chalmers Johnson's *MITI and the Japanese Miracle*. MITI's specific role in promoting the computer industry was brought to light in books and articles by scholars such as Marie Anchordoguy, Martin Fransman, and Fumio Kodama.[65]

However, at about the time that the rest of the world was becoming aware of MITI's role in directing Japan's industrial development, MITI found itself facing competition for policy leadership in the information technology sector from an unexpected rival, the Ministry of Posts and Telecommunications (MPT). The catalyst of this competition came in the early 1980s with the arrival of value-added networks (VANs) that provided on-line information and digital communications services. VANs were an early form of convergence between computers and communications, and since communications were involved, MPT saw regulation of VANs as falling under its jurisdiction. From 1981 to 1984, MPT battled MITI over how to regulate VANs, with MPT favoring stricter regulation and MITI favoring more competition. In the end a compromise was reached, but MPT had successfully staked its claim to a piece of information technology policy turf.[66]

MPT's strength relative to MITI continued to grow as convergence accelerated, and as MPT strove to join the elite ranks of Japanese bureaucracies. The battle with MITI reached its peak in the mid-1990s when Vice-President Al Gore announced the U.S. national information infrastructure (NII) initiative. The Japanese government viewed Gore's NII, or "information superhighway," plans as a major threat, fearing that the United States would gain a critical competitive advantage both as a producer and user of information technologies by building such an infrastructure. Both MPT and MITI developed their own NII plans for Japan, as did telecommunications giant NTT, and competition ensued over who would lead the Japanese NII response. Rather than cooperate, the two ministries and NTT all developed their own NII test-bed projects and trials, often duplicating each others' efforts.[67]

Meanwhile the two ministries disagreed over the issue of NTT's future. NTT had gone from being a government corporation to a private company in

1985, although the government retained about two-thirds of NTT's stock. MPT favored breaking NTT up into competing local and long distance companies to promote a more dynamic domestic market and reduce telecommunications prices via competition. MITI sided with NTT, which opposed the breakup and wanted to be allowed to compete in international markets. In the end, a compromise was reached which broke NTT into three companies under the control of a parent holding company and allowed NTT to compete internationally. This decision was a transparent move aimed at giving the appearance of promoting competition while actually increasing NTT's power, since no real breakup had occurred.

The victory of NTT was a setback for MPT, but it was also not much of a victory for MITI. MITI has not found a major role in important new policy areas such as the Internet and network computing. Instead, the stalemate between MITI and MPT has prevented Japan from developing coherent, coordinated strategies to deal with the policy issues raised by convergence, network computing, and the Internet. The two are pursuing their independent NII strategies, while NTT will be left to make the major investments and decide the form that Japan's NII will take. The future of Japan's computer industry is likewise being shaped by the management decisions of NEC, Fujitsu, Toshiba, Hitachi, and the other major companies. Japan's bureaucrats have not become irrelevant, but they are hardly the visible hand guiding the computer industry that they were in the past.

## Conclusions

Japan seemed to have all the ingredients for success in the PC era, from strong manufacturing skills and control of many key components technologies to a corporate structure that could support a sustained drive into export markets. Yet in spite of their success in components and peripherals, the Japanese computer makers have had only limited success in PCs, and have been virtually shut out of the software industry.

The reasons for this mixed record are complex, yet the most important have to do with Japan's industry structure. Japan's large, vertically integrated firms were well suited to high-volume, capital-intensive components production. They also did quite well in the relatively stable mainframe industry, because they could marshal the necessary resources within their *keiretsu* groups and count on the members of those groups as captive customers. However, in industry segments such as PCs and hard disk drives, where product cycles are short and timing critical, the Japanese industry structure was a liability. Unable to make decisions quickly, Japan's computer makers had limited success in such businesses.

Japan's industry structure has been even more of a barrier to the growth of a competitive software industry. Small software companies found it difficult to raise capital or develop adequate distribution channels. Large users long favored custom software rather than packaged applications and relied on hardware vendors or their own subsidiaries to develop applications; thus the market for general purpose packaged applications was slow to develop.

Japan also suffered weak linkages to the global production system and to global markets due to the isolation of its domestic market from international standards. Due to language differences, closed distribution channels, and conservative users, Japan's PC market developed slowly, with high prices and low adoption rates. The prevalence of incompatible standards in Japan meant that its PC makers could not use the domestic market as a base to develop products for international markets. It also meant that Japanese components suppliers could not export many components developed for domestic PCs, particularly components like motherboards that require close interaction with PC vendors at the design and engineering level. Low levels of PC use and fragmentation of the market also stunted the development of Japan's packaged software industry; by the time the PC market began to grow rapidly in the 1990s, it was foreign software vendors that benefited most.

Meanwhile, industrial policy, which was so important in Japan's earlier success in mainframes, has been at times irrelevant and counterproductive in the PC era. MITI's industrial policies emphasized catching up in the declining mainframe and supercomputer industries. The major R&D consortia were poorly conceived and failed to overcome the tensions between cooperation and competition inherent in such projects. The failure of the R&D consortia and other industrial policy efforts was less important than the obstacles created by Japan's regulatory apparatus. The Ministry of Finance has been slow to loosen its control over capital markets and has made it difficult for venture companies to raise capital, thus stifling the entrepreneurial energy that Japan's PC industry badly needed. In addition, regulation by the Ministry of Posts and Telecommunications has meant high prices for telecommunications services, which slowed the adoption of computer networks and the Internet in Japan. The Japanese government has embraced the rhetoric of deregulation and liberalization for many years, but so far it has made limited progress in those policy areas important to the computer industry.

The situation began to change significantly in the mid-1990s. The Japanese market unified on the global Wintel standard and PC prices dropped drastically, causing a demand boom in the domestic market. Japanese PC makers finally targeted international markets and tapped the Asian production network to lower production costs. Some Japanese companies also are targeting new hardware such as network computers, set-top Internet TV boxes, and handheld PCs, and some are gearing up to make Digital Versatile Disk (DVD) the new standard for multimedia storage. But those markets are all decreasing returns markets in which Japan will face strong competition right from the start. Samsung had a DVD player on the market as soon as Toshiba or Matsushita, and if the experience of DRAMs is any guide, the Korean companies will ensure that there are no cozy profit margins for anyone to enjoy.

The most important question for Japan is whether its companies will be able to move beyond commodity hardware to compete in the new increasing returns segments of the industry. So far the evidence is not promising. The new battles over architectural standards for the Internet are being fought among Netscape, Sun, Microsoft, Oracle, Cisco, IBM, and other U.S. companies. In spite of the growing popularity of the Internet in Japan, the Japanese computer industry has again been slow to respond to the new market opportunities being created by the network era.

Japan's dominance of many important hardware technologies means that it will retain its leadership in key components, creating strong profit opportunities for the companies that control such technologies. The revival of the Japanese economy should also revive the growth rates of the Japanese hardware industry as a whole. However, for Japanese companies to go beyond the diminishing returns commodity hardware business and start to compete in the profitable, dynamic increasing returns segments of the computer industry, they will need to make serious changes in their corporate cultures. This means changing the way that large companies are managed and also creating space for newcomers to spur innovation and tap niche markets. Government deregulation of financial and telecommunications markets is vital as well. Major change is not likely in the short run by either business or government, but it is happening gradually. In the words of Mochio Umeda, "they will get somewhere, somehow."[68] But by the time they get there, will the market have gone somewhere else?

# 4

# Asia's New Competitors

## Korea and Taiwan

The personal computer revolution created opportunities for new countries to become integrated into the production network of the PC industry. The most notable entrants were the newly industrializing economies (NIEs) of Asia: Korea, Taiwan, Singapore, and Hong Kong. The NIEs' economies had grown at exceptional rates on the strength of labor-intensive manufacturing and rising exports, but by the late 1970s, labor costs were going up and new competition was developing from lower wage countries in the region. The governments of Korea, Taiwan, and Singapore were convinced that their economies needed to "graduate" to more capital- and technology-intensive industries. In the electronics industry, the governments promoted production of more advanced consumer products, such as VCRs and microwave ovens, and sophisticated components such as semiconductors. They also laid the groundwork for computer production by encouraging foreign investment and technology transfer, and by developing domestic technical and manufacturing capabilities.

As U.S. PC companies looked for low-cost suppliers and subcontractors, they created opportunities for Asian companies to enter the PC industry without having to master a wide range of technologies or develop their own marketing and distribution channels. A company could produce a cable, power supply, keyboard, or monitor based on IBM's architectural standards and sell the components to any PC maker. Or it could assemble PCs or circuit boards for U.S. companies that preferred to outsource some parts of the production process. The barriers to entry were low, and East Asian producers flooded into the market.

The direct investment and outsourcing by multinational computer makers and efforts by local companies to become part of the supply chain combined to create a boom in computer production in East Asia. The mix was different in each case. Singapore depended heavily on production by foreign multinationals, Taiwan and Hong Kong had a mix of foreign and domestic producers, and Korea's industry was led by domestic firms. During the 1980s, each of the four saw rapid growth in production of computers and peripherals (figure 4-1). However, in the late 1980s and early 1990s, production levels stagnated in Korea and Hong Kong but surged in Taiwan and Singapore.

By the mid-1990s, the NIEs had established leading positions in many segments of the personal computer hardware industry (table 4-1). Taiwan was the world leader in production of notebook computers, monitors, motherboards, scanners, keyboards, and mice. Its companies were moving into higher technology products and providing design and distribution as well as production. Singapore led the world in production of hard disk drives and sound cards, and was fourth in PC assembly. Korea was challenging Japan's control of the DRAM market, but at the same time, its PC industry was losing its edge as global competition intensified. Hong Kong lost much of its manufacturing base, but retained a vital position in the industry by managing production in southern China.

While the Asian NIEs became major centers of hardware production, they failed to make a mark in the software and services industry—with the exception of Singapore, whose software industry nearly matched that of the United States as a percent of GDP (table 4-2). Software production in the NIEs consists mostly of custom programming or localization of imported products. There are few commercially successful packaged applications, and software exports are very low. Another problem for the NIEs has been low levels of computer use, again with the exception of Singapore (figure 4-2). While Singapore's government has promoted computer use and the private sector has been enthusiastic in investing in information technology, the other three NIEs have inconsistent records as users. Large companies and government agencies

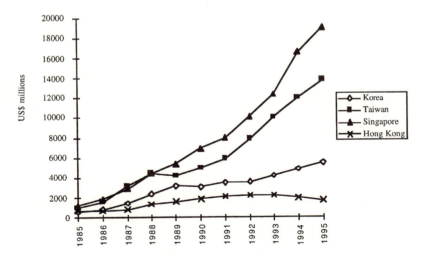

FIGURE 4-1. Computer Hardware Production in Asian NIEs, 1985–1995.
*Source:* Reed, 1996.

TABLE 4-1. Computer Hardware Market Shares for Asian NIEs, 1995

| Region | Desktop PCs | Notebook PCs | Monitors | Motherboards[a] | Hard Disk Drives[b] | DRAM |
|---|---|---|---|---|---|---|
| | % Share of Global Production (in units) of: | | | | | |
| Korea | 5 | 1 | 25 | n.a. | 3 | 30 |
| Taiwan[c] | 10 | 27 | 57 | 65 | 0 | 5 |
| Singapore | 3 | 12 | 5 | n.a. | 45 | n.a. |
| Hong Kong | 1 | 0 | 0 | n.a. | 0 | 0 |
| NIEs share of world | 19 | 40 | 87 | n.a. | 48 | 35 |

*Sources:* Market Intelligence Center/Institute for Information Industries (MIC/III), *Asia IT Report* (February 1996 and November 1996) and data provided to authors; Electronics Industries Association of Korea (EIAK), *'95 Statistics of Electronic Industries* (Seoul: EIAK, 1996). Peter Gourevitch, Roger E. Bohn, and David McKendrick, "Who is Us? The Nationality of Production in the Hard Disk Industry," The Data Storage Industry Globalization Project, Graduate School of International Relations and Pacific Studies (La Jolla, Calif.: University of California, San Diego, 1997).

[a]Includes merchant sales only. Does not include captive production by PC vendors.

[b]Final assembly.

[c]Includes offshore production by Taiwanese companies.

have computerized, but smaller companies and households have been slower to adopt the technology. High rates of software piracy and an unwillingness to pay for services are also factors in the underdevelopment of local software and services industries.

The following sections detail the experiences of Korea and Taiwan during the PC era of the 1980s and 1990s. The next chapter discusses Singapore and Hong Kong. While there are similarities and interesting comparisons to be found among the four countries, the two countries paired in each chapter offer especially good comparisons and contrasts. Korea and Taiwan are both medium-sized economies that have experienced high-speed economic growth and developed strong manufacturing bases since the early 1960s. Singapore and Hong Kong are both city-states whose economies were historically based on trade and commerce, but each developed a large, export-oriented manufacturing sector during the same period as Korea and Taiwan. As computer producers, Taiwan and Singapore have had remarkable success, while their counterparts in Korea and Hong Kong have had a more mixed record.

## Korea

Korea presents an intriguing case in the computer industry, because its difficulties in the PC industry contrast with its great success in consumer electronics and semiconductors. The Korean case shows that an industry structure that is well suited to one business can be dysfunctional in another, and that a structure that works well at one time can become a liability as an industry changes. Also, it points out that protectionist industrial policies are counter-

TABLE 4-2. Packaged Software Production in United States and Asia

| Country | Software Production, 1995 (US$ millions) | Software Production as % of GDP | Software Exports, 1995 (US$ millions) |
|---|---|---|---|
| United States | 60,000 (1996) | 0.86 | 23,000 (1993)[a] |
| Japan | 7,200 | 0.15 | 2,300[b] |
| Korea | 496 | 0.13 | 31 |
| Taiwan | 285 | 0.12 | 80 |
| Singapore | 556 | 0.84 | 214[c] |
| Hong Kong | 50[d] | 0.04 | 167 |

*Sources:* For Japan, Korea, Taiwan, Hong Kong: U.S. Department of Commerce, National Trade Data Bank, www.stat-usa.gov (various country reports).

For Singapore: National Computer Board, *IT Focus,* special issue (1996).

For United States: U.S. International Trade Commission (USITC), *Advice Concerning the Proposed Modification of Duties on Certain Information Technology Products and Distilled Spirits* (Washington, DC: USITC, April 1997).

[a]International sales of U.S. packaged software vendors, from U.S. Department of Commerce, *U.S. Global Trade Outlook 1995–2000* (Washington, D.C.: USDOC, 1995).

[b]Includes video game software.

[c]Authors' estimates based on ratio of exports to production in earlier years.

[d]Hong Kong Bureau of Census and Statistics data cited in chapter 5 includes some services.

productive in a dynamic industry that requires close linkages to the global production system.

Korea's troubles in the computer industry were a great surprise to those who followed its rapid growth into a manufacturing power since the 1960s. By the late 1980s, Korea was being touted as "Asia's Next Giant,"[1] thanks to its record of economic growth and industrialization. The Seoul Olympics in 1988 helped the world discover Korea, and a peaceful transition from military rule to democratic government challenged the notion that the East Asian miracle was inseparable from authoritarian rule.

The Korean electronics industry was one of the pillars of the economic miracle. From TVs to VCRs to microwave ovens, Korean companies challenged the Japanese giants that dominated much of the consumer electronics industry. This turned out to be just a warm-up for the semiconductor industry, where Korea caught up to both Japan and the United States in DRAM technology. The Korean PC industry was also enjoying rapid growth, with production and exports tripling just between 1987 and 1989. The PC industry seemed to be one more success story for Korea's electronics industry, providing additional evidence that Korea had arrived as an economic and technological power.

As it turned out, the late 1980s were a turning point in many ways for Korea. Democratization had opened the door for workers to demand a greater share of the benefits from the economic miracle, and average wages in manufacturing soared from US$1.23 in 1985 to US$7.40 in 1995.[2] Meanwhile, competition was intensifying from lower wage countries such as China, Ma-

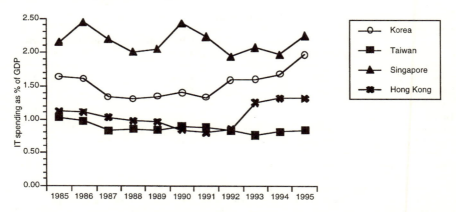

FIGURE 4-2. Computer Use in Asian NIEs. *Source:* IDC, "Revenue Paid to Vendors for Systems, Software and Services, 1985–1995, (Framingham, MA: IDC, 1997).

laysia, and Thailand. Korean companies tried to upgrade their product mix, but found it harder to compete against U.S. and Japanese companies that now saw the Koreans as competitors in their core businesses. Korea's fast-growing electronics industry turned out to be dependent on Japanese components and manufacturing equipment, and its very success exacerbated a large trade deficit with Japan.

Korean companies also had problems with quality and marketing, which hurt their image in foreign markets. The chairman of Samsung Electronics was shocked when he visited electronics outlets in the United States and found his company's products languishing in the back corners of the stores. The image of Korean products in general was tarnished in the United States by the Hyundai Excel automobile, which was initially a hit with its low prices but was soon found at the bottom of *Consumer Reports* rankings for reliability.

The Korean electronics industry responded to these challenges in several ways. Labor-intensive production was moved offshore to Southeast Asia, China, Mexico, and elsewhere to reduce costs. Korean companies have invested heavily in R&D to move to the leading edge of DRAM technology, and Korea's DRAM technology is now so good that U.S. and Japanese chip makers have sought out the Korean companies for strategic alliances. The electronics companies have entered the flat-panel display industry with high-volume production, challenging another Japanese stronghold. There is also an increased emphasis on quality throughout the industry.

The PC industry is a different story, however. Production and exports dropped sharply in the early 1990s, to less than half of their 1989 levels. The same companies that were challenging Japan's giants in semiconductors were being left in the dust by much smaller Taiwanese companies in the PC industry. Even when production started rebounding to meet growing domestic demand, exports continued to decline. Meanwhile, Korea was locked out of increasing-returns sectors such as software and microprocessors, while competition continued to intensify in its commodity hardware businesses.

Korea's experience supports the argument that the PC industry favors different industry structures, national capabilities, and industrial policies from the high-volume components and consumer electronics industries. It also shows the importance of linkages to global markets and technology sources, and how successful linkages have different characteristics in PCs than they do in other electronics sectors.

### Electronics: Challenging Japan

The history of Korea's electronics industry presents a recurring narrative of success against great odds. There are heroic tales of engineers working round-the-clock to meet deadlines, of finding ways to get key technologies after being rebuffed by American and Japanese leaders, and of resilience in the face of discouraging setbacks.[3] In the end, the Korean companies have won impressive victories against large, technologically sophisticated Japanese companies in markets that had been forfeited by most U.S. and European competitors.

The Korean government began targeting the electronics industry in 1969 by enacting the Electronics Industry Promotion Law. The Ministry of Trade and Industry (MTI)[4] established programs for technical development and training, and it promoted electronics production through tax incentives, low-cost loans, and direct subsidies. Korea selectively allowed investment by foreign multinationals, which accounted for about half of Korea's electronics exports during the 1970s, but favored development of a locally owned industry. The government provided tax incentives, low-cost loans, and foreign loan guarantees to domestic conglomerates (*chaebol*) such as Samsung, LG (formerly Lucky Goldstar), and Daewoo, demanding in return that they meet aggressive export targets. These companies at first found export opportunities as suppliers and subcontractors to multinationals, and they sold their own brand products in the protected domestic market.

Starting with black-and-white TVs, and moving on to color TVs, VCRs, and microwave ovens, Korean companies quickly learned and applied the necessary technologies and manufacturing processes to compete internationally. They used reverse engineering, licensing, OEM relationships with companies like General Electric, and any other means available to get technology. Once one Korean company had entered the market, others would hire away some of its engineers to catch up. This way, technology was diffused across the industry and the big electronics companies could all participate in each new market.[5]

Electronics production grew from US$140 million in 1971 to US$3.8 billion in 1981, while exports grew from US$89 million to US$2.2 billion.[6] By the end of the 1970s, foreign electronics producers began to leave Korea for lower cost locations elsewhere in Asia. Taking advantage of their experience as suppliers and subcontractors, Korean companies surged into the export market on their own. Many U.S. retailers such as J. C. Penney and

K-Mart were filled with Korean-made electronics products, often selling under store-brand labels. Through heavy investment and continuous learning, the Korean manufacturers became low-cost producers of many consumer items. When the Japanese yen soared in value after 1985, Korean products became even more competitive. Production of consumer electronics soared to more than US$13.8 billion by 1995, with exports of US$7.8 billion.[7]

The Korean government, however, was not satisfied with just having a consumer electronics industry, so it began promoting industrial electronics such as telecommunications equipment and semiconductors in the late 1970s. Industrial electronics production grew rapidly, reaching nearly US$13 billion with exports of US$7.6 billion in 1995, while electronic components production reached US$36.8 billion, with exports of US$28 billion.[8] The biggest success story was in DRAMs, where Korean companies went from zero to nearly 30% of the worldwide market in less than a decade. Surprisingly, the government was slow to get on board in supporting the DRAM industry. Instead it was Samsung that instigated the move into DRAMs, followed by Hyundai and LG. While the government's role in the DRAM industry was more marginal, its earlier promotion of the electronics industry was responsible for the very presence of companies with the ability to compete in the DRAM industry.

### Semiconductors: Becoming a World Leader in Memory Chips

The rise of Korea's semiconductor industry was both dramatic and unexpected.[9] Certainly the big Japanese chip makers that had driven most of their U.S. competitors out of the memory chip business were not expecting to be challenged by Korean upstarts just a few years later. Yet by 1994, Samsung was first in the world in DRAM production, with 15% of the market, and LG and Hyundai ranked sixth and seventh, with about 6% market share each. Korea's semiconductor industry grew from just more than $1 billion in 1985 to $14.8 billion in 1994, making Korea the third largest semiconductor producer in the world.[10] The story of the DRAM industry illustrates the Korean electronics industry at its best, using hard work, technological resourcefulness, manufacturing prowess, and heavy investment to challenge the Japanese at their own game.

The Korean semiconductor industry began in the 1960s when several MNCs began assembling devices there. Local companies got involved in the 1970s, with the help of the government, which began promoting the industry in 1975. The government established a public research institute, the Korea Institute of Electronics Technology (KIET) to conduct R&D on very-large-scale integrated circuit (VLSI) processes. KIET was not successful in developing commercially viable products, but it trained many engineers who later played important roles in the private sector.

In 1974, Dr. Ki-Dong Kang, a Korean-American scientist, started the Korea Semiconductor Company, which got into financial trouble and was bought out by Samsung in its first year. Kang, who had previously worked for Motorola, helped train Samsung's engineers in the technology and processes needed for chip production. This was the first of many instances in which Korean companies would draw on the knowledge of Korean-Americans or overseas Koreans to develop semiconductor technologies.

In 1983, Samsung, Hyundai, LG, and Daewoo all began investing in VLSI production, a key step to competing in the high-end memory business. Interestingly, while the government had promoted the semiconductor industry, it was initially opposed to the *chaebols'* decision to enter the DRAM business and compete directly with U.S. and Japanese companies. The companies were on their own in developing the 64 kilobit (64K), 256 kilobit (256K), and 1 megabit (1M) generations of DRAMs. The Korean companies were consistently turned down when they tried to license technology from leading U.S. and Japanese semiconductor firms. So they turned to other sources.

Samsung consulted with Korean-American engineers working in U.S. companies and universities for advice on entering the DRAM business. The company set up an R&D lab in Silicon Valley in 1983, with five Korean-American Ph.D.s from U.S. universities and 300 American engineers; then it organized another task force in Korea that included two Korean-Americans. The two teams worked together to develop 64K DRAMs, using technologies licensed from Micron Technology and Zytrex, two small U.S. companies that needed the cash. The teams worked round the clock to achieve Samsung's goal of developing a working production system for 64K DRAMs in six months. Samsung was able to bring 64K DRAMs to market eighteen months after the Japanese had introduced their first commercial versions. While Samsung relied on U.S. sources for design and process technologies, it turned to a Japanese firm to design and supervise construction of its mass-production plant.

Hyundai was a latecomer to semiconductors and to electronics in general. With no experience in semiconductors, Hyundai turned to Dr. Kang (who had left Samsung and returned to Silicon Valley) to develop a strategic plan for the electronics industry. It then hired four Korean-American Ph.D.s from U.S. universities who had experience at Xerox, System Control, Fairchild, and Ford. Hyundai began by producing DRAMs as an OEM for Texas Instruments in order to gain experience in production processes; then it purchased designs from Vitelic to enter the DRAM industry on its own.

LG and Daewoo were more conservative in the semiconductor business. LG purchased KIET's obsolete labs and production facilities in 1984, licensed designs from Advanced Micron Devices and Zilog, and entered a joint venture with AT&T's Western Electric in DRAMs. All these moves helped LG gain knowledge and experience, but it still lagged behind Samsung and Hyundai in introducing 64K and 256K DRAMs. Finally, LG licensed 1M DRAM technology from Hitachi, which wanted a reliable OEM source so Hitachi could concentrate on newer product generations. Daewoo decided to concentrate on making chips for its telecommunications business and stayed out of the DRAM business.

With each succeeding generation of DRAMs, the Korean companies closed the technology gap with the advanced countries. As the Koreans began to catch up technologically, the Japanese producers tried to cut prices to crush them as they had most of their U.S. competitors. But luck and timing were on the side of the Koreans. Responding to charges that Japanese chip makers were dumping, the U.S. government slapped tariffs on Japanese DRAMs, then negotiated the U.S.–Japan Semiconductor Trade Arrangement of 1986, which required the Japanese to maintain "fair" prices and establish quantitative export controls.[11] This created an opening for the Koreans to expand their market share and turn a profit as well. Many industry analysts in Korea point to the U.S.–Japan trade dispute as the turning point for the Korean semiconductor industry, especially coming at a time when Korean companies were making heavy investments to expand their production capacity.

As they moved closer to catching up with the American and Japanese companies in DRAM technology, Korean companies found themselves under more pressure to develop their own R&D capabilities. Most of the smaller companies from which the Koreans had licensed technology in the mid-1980s had been driven out of the market or were falling behind technologically due to lack of capital for R&D. Also, Samsung and Hyundai were forced to pay royalties to Texas Instruments and Intel for patent infringement on DRAM designs. The time had come for the Koreans to make it on their own, and now the government decided to get involved.

In 1986, the Korean government announced a national R&D consortium for 4M DRAMs, to be coordinated by the Electronics and Telecommunications Research Institute (ETRI). The consortium involved Samsung, LG, and Hyundai and six universities, with the goal of mass producing 4M DRAMs by 1989. The ETRI program never got off the ground, however, because the companies refused to work together. Samsung had nearly caught up with the market leaders by hitting the market with 1M DRAMs in 1987, in time to catch the rise in demand. It was not interested in sharing its technology with laggards Hyundai and LG. The consortium spent $110 million over three years, but there was little cooperation or sharing of technologies. Instead, the three companies moved independently on development of 4M designs, each investing heavily in their own R&D.[12]

It was at the 4M generation where the Koreans' efforts truly paid off. The *chaebol* got another break in the early 1990s, when Japan's financial troubles forced its semiconductor makers to cut back on capital investment just as PC sales were rebounding. DRAM demand also was being stoked by the success of Windows-based software, which required more memory to run. The Koreans benefited when the market for 4M DRAMs lasted longer than earlier product generations, allowing the Korean companies to gain market share from their heavy investment in 4M capacity while the Japanese were shifting to 16M production.[13] Samsung passed NEC to become the top DRAM producer in the world in 1994. Global demand soared and prices stayed high through the end of 1995, allowing the Koreans to earn huge profits in DRAMs and invest heavily in next generation technologies.

By the mid-1990s, the Koreans were at or near the leading edge of DRAM technologies, and they were being courted by the U.S. and Japanese companies who had once rebuffed them. Samsung, the leader, developed strategic alliances with Toshiba, NEC, Mitsubishi, Fujitsu, and DEC. All three Korean DRAM makers have also invested in R&D facilities in the U.S., Japan, and Taiwan, as well as in Korea. Through their own R&D and investments in foreign companies, the Korean chip makers are trying to bolster their position in DRAMs as well as to move into ASIC, microprocessors, and other non-memory chips.

The collapse of DRAM prices in 1996 showed how vulnerable the Korean companies remain, given their heavy dependence on commodity memory chips. The *chaebol* are a long way from being leaders in the nonmemory business, and the Korean industry structure becomes more of a liability in those segments of the industry. ASICs and other specialized chips are design-intensive, requiring innovation and flexibility more than mass-production skills. As one U.S. semiconductor industry executive remarked to the authors, "The Koreans are great at high-volume production, but don't ask them to make model changes in the middle of a run."

What explains Korea's amazing success in semiconductors? The answers lie in the structure and strategies of the Korean companies. There was a close fit between the structure of the Korean companies and the demands of the DRAM industry. The *chaebol* drew on large pools of internal capital to support the heavy investment required to compete in DRAMs. These sources include profits from other businesses, and loans from nonbank financial institutions controlled by the *chaebol*.

The management style of the *chaebol* also worked in their favor. The president of a *chaebol* has full authority over the company and can take it into a new risky business without worrying about the threat to stock prices or about achieving consensus among the management team. There were many people both inside and outside Samsung who questioned its entry into the DRAM business, but then-chairman Byung-Chull Lee made the decision and directed huge resources into the industry. Likewise, the Koreans do not give up easily. Hyundai lost money in DRAMs for a decade before finally making big profits on the 4M generation. The nature of DRAM production also fit well with the companies' mass-production orientation. The *chaebol* are at their best when they can take a single product and produce millions of units, steadily improving production yields and reducing costs.

Money and mass production alone was not enough, though. The Koreans also overcame the steep technological barriers to entry with innovative strategies for acquiring and developing technology. Hiring Korean-American scientists and engineers with experience in U.S. companies gave the *chaebol* access to the knowledge base of leading semiconductor vendors. While only a few of such specialists were hired, they served as a cadre to train entire teams of Korean engineers and to help guide top management strategy for the industry. The *chaebol* took advantage of their financial resources to license technology from struggling U.S. chip makers, who had developed product designs that they could not afford to commercialize. In order to improve their production processes, the Koreans hired retired Japanese engineers on temporary assignments. Finally, the Koreans developed their own R&D capabilities to end their dependence on foreign technology and catch up to the world's leaders in DRAM design and process know-how.

In addition to their own considerable efforts, the Korean companies were also helped by good timing, entering the industry just as the trade dispute between the United States and Japan created an opening in the DRAM market. The Koreans were prepared, both technologically and financially, to seize the opportunity when it came, but without the trade dispute they would have faced a stronger reaction from the Japanese companies that controlled the industry.

One factor that turns out to be less important in semiconductors than in other Korean industries is government policy. The R&D consortia and other initiatives were too small and too late to make much of a difference, given the resources already available to the *chaebol*. Government policy was important mainly in educating the large numbers of engineers that the industry required. In Linsu Kim's words, "Korea's success in the semiconductor industry should be attributed to business initiative rather than state initiative."[14] From a broader historical perspective, however, government policy was indeed important. The government pushed the *chaebol* into the electronics industry in the 1960s and began promoting semiconductors in the 1970s. And decades of government subsidies helped create the giant conglomerates with the resources to compete in such a capital-intensive industry.

### History of Korea's Computer Industry

Korea entered the computer industry in the early days of the personal computer era. There was no mainframe or minicomputer industry, and almost no hardware or software production, in Korea before 1980. The PC revolution coincided with the Korea's entry into industrial electronics markets such as semiconductors and telecommunications. But the *chaebol* were not initially interested in the nascent PC industry, which looked too small to fit their mass-production strategies. Instead, the pioneers of the Korean PC industry were small start-up companies such as Trigem and QNIX. Most of these fell by the wayside, but Trigem survived and became Korea's second largest PC maker.

The *chaebol* became interested in the PC industry after the government banned PC imports in 1982 and began investing in government computer networks. Then the big electronics companies all jumped in, taking advantage of the protected domestic market and making forays into the export market. PC production surged from $39 million in 1983 to $1,733 million in 1989, and exports rose from $19 million to $971 million (figure 4-2). Production of peripherals, especially monitors, also grew rapidly. The biggest success story among the *chaebol* was Daewoo, which designed and manufactured IBM-compatible PCs for Leading Edge in the United States.

*Trigem.*    In a national market dominated by huge conglomerates, Trigem has been a surprising success as an independent start-up. Trigem's edge has been its focus on the PC industry and its flexible, innovative strategies to find and develop markets that the *chaebol* had ignored. Trigem was started in 1980 by Y. T. Lee and some of his fellow alumni of the Korean Advanced Institute for Science and Technology (KAIST). Lee, who is considered the godfather of the Korean computer industry, later became the first president of Dacom, a state-owned data communications company, and remains the chairman of Trigem.

Trigem made Korea's first PC in 1981 and its first IBM-compatible PC in 1984. The company was able to grow and survive in spite of competition from the big *chaebol*. Because of its links to the government-sponsored KAIST, Trigem has symbolic importance to the government and has received some of the same kinds of subsidies and access to government procurement that the *chaebol* receive.

Trigem has been aggressive and creative in finding ways to counteract the strengths of the giants with which it competes. It set up its own network of 350 exclusive dealers in Korea in order to compete with the extensive distribution networks of the *chaebol*. Trigem knows it cannot easily sell PCs to businesses that are part of a *chaebol* with its own PC company, so it has targeted the home market, which now accounts for 45% of its sales. To compete with Samsung, LG, Hyundai, and Daewoo, which offer free training at any of their thousands of dealer outlets, Trigem offers training classes broadcast via satellite from Seoul to locations around the country.

Trigem is also more internationally oriented than other Korean PC makers. Thirty-three percent of its revenues come from foreign sales, including US$200 million in the United States and US$100 million in the United Kingdom. In the late 1980s Trigem tried to establish its brand name overseas and improve its design capabilities by investing in several U.S. computer firms. Unfortunately, these investments were made just as the PC market was slumping in 1990, and Trigem was forced to pull out of most of its acquisitions.[15] Trigem's own brand accounts for nearly all of its PC sales, but it makes motherboards for IBM, Olivetti, and Epson (which owns a 5% stake in Trigem).

In the Korean market, Trigem sells Epson printers with Korean-language fonts implemented by Trigem's engineers; it also sells laser printers using its own controller boards and engines from Canon, Samsung, and LG. Trigem's other Korean businesses include systems integration, an Internet service provider called Thrunet (in a joint venture with Korea Electric Power Company), a joint venture with Japan's Softbank for distribution of software, and a financial services company.

Trigem's main business is still PCs, and it has ranked first or second in the Korean market almost every year since its inception. That business ran into trouble in 1995, however, as Samsung made an aggressive push for market share, cutting prices and introducing a successful line of notebook PCs. Trigem had not developed its own capabilities in notebook design and production, and only sold 30,000 units in 1996, compared to 100,000 for Samsung. Trigem's market share dropped to 18%, while Samsung increased its share to 28%. Only two years earlier, Trigem had been in a virtual tie with

Samsung. Even worse, Samsung's price cuts forced Trigem to respond and cut into profit margins, which were already only a slim 1.6% of sales in 1995.[16]

Trigem began to fight back, developing a line of high-end notebooks and improving its dealer support. Some in Korea feel that Trigem cannot compete against Samsung, which can afford to lose money to gain market share. However, with DRAMs no longer a cash cow, Samsung may be less willing to try to increase market share at the cost of losing profits. For Trigem to stay competitive, it will have to rely on the focus and international orientation that have been the keys to its success, but it must also look for new opportunities offered by the network era. Leveraging its brand name, its distribution channels, and its relationships with companies like Epson and Softbank, Trigem could succeed in systems integration, network services, content, and perhaps in newer consumer products such as handheld PCs or set-top boxes. The company will also have to target new international markets, especially in the fast-growing Asian region.

*Daewoo and Leading Edge.*   The 1980s were a good decade for Korea's PC industry, and Daewoo was the most successful in penetrating international markets. Daewoo's path to the U.S. market went through Leading Edge, one of the early IBM PC clone makers. Leading Edge was started in 1980 by Michael Shane, a former wig and designer jeans salesman. The Massachusetts company had contracted with Mitsubishi for production of PCs until 1984, when the two companies became involved in a legal dispute; at that point, Leading Edge turned to Daewoo to manufacture its PCs.

Daewoo designed and built Leading Edge PCs that received high marks for quality and innovation from PC magazines and *Consumer Reports*. While IBM's machines required add-on cards to expand their capabilities, the Leading Edge PC put many of those features on the motherboard and made them standard. Daewoo also designed a motherboard for Leading Edge that was half the size of IBM's, making the machine lighter and less bulky. Leading Edge sold its PCs at 60% of IBM's price, and developed a creative advertising strategy to promote them. In its first year on the market, Leading Edge's Model D sold 100,000 units and succeeding x286 and x386 models sold well from 1985 to 1987. The relationship between Daewoo and Leading Edge worked well, with Daewoo providing product innovation and low-cost production, while Leading Edge provided marketing, distribution, and good product feedback to Daewoo's engineers.

By 1988, however, Leading Edge got into serious financial trouble due to its own mismanagement. The company had required dealers to pay up front for PC shipments, unlike other vendors that extended credit. When some Leading Edge dealers failed to receive shipments for which they had paid, they banded together to sue and forced the company into bankruptcy. Daewoo stepped in and took over Leading Edge in 1989 to try to maintain its position in the U.S. market. But the transition took time and many customers abandoned Leading Edge, as did many of the company's key employees.

Daewoo's PC business was very vulnerable, because it had depended entirely on Leading Edge for marketing, distribution, and market information. From 1989 to 1991, Daewoo tried to develop its own capabilities while stabilizing the Leading Edge product line. The situation worsened in 1992, when Compaq launched a price war that put tremendous pressure on the PC clone industry. Daewoo tried to develop new distribution channels, moving from dealers to national distributors, then to mass marketers and wholesalers, with little success. Daewoo finally sold Leading Edge to a Swiss company in 1995, and Leading Edge soon went out of business altogether. Since disposing of Leading Edge, Daewoo's PC business has been limited to doing some OEM business for the export market and selling its own brand PCs in Korea, where it has less than a 5% market share.

Daewoo's experience in the PC industry contrasts with the more successful Taiwanese PC makers in a few important ways. First of all, while Taiwanese companies usually have multiple OEM customers, Daewoo was entirely dependent on Leading Edge. When Leading Edge got into trouble, Daewoo was unable to rescue it or to find other OEM customers to take up the slack. Second, Daewoo lacked the strong intelligence networks that Taiwanese PC makers rely on in the U.S. market. As Leading Edge faltered, Daewoo was flying blind in the U.S. market, just as major shifts were taking place in the early 1990s. Also, PCs are not Daewoo's main business, and the PC industry was never the life-or-death business that it is for many Taiwanese companies, or for Trigem. Once it lost the Leading Edge connection, Daewoo simply lacked the focus, flexibility, and global linkages it needed to compete.

*The 1990s: Market Whirlwind Hits Korea's PC industry.*   Korean PC makers thrived in the 1980s competing on price in standardized products for the IBM-compatible market. While Daewoo made some innovations for the Leading Edge line, most Korean makers concentrated on high-volume assembly with little value added through design or engineering. But the global PC industry entered a shakeout period in the late 1980s and early 1990s, and the Korean companies were big losers.

In particular, three changes in the PC industry severely damaged Korea's global competitiveness. First, product cycles accelerated, meaning that long production runs could not be used to bring down average costs. Instead, shorter runs and frequent changes were required, placing a premium on flexibility—never a Korean strong suit. Second, product differentiation became more important as customers looked for networking and multimedia features. Companies could no longer make one or two models for all markets; they needed a variety of configurations for various business, household, and education buyers. The need to differentiate products not only required more flexible production, but also demanded higher levels of design and engineering skills, especially at the motherboard level. The Korean PC companies lacked the capabilities of their Taiwanese counterparts, which had been designing and building motherboards and systems for multiple OEM customers and had developed high-level PC design skills. Thus, most U.S. PC makers turned to nimbler Taiwanese suppliers as they tried to keep up with accelerating product cycles and technology changes.

Finally, price wars broke out in the PC industry, squeezing profit margins for all companies, but especially for clone makers and OEM suppliers. The *chaebols'* high overhead costs along with rising domestic wage rates made it difficult to survive in such a market. The Korean PC industry was battered by the hypercompetitive global market, and in just a few years production and exports dropped to a fraction of their peak in 1989 (figure 4-3). The *chaebol* were, of course, reaping the benefits of a growing global PC market through their DRAM sales, but they were forced to retreat to the domestic market for PC systems. Hyundai, for instance, had a 3% share of the U.S. market in 1989, but by 1993 had pulled back from the U.S. market to concentrate on Korea and Europe, where it still was competitive. Daewoo also gave up on the U.S. market after selling its Leading Edge subsidiary in 1995.

Korea has done better competing in peripherals, with production and exports continuing to grow through the 1990s (figure 4-4). Nearly half of the value of Korea's peripherals output is accounted for by monitors, and the big four *chaebol* are ramping up flat-panel display production to catch the wave in demand for notebook PCs with large, high-quality screens. But those achievements, as important as they are, cannot disguise Korea's weakness in the rest of the PC industry. Korea remains far behind Taiwan, Singapore, and Southeast Asia in production of motherboards, hard disk drives, add-on cards, modems, scanners, and most other PC parts and peripherals.

Unwilling to abandon the global market altogether, the *chaebol* shifted their strategy to pursue acquisitions of U.S. companies. In 1994, Samsung purchased a 40% stake in PC maker AST Research, and Hyundai bought a

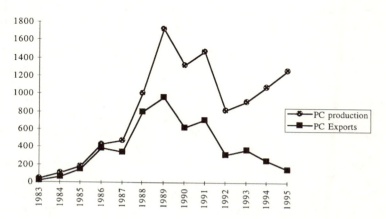

FIGURE 4-3. Korean PC Production and Exports, 1983–1995 (US$ millions). *Source:* Electronics Industry Association of Korea (EIAK), *Electronics Industry Yearbook,* (Seoul: EIAK, various years).

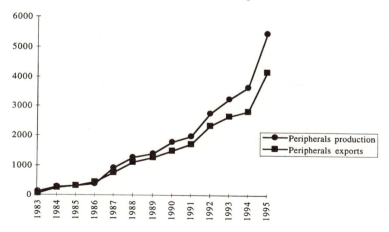

FIGURE 4-4. Korea's Peripherals Production and Exports, 1983–1995 (US$ millions). *Source:* EIAK, various years.

40% stake in disk drive maker Maxtor. The logic of these investments was to acquire technology and access to distribution channels, but in each case, the Korean company was buying into a distressed U.S. company whose market share was plummeting. Maxtor quickly burned through Hyundai's $150 million investment and lost market share as the disk drive industry consolidated.

AST had been floundering since its ill-fated purchase of Tandy's PC business, and in 1995 it went into a free fall, with U.S. PC shipments declining by 26%.[17] Samsung installed Apple veteran Ian Diery as CEO to turn the company around, but a year later the company replaced him with Samsung's own Y. S. Kim. As losses mounted, Samsung finally acquired the remaining shares of AST, feeling that if it was going to keep pumping money into the company, it should have complete control.

Unfortunately for Samsung, its troubles with AST have overshadowed its own success in the domestic market, where it moved ahead of Trigem to capture 28% of the market in 1995. The company also used its joint venture with Hewlett-Packard to gain a large share of the workstation market, and it developed relationships with DEC and AMD to produce microprocessors based on DEC's Alpha and AMD's Intel-compatible designs. Rapid growth in the domestic market helped revive growth in total production, starting in 1993, but the other *chaebol* did not participate strongly in the rebound. LG Electronics, placing a weak third behind Samsung and Trigem in 1995, finally joined IBM in a joint venture to sell PCs in the Korean market. Daewoo and Hyundai were even passed in 1996 by upstart electronics retailer, Sejin, which began selling its own brand of PC.

*Software and Services.*    Korea has a very small software industry, as shown in table 4-2. Most software used in Korea is either a translation of an imported program or an illegal copy of such a program. In 1995, Korea imported US$350 million worth of software, while exporting just US$21 million.

Korea's business and technology culture does not offer a good breeding ground for a successful software industry. The electronics industry grew by producing imitative products based on well-established designs. Even in DRAMs, where the Koreans are now at the leading edge technologically, they are still aiming at well-defined product generation targets. The software market has no such clear road maps. In such a business, the key to success is to define new solutions or create new capabilities for users. This is new terrain for Korean companies and workers, and so far there have been only a few success stories.

The best-known software entrepreneur is Chan-jin Lee, founder of Hangul and Computer Company, which developed a successful Korean word processing program. Lee received a lot of media attention for his business activities, and even more for marrying a movie star after his company became successful. Another successful software start-up is Handysoft, a developer of groupware started by Yung-Gyung Ahn. Many younger Koreans see entrepreneurs such as Lee and Ahn as role models and would like to start their own companies. It is still very difficult for independent software companies to raise venture capital from Korean financial institutions, but some venture capital is available from government funds and from wealthy individuals such as Trigem's Y. T. Lee, who has financed ten start-ups himself.

Within the *chaebol*, there has been little interest in the software business until recently. Samsung is now leading the push into software and services via its Samsung Data Systems (SDS) subsidiary. Samsung believes much of its future growth will come from knowledge-based businesses such as software and telecommunications. SDS managing director Hye-Keun Kwag worked for DEC, and he is pushing his workers to develop the problem-solving orientation of American engineers.[18]

SDS had 5,500 employees and sales of more than $1 billion in 1996, mostly in systems integration and custom programming. The company is now developing packaged programs for vertical markets such as hospitals but feels it must export to reach a large enough market to make money in these markets. If Samsung succeeds in the packaged software industry, it will serve as a model for the Korean industry. But success will not come easily outside the friendly confines of the Korean market. Samsung and any other Korean software maker will not only have to translate programs into other languages, they will also have to develop distribution channels, customer support, and market intelligence networks in each market.

*Domestic Market and Computer Use.*    Korea's domestic computer market is by far the largest of the four NIEs. Personal computer sales were 1.97 million units in 1996, compared to just 525,000 in Taiwan, 342,000 in Hong Kong, and 306,000 in Singapore.[19] Foreign PC makers have less than 10% of the market. From 1983 to 1988 they were kept out by a near total ban on imports of PCs and many peripherals. Tariffs of 8%–15% were retained on PCs, peripherals, and most components; in 1998, these were removed to comply with World Trade Organization rules. Even with formal trade barriers being lowered, Korea's distribution system remains a formidable barrier to entry. Samsung, LG, Daewoo, and Trigem all have extensive dealer networks covering the entire country, and they offer levels of training and support that outsiders cannot easily match.

The domestic market is led by Samsung, with about 28% of the market in 1996 and Trigem, with 18%. The rest of the market is divided among LG, Daewoo, a handful of foreign firms, and Sejin, an electronics retailer that introduced its own brand of PCs and took 13% of the market in 1996, before being purchased by Daewoo in 1997 (table 4-3). Samsung increased its market share rapidly in the mid-1990s, using profits from DRAM sales to subsidize a price-cutting strategy and new product introductions. Trigem was hurt the most by Samsung's market share drive, because it could not buffer the impacts of a PC price war with profits from other businesses. The tables started to turn in 1996, however, when a 75% drop in DRAM prices hurt Samsung badly and actually benefited Trigem by giving it access to cheaper memory for its own PCs.

The size of the Korean market has had an ambiguous impact on the PC industry. It is large enough to provide a significant base for two or three companies, as long as foreign competitors are excluded. But it is also large enough to lull those companies into concentrating on the domestic market, rather than seeking opportunities in the global production system. A Taiwanese or Singaporean company knows that it can't survive on the domestic market, but Korean companies can be tempted to concentrate on the domestic market and treat the global market as a place to sell excess capacity and smooth out production levels. This is exactly how Trigem and others have treated their OEM businesses. In fact, executives from two different *chaebol* admitted in interviews that they had no interest in trying to compete with Taiwan and China as OEM producers, because margins are too thin to make it worth the effort.

TABLE 4-3. Korea's PC Market Share by Vendor, 1991–1996 (% of units sold)

| Vendor | 1991 | 1992 | 1993 | 1994 | 1995 | 1996 |
|---|---|---|---|---|---|---|
| Samsung | 15% | 13% | 17% | 23% | 26% | 28% |
| TriGem | 16 | 15 | 19 | 22 | 22 | 17 |
| Sejin | 0 | 0 | 0 | 0 | 0 | 13 |
| LG | 10 | 10 | 13 | 12 | 10 | 9 |
| Hyundai | 5 | 6 | 6 | 9 | 7 | 7 |
| Daewoo | 10 | 9 | 8 | 7 | 8 | 5 |
| IBM | 7 | 5 | 4 | 3 | 1 | 1 |
| Others | 56 | 47 | 37 | 27 | 26 | 20 |
| Total units | 590,000 | 690,000 | 970,000 | 1,200,000 | 1,514,000 | 1,973,000 |

*Source:* IDC Asia/Pacific Research Center, data provided to authors.

Korea's PC market has grown rapidly, but by 1995 there were just 78 computers in use per 1,000 people, compared to 98 in Taiwan, 171 in Hong Kong, and 189 in Singapore.[20] Computer use is high in the finance, manufacturing, and government sectors, but small businesses and the service sector have been slow to computerize. The domestic market could be expected to provide opportunities for local software firms, but the slow adoption of computers in many segments of the economy, along with high piracy rates, have been barriers to the development of software and information services industries.

### Industry Structure

The Korean computer industry, like the electronics industry, is dominated by Korea's four largest industrial conglomerates: Samsung, LG Electronics, Hyundai, and Daewoo. The Korean *chaebol* are groups of companies controlled by the families of the founders, with sons and other relatives often running member companies. These groups receive preferential treatment from the government in return for political support, and they have grown into multibillion dollar empires, with businesses ranging from automobiles to steel, shipbuilding, construction, electrical appliances, and electronics. The *chaebols'* size and diversity have been important assets in entering commodity electronics markets such as DRAMs, which require huge capital investments. The *chaebol* not only can subsidize such investments with money from other businesses, but they also have financial institutions within their groups they can turn to for capital.

The most successful businesses for the *chaebol* have been those that demanded an export orientation, either because of the nature of the business or because of government policy. In the case of consumer electronics, textiles, and other labor-intensive businesses, the government required that companies achieve export targets in return for subsidies and protection in the domestic market. Capital-intensive businesses such as steel and DRAMs require large-volume production to support the heavy investments required in plant and equipment, so it was necessary to export. Forced to compete globally, the Koreans achieved high levels of productivity in these industries.

However, the logic of the *chaebol* has been to compete in every industry sector possible, not just those in which they can compete internationally. They entered industries such as heavy machinery, petrochemicals, telecommunications equipment, and minicomputers in response to government policies aimed more at achieving self-sufficiency in strategic industries than at competing internationally.

Rather than expanding vertically within core industries, the *chaebol* continue to move horizontally into entirely new industries. Encouraged by government subsidies that were based on output rather than value added, they emphasized large-scale assembly rather than developing upstream industries. For instance, Samsung has not made a serious effort to develop semiconductor equipment or materials suppliers within its group. Yet it defied the government's wishes by entering the overcrowded passenger car business.

This type of horizontal diversification has led the *chaebol* to compete furiously with each other across dozens of markets, while depending on Japan or the United States for key components, equipment, and technology in even their most successful businesses. Even after the government started trying to rein in the *chaebols'* economic power with the Fair Trade Act of 1980, they continued to expand into new industries. In the mid-1990s, the government of Kim Young Sam was unable to carry out its plans to force the *chaebol* to concentrate on a few key industries.

In the computer industry, the specific problems have been the lack of focus and flexibility. The computer business is not a core business for any of the *chaebol* (table 4-4). As a result, computers do not get the attention of top management that semiconductors, consumer electronics, or automobiles receive. The *chaebol* are also hampered by a hierarchical structure that makes decision-making cumbersome. When it comes to major decisions, the *chaebol* can actually change direction fairly quickly, because the president can simply rule by decree. But for day-to-day decision-making, the process is more bureaucratic and inflexible. And it is those day-to-day decisions about product features, prices, suppliers, and logistics that are critical to the PC business.

Several events started to change the *chaebols'* strategic orientation in the 1990s. The rapid decline of the Hyundai automobile in the U.S. market pointed out the importance of product quality. The collapse of the PC industry showed the importance of innovation, design, and responsiveness to the market. Some changes have already taken place as a result. For instance, during an overseas trip marked by complaints from customers and advisers, Samsung Chairman Lee Kun-Hee issued his so-called Frankfurt Declaration: "Quality first, no matter what." Lee told his managers to "change everything except

TABLE 4-4. Korea's Largest Computer Makers, 1996

| Company | Computer Revenues (US$ millions) | Corporate Revenues (US$ millions) |
|---|---|---|
| Samsung Electronics | 1,890 | 19,832 |
| Samsung Display Devices | n.a.[a] | 3,074 |
| Trigem Computer | 1,070 | 1,070 |
| LG Electronics | 425 | 9,373 |
| | (1,935)[b] | (10,256) |
| Hyundai Electronics | 230 | 3,957 |
| Daewoo Telecom | 180 | 1,053 |

*Source:* Company data provided to authors; "Riding the Roller Coaster," *Electronic Business Asia,* 8 (June 1997): 42–45.

[a]Revenues include monitors, displays, and related components. No breakdown available.

[b]Data includes peripherals and components as well as systems and applications. Communication from K. S. Park, LG IBM PC Co.

how they treat their families." Decision-making is supposed to be decentralized, in a more American style of management. Samsung launched a CEO school in 1993 to put all its top executives through six months of retraining, three months of which is overseas. Managers are forbidden to travel by plane in their foreign locations; instead they must rub elbows with the local population and try to understand the countries in which they are studying.[21] The goal is to overcome Samsung's insular, Korea-centric mentality and equip it to compete in global markets.

However, there is a strong resistance in Korean companies accustomed to rigid hierarchical management structures. Discussing Lee's management style, Bae Soon-Hoon, president of rival Daewoo Electronics, said, "It's a big risk. You can't make a good organization innovative in one day."[22] Even a Samsung executive admitted that top managers are used to being considered experts in all areas, and they find it difficult to take advice from younger people, even if a younger person has more expertise in a particular area.

The ability of the *chaebol* to change their management styles and become more globally oriented will be important to their future success, especially as the Korean market opens up. Still, companies like Samsung, Hyundai, LG, and Daewoo have tremendous human and financial resources to meet the challenge of global competition in their high volume manufacturing industries. A bigger issue facing Korea is how to keep the *chaebol* from smothering the smaller companies that could provide a needed dose of innovation, flexibility, and entrepreneurship to the Korean electronics and computer industries.

*Weakness of Small- and Medium-Sized Enterprises.*   Until the mid-1980s, the *chaebol* tried to produce most of their components in-house. However, as a result of labor strife and rising wages since 1987, the *chaebol* have been anxious to shift labor costs to their suppliers.[23] Most of these suppliers are small- and medium-sized enterprises (SMEs) that are each locked into the production network of one *chaebol* and lack the ability to innovate and improve their competitiveness.

The situation is similar to Japan's *keiretsu* system but is actually worse for the Korean suppliers. Most Japanese equipment and components suppliers are part of a *keiretsu*, but they also sell outside their own group to both domestic and foreign customers. Many larger suppliers in Japan have strong technological capabilities in their own right. In addition, Japan's electronics industry has seen the growth of several independent companies such as Sony, Canon, and Kyocera into market and technology leaders. This is not the case in Korea. There are few major independent companies in Korea's electronics industry (an exception is Trigem), and Korea's smaller suppliers are tightly bound by the *chaebol* system. It is said that the *chaebol* use their suppliers as shock absorbers in economic downturns, making them pay cash when they buy from the *chaebol* but delaying payment when they sell to them.[24]

The weakness of the SMEs is one reason for Korea's continued dependence on Japan for critical production equipment and components. Most Japanese suppliers were nurtured in the *keiretsu* network, which provided a secure market and access to capital, but they have matured into global competitors. Korea's semiconductor giants must rely on Japanese and U.S. suppliers for virtually all of their capital equipment, because there is no Korean equivalent to a major independent equipment supplier such as Nikon, Canon, or Applied Materials.

The lack of strong independent SMEs has prevented Korea from entering the smaller niche markets that the *chaebol* tend to ignore as they focus on high-volume production. Some of these markets can grow into very large markets, yet by the time that happens, it is very expensive to try to break in. Taiwan's SMEs were able to gain a leading position in many computer components and peripherals while the PC industry was in its early development, and Korea has yet to make a dent in those now-large markets.

A major problem for the Korean SMEs has been the predatory nature of the *chaebol*. If a small company becomes successful, one of the *chaebol* will often try to purchase it. For instance, after Sejin began making inroads into the Korean PC market in 1996, it was bought by Daewoo's PC division in 1997.[25] If the company resists being bought, the *chaebol* might retaliate by starting rumors that the company is in trouble or persuading a bank to call the company's loans. Most SMEs don't have the capital to survive such an attack and end up capitulating. Another tactic for the *chaebol* is to create its own subsidiary and use its market power to try to overwhelm a successful SME.

The government has attempted to support the SMEs through a number of schemes, including venture capital funds and SME sanctuaries—industry segments from which the *chaebol* and their affiliates are excluded. However, these efforts have not been successful in creating an entrepreneurial SME sector. A survey by Soongsil University found 70% of government-allocated credit going to a few larger SMEs with ties to the leading *chaebol*.[26]

The environment for SMEs is changing somewhat, partly because the *chaebol* are coming to appreciate what independent companies can offer. When independent SMEs are able to innovate and sell to multiple customers, the *chaebol* get the benefits of economies of scale that their usual suppliers cannot offer. They can also help reduce Korean's dependence on Japanese suppliers of equipment and components.

The government has also made some legal and regulatory reforms that should help SMEs. Bankruptcy laws were changed so that going bankrupt no longer means an entrepreneur might end up in prison, as was previously the case. Also, in 1996, the Fair Trade Commission was elevated to cabinet-level status, giving it more power to enforce antitrust laws and rein in the *chaebol*.

*Comments on Industry Structure.* Korea's computer industry structure is a reflection of the structure of the electronics industry and the Korean economy as a whole. The *chaebol* use their control of distribution channels and access to a large customer base among their fellow *chaebol* members to dominate the domestic market. The *chaebol* structure has real advantages for competing in mass markets such as consumer electronics, DRAMs, flat-panel displays, and monitors, but it has been a liability in other parts of the computer industry. There is not enough flexibility to manage in a dynamic environment such as the PC industry, and little room for innovation within the system.

Perhaps the biggest problem is the lack of focus. Computers are just not important enough to the companies that produce them in Korea. Only Trigem depends on PCs for its survival. The big conglomerates are busy with everything from microwaves and semiconductors to cars, shipbuilding, finance, and real estate. Even within the electronics industry, there is a lack of strategic focus on PCs.

### Industrial Policy

The difficulties faced by the Korean PC industry in the 1990s are clearly a result of the inability to respond to market conditions or develop the necessary capabilities to do so. The dominant position of the *chaebol* in Korea's domestic market also tends to smother smaller companies. However, the strengths and weaknesses of the Korean electronics and computer industries are not just attributable to character of the private sector. Just as the Korean government deserves credit for successful industrial policies in some sectors, it must take some of the blame for the misfortunes of the computer industry. Its strategy of protecting the domestic PC market isolated, rather than nurtured, the fledgling industry.

The Korean government has promoted the computer industry for two decades as part of its strategy to diversify the electronics industry beyond consumer electronics. The three major sectors targeted were computers, semiconductors, and telecommunications. Plans for the promotion of the computer industry were first announced in 1977, and a National Information Technology Plan was finalized in 1983.[27] During the 1980s and 1990s, the Korean government employed a combination of import protection, financial subsidies, and R&D consortia to promote computer production. It also developed government computer networks to promote computer use and create demand for domestic producers. Finally, in the 1990s, the government took steps to promote software development and has begun implementing a major plan called the Korea Information Infrastructure.

*Trade and Investment.*   From 1983 through 1987, the government banned imports of personal computers and many peripherals to give the domestic industry a chance to develop.[28] After the ban was lifted (partly as a result of U.S. trade pressure), Korean products continued to receive favored treatment in government procurement. One effect of the import ban was to keep prices high and inhibit domestic demand for PCs. Korean PC makers used the protected domestic market as a profit sanctuary, but they failed to integrate themselves into the developing Asian production network.

By the late 1980s, it was clear that Korea had fallen behind Taiwan in the critical processes of designing and producing PC motherboards. In an attempt to nurture the domestic industry, the government raised duties on imported motherboards from 3% to 15–20%.[29] In the end, this decision raised costs for Korean PC makers (which depended on Taiwanese suppliers) and made them less competitive just as price wars began to break out in the industry. Korean companies failed to catch up with the Taiwanese in motherboards, hurting the competitiveness of the PC industry.

The domestic market remains protected by the structure of the *chaebol* system, which provides a sort of informal import protection through its internal market links. *Chaebol* members generally buy products from within the group, and since the four *chaebol* involved in computer production account for a large share of Korea's GDP, this effectively closes off a significant share of the Korean business market to imported products.[30] By doing so, it also discourages foreign MNCs from investing in Korea, further distancing Korea's industry from the spillover benefits obtained when people and technology move from company to company.[31]

*Industry and Technology Promotion.*   Financial subsidies have been given to Korea's computer industry to support R&D and to provide venture capital to smaller companies. A number of funds have been developed to support investment in high-technology industries. These include the Electronics Industry Promotion Fund, which made low-interest loans available for the development of prototypes. Another was the National Investment Fund, which provided loans for the purchase of domestically made equipment and materials by the electronics industry. A third fund was the Industrial Technology Improvement Fund, which provided loans for development of machinery, components and materials. About US$180 million of loans were disbursed by these three funds during the 1980s.

In order to promote domestic R&D, the government has provided financial incentives to the private sector including preferential loans, tax incentives, reduced tariffs on imports of R&D equipment, deduction of R&D expenditures and human resource development costs from taxable income, and support for small technology-based companies. Total R&D spending in Korea grew from 0.6% of GDP in 1980 to 2.6% in 1994 and the number of corporate R&D laboratories grew from 65 in 1981 to 2,272 in 1995.[32] Private sector R&D grew at an extraordinary rate to nearly US$10 billion in 1994, from just US$1.5 billion in 1985. This is not to say that government subsidies were the main impetus for private R&D. The companies were moving into higher technology industries such as DRAMs and had to increase their R&D to compete, but government incentives no doubt eased the way for companies to invest in riskier R&D projects.

The government's own R&D spending continued to grow quite rapidly, quadrupling between 1985 and 1994, although government R&D has been dwarfed by the private sector. The government tends to spread its R&D efforts over a wide range of technologies rather than focusing on a few places where it could have a greater impact. University research also has been poorly funded, and Korea's universities have failed to produce significant research outputs or to train sufficient numbers of researchers. Basic (as opposed to applied) research was especially neglected, and the government finally enacted the Basic Research Promotion Law in 1989. By 1993 the government had established fourteen science research centers and sixteen engineering research center in various universities.[33]

Another ongoing project is Taedok Science Town, located adjacent to the city of Taejon. Taedok is modeled after Tsukuba Science City in Japan; since 1973, the government has spent US$3 billion on R&D facilities in Taedok. Located in Taedok are fourteen government labs, including the Electronics and Telecommunications Research Institute (ETRI). There are also eleven corporate laboratories. But in spite of twenty years of investment, Taedok has not attracted the best scientists in Korea, nor has it become a major industrial park. This is largely due to its distance from Seoul, which remains the center of industry, technology, and government in Korea.

In addition to providing financial incentives to the private sector, the Korean government has organized several public–private R&D consortia to tackle particular technology problems, such as the 1986 project to develop 4M DRAMs. The first major R&D project aimed specifically at computers was the TICOM minicomputer, developed by researchers from ETRI, Samsung, Hyundai, Daewoo, and Goldstar. This project was initiated by the Ministry of Communication (MOC) and the Ministry of Science and Technology, initially to develop computers for use in the government's National Administrative Information System. The first generation of TICOM was based on technology from a U.S. company, Tolerant, which proceeded to go out of business. The next generation had to start over with Intel x86 processors and a Unix operating system, but it was hampered by the need for compatibility with the original machines. TICOM minicomputers have been purchased by government agencies and public institutions, but they have had virtually no sales to the private sector outside of purchases by the four *chaebol* who produce the TICOM. The third generation of TICOM reached the market in 1995, but it is still unclear what market potential exists for TICOM in a shrinking global minicomputer market dominated by IBM, Hewlett-Packard, and DEC.

In 1994, the Ministry of Trade, Industry, and Energy (MOTIE) began a new joint project with AT&T GIS (now NCR) to develop large-scale computers based on massively parallel processing (MPP) technology. MPP is a relatively new technology that might offer opportunities to newcomers, but the market potential for such systems is unclear. MPP systems require highly sophisticated software to function, and it may not be a good match for Korean companies whose software capabilities are very limited. Meanwhile, the MOC and ETRI also launched their own R&D project to develop mainframe computer technology. The government at the time stated its intention to move Korea's computer industry "into high-end computers and away from price-competitive personal computers."[34] A more pessimistic perspective would be that Korea is trying to move into declining markets for large-scale systems dominated by U.S. and Japanese firms with huge advantages in technology, customer base, and software availability.

In the 1990s, the government developed new programs to support research across a wide range of technologies with the goal of boosting R&D to 4% of GDP by the end of the decade. For instance, the Highly Advanced Nation R&D project, also referred to as the G-7 project, is aimed at lifting Korea to the level of the G-7 countries technologically by 2020. The G-7 project involves specific product technologies including new drugs and chemicals, broadband ISDN, and high-definition television, as well as basic technologies such as new materials and ultra-large-scale integrated circuits. During the first three years, $1.3 billion was spent on the G-7 project, which produced 2,500 patent applications and 2,000 academic articles.[35] An initiative called the Spin-off Support program was introduced in 1992, with the goal of encouraging researchers in government labs to establish their own high-tech companies. Another program is the New Technology Commercialization Program, which offers preferential financing to R&D and commercialization of technologies that are new to Korea.

Like Korea's computer industry, the Korean government generally ignored software. Then the decline of Korea's computer hardware industry in the 1990s revealed the country's weakness in software and design, and in 1993 the government drafted a Basic Plan of National Strategy for Software Industry Promotion. Responsibility for software policy was given to the newly created Ministry of Information and Communications (MIC). In 1995, MIC announced that it would invest about US$1.84 billion by the year 2010 (about US$125 million annually) in order to foster the nation's software industry. Under the plan, MIC will support creative ideas on multimedia, games, and PC applications, strengthen protection of intellectual property rights, and establish software research centers and public databases.[36] It should be borne in mind that actual spending often falls short of initial plans, since most projects must be funded annually as part of the budget process.

*Promotion of Computer Use.*   The Korean government has initiated several large-scale network projects and invested in computerization of public agencies to promote computer use and create demand for the domestic industry. The National Computerization Board (NCB) began building a national computer network in 1987 called the National Basic Information System (NBIS). The NBIS included networks of government agencies, financial institutions, educational institutions, and defense and security agencies.

The government invested about US$200 million in the National Administrative Information System (NAIS), a network of government agencies, while the banks spent about US$650 million on the financial network. Preference was given to domestically produced computers, particularly the TICOM minicomputer, in government procurement. Initial funding for NAIS came through a special process, with five-years' funding arranged in advance by the NCB. However, funding for the second stage of the NBIS was put under the normal budget process, where it faced strong competition from competing government projects. Those in charge of budget allocations did not see visible benefits from IT investments under NAIS, partly because of the difficulty in measuring such impacts, and support for the project waned.

Government interest in information technology use was resurrected around 1993–1994 when the United States and Japan announced national information infrastructure plans. Leaders in business and government became concerned that failure to develop an advanced information infrastructure would cause Korea to lose ground against more advanced countries, and that Korean companies would then be isolated from the global marketplace. The government responded with a major initiative called the Korean Information Infrastructure (KII).[37]

The KII is a fifteen-year plan (1995–2010) to upgrade Korea's communications infrastructure, develop new IT applications, and promote use of the technology throughout the economy and society. Government is expected to be a leading user, and the first stage of KII involves creating a high-speed network called the New Korea Net—Government (NKN-G) that will link government agencies, universities, and other public institutions. The next stage will involve rolling out applications and technologies to the private sector via the New Korea Net—Public. The KII plan is being guided by a high-level steering committee headed by the prime minister and including key ministers and representatives of the National Assembly and Supreme Court. The steering committee is expected to resolve conflicts among government agencies involved in the project, and to sustain support for the project at the highest levels of government. Jurisdiction over the project mainly falls to the Ministry of Information and Communications, although MOTIE argues that it should have a role as well.

The cost of the KII plan is estimated by the government at about US$56 billion over twenty years. Only US$2.25 billion is expected to come from the public sector to establish pilot projects, promote the project to the public, support core technology development, and construct the NKN-G. The rest of the investment is to come from the private sector and from Korea Telecoms, the state-owned telecommunications company that is being privatized gradually. As in the United States and other countries, there is concern about whether the private sector will make large risky investments in technologies, infrastructure, and services that could become obsolete or fail to attract sufficient demand to turn a profit. There is also concern about emphasizing supply over demand, which has been the case in other Korean initiatives such as the NBIS. The government agencies involved are trying to focus on applications and use as well as infrastructure and supply, but in the words of the National Computerization Agency's Kuk-Hwan Jeong, "To a considerable degree, the KII plan must proceed on the faith that demand will rise in response to supply."[38]

*Policy Coordination.*    The development of effective computer policy in Korea has been hampered in recent years by bureaucratic competition, similar to the situation in Japan. Computer industry policy in Korea was originally the province of the Ministry of Trade and Industry (MTI), but with the convergence of computers and communications, competition developed between MTI and the Ministry of Communications. The government restructuring of 1994 shifted the balance of power toward the newly created Ministry of Information and Communications (MIC), which is responsible for software, information services, and information infrastructure, as well as telecommunications. Still, there is competition between the two ministries, because computer hardware and semiconductors remain under MOTIE (the former MTI). After the 1997 elections, the government was expected to clarify the roles of different ministries, which could help resolve some of the conflicts and help officials come up with a more coordinated approach to computer policy. However, Korea's financial crisis took precedence on the new government's immediate agenda.

*Comments on Industrial Policy.* Korea's policies for the computer industry must be judged as less than effective. There has been a lack of focus as the government has directed resources into a broad range of hardware technologies. There has been no clear emphasis on leveraging Korea's strengths in components manufacturing, nor has the government effectively addressed shortcomings in design and software capabilities. Accordingly, Korean computers and peripherals (outside of monitors) have been uncompetitive in world markets, and the software and services industries remain small. Especially damaging has been the inability to promote competition to the *chaebol* in the domestic market, either through SMEs or foreign companies. This has allowed the *chaebol* to avoid making the necessary changes to be more competitive in the global industry.

Part of the problem is that those responsible for Korea's technology policy seem fixated on following Japan and the Japanese model for computer industry promotion. Hence, Korea's policies have suffered from many of the same shortcomings as Japan's policies in the PC era. While the government and the *chaebol* have focused on beating Japan, the Korean computer industry has been left behind by competitors in Taiwan, Singapore, and elsewhere. Meanwhile, Korea has still failed to reduce its dependence on Japanese suppliers of key components and equipment.

It is unclear whether policies to strengthen the software industry and promote venture companies will have much impact. Innovation is not easily supported directly; it is more likely to be nourished by creating a favorable environment. The government could help do this by limiting the influence of the *chaebol* (especially in the distribution system), by protecting intellectual property rights, and by continuing to encourage computer use. In Korea, the software industry must have the *chaebol* as customers, but will be stronger if there are many independent companies free from the management hierarchies of the *chaebol*.

## Conclusions

Korea's extraordinary success in high-volume semiconductors and other commodity components has contrasted with its mixed record in PCs and outright failure in software. These contradictions are primarily explained by industry structure, and the nature of linkages with the global economy. Industrial policy has played a lesser, but still important role.

The Korean industry structure, dominated by large diversified conglomerates such as Samsung, LG, and Hyundai, is well suited to the demands of high-volume manufacturing. The *chaebols'* size and diversification give them the resources to make heavy investments in capital-intensive industries such as DRAMs and flat-panel displays, and their strengths in consumer electronics translated into success in computer monitors. On the other hand, the size and hierarchical structure of the *chaebol* limit their speed and flexibility and have been a liability in PCs, software, and services. The diversification of the *chaebol* also has led to a lack of focus on the PC business. Equally problematic is the tendency of the *chaebol* to squeeze out smaller companies that might otherwise provide the dynamism and flexibility that Korea needs to compete in the PC industry.

The Korean PC industry also has had less success in developing global linkages than, for instance, the DRAM industry. Samsung, LG, and Hyundai were all highly resourceful in gaining access to foreign sources of technology for DRAMs, whether through hiring Korean-American engineers, bringing in Japanese consultants, or licensing technology from small U.S. companies. There was a strong linkage developed between Korea and Silicon Valley, as exemplified by Samsung's two teams of engineers collaborating across the Pacific. The Korean companies developed a web of strategic alliances with U.S. and Japanese companies. In PCs, however, the linkages were weaker. Daewoo used its Leading Edge connection to enter the U.S. market, but when Leading Edge floundered, Daewoo could not resurrect it, nor could it develop alternative marketing channels. The other PC makers mostly focused on the domestic market, and when they tried to expand globally through acquisitions of U.S. firms, the results were disappointing.

It is difficult to explain why the same companies that developed strong ties to the United States and Japan in semiconductors remained rather isolated in PCs. Perhaps the answer lies in the nature of the two industries and the types of linkages demanded. The DRAM industry required obtaining advanced design and process technologies, which could be obtained through licensing, poaching of engineers, or other means. There is little demand for collaboration with the customer, since DRAMs are all fundamentally the same. This is not the case in the PC industry. It is not enough to get the product and process right and then sell millions, as in DRAMs. Selling a motherboard, add-on card, or complete system requires meeting product specifications set by the final system vendor, and every new model is somewhat different. This requires a close interaction between the supplier and customer to solve problems and get a product to market, and the Koreans did not develop these types of close ties to the global production network.

The government's computer industry policies have often served to reinforce the industry's tendency toward isolation. By protecting the domestic market, the government created a profit sanctuary in which the industry could operate comfortably and did not need to fight it out in the global market. When the PC industry went through major shifts in the late 1980s and early 1990s, Korean companies did not know how to respond, and they chose to retreat to the domestic market. The government's import substitution approach also led to distracting efforts to build a minicomputer and mainframe industry rather than developing better capabilities in PCs. The best thing the government has done is to promote computer use by putting computers in schools and creating a new generation of computer-literate people who are now entering the workforce. This, as much as anything, bodes well for both the production and use of computers in the future.

In the future, Korea's DRAM industry will benefit from the continued growth in demand for more powerful PCs and associated software. There is also continuing growth in demand for larger flat-panel displays, and Korean companies should be able to expand their share of that market as a result of their recent large investments in LCD capacity.

It is less certain that Korean companies can themselves become serious competitors in the PC market outside Korea. So far there is no evidence of a Korean resurgence in PC exports. Other than Samsung, the leading electronics companies seem to be more interested in developing newer consumer-oriented hardware platforms rather than trying to compete in the global PC business. Their continued involvement in the PC industry is justified more on strategic than on business grounds, because the PC is considered a technology driver for the electronics industry.

A more critical question is whether Korean companies can move beyond competing in the diminishing returns, commodity manufacturing segments of the computer industry. To do so, they need to diversify into higher value, innovation-intensive markets such as ASICs, microprocessors, and software. For Korea as a country, the problem is to find higher value activities to replace the labor-intensive production that is being moved offshore. This means developing new capabilities emphasizing "soft" skills and creating an environment that nurtures those capabilities.

To develop the soft skills that Korea lacks will take more than just the usual government incentives or technology programs. It will require a shake-up of the entire industry structure as well as the education system to create a culture in which innovative people and firms can operate. So far, such a restructuring seems unlikely. The government has found itself less able to exert influence over the *chaebol* and their tremendous economic power, but stronger enforcement of antitrust laws could help put some boundaries on that power. In the end, the Asian financial crisis of 1998 appears to be doing what the government could not. The major *chaebol* have begun to cut back on some of their expansion plans and announced that they would focus on core industries.

The more fundamental reforms needed to open up the industry structure and create new capabilities will take tough political choices and an acceptance by the private sector of the need for significant reform. But as Linsu Kim reminds us, Korea has a long history of responding to internal and external challenges (such as surviving 950 foreign invasions during 2,000 years of written history), so it would be premature to write off Korea as a competitor in the computer industry. It will certainly remain a major force in the commodity hardware industry, and it may ultimately find a broader role in new markets created by the convergence of computers and consumer electronics.

## Taiwan

While Korea's PC industry went on a roller coaster ride—up in the 1980s and down in the 1990s—Taiwan's industry slowed momentarily in the early 1990s then resumed its upward trajectory. Taiwan is a world leader in a wide range of PC systems, components and peripherals, and it is moving both upstream into memory chips and flat panel displays, and downstream into distribution, service, and support. Taiwanese companies have developed strong capabilities in design and systems engineering and provide a full range of services to foreign PC makers, from design and manufacturing to distribution and after-sales support. Taiwan stands out as Asia's greatest national success story in the PC era, especially considering that its success was built on the efforts of domestic entrepreneurs.

How did Taiwan's small companies succeed in the perilous PC era, while Japan's and Korea's giants stumbled so badly? That is a story whose cast includes a visionary government official, an entrepreneur of humble origins who is now an international business star, hundreds of engineers and entrepreneurs who have brought the technology of U.S. universities and companies back to Taiwan, and thousands of people working long hours and honing their skills just to survive in the brutally competitive PC industry.

It is also a story of U.S. companies that helped create the Taiwanese industry by sourcing components from Taiwan and contracting assembly out to Taiwanese companies, and of Japanese companies that transferred mature technologies to Taiwan as they moved into new product generations. Meanwhile, Taiwanese companies used overseas Chinese connections to monitor technology and market developments in the United States and elsewhere. Taiwan's success story is also a model of well-conceived government policies that supported a fledgling computer industry by developing technology, training engineers, gathering market intelligence, and providing financial support. Finally, there is an underside to the story—one of stolen chips from California ending up in Taipei electronics shops, "reworked" Pentium chips being installed in PCs, and blurred lines between reverse engineering and direct copying of other companies' designs.

These elements make for a story as complex and interesting as that of Silicon Valley itself, and one that is much less understood. To understand Taiwan's success in computers, we must first go back more than thirty years to a time when the island's economy was still based on agriculture and light industry, and a few foreign companies came to Taiwan to build its first electronics factories.

## History of Taiwan's Computer Industry

Although a few Taiwanese firms had begun to assemble radios and simple electrical equipment in the 1950s, Taiwan's electronics industry really got off the ground in the early 1960s, when companies such as General Instruments, Texas Instruments, Sanyo, and Matsushita invested in Taiwan to produce consumer electronics products and parts. During the 1970s, they were followed by a new wave of investment and components sourcing by companies, such as RCA, Philips, and IBM, for a variety of consumer products and computer components. As foreign companies invested in Taiwan, Taiwanese companies responded by setting up as suppliers and subcontractors. Many of Taiwan's electronics firms were started by engineers with experience working for the MNCs, and much of their technology was licensed from those foreign firms.[39] The Taiwanese electronics industry grew rapidly in the 1970s, accounting for 18.2% of exports in 1980 (compared to 12.3% in 1970). Television production grew from 1.8 million sets in 1971 to 7 million in 1980.[40]

Taiwan's government began to promote electronics production in the 1960s by creating incentives for investment in electronics and establishing export-processing zones. These incentives and Taiwan's cheap labor attracted many foreign firms to invest in production of consumer electronics and simple assembly of semiconductors.

By the late 1970s, some Taiwanese companies were assembling imported PC kits, and others began making unauthorized clones of the Apple II computer. The Taiwanese government cracked down on such illegal clones in 1982–1983, partly due to pressure from Apple and the U.S. government. In response, Taiwan's PC makers shifted to producing IBM-compatible PCs.

During the 1980s, foreign computer makers invested in production facilities in Taiwan to take advantage of low-cost labor from factory workers to technicians and engineers. Local companies moved quickly to take advantage of opportunities for subcontracting and OEM production. A dense network developed of small PC component suppliers, many of whom had previous experience in producing consumer electronics and components. Some companies began to produce components and peripherals such as cables, power supplies, keyboards, and mice, while others assembled complete PCs for foreign customers.

As they gained experience and manufacturing capabilities, domestic companies moved into more advanced products such as motherboards, scanners, graphics cards, and monitors. Personal computer production was led by MNCs in the early 1980s, but domestic companies accounted for 70% of hardware production by 1990.[41]

In spite of its accomplishments, Taiwan's computer industry has not had a smooth ride. During the 1980s, the PC industry was growing almost in spite of itself. The mentality of the industry was mercantilist—that of traders rather than manufacturers—and companies lacked a long-term strategic vision. An early company, ARC, shipped 2,000 faulty motherboards to Dell and ruined its relationship with Dell—a mistake from which ARC never recovered. Michael Dell berated the Taiwanese industry for its quality problems and warned its companies to prepare for hard times, but few in Taiwan listened.[42] A number of companies tried to move away from OEM production to promote their own brand names in the late 1980s, but most failed due to an inability to differentiate their branded products from no-name clones. They also failed to develop effective distribution channels in foreign markets and did not provide good service to customers or resellers. By the 1990s, the surviving PC makers had returned to OEM production, except for Acer, which was able to develop successfully its own brand name internationally.

Like Korea, Taiwan was heavily dependent on Japan for critical technologies, components, and equipment, and its products had a reputation for poor quality. The industry was still involved mostly in labor-intensive product segments, and it faced rising wage rates at home and competition from low-cost production locations elsewhere in Asia. However, Taiwan had received a break in 1987 when the United States placed 100% tariffs on Japanese PCs in response to charges that Japanese companies were dumping semiconductors in the United States. This gave Taiwan's PC makers an opening (the tariff lasted one year) to show the U.S. companies that they could replace the Japanese as suppliers and contractors for more advanced products. As Poh-Kam Wong points out, this event created an opening, and the responsiveness and capabilities of Taiwanese firms enabled them to "lock-in the window of opportunities into permanent gains."[43]

As the industrial countries entered a recession in the 1990s and price wars ravaged the computer industry, Taiwan's computer industry struggled to stay afloat. Taiwanese firms were hurt by an appreciating NT dollar that made their products more expensive in export markets. Unlike the Japanese and Korean industries, however, Taiwan's computer industry responded quickly and was able to resume its rapid growth rate by 1992. The industry continued to increase its technological capabilities, moving into production of notebook computers and workstations. Leading firms such as Apple, IBM, Compaq, Packard Bell, and Dell contracted with Taiwanese firms for production of desktop and notebook computers, motherboards, printed circuit boards, and monitors. Those five companies contracted with Taiwanese firms for more than US$2 billion in OEM production in 1994 alone (table 4-5). In 1995, the world's top eight PC makers were all sourcing significant amounts of desktop and notebook PCs, as well as motherboards, from Taiwanese suppliers (table 4-6). Local companies also began to do original design manufacturing (ODM), in which foreign PC makers would contract with them for design as well as manufacturing.[44]

By 1995, Taiwan was the number one producer worldwide of notebook PCs, monitors, motherboards, scanners, mice, and keyboards. Total hardware production in Taiwan had reached US$14.3 billion, and Taiwanese companies were producing another US$5.3 billion in hardware offshore. Taiwan's position in the world computer industry is shown in table 4-7.

The combination of engineering capabilities and highly flexible manufacturing techniques has enabled Taiwanese companies to take an engineering

TABLE 4-5. Taiwan OEM Production for Major PC Vendors

| Buyer | OEM Product | Taiwan Maker | 1994 OEM expend. (US$ millions) | 1995 OEM expend. (US$ millions est.) |
|---|---|---|---|---|
| Apple | Monitor<br>Notebook<br>PDA<br>SPS | Tatung<br>Acer<br>Inventa<br>Delta | $300–400 | $300–400 |
| Compaq | Monitor<br>Mouse<br>Notebook<br>PCB<br>SPS | ADI, Philips, TECO<br>Logitec, Primax<br>Inventa<br>Compeq<br>Lite-on, Delta | $400 | $500 |
| Dell | Monitor<br>Notebook<br>Motherboard<br>PCB<br>SPS | Lite-on, Royal<br>Inventa, GVC<br>Lung Hwa, FIC<br>Compeq<br>Lite-on | $450 | $450 |
| IBM | Monitor<br>Motherboard<br>Notebook<br>SPS | Sampo, Capertronic<br>GVC, Lung Hwa<br>Sun-Moon-Star, Delta,<br>ASE | $400 | $450 |
| Packard Bell | PC<br>Motherboard<br>Keyboard | Tatung<br>Tatung, GVC<br>BTC | $450 | $500 |

Source: Market Intelligence Center/Institute for the Information Industry (MIC/III), data provided to authors.

concept from the drawing board to volume production in less time than anywhere in the world. The biggest problem facing Taiwan's hardware industry in the mid-1990s was a continuing reliance on Japanese and U.S. sources for critical components, including flat-panel displays, cathode-ray tubes (CRT), DRAMs, and microprocessors. However, the government and industry were taking steps to develop domestic capabilities in each of those areas. A number of DRAM facilities were under construction and the leading monitor maker, Tatung, was developing its own CRT and LCD technology.

*Offshore Production.* Taiwan's computer makers have responded to rising labor costs by moving their own labor-intensive production to mainland China and Southeast Asia. By 1995, offshore production accounted for 49% of monitors, 37% of motherboards, 77% of power supplies, 47% of graphics cards, 24% of mice, and 65% of keyboards (table 4-8). They also moved assembly and sales operations closer to their customers, especially in the United States and Europe. In 1995, Acer was assembling more than 50,000 PCs per month in the United States in order to be quick to market with new products.

TABLE 4-6. Leading PC Vendors' Procurement in Taiwan

| Top 8 PC Vendors Worldwide, 1995 | % of Desktop PC or Motherboard Procured from Taiwan and Name(s) of Taiwanese OEM | % of Notebook PCs Procured from Taiwan and Name(s) of Taiwanese OEM |
|---|---|---|
| Compaq | 20%–25% Mitac | 15% Inventa |
| IBM | 20%–30% ECS, USI | 15%–20% ASE |
| Apple | — | 25% Acer, Quanta |
| Packard Bell | 30%–60% GVC, Tatung | — |
| NEC | 25%–30% ECS | — |
| Acer | 100% Acer | 100% Acer |
| Hewlett-Packard | Started during 1995 GVC | 60%–70% Twinhead |
| Dell | 30%–50% GVC | 25% Quanta |

*Source:* Market Intelligence Center/Institute for the Information Industry (MIC/III), data provided to authors.

The shift of production offshore has not hollowed out the domestic industry, because local manufacturers have moved up to higher value-added production or more advanced production technologies. For example, they have employed surface mount technology (SMT) to stay competitive in production of motherboards and PCs. They have also kept in Taiwan production of the latest generations of hardware and more technologically advanced products such as notebooks, scanners, network cards, and video cards.

*The Intel Challenge.* Taiwan's motherboard and chipset makers have succeeded on the basis of excellent design and engineering capabilities and the ability to develop and produce a variety of designs to meet the needs of different PC vendors. In 1995, however, Intel began designing and producing large numbers of chipsets and motherboards. Some estimates put Intel's motherboard output as high as ten million units, a total close to Taiwan's 1994 output of twelve million units.[45] A number of major PC vendors turned to Intel to supply motherboards for their Pentium-class PCs. Intel claimed that it started producing chipsets and boards simply to accelerate the acceptance of the Pentium chip, not to take business away from other board makers. However, there were fears in Taiwan that Intel was planning to move downstream and would eliminate some of the biggest segments of the Taiwanese industry.

Naturally, Taiwan's PC and motherboard makers were concerned about the new challenge. Having Intel as a competitor rather than a partner was disquieting, to say the least. More troubling was the idea that if Intel was able

TABLE 4-7. Taiwan's Market Share and Unit Output of Hardware Products, 1995

|  | Total Production (1,000s of units) | Share of World Market (%) | Offshore Production (% of total) | Value (US$ millions) |
|---|---|---|---|---|
| Monitor | 31,329 | 57 | 49 | 7,271 |
| Notebook PC | 2,592 | 27 | 0 | 3,339 |
| Desktop PC | 4,667 | 10 | 9 | 2,314 |
| Motherboard | 20,864 | 65[a] | 37 | 2,222 |
| Scanner | 2,481 | 64 | 0 | 434 |
| Switching power supply | 34,320 | 35 | 77 | 895 |
| Graphics card | 9,300 | 32 | 47 | 516 |
| Terminal | 956 | 27 | 0 | 161 |
| Network card | 10,246 | 38 | 3 | 298 |
| Hubs | 933 | 22 | 1 | 123 |
| Sound card | 3,750 | 22 | 15 | 123 |
| CD-Rom drive | 3,572 | 11 | 26 | 305 |
| Mouse | 40,904 | 72 | 24 | 191 |
| Keyboard | 32,780 | 65 | 86 | 369 |

*Source:* Market Intelligence Center/Institute for the Information Industry (MCI/III), *Asia IT Report* (December 1996 and January 1997). Also tables provided to authors by MIC.

[a]World market includes merchant sales only, not motherboards produced for captive use by PC vendors.

to convince PC makers to standardize on a few board and chipset designs, Taiwan's design strengths could be negated. The concern about Intel dominating the motherboard business did not last long; Intel took a big loss in early 1996 when it got stuck with a large inventory of unsold DRAMs that it had bought just before prices plummeted. The bigger concern remains, however, that Intel is reducing the ability of Taiwanese board and chipset makers to differentiate their products.

Another concern is the fact that Intel can continue to include more capabilities into the microprocessor with each generation of more powerful chips, as it has already done with multimedia features on its MMX processor series. Networking and other features may eventually be built into the processor, destroying the business for some of Taiwan's hardware makers.

*Diversifying and Extending Capabilities.* Taiwanese companies have responded to the Intel challenge by diversifying and by extending their OEM services. For example, Acer makes DRAMs in a joint venture with Texas Instruments, motherboard leader FIC is making notebooks, Elitegroup is focusing on scanners and semiconductors (in a venture with Mitsubishi), while scanner maker UMAX has licensed the Macintosh operating system to compete in the Mac clone market. Taiwan also has diversified its customer base, as a number of major Japanese companies now source components and complete systems in Taiwan.

Taiwan's computer makers also have expanded their capabilities as OEM producers. OEM production used to involve a U.S. company coming to a

TABLE 4-8.  Domestic and Offshore Computer Production

| | 1992 | 1993 | 1994 | 1995 | 1996[a] |
|---|---|---|---|---|---|
| Hardware production (US$ millions) | 8,391 | 9,693 | 14,582 | 18,871 | 24,347 |
| Domestic | 7,418 | 8,002 | 11,579 | 13,587 | 16,587 |
| Offshore | 973 | 1,691 | 3,003 | 5,284 | 7,760 |
| Offshore as % of total | 12% | 17% | 21% | 28% | 32% |

*Source:* MIC/III, *Asia IT Report* (December 1996).

[a]Estimate

Taiwanese company with a new design and contracting for production. However, Taiwan's OEM leaders (such as FIC, Mitac, Acer, and others) provide design, distribution, and service, as well as manufacturing. A foreign PC vendor can come to Taiwan, be presented with a catalog of motherboard designs, and choose one that meets its system configuration requirements. If the Taiwanese company is producing the entire system, it may also distribute the finished product to the U.S. company's resellers and even provide warehousing, logistical, and service support. The U.S. company might never actually take possession of the computer. Its only functions are marketing, channel support, and finance. This new arrangement puts a premium on capabilities that go far beyond low-cost manufacturing to include market intelligence, product design, logistics, and customer support. By developing these capabilities, the Taiwanese companies have increased their share of the value chain in the PC industry and have created competitive advantage against competitors in other countries.

*Acer.*   Acer is Taiwan's biggest and best-known PC company, having risen from OEM anonymity to become the eighth leading brand in the global market in 1995. More than just a PC maker, Acer also produces a wide range of peripherals and components and is in the publishing and information content business. Acer's sales tripled from US$1.88 billion in 1993 to US$5.7 billion in 1995, before slowing to US$5.86 billion in 1996. Acer's founder and chairman, Stan Shih, has become the face of the Taiwan computer industry both at home and overseas.[46]

The company, originally called Multitech, was started in 1976 by Shih, his wife, Carolyn, and five other partners with $25,000 in capital. The company started by providing engineering and consulting services, with an eye toward developing products based on microprocessors. The initial years were difficult. After one year, three of the partners bailed out, and Shih had to cut his salary in half while his wife worked for free to help the company survive. Acer's first PC, called the Microprofessor, was an educational learning kit introduced in 1981. In 1982, Acer began assembling IBM-compatible PCs for ITT and in 1984, developed its own 16-bit PC. In 1986, Acer became the second company, after Compaq, to introduce a 386-based PC.

The 1980s were a time of rapid growth and expansion for Acer, but trouble arrived in the early 1990s, when the company's rapid expansion ran up against a slowdown in the global market. In 1989, Acer hired a former IBM executive named Leonard Liu as president of Acer America. Under Liu, Acer acquired multiuser system maker Altos Computer Systems for US$94 million, after having acquired minicomputer maker Counterpoint Computers in 1988. These acquisitions were a financial burden and turned out to be difficult to assimilate, straining Acer's managerial structure at a time when it was already under pressure from rapid expansion. Liu's control-oriented management style conflicted with Acer's culture, leading to a divisive atmosphere in the company, and even in the Shih household, where Carolyn criticized Liu's leadership.[47] Shih offered his own resignation, but Acer's board refused it and affirmed its support for Shih.[48]

Liu finally left the company, and Shih initiated a major restructuring. This restructuring helped Acer recover, but it did not come about painlessly, or without some outside help. The pain involved identifying 400 "non-performing" managers, who were asked to retire or leave. Acer hired McKinsey & Company to prepare a consulting report on the global computer industry, advising Acer on how to restructure itself to respond to the changing market. The report helped guide the restructuring and also provided top management with some cover for violating Taiwan's unofficial "no layoff" policy for larger companies. Acer went further to ease the stigma of the layoffs, writing letters to each of the managers and their families, as well as letters of recommendation to prospective employers explaining that the layoffs were a result of uncontrollable market forces and did not reflect badly on the abilities of the managers.[49]

Outside help came in the form of a private cash infusion from Continental Engineering and Construction, whose owner was an alumnus of the same university as Stan Shih. It also came in the form of government assistance in arranging bank loans. The government felt that it could not afford to let Acer fail, partly because of the jobs involved and partly because of Acer's position as one of Taiwan's few well-known international companies. Acer did not waste the opportunity provided by its own cost cutting and outside cash infusions. The restructuring, along with resurgence in global demand, helped the company resume rapid growth while returning to profitability.

Acer was reorganized on an innovative business model based on decentralizing management to achieve rapid response to market conditions. As of 1995, Acer was divided into eleven semi-independent business units. Five were regional business units (RBUs), serving Taiwan, North America, Europe, Latin America, and the rest of the world. The other six were strategic business units (SBUs), including Acer Inc., Acer Peripherals, Acer TWP, Ambit Microsystems, Acer Laboratories, and TI-Acer (table 4-9). Acer's business units are organized under what the company refers to as the "client-server" model, in which each unit might be buying from another unit (as a client) at one time and selling to that unit (as a server) at another. The idea is to create a network-style organizational structure rather than a hierarchical one.

TABLE 4-9. Acer's Organization Structure

| Strategic Business Units | Regional Business Units |
| --- | --- |
| Acer Inc.—Acer's core business group. Responsible for headquarters functions, manufacturing of PCs and components, and technology development. Manufacturing plant is in Hsinchu. 1994 revenues: US$1,252 million. | Acer America—Headquarters in San Jose, Calif. Responsible for marketing, sales, assembly, and service of Acer brand products in North America. 1994 revenues: US$858 million. |
| Acer Peripherals—Produces monitors, keyboards, laser printers, CD-ROM drives, terminals, and fax machines. Factories in Taoyuan, in Penang, Malaysia, and under construction in Suzhou, China. 1994 revenues: US$564 million. | Acer Computer B.V. (Acer Europe)—HQ in the Netherlands, with subsidiaries in major European countries. Responsible for marketing, sales, and service for Europe, with assembly in three European plants. 1994 revenues: US$289 million. |
| TI-Acer—Joint venture with Texas Instruments to make DRAMs. Plant in Hsinchu. 1994 revenues: US$319 million. | Acer Computer International—HQ in Singapore. Responsible for marketing, assembly, distribution, and service for Asia-Pacific, India, Africa, Russia, and Middle East. 1994 revenues: US$214 million. |
| Ambit Microsystems—Joint venture with German company, Temic, a Daimler-Benz Group company. Produces electronic components for computer, telecoms, and automotive products. 1994 revenues: US$319 million. | Acer Computec Latino America—Joint venture between Acer Latin America and Mexico's largest computer distributor, Computec de Mexico. Responsible for marketing, sales, assembly, and service in Latin America, with subsidiaries in Columbia, Venezuela, Argentina, Chile, and Peru. 1994 revenues: US$214 million. |
| Acer Laboratories—Designs and manufactures ASICs for computer motherboards. 1994 revenues: US$66 million. | Acer-Sertek—Responsible for marketing Acer products in Taiwan. Acts as sales agent for other computer brands; develops multimedia equipment and military/industrial use computers. Operates 130 AcerLand computer stores and 100 resellers in Taiwan. 1994 revenues: US$245 million. |
| Acer TWP—Taiwan's largest publisher of high-tech books and magazines. Now focusing on multimedia products such as CD-ROM titles. 1994 revenues: US$18 million. | |

*Source:* Acer company documents.

Acer's strategy is for SBUs to develop and manufacture core products and services that are marketed by the various RBUs. Under the so-called "fast food" model, Acer produces components in centralized facilities in Taiwan and ships them to local assembly sites near the final customer. The RBUs choose designs and configure the products to meet local demand. In order to deliver "fresh" PC models to the market, Acer ships the latest motherboard designs by air freight to the market. Cheaper sea freight is used for components that do not change so quickly, including housings, power suppliers, and floppy disk drives. CPUs, memory chips, and hard disk drives are bought locally and installed in order to get the lowest price and most up-to-date technologies.[50] Acer's modular designs allow easy upgrades to newer CPUs.

One of Acer's most important strategic moves was a joint DRAM venture with Texas Instruments, TI-Acer. Moving into the volatile DRAM business was a risky move for Acer, even with an established partner like TI. But Acer felt it needed to secure its own DRAM supply, so it went ahead. When DRAMs were in short supply in 1994–1995, TI-Acer paid off handsomely, accounting for over half of Acer's profits, but the DRAM price crash of 1996 cut deeply into those profits.

Acer now has the capacity to make most components in a PC, with the notable exceptions of the CPU and hard disk drive. It is also moving into the soft side of the business through its newest RBU, Acer TWP, which is involved in publishing and multimedia products. Shih is pushing Acer toward high-value-added business segments in components and marketing and away from depending on low-value PC assembly. Shih's theory of value added is illustrated in "Stan Shih's Smiling Curve" (figure 4-5). This value-added curve could overlap Acer's business structure, with the SBUs on the left side of the curve and the RBUs on the right side.

Acer's expansion plans are based on Shih's "21 in 21" plan to have twenty-one publicly listed companies around the world by the twenty-first century, with Acer keeping a 19% to 40% stake in each company.[51] This will provide Acer with access to capital markets around the world and give local managers clear incentives to maximize the performance of their own business unit. Regional and country units will be managed by local managers (as is done already in existing units), with headquarters acting as a strategic coordinator.

The company has already gone far in developing its global presence. Its motto of "Global Brand, Local Touch" focuses on creating favorable brand name recognition around the world, but tailoring products, services, and management styles to local conditions at the country level. Acer's stylish charcoal gray Aspire model was designed for the U.S. consumer market and was a hit in 1995. Acer is also the number one brand in several Latin American and Southeast Asian companies, and it is targeting India through a joint venture with Indian PC leader Wipro. Acer was even number one in Mexico for a time, in spite of Mexico's proximity to the U.S. PC industry. By targeting emerging countries, Acer has established its brand name and developed local infrastructure in markets with high growth potential for the future. Ironically, Acer's biggest disappointment so far has been in mainland China, where it ran into trouble with its local partner and had to regroup for a new market push.

Acer's networked business model is intriguing, yet it is not easy to allow units to have autonomy while maintaining some sort of central strategic direction. Unlike most Taiwanese companies, whose management is highly centralized, Acer is gambling on a new structure that has few precedents, even in the United States.

Acer is not a typical Taiwanese company in some ways, yet it exemplifies many characteristics of the Taiwanese computer industry. Its humble origins,

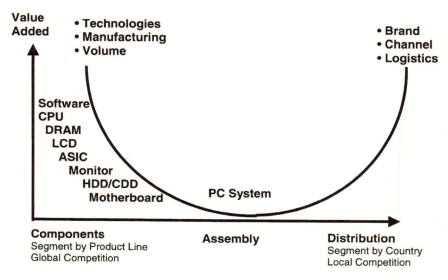

FIGURE 4-5. Stan Shih's Smiling curve. *Source:* Acer company documents. Reprinted by permission.

its rapid growth, the strong role of the founder and his wife (who, as in many Taiwanese companies, is a powerful force behind the scenes), and its strong export orientation are common to much of the industry. However, Acer has gone further than the rest of the industry, particularly in developing a successful brand name. Acer still relies on OEM sales for about 35% of its revenues, but the Acer brand is increasingly the mainstay of its business.

Shih's management style might seem on the surface to be management-by-cliché,[52] but behind the buzzwords is an innovative model for organizing a global high-tech company. A key reason for Acer's global success has been the high quality of managerial talent the company has assembled and the responsibility it gives to those managers. Its business unit heads are some of the best in Taiwan and, according to local analysts, could work for any company in the world. Acer sets goals for its business units in an annual meeting of unit heads called the Acer Summit. Each unit presents its budget, projections, and business plans, and each is pushed to set targets as high as is reasonable.

While Acer now downplays the role of the Taiwanese government in its success, the government has clearly been a factor. Acer's original IBM-compatible PCs employed the BIOS developed in a government research institute, the Electronics Research and Services Organization, and the company benefited from other technologies developed in government labs. The government had also helped in the 1980s; when IBM charged Acer with infringing on IBM's BIOS, the government negotiated a lower royalty payment. Acer now develops much of its own technology, and Shih has called for breaking up and privatizing government research institutions over the next decade to free up resources for the private sector.

Acer has long been a favorite of government leaders such as K. T. Li, who see Stan Shih and Acer as the prototypical success stories for Taiwan. By comparison, Tatung is an old-line family conglomerate, FIC is part of the Formosa Plastics group, Elitegroup's founder comes from a wealthy family, and semiconductor leaders UMC and TSMC are government spin-offs. But Acer is a true start-up company, and Shih is a true self-made man of humble origins—and the government has been willing to provide a hand when necessary.

One striking impression that the authors had in talking to people in Taiwan was the pride the country feels about Acer's success. Even Acer's competitors have an obvious, if grudging, respect for Acer. It is said that Taiwan's President Lee owns stock in only one company, Acer. The combination of entrepreneurial energy, shrewd business strategy, and an occasional well-timed helping hand from the government has made Acer one of Asia's success stories in computers, and a good illustration of Taiwan's national success.

*Software and Services.*   While the hardware industry was booming, Taiwan's software industry remained small and developed only limited capacity for design and engineering. Taiwan's software and information services market has grown steadily, however, and has reached sales of US$1.75 billion in 1995, compared to just US$600 million in 1989. Of the total, packaged software accounted for 38%, or US$672 million. The rest consisted of turnkey systems (15%), systems integration (22%), professional services (11%), and processing and network services (14%).[53] Local production of packaged software reached US$390 million in 1996, up from $280 million in 1995.

The most successful software companies have been Trend (antivirus programs), Dynalab and E-ten (Asian language fonts), U-Lead (multimedia tools), and D-Link (LAN software). The fastest growing segment of the Taiwanese software industry has been computer games, where Taiwanese companies have developed successful export products such as Three Kingdom, Monopoly, and Japanese Mahjong. Taiwanese game developers have worked with Japanese vendors to develop games for their platforms. For instance, in 1995, four Taiwanese companies got development licenses from Sega to develop games for Sega's new Saturn game machine. Meanwhile, Acer's subsidiary, Acer TWP, is developing multimedia CD-ROM titles based on Eastern cultures for both Asian and Western audiences.

The failure of Taiwan to develop a large software industry is something of an enigma, since the country's industry structure would seem to be well suited to supporting an entrepreneurial software industry. One explanation is that many hardware firms started out producing other electronic gadgets, and the move to computer hardware was a natural one. Software, however, involved an entirely different set of skills. Another problem was the lax protection of intellectual property rights (IPR), a fact that made development of original software an unattractive prospect. Also, most of the government's software and systems integration projects were contracted to the state-owned Institute for Information Industries (III), which only subcontracted out the more basic programming functions to the private sector. These factors helped limit the market opportunities for Taiwan's software industry. As the government has begun to enforce IPR laws and outsource more of its own software development, the software and services industries have been expanding, but they are still far behind the size and capabilities of the hardware industry. Probably the main reason has been the slow development of the domestic market.

*Domestic Market and Computer Use.* Taiwan's development into a leading computer producer has not been accompanied by similar success in computer use. The diffusion of computers in Taiwan lags far behind that of Japan, Singapore, and Hong Kong, and is slightly ahead of Korea. Taiwan's total spending on computer hardware, software, and services is also far behind its neighbors (figure 4-3). The adoption of information technology (IT) has been especially slow in the private sector, where the SMEs have been hesitant to adopt computers as a business tool. The SMEs are said to lack familiarity with the value of IT use. As one interviewee stated, "Chinese businessmen can appreciate the value of a $50,000 Mercedes immediately. They don't see the value of spending $50,000 for computers in their business." While such a statement may sound like a stereotyping of Chinese businesspeople,[54] and may not fully explain the low levels of IT use, the data do bear out the fact that Taiwanese businesses have been slow to embrace IT. A more fundamental reason for the low level of use is the limited resources available to SMEs to invest in computers, and the fact that business transactions are still largely carried out face-to-face in tightly clustered industry sectors.

### Industry Structure

The domestic Taiwanese computer industry is roughly divided among three tiers of companies. The first tier consists of about ten relatively large companies with annual sales of more than US$500 million (table 4-10). While large by Taiwanese standards, these companies are still only a fraction of the size of the Korean and Japanese leaders.

The next tier consists of a few dozen medium-sized companies, with sales of US$50 million–500 million. These companies tend to specialize in a few products, often shifting to take advantage of new opportunities. They include Umax, Elite, Inventa, Primax, Quanta, Compal, Logitech, and others. Some of these have been able to move up into higher technology products such as scanners and add-on cards, while others have remained in lower end products such as keyboards and mice. Most of their business is done on an OEM or subcontracting basis, although Umax broke out of the pack by introducing its own brand of Macintosh-compatible PCs in 1996.

The third group consists of thousands of small companies with less than US$50 million in sales. These companies form the foundation of Taiwan's

TABLE 4-10. Taiwan's Largest Computer Makers, 1996

| | Computer Revenues (annual) (US$ millions) | Corporate Revenues (annual) (US$ millions) |
|---|---|---|
| Acer | 5,860 | 5,884 |
| Inventec | 1,585 | 1,585 |
| Lien Hwa-Mitac Group | 2,081 | 2,439 |
| (Mitac) | (1,371) | (1,371) |
| First International Computer (FIC) | 1,100 | 1,100[a] |
| Tatung | 935 | 4,450 |
| GVC | n.a. | 871 |
| Lite-on | n.a. | 773 |
| Compal | 719 | 719 |
| Chuntex Electronic | 613 | 613 |
| ADI | 608 | 612 |

[a]Does not include revenues of parent company, Formosa Plastics.

Sources: "Riding the Roller Coaster," *Electronic Business Asia*, 8 (June 1997): 42–43; "The Datamation 100," *Datamation* (July 14, 1997). *Electronic Business Asia* gives data for Lien Hwa-Mitac Group, while *Datamation* gives data for Mitac alone. The two sources give different figures for Acer, with *Datamation* possibly including other Acer Group members' revenues to arrive at a larger figure of US$7 billion for both computer and total revenues; *Electronic Business Asia* figures are used in this table for Acer. No separate computer revenue data is available for GVC and Lite-on, both of which produce other electronics equipment.

computer industry and give Taiwan the deepest and broadest PC supply base in the world. They do everything from plastic molding, metal plating, and printed circuit board production, to producing resistors, capacitors, connectors, cables, and transformers. Most of these companies are located within a sixty-km radius centered between Taipei and Hsinchu.

In addition to the three groups of domestic companies, there are also a number of foreign MNCs manufacturing in Taiwan, including DEC, AST, Philips, and IBM. Foreign investment helped drive the early growth of Taiwan's PC industry, as it had in the electronics industry in general. During the 1980s, U.S. firms replaced Japanese firms as the leading source of foreign investment in Taiwan's electronics industry, a shift that helped precipitate Taiwan's move from consumer electronics to computers.[55] Foreign multinationals were an important element in Taiwan's PC industry structure, serving as conduits to international markets and bringing valuable technology with them. More important, they served as a training ground for hundreds of engineers who eventually spun off their own companies. There are more than thirty chipset makers alone in Taiwan, most of which are spin-offs from the U.S. firm, Chips & Technologies.[56] While foreign MNCs have played an important role, the majority of production and exports now comes from Taiwanese companies.

The entrepreneurial bent of the private sector is at least partly cultural, but it was nurtured by government policies since the 1950s which favored small-scale industrialization.[57] Taiwan's entrepreneurs were supported by a vast web of subcontractors, which allowed them to pursue new markets with small investments, because they could contract out much of the subcomponent production. Thus, Taiwanese producers could enter markets that were not yet well defined and where the risk of failure was high, because the cost of failure was relatively low.[58] Taiwan's competitive edge is attributed in part to the breadth and depth of its supplier base, or "lots of companies doing different things, lots of companies doing the same thing," in the words of Mitac vice-chairman C. S. Ho.[59] This enables Taiwan's firms to achieve fast turnaround and technology cycles, because the presence of many small, flexible suppliers allows quick delivery of parts necessary to achieving fast production ramp-up.

Near Taipei, there are thousands of these companies able to supply almost any component. They are willing to work weekends to meet deadlines that seem unrealistic, and they are resourceful in finding scarce parts, sometimes even from less-than-reputable sources. There is a gray market for many electronics components, some allegedly stolen, and there are reports that some companies in Taiwan are involved in "reworking" chips, for example, relabeling a 100 mHz Pentium chip as a 133 mHz chip and reselling it.

Another source of strength is the design capabilities of Taiwanese companies. As a Singaporean PC maker put it, "They can fax designs to you that afternoon. For years they have been building up design cells, so when they need a new design, they pull together the appropriate cells, make some small changes, and they have a new design."[60] As a result, Taiwanese companies can compete in fast changing markets such as motherboards and notebook computers, where time to market with the right product features is critical to success. These design capabilities are closely tied to the presence of a large pool of engineers with specialized PC skills. Coopers & Lybrand estimates that Taiwan has around 15,000 PC hardware design engineers and analysts, most of whom came of age in the PC era and are at the top of the "PC design learning curve."[61]

Most of the small producers are involved in subcontracting and supplying subcomponents to a smaller number of relatively large firms who control most of the major assembly activities (table 4-11). For instance, the top five companies accounted for more than 60% of production in desktop PCs, scanners, keyboards, mice, and switching power supplies. Unlike Korea, however, the group of top five producers is a different set for each market segment. Only a few companies, such as Acer, Tatung, and Primax, appear on more than one list.

The small companies have some important advantages over larger competitors, thanks to their flexibility and responsiveness. However, small companies are at a disadvantage as exporters, since they lack the resources to set up marketing and distribution channels in export markets. At least three factors helped the Taiwanese companies overcome that disadvantage by providing access to foreign markets. One is the presence of many Taiwanese trading companies that had the ability and willingness to explore export prospects for specialized products with niche markets. For instance, a producer of cables

TABLE 4-11. Computer Output by Taiwan's Major Producers, 1994

| | Desktop PCs | Portable PCs | Scanner (desktop) | Scanner (handheld) | Keyboard | Mouse | Switching Power Supply | Graphics Card | Monitors |
|---|---|---|---|---|---|---|---|---|---|
| Company[a] | Acer | Quanta | Microtek | Mustek | BTC | Logitech | Delta | Great Tek | Acer |
| | Tatung | Acer | Umax | Logitech | Silitek | SysGration | Dee Van | TNC | Philips |
| | FIC | Compel | Plustek | Primax | Acer | Primax | Lite-on | Prolink | ADI |
| | Mitac | Inventa | Mustek | N/A | Chicony | Chic | Skynet | BTC | Tatung |
| | DEC | Twinhead | TECO | N/A | Monterey | Kye | Prior | Compro | Lite-on |
| Top 5 Output | 2,507 | 1,082 | 480 | 962 | 14,136 | 23,644 | 21,720 | 2887 | 10,450 |
| Total Industry Output | 3,090 | 2,057 | 557 | 1,106 | 22,800 | 29,800 | 25,981 | 8748 | 24,023 |
| Top 5 Share | 81% | 53% | 86% | 87% | 62% | 79% | 84% | 33% | 44% |

*Source*: Market Intelligence Center/Institute for the Information Industry (MIC/III), "Upgrading Taiwan's IT Industry: New Challenges and the Role of International Cooperation," (Taipei: MIC/III, 1995), overhead presentation by T. C. Tu.

[a]List does not show ranking; companies are listed randomly.

could rely on trading companies to locate purchasers abroad. Another conduit to export markets was provided by the multinational computer companies that had invested in Taiwan. Taiwanese firms supplied components and became subcontractors for the MNCs, thus becoming integrated into the production and distribution chains of the MNCs. Finally, Taiwanese firms developed links to export markets through connections with overseas Chinese living in those markets.

Taiwan's computer industry developed into almost an extension of Silicon Valley. The U.S. multinationals in Taiwan served as the initial core of an industry structure that was deeply enmeshed into the global PC production chain. Eventually, some Taiwanese firms grew into being major producers in their own right and developed their own production chains both in Taiwan and offshore. Most still rely on OEM sales for much of their international distribution, however.

The initial strengths of the Taiwanese companies were their sharp ear for market opportunities and their ability to respond rapidly to those opportunities. These skills enabled them to succeed in unstable markets in which product generations are measured in months. It also enabled them to share in the higher profit margins associated with new product introductions and to withstand later price competition. Over time, they also developed strong design capabilities and improved their manufacturing skills. It was crucial that the smaller companies focused on integrating into the global PC production chain in niche markets where their flexibility gave them a competitive edge. Only the larger firms entered into high-volume, more sophisticated products such as monitors, scanners, and notebook computers. The Taiwanese industry caught the growth wave of the PC market and avoided direct competition with foreign industry leaders, except in cases in which they had developed sufficient experience and technological capabilities.

A pattern of consolidation appears to be taking place in Taiwan's computer industry. The PC industry has evolved to a point where economies of scale are more vital to success. Only large producers can get volume discounts on components or offer the scale of production necessary to handle major OEM accounts. In the words of one analyst, companies need to be "big enough or small enough" to survive. Big companies are able to tap the formal financial markets for capital, while small companies can use family money and focus on niche markets. The companies hurt most by the consolidation are medium-sized firms that lack the size to compete in volume markets but are too big to survive on small, irregular orders.

### Industrial Policy

The driving force behind Taiwan's computer industry strategy was K. T. Li, a former Minister of Finance and Minister of Economic Affairs who mobilized the government to support the computer and semiconductor industries in the late 1970s. As Minister of State, Li used his influence at the highest levels of government to initiate a number of government programs that were critical to Taiwan's move into advanced electronics production.

Li created a formal advisory group of about fifteen people, mostly foreigners, who advise the government on electronics policy. These include executives from IBM, AT&T, and various other leading MNCs. Taiwan's policies have thus focused on finding opportunities in international markets and developing the capabilities necessary to exploit those opportunities.

Taiwan's strategy involved a large role for government, but it was much different from those of Japan and Korea. Without large private sector groups like the *keiretsu* and *chaebol* available to carry out its computer strategies, the government had to rely primarily on MNCs and many small-and medium-sized enterprises that were already active in consumer electronics and components.

Initially, however, the SMEs lacked technological capabilities, capital and human resources, and marketing abilities to move into international PC markets. The government targeted its computer industry policies at overcoming those deficiencies through financial subsidies, initiatives to upgrade Taiwan's technological capabilities and human resources, and provision of market intelligence services. More recent policies have promoted computer use to create domestic demand for software and information services. Finally, the government has tried to reduce Taiwan's dependence on Japanese semiconductors and LCDs by encouraging domestic production.

*Industry and Technology Promotion.* The government has provided subsidies to compensate for the problems faced by SMEs in raising capital beyond their own family resources. The government provided grants and low-interest loans to support investments in product design, process technology, quality improvement, automation, and personnel training. Finance was provided to electronics and computer industries by the Bank of Communications through five-to seven-year loans at an interest rate 2.5% lower than the commercial rate. In addition, a manufacturer could apply to the Bank for equity investment up to 25% of its paid-up capital. The Small Business Bank made short-term, low-interest loans for investments in computers and development of computer-related products. Such direct subsidies were supplemented by business tax exemptions, accelerated depreciation of fixed assets, and deductions for investments in R&D, machinery, and equipment.[62] Government officials also have negotiated with foreign suppliers of components, such as DRAMs, on behalf of groups of companies to gain better terms than what they could get on their own.

The government also has taken a number of steps to upgrade Taiwan's technological capabilities. In addition to promoting R&D by the private sector through tax incentives, it financed R&D in semiconductors, computer hardware, and software at public research institutions. The technologies developed in these centers have been transferred to private sector companies for commercialization. These institutions include the Industrial Technology Research Institute (ITRI), and its subsidiaries, the Electronics Research and Services

Organization (ERSO) and the Computer and Communication Research Laboratory (CCL). ERSO conducted R&D in semiconductors and computer hardware, and in some cases it created spin-off companies run by its own engineers to commercialize the technology. CCL conducted research in communications and computer hardware. The Institute for Information Industries (III) trained computer professionals and carried out software development and systems integration for government agencies.

One key to Taiwan's success in the IBM-compatible PC market was ERSO's reverse engineering of the IBM BIOS, which allowed local companies to avoid paying licensing fees to IBM. IBM threatened to sue ERSO for patent infringement, but after losing a similar case against Phoenix Technologies in the United States, IBM decided not to take action against ERSO.

In 1980, the Industrial Development Board of the Ministry of Economic Affairs (MOEA) began building the Hsinchu Science-based Industrial Park as a center for high-tech companies and R&D facilities. The park is modeled on Silicon Valley and achieves similar opportunities for close interaction among researchers and manufacturers. The government relocated the research labs of ERSO and other institutions to Hsinchu to facilitate technology transfer. Plans are underway to expand Hsinchu and to develop other technology-based parks.

The government also has promoted collaboration between the public and private sectors to develop and commercialize technology. One of these was a heavily criticized notebook computer consortium consisting of forty companies, many of whom went out of business during the market downturn of the early 1990s. Critics argued that too many companies were invited to develop products based on a common platform, and it was inevitable that many would fail. Still, the survivors have helped make Taiwan a leading producer of notebook PCs.

Another Taiwanese strategy has been the strengthening of ties to international sources of capital and technology. Foreign investors are attracted to Taiwan through various incentives, and incentives are offered to Taiwanese engineers in the United States to return and start businesses in Hsinchu. The government has promoted alliances with multinational corporations to gain access to technology and markets. An early example was the establishment of Neotech Development Corporation (NDC) in 1983 by III and IBM to provide software development services to IBM. ERSO has also cooperated with IBM and Motorola in a PowerPC consortium, with participation from most of Taiwan's leading PC makers. Taiwan's Umax was one of the first companies to produce PowerPC computers based on the Macintosh operating system.

ITRI has come under criticism from the legislature for its supposed lack of commercial orientation. At the same time, it has been criticized by the private sector for being too commercially oriented and competing directly with private companies. ITRI's response has been to develop more projects with private sector partnership from the beginning.

*Developing Human Resources.* Taiwan's electronics sector is supported by a large supply of technical talent available on the island. Taiwan had more than 170,000 people with scientific and technical degrees in 1992, compared to just 9,200 for Singapore and 1,400 for Hong Kong. The government has provided subsidies to the private sector for personnel training and has offered training of computer professionals through III. Taiwan's universities also have trained thousands of engineers, giving the country a large supply of relatively low-cost, skilled engineers.

In addition, both the government and private companies have taken advantage of the large number of Taiwanese who have migrated to the United States to study and work. They have lured executives as well as lower level engineers back to Taiwan by offering opportunities to head up new companies, either immediately or after helping an established company develop a new technology or move into a new market. One key returnee to Taiwan was Morris Chang, former Vice-President of Texas Instruments and President of General Instrument, who left GI to become director of ITRI and later chairman of Taiwan Semiconductor Manufacturing Corporation (TSMC). Hundreds of other engineers and executives with experience in leading U.S. corporations have returned to Taiwan or have left positions with U.S. companies in Taiwan to work for Taiwanese companies. Taiwanese companies also hire engineers from U.S. companies to moonlight for them on R&D projects. Two major sources of talent for ITRI in particular have been AT&T's Bell Labs and IBM's research labs, both of which laid off thousands of researchers in the 1990s.

*Market Intelligence.* Information on overseas markets is gathered and distributed to the private sector by III's Market Intelligence Center (MIC). MIC has a staff of ninety people, including sixty professionals, making it the largest market researcher in the Asia-Pacific region. It receives 70% of its funding from the government and 30% from industry, mainly through running seminars and providing consulting services. These services include business plan development, market research, and training companies to do their own market research. MIC also publishes *Asia IT Report* monthly and the *Annual Monitor Industry Report*, and every month it puts out special reports on the Asia-Pacific market, telecommunications, hardware, software, and legal issues. In 1996, 233 companies were members of MIC, paying an annual fee to receive MIC's publications and attend its seminars.

MIC plays a vital role in supplying information to the many SMEs in the IT industry. Larger companies often buy market information from companies such as Dataquest and IDC. However, this information is expensive and tends to concentrate on larger markets and producers. MIC responds to inquiries from Taiwanese companies, often about smaller market segments not covered by the big research firms. As one MIC official told the authors, "IDC and Dataquest usually report market information about the top nine companies and then 'all others.' We focus on 'all others.' Also, we focus on specific industry segments like monitors or motherboards and on the short- to mid-term (one to two years) rather than the long term. We respond to questions that industry needs answers to now."

*Software, Services, and Computer Use.*    While earlier policies focused on promoting the hardware industry, officials have come to realize the importance of software, services, and computer use, and to address Taiwan's weaknesses in those areas. The Industrial Development Board gave III responsibility in 1993 to implement a five-year development plan for the software industry. The plan, called the New Product Development Grant Program, was funded starting at the end of 1994 as part of the government's broader Leading Product Development Grant program (LPDG). The LPDG provides grants for leading technologies in a number of sectors, but most of Taiwan's software companies were too small to qualify for the LPDG program, which requires revenues of NTD 200 million to be eligible. The qualifications were lowered for the software industry and about fifteen companies received grants in 1995.

The program initially focused on export products, mainly for the U.S. market. Although the mainland China market would appear to be a natural target, the prevalence of pirating there dimmed the prospects of success. The III officials in charge of the program originally thought that the industry needed technical help, but they discovered over time that the biggest need was for business support. This is being provided in several forms. One is market intelligence, where III is working with Arthur D. Little and Dataquest to project world market trends for software. Another is matchmaking. III has introduced local companies to foreign software firms and distributors; they have also hooked up software developers with hardware companies or other distribution channels. They have linked venture capitalists from the United States with local companies and helped local hardware companies that were looking to invest in software. Another role is in product definition, that is, helping software companies identify market opportunities and improve their product development processes.

In addition to helping companies export, the government also commissioned software companies to develop generic applications for about forty local industries such as laundries, bicycle shops, and restaurants. The development of such applications is designed to help small businesses computerize but avoid the costs of creating custom applications. It also provides software companies with a subsidy for writing applications that they can commercialize and eventually export to Chinese-owned businesses around the world. So far, most of the products developed with government help have not been commercial successes, and they have failed to generate sufficient revenues to go beyond the first generation of the product.

To promote small business computerization further, in 1991 the Ministry of Economic Affairs appointed information systems experts to conduct diagnoses of information systems needs at 196 small firms and provide consulting to those asking for assistance. The government offered a 50% subsidy for expenses under US$6,000 and made low-interest loans available for small firms to buy hardware and software.[63]

*Government Computerization.*   Government historically has been the leading user of computers in Taiwan. Other sectors are making up ground, however, and the public sector's share of the market dropped from 38% in 1985 to just 26% in 1992. Government computerization has been promoted through development of a network of administrative information systems, which helped drive a doubling of public sector IT spending from 1985 to 1992.

In the past, III has been accused of monopolizing too much of the software development for government projects. In order to increase the opportunities for the private sector, the government has asked III not to bid for government projects as part of III's funding requirement since 1994. However, local systems integrators and other service providers still claim that III keeps the most lucrative parts of government contracts for itself, and that they "dish out the high risk business that's not worth doing (actual software development)." In competition for a complete systems development project, the private sector finds it difficult to compete with III because government agencies are protected if they choose III.

In 1996, in an effort to improve the quality of information services and help the private sector bid on government contracts, III set up an outsourcing office to act as a consultant for both government and the private sector. It also started to evaluate the quality and credit of companies making bids rather than just taking the lowest bid.

*Developing Upstream Technologies.*   As Taiwan's computer industry grew, it was heavily dependent on imported semiconductors, cathode ray tubes (CRTs) for monitors, and flat-panel displays. During times of supply shortages, Taiwan's computer makers faced rationing of DRAMs and were forced to limit production. Also, Taiwan's smaller PC makers apparently must pay an average of 12% higher prices for DRAMs than their larger competitors. Taiwan's world leadership in motherboard production increased its dependence on imported chips. The government has responded with initiatives to promote domestic DRAM production.

The Taiwanese government actually has been promoting semiconductor technologies since the 1970s. In 1977, ITRI contracted with RCA for technology transfer in integrated circuit design. In 1979, ERSO set up a private company called United Microelectronics Company (UMC) to develop commercial products based on ERSO's own research. UMC was staffed by ERSO engineers, but operated as a for-profit company producing chips for consumer electronics products. In 1983, ERSO began developing very large-scale integrated circuit (VLSI) technology in conjunction with a Silicon Valley company, Vitelic, that had been formed by overseas Chinese that year. During the 1980s, Taiwan's semiconductor industry consisted mostly of design and specialized production for niche markets, rather than large-scale production of commodity products such as DRAMs.

This strategy would change, however. There are inherent problems involved in trying to be a company that designs chips but does not produce them. Companies that do both have an advantage in integrating the design and production processes, with design engineers receiving valuable feedback from production engineers. Also, designers of chips that depend on outside silicon foundries can be squeezed when there is a shortage of manufacturing capacity. Therefore, reliance on external facilities can be a risky strategy.[64]

In response to these concerns, as well as the predicament faced by the computer industry's dependence on foreign semiconductors, the government began to encourage domestic investment in semiconductor manufacturing. The government negotiated an agreement with Philips to establish the Taiwan Semiconductor Manufacturing Corporation (TSMC) in 1985. The government put up 48% of the capital, Philips gave 27.5%, and private investors the rest. TSMC began producing wafers at ERSO's plant then built its own facilities to produce six-inch wafers. UMC likewise built its own wafer fabrication facility (fab). In the mid-1990s, there was a flurry of investments in new wafer fabs for the purpose of undertaking DRAM production. These included:

- TI-Acer, using Texas Instruments' technology;
- Mosel-Vitelic, a subsidiary of the U.S. company Vitelic using technology from the Japanese firm Oki;
- Nan Ya Plastics, a private firm also using technology from Oki;
- Vanguard, a subsidiary of TSMC created when TSMC took over ITRI's submicron laboratory in 1995;
- Formosa Plastics, a large petrochemical conglomerate, using technology from Toshiba and Siemens; and
- Umax, a private company known for making computer scanners, using technology from Mitsubishi.

In 1994 and 1995, as DRAM prices remained high due to global supply shortages, plans for wafer fabs were announced by a number of other companies, some of whom had no experience at all in semiconductors. These companies saw TSMC, UMC, and TI-Acer making fat profits in memory chips and wanted a piece of the action. By 1996, however, DRAM prices were plummeting and many of these plans were in doubt. Shortages of water and electricity further complicated the situation, and rather than continue expanding in Taiwan, TSMC announced plans for a US$1 billion facility in Oregon.

*Policy Coordination.* The ability of the Taiwanese government to play a positive role in the industry's development is closely related to its ability to coordinate policies across a wide range of issues, including R&D, training, industry promotion, and market intelligence. K. T. Li's strong leadership was instrumental in establishing Taiwan's computer policies and helped institutionalize support for the industry at the highest levels of government. Taiwan's government has consolidated most policies for computer production and use under the Ministry of Economic Affairs and its affiliated institutions (primarily the Industrial Development Bureau, III, and ITRI). This is not to say that there are no complaints about Taiwan's policy institutions. The private sector has complained about competition from both ITRI and III, claiming that ITRI subsidizes research that is then spun-off into commercial products by its own engineers, and that III competes unfairly for government services contracts. But Taiwan has been able to avoid the bureaucratic competition that has marked Japan and Korea, and it has usually worked with and through the private sector to make and implement policy. The government also has tapped the knowledge of overseas Taiwanese and foreigners to guide its policymaking, thus avoiding the insularity that sometimes afflicts Japan and Korea.

*Comments on Industrial Policy.*   Taiwan's government has played a critical function in supporting the computer industry, by developing technology, providing market intelligence, and training engineers and computer professionals. Its role has been to fill the gaps in the capabilities of the private sector, while letting the private sector make its own investment and production decisions. This approach has been effective in tapping the energy of Taiwan's entrepreneurs rather than trying to direct the industry from above.

As Taiwan's computer industry continues to grow and diversify, the need for direct government support and promotion will decrease. Already, the focus of policy is shifting to development of the national information infrastructure (NII) and promotion of computer use, linked to efforts to promote the software industry.

The biggest policy issue affecting Taiwan's computer industry in the future will not directly involve industrial policy, however. Instead, it will involve Taiwan's relations with mainland China. Already a large amount of production has moved from Taiwan to China, which offers both cheap labor and engineering talent for Taiwanese companies. More important is the China market, which is the most likely large growth market for Taiwan's computer makers in the future. If political relations improve so that direct trade and investment are permitted, Taiwan would be in a great position to take advantage of the China market. But if relations deteriorate, the consequences for Taiwan's computer industry would be serious.

## Personal Networks: Linking Policy, Structure, and the Global Market

In every country, business decisions and government policies are propelled by forces that are not visible in any annual report or government white paper. Japan's "old boy" networks of former university classmates meet in bars and on golf courses and make decisions that affect both government and business strategies. Korea's *chaebol* have operated more as family dynasties than as modern corporations, and new business ventures are usually headed up by family members rather than outsiders.

Taiwan's thriving computer industry is clearly a function of an appropriate industry structure and shrewd policy choices. But underlying both business and government strategy are less visible personal and business relationships, referred to as *guanxi*, along with a strong sense of nationalism mixed with a pragmatic sense of self interest. Business and policy decision-makers not only take these factors into account, but also depend on them to make their strategies work.

Relationships in Taiwan are organized in concentric circles, in which the inner circle is the immediate family, the next circle is the extended family, the next is classmates, and the next is graduates of the same school. Outside all of that is the company and its customers. Taiwan's fast turnaround time on new products is partly due to these relationships, where an engineer can call his former classmate at midnight to solve a technical problem. Taiwanese companies do business on the basis of these personal relationships rather than on the legalistic, contractual basis favored by most American companies. The U.S. companies that have most successfully tapped the Taiwanese production network, such as Dell, Gateway 2000, and Packard Bell, operate like Taiwanese companies. Their presidents come to Taiwan and meet directly with the presidents of their Taiwanese partners, rather than sending their lieutenants. Some foreign MNCs have tried to operate outside the relationship network and had serious problems.

Personal relationships, combined with nationalism and the entrepreneurial bug, help explain the return of Taiwanese expatriates from the United States to work in Taiwan. The authors heard a number of anecdotes about people working in the United States who were lured back to Taiwan to work in a Taiwanese company, with the promise being held out that if things worked out, the returning national would be set up in his own business in a few years. For instance, an engineer who had worked for fifteen years at Hewlett Packard specializing in computer networks was invited back to give seminars at a major Taiwanese company and some of its customers. After two years he was offered a salaried position to set up the company's networks and help restructure the company's organization to take advantage of the new information systems. After working for a year on a trial basis, his boss told him he would set up a new company for him to run after the parent company's networks were stabilized. This new company could sell network development services to other companies. The implied agreement behind such relationships is, "You do a good job for me, and later I'll help you set up your own business." Overseas Taiwanese are also lured back to Taiwan by a sense of nationalism, often returning to work for smaller salaries than they were making in the United States.[65]

Even those Taiwanese who are working in the United States are a valuable source of information. Some of them have been hired to moonlight for Taiwanese firms developing new products. Others work for U.S. companies but are said to provide information to Taiwan on the direction of leading companies or particular technologies. One Taiwanese executive referred to overseas Taiwanese as "human resources on deposit," and said that in a day or two he can get most information he needs from Taiwanese working in U.S. companies. He also said that Taiwanese from around the world hold their annual class reunions at the Comdex computer trade show in Las Vegas, maintaining personal connections that span the Pacific and the globe.

Taiwanese workers are footloose, moving between companies or starting their own companies much more readily than their counterparts in Japan and Korea. This flow of people helps diffuse technology and energizes the industry in a manner reminiscent of Silicon Valley. Companies, particularly MNCs, risk leakage of their own technology in this environment, but they also benefit from the increasing capabilities of their partners and suppliers.

Taiwan's business culture is also similar to that of Silicon Valley in the ability of entrepreneurs to fail once or twice and still bounce back with a new idea or get a job with an established company. In the United States, venture capitalists actually consider a previous failure to be a plus. The previous attempt is considered to be a valuable learning experience, and the fact that the entrepreneur has bounced back with a new venture is considered evidence of having the true spirit and energy needed to succeed. By contrast, in Japan a failed entrepreneur is stigmatized by the failure, and it is considered almost crazy to leave a large company and start a new venture.

Another side of the personal connection equation is the importance of successful entrepreneurs as role models to attract young people into the PC industry. No other industry in Taiwan has created so many millionaires, and many of them are relatively young. While some veterans fear that Taiwan is losing some of its drive as more people get rich, those success stories provide the impetus for a great deal of the entrepreneurial energy in the industry. Salaried computer professionals actually earn considerably lower salaries than their counterparts in other countries,[66] but the possibility of starting the next Acer or Mitac lures thousands into technical fields every year.

Government research institutes such as ITRI and ERSO capitalize on the entrepreneurial bent of Taiwanese engineers and scientists by allowing them to commercialize technologies they develop in the government labs. The most famous ITRI spin-offs are semiconductor companies UMC and TSMC (and its subsidiary, Vanguard), but dozens of companies have been started over the years by ITRI engineers, including many computer hardware companies and a few software companies.

ITRI has also tapped the overseas Taiwanese community for high-level scientific and managerial talent. The best known is Morris Chang, but there have been others who have left leading U.S. firms such as IBM and AT&T to take senior positions at ITRI. These people bring not only technology or "know how," but also market knowledge or "know what" (i.e., what to invest in) to the government labs.

Both the government and private sector keep close tabs on the overseas Chinese community. A government agency under the Executive Yuan has kept a database of Taiwanese working in U.S. companies, although there has been debate about closing the office. A private organization called Jade Mountain run by Taiwanese-Americans holds events in U.S. cities in which Taiwanese companies make presentations and recruit people. Government policy and business strategy count on personal connections as an asset and take steps to nurture and capitalize on those assets. This is not unique to Taiwan. Korean companies hire Korean engineers in California and encourage them to return to Korea; the governments of India and Vietnam have tried to tap their overseas "human resources on deposit" in the United States as well. But no one has done this as effectively as Taiwan, nor has anyone else created such a favorable environment for entrepreneurial activity as has Taiwan. The ability to take advantage of its cultural idiosyncrasies is a critical factor in the success of Taiwan's business and government strategies for computers, and the network of personal connections can be seen as the "invisible hand" behind Taiwan's computer industry.

### Conclusions

Taiwan's success in computer production can be explained primarily as a result of private sector initiative supported by government efforts to develop capabilities and resources lacking in Taiwan's SME-dominated industry structure. Taiwan also was fortunate that the PC revolution created an international industry structure that lowered entry barriers to the computer industry and presented opportunities for small players to participate in the industry's global production system. Conversely, U.S. companies were fortunate to find such a source of low-cost suppliers, allowing them to avoid the dependence on Japanese suppliers that had been so costly to the consumer electronics industry. This convergence of interests has been generally beneficial to both the United States and Taiwan, although there have been winners and losers at the company level.

One key to Taiwan's success has been an industry structure consisting of a large number of highly focused companies that together make up a broad and deep industry cluster for the PC industry. Those companies not only move quickly on their own, but the network structure of industrial relations also allows for rapid coordination among companies to respond to new market opportunities. Another key success factor has been the breadth and dynamism of Taiwan's global linkages. Access to information, technology, and overseas markets through the web of personal, company, and multinational connections has given Taiwan a tremendous advantage in the PC industry. Finally, the role of government industrial policy in stimulating and coordinating private sector efforts has been vital to Taiwan's success.

Ultimately, both business and government strategy have depended on the web of personal relationships that make it much easier for companies to work together and with government than is the case in most countries. The fact that these connections extend far beyond the borders of the small island of Taiwan is especially important in helping Taiwan integrate into the global PC production network and avoid the isolation that has plagued the Japanese and Korean PC industries.

Taiwan's ability to compete in computers has been exceptional at both the company and country level, but like the other Asian NIEs, the country faces continuing challenges as it tries to sustain its momentum in the industry. The shift of labor-intensive production offshore has helped Taiwanese companies stay competitive in the most cost sensitive market segments, such as keyboards, motherboards, and various peripherals. But in order to sustain growth and profitability, those companies need to develop the capabilities to compete in both the technology-intensive and market-oriented segments of the industry. Likewise, Taiwan needs to develop those capabilities to replace the production that is moving offshore.

Success in technology-intensive businesses such as semiconductors and flat-panel displays will require developing stronger technological capabilities rather than just depending on technology developed elsewhere. This is a challenge for both the private sector and government research institutes. Companies must also continue to add value in their core OEM businesses by innovating in distribution, logistics, and service, and perhaps to follow the examples of Acer, Umax, and a few others to develop stronger brand names. Finally, both the private and public sectors need to put much greater emphasis on computer use and on production close to use, in the form of software and services. There is great potential for developing software and services for the Greater China market (including the mainland, Hong Kong, and other Chinese-speaking populations), but Taiwan's low levels of use and its strong hardware emphasis are a major barrier to tapping that potential. Capitalizing on these increasing returns opportunities will require a fundamental shift in orientation to realize the value and potential of software and services, and the importance of computer use.

# Asia's New Competitors

## Singapore and Hong Kong

The city-states of Singapore and Hong Kong are extraordinary economic success stories and highly competitive rivals. The two have long been the leading
trading centers in the region and more recently have developed strong export-
oriented manufacturing sectors. These two competitors could hardly be more
different, however, in economic and social ideology. Since gaining independ-
ence in 1965, Singapore has pursued a state-guided economic strategy with
large state-owned enterprises controlling key sectors such as housing, petroleum refining, and the national airline. It has also pursued a paternalistic (or
in Singaporean parlance, "communitarian") social policy that has created a
clean, safe environment for foreign investors while cobbling together a common identity in a multicultural society. Hong Kong, by contrast, has a strong
belief in laissez faire economics and an abhorrence for government intervention in the economy.[1] Singapore's careful censorship and constant campaigns
to promote cleanliness and courtesy likewise contrast with Hong Kong's more
open, free-wheeling environment.

The competition between Singapore and Hong Kong has been the subject
of a good deal of academic debate over the merits of their different economic
models. The two are in competition for foreign investment and commerce,
with each hoping to be the key hubs for transport, telecommunications, and
finance in Southeast Asia. Hong Kong's position as the gateway to China
remains a source of competitive advantage, but Singapore's government has
been more aggressive in courting multinationals, especially in manufacturing.
There are probably few industries that better illustrate the contrasts between
the Singapore and Hong Kong economic models than the computer industry.

## Singapore

One of Singapore's most impressive economic achievements has been the creation of a large computer industry virtually from scratch in less than fifteen

years. When the government first targeted information technology as a strategic industry in 1981, Singapore had almost no computer production[2] and was far removed from the key technology and market centers of the world's computer industry. By 1995, total hardware production topped US$19 billion and most of the leading multinationals in the computer industry had set up shop in Singapore, doing manufacturing, design, marketing, and logistics. Companies such as Compaq, Seagate, Hewlett-Packard, Apple, and Western Digital now use Singapore as the hub of a production network that spans Southeast Asia and is linked to the global distribution systems of these companies. The MNCs were followed to Singapore by many of their American and Japanese suppliers, who were joined by local companies to create an extensive industry cluster supporting the computer industry. Singapore leads the world in production of hard disk drives, earning it the name "Winchester Island" after a popular name for such drives. It is also a large producer of PCs, printers, and other peripherals, and it is investing heavily in semiconductor production.

Unlike the other East Asian countries, Singapore has put as much emphasis on computer use as on production. Singapore invests a higher percentage of its GDP on computers than any of the other NIEs. This investment in computer use, along with the creation of a superb telecommunications network, created a high quality, low-cost information infrastructure that is a strong attraction to companies investing in Singapore. It has also provided the basis for a new strategy of promoting Singapore as a regional hub for information services, entertainment, multimedia and finance.

None of this has come about by chance or through pure market forces. The growth of the industry has been guided by carefully coordinated policies to promote computer production and use. Unlike Japan, Korea, and Taiwan, Singapore relied mainly on foreign multinationals, rather than domestic companies, to make the necessary investments and develop the industry. Singapore's Economic Development Board persuaded major computer makers to locate in Singapore and coordinated the effort to improve the country's technical capabilities and infrastructure. Given the potential risks of government-led industrial targeting, it is interesting and enlightening to look more closely at how Singapore's government was able to turn the island into a hub in the global production network.

## History of Singapore's Computer Industry

Singapore's electronics industry employed 120,000 people and accounted for about 10% of GDP in 1995. Of that amount, a little over half is accounted for by computers, disk drives, and peripherals. Yet the electronics industry in Singapore is less than thirty years old, and the computer industry half of that. The history of computer production in Singapore can best be understood by tracing the investment decisions of MNCs who have located there over the years.

The first electronics production in Singapore began in the late 1960s when U.S. semiconductor companies such as National Semiconductor, Fairchild, and Texas Instruments began assembling simple chips. At this time, Singapore was one of the few developing countries offering cheap labor, incentives for foreign investors, and a stable business environment. While most countries in the region restricted trade and foreign investment in an effort to nurture domestic manufacturers, Singapore was encouraging foreign investment and building the necessary infrastructure to support an export-oriented manufacturing base.

From the beginning, the Singapore electronics industry was producing for world markets, and Singapore began to gain experience in producing to world class standards. In the 1970s, a number of consumer electronics makers came to Singapore to take advantage of its experience and low costs to make television sets, radios, and audio equipment. These companies included major MNCs such as General Electric, Matsushita, Philips, and Thomson.

The growth of consumer electronics production created demand for parts and components, and local suppliers began producing metal and plastic parts, packaging materials, and electrical parts for the MNCs. During this time, the Singapore government began to train workers in precision engineering and electrical technology in cooperation with MNCs. The Singapore Economic Development Board (EDB) set up joint training institutes with Philips, Tata, and Brown Boveri.[3]

Singapore began targeting computer production in the early 1980s at the same time U.S. computer companies began to look abroad for less expensive places to manufacture. The first place where these forces meshed was in the disk drive industry. The first company to come to Singapore was Tandon, which began producing floppy disk drives in the late 1970s. Tandon was joined in 1979 by Magnetic Memories International (MMI), which produced hard disk drives for a year then closed down. Tandon and MMI helped create supporting industries for the hard drive industry, including precision metalworking and mechanical components. The real take-off point for Singapore's disk drive industry came when an upstart called Seagate Technology decided to come to Singapore. Seagate's rise to become the world's largest disk drive maker was paralleled by Singapore's growth into a world center for disk drive production.

*Seagate Technology and Singapore's Disk Drive Industry.*   The key event in the creation of Winchester Island was Seagate's choice of Singapore as its main manufacturing location in 1982. Seagate needed to expand production after just a year of operation to keep up with rapid demand growth. David T. "Tom" Mitchell, one of Seagate's cofounders, had run plants in Singapore, Hong Kong, Seoul, and Jakarta while he was with Fairchild Semiconductor in the 1970s. During a two-week period when Seagate's U.S. plant was shut down, he visited Hong Kong and Singapore to select a production site. While Hong Kong offered the usual laissez faire attitude toward new investment, Singapore's Economic Development Board put on a full court press to bring Seagate to Singapore.[4]

The EDB helped Mitchell with every step of setting up a facility. They took him to meet with other companies who were doing mechanical assembly in Singapore, gave him an assistant to help type up a business plan, and hooked him up with a search firm to locate and interview managers. The government also gave Seagate a ten-year tax holiday and made factory space available in the Jurong Industrial Estate. In less than two weeks, Mitchell left his new management team to start operations and returned to California. In the case of Seagate, the initiative taken by the Singapore government clearly made a big difference in the location decision.[5]

Seagate's investment set into motion a virtuous cycle, as suppliers of components and subassemblies set up production in Singapore, improving the local supply infrastructure and attracting further investment by other disk drive makers. Seagate was followed to Singapore by Miniscribe, Maxtor, Micropolis, Rodime, Conner, Control Data, and Western Digital between 1983 and 1989. In the mid-1990s, IBM's Storage Systems Division started production in a new plant in Singapore, and about ten more disk drive components manufacturers moved to Singapore.[6] Since 1982, Seagate has continued to invest in Singapore, and now has six facilities there (including facilities that came with Seagate's purchase of Conner), which assemble 5.25 inch, 3.5 inch and 2.5 inch disk drives and produce printed circuit boards (PCBs) and disk media. In 1997, Seagate opened a new 1,000,000 square foot facility in Singapore called Seagate City, with plans to consolidate much of its Singapore production in that plant.[7]

Interestingly, Japan's disk drive manufacturers chose to keep their production at home, in spite of EDB efforts to attract them. Scott Callon quotes an EDB official as saying, "We tried very hard of course. But the Japanese believed that the complexity of the drives were such that Singapore wasn't good enough. They thought they should do it in Japan, what with the clean rooms and the precision requirements. They finally went offshore very late in the game, in 1988–1989. They went to Thailand, where Seagate had already gone in 1987."[8] This is a telling case of the Japanese companies' slowness to take advantage of the capabilities of the Asian production network that the U.S. companies had helped create and were tapping so effectively.

As the MNCs increased their production, Singapore gained experience and valuable knowledge of the complex processes involved in disk drive manufacturing. Meanwhile, the government trained thousands of engineers and computer professionals and initiated joint research projects with various MNCs. These capabilities enabled the MNCs to conduct higher value added activities in Singapore. The U.S. disk drive makers can design and develop prototypes of new generation drives in the United States, then ramp-up full scale production of new product generations in Singapore. Singapore serves as an "engineering transfer station,"[9] responsible for the process engineering to start-up and optimize the production process for new product lines and transfer older generations to other locations in the region. This process requires strong engineering and manufacturing capabilities, because timing is essential to hitting the "sweet spot" in the market with ever larger capacity drives. Once the production process is stabilized, it is often moved to a factory in Thailand or Malaysia (and, increasingly, China) and a new generation is ramped-up in Singapore.

*Apple Computer and Singapore's PC Industry.*    A similar process of MNC investment, local supplier development, and technological upgrading can be seen in PCs, as illustrated by the experience of Apple Computer in Singapore. Apple first came to Singapore in 1981 and produced PCBs for its Apple II product line for the next four years, outsourcing assembly to a number of Singaporean companies. In 1985, Apple began doing final assembly of the Apple II in Singapore. Over the next few years, the company expanded its operations in Singapore and began designing some components there. In 1990, it began final assembly for two new Macintosh systems, as well as designing and manufacturing monitors for those models. Apple Singapore was able to move from design to production roll-out in about half the time of Apple's other facilities. By 1992, Apple Singapore had taken responsibility for final assembly for all Asia-Pacific markets and was designing and producing boards, monitors, and peripherals for the global market.[10]

In 1993, Apple set up a hardware design center in Singapore, its first such center outside the United States. The Apple Design Center designs products for the global market, as well as products and solutions specifically for Asian markets. Singapore is now part of Apple's "follow the sun" design process, in which engineers in California, Ireland, and Singapore work together taking advantage of the differences in time zones to work continuously and speed the design process. Singapore's telecommunications infrastructure is critical to that strategy, because huge engineering files must be sent and received for the process to work.

By 1995, Apple was sourcing about US$2 billion from the Asian region (about 20% of Apple's revenues that year). About US$450 million was from Singapore, with much of that coming from other MNCs such as Texas Instruments (DRAMs) and the various disk drive makers. Only plastic moldings, packaging, and PCB assembly are done by Singaporean companies. Motherboards are made both at the Apple Singapore factory and by subcontractors in Taiwan. Notebook and desktop PCs as well as monitors are made in the Singapore plant. Apple's strategy has been to make higher end models in its own plants and outsource lower end models to OEMs in Taiwan and elsewhere.[11]

Similar stories could be told in different segments of the computer industry for Compaq, Hewlett-Packard, AT&T, IBM, and DEC. Likewise in semiconductors for Motorola, Texas Instruments, SGS-Thomson, Siemens, and National Semiconductor. The underlying theme of each of these cases is the steady upgrading of local activities by MNCs, with associated growth in the capabilities of local suppliers.

*Industry Performance.*    The growth of Singapore's computer industry has been sensational, with output soaring from US$1.2 billion in 1985 to more than US$19 billion in 1995 (figure 5-1).[12] The computer industry accounts directly for more than 40% of Singapore's electronics output, and indirectly for considerably more, because most of the electronics components produced there go into computer hardware.

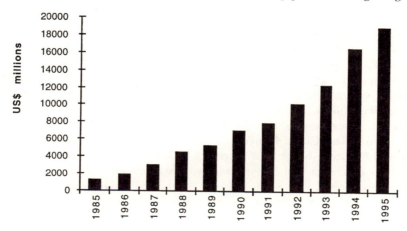

FIGURE 5-1. Computer Hardware Production in Singapore, 1985–1995. *Source:* Reed, *Yearbook of World Electronics Data*, Surrey, UK: Reed Electronics research, 1991–1997. Annual yearbooks and electronic data.

In spite of a small domestic market, Singapore's software and services industries have also grown quickly, to reach about US$1.18 billion dollars in 1995. Heavy public and private investment in computerization has created opportunities for the local industry, especially in vertical business applications such as banking and shipping.[13] Still, Singapore's computer industry is heavily weighted toward hardware, and it has been dominated by foreign multinationals, although there are a few exceptions, particularly in the sound card business.

*The Sound Card Business: An Exception to MNC-Led Growth.* A major exception to MNC dominance in Singapore's computer industry has been the success of Creative Technologies and Aztech Systems in sound cards. Creative's Sound Blaster brand is so well known in the U.S. market that its name is almost synonymous with sound cards. The two local companies controlled 75% of the market in 1994, with Creative Technologies leading the world at 60%. Both companies have been expanding their product lines to include a broader range of multimedia hardware and software.

Creative's rise to the top is especially striking, a true homespun Singaporean success story in a country where foreign MNCs generally rule the computer industry.[14] Creative was started in 1981 by two childhood friends, Sim Wong Hoo and Ng Kai Wa, whose common interest was music and who led a harmonica troupe while attending Singapore's Ngee Ann Polytechnic. The two were joined in 1986 by their university classmate Chay Kwong Soon. Creative started out producing add-on cards for Apple II computers and doing other odd jobs such as training and servicing. Eventually, Creative developed a clone of the Apple II that did not infringe on Apple's patents and copyrights, and which could even "talk" in Chinese.

As the Apple II line was overwhelmed by the IBM-PC in the mid-1980s, Creative launched a new product called the Cubic CT, a multimedia computer with enhanced color graphics, built-in audio board, and a built-in Chinese operating system and fonts. Unfortunately, the PC market was not ready for multimedia, mainly due to a lack of software applications. Creative tried to get local teachers to develop educational software for the Cubic, but they got no response. The Cubic turned out to be a commercial failure and almost destroyed Creative, which had spent $500,000 developing it. In Sim's words, "I had hoped that a multilingual society like Singapore would need a multilingual computer. I was wrong. Also I realized, by looking only at Singapore, we were just like a frog looking at the sky from the bottom of a well."

After this failure, Creative decided to switch its focus from language to music, and created a PC add-on card called the Creative Music System. Sim then took a big gamble by going to the United States and setting up Creative Labs, Inc. His breakthrough came when he convinced some software makers to support Creative's sound card, renamed Game Blaster, for their PC-based video games and educational products. In 1989, Creative developed a new, advanced sound card called Sound Blaster, which was introduced at the Comdex Show in Las Vegas. Sound Blaster hit the market just as Intel's 386 card and Microsoft Windows 3.0 were arriving and the home PC market began to take off. Creative rode the multimedia wave and saw its sales soar from US$5.4 million in 1989 to US$658 million in 1994.

Sound Blaster was never an outstanding technical achievement, although the company has continued to upgrade its technology by licensing and purchasing companies such as E-mu Systems, a leading U.S. maker of music synthesizers. Instead, the product succeeded because of effective marketing and strong technical support for users—and because it hit the market at the right time. In addition, Creative has collaborated with Microsoft, Intel, and IBM to secure its position as the de facto industry standard for sound cards.

Creative succeeded in large part because of its ability to tap the U.S. market and because it was able to establish an important standard in the PC industry. Defending that standard has not been easy, however. Other companies have entered the sound card market to compete with Creative, but a bigger challenge is Intel's continuing drive to establish control over nearly all PC hardware standards. As microprocessors become more powerful, multimedia capabilities can be built into the chip, reducing the need for add-on cards. Microsoft has also added more multimedia capabilities into its operating systems, squeezing Creative from another direction.

The sound card business is an anomaly in Singapore's computer industry, a case in which local companies found a niche opportunity and made an impact in the global PC market. Otherwise the country's emphasis on MNC-led growth has kept domestic companies from growing into international competitors. The MNCs are able to attract the most talented people to work for them, and only recently have some of those people begun to start their own companies. There is also no equivalent to Taiwan's government labs that develop domestic technologies and then spin-off companies to commercialize those technologies.

Even those companies who have grown relatively large, such as Creative, Aztech, and PC maker IPC, have struggled to stay profitable in the hypercompetitive hardware business. Creative actually plunged into the red in 1996 even though sales grew to US$1.3 billion, because its core sound card business came under attack and it failed to develop successful new products. Creative tried to compete in the CD-ROM manufacturing business but lost money in the already crowded market.

Meanwhile, Singapore's top PC maker, IPC, was also running into hard times in the global market. IPC had focused initially on the European and Asian markets and then entered the U.S. market by purchasing a small PC maker, Austin Computer. However, after suffering setbacks in 1995 and 1996, IPC retreated from the retail PC market in the United States, as well as Australia, to focus on the corporate market and OEM business.[15]

The government has started to promote domestic companies in recent years, but the results of this effort will not be known for a while. In the meantime, Singapore must continue to attract and retain MNC investment as its main hope in the computer industry.

### Industry Structure

The computer industry in Singapore is concentrated on disk drives, PCs, and peripherals. Historically, disk drive production has been the leading segment of Singapore's computer industry, but in 1993, exports of computers and subassemblies equaled those of disk drives, at about US$6 billion each. A fast-growing segment of the industry was printers, which nearly doubled in exports in 1993, reaching US$1 billion.[16] Each of these industries is dominated by foreign MNCs. The disk drive industry consists entirely of MNCs, including Seagate, Conner (now part of Seagate), Maxtor, and Western Digital (table 5-1). While Singapore increasingly faces competition from Thailand, Malaysia, and China as a production site for hard drives, its superior infrastructure (human resources, physical infrastructure, and supplier base) has enabled it to move into higher value activities such as process engineering and manufacturing coordination.

Most production of PC systems is done by MNCs as well, although there are several Singaporean companies in the industry. The largest PC makers are Apple and Compaq. In 1995, Apple employed 1,800 workers producing PCs, monitors, and various components in a US$250 million plant. Compaq operates two plants in Singapore, with responsibility for design and manufacture of notebook PCs for worldwide sales and desktop PCs for Asia. Hewlett-Packard's Singapore operations are involved in manufacturing and process design for printers, desktop PCs, and servers.[17] Among the multinationals in Singapore, Hewlett-Packard is becoming known as a source for local spin-offs, because several people have left HP to start new companies.

TABLE 5-1. Major Multinational Computer Companies in
Singapore, 1994

| Company | Number of Employees |
| --- | --- |
| Seagate/Connor (disk drives) | 17,000 |
| Maxtor (disk drives) | 4,800 |
| Western Digital (disk drives) | 4,200 |
| Compaq (PCs, PCBs) | 4,000 |
| Apple (PCs, monitors, PCBs, software) | 1,800 |
| IBM (PCs, disk drives) | n.a. |
| DEC (systems assembly) | n.a. |

Source: Berkeley Roundtable on the International Economy, University of California;
compiled by Greg Linden.

In 1994, total employment in the labor-intensive disk drive industry was 27,000, compared to just 8,500 in the PC industry and 9,000 in office automation, as shown in table 5-2. However, value added is nearly the same in all three categories. The situation in disk drives is somewhat risky in that labor is becoming very expensive and workers are difficult to retain, leading disk drive makers to look elsewhere in the region for new production sites. It is generally agreed that Singapore will retain an important position in the industry, but that most new production facilities will be located elsewhere. It is also argued by at least one MNC manager that Singapore's edge in initial production ramp-up is disappearing, as Malaysia gains more experience in disk drive production.[18]

The large network of supporting companies, including subcontractors, suppliers, and OEMs, is a mix of domestic companies and foreign subsidiaries. While most local companies are relatively small and limited to supplying MNCs, a few have entered international markets themselves. The largest domestic computer makers in 1996 were Creative Technology, IPC, and Aztech Systems (table 5-3).

Supporting Singapore's MNC-based computer industry are many small- and medium-sized foreign and domestic companies that produce various components such as resistors, capacitors, PCBs, plastic cases, and metal parts. There are also dozens of contract manufacturers providing a full range of PCB assembly services. While most of these are very small companies, six reported revenues of over US$100 million in 1994, and another eight had between US$10 million and US$100 million in revenues.[19] Singapore cannot match the depth of Taiwan's local industry cluster, but Singapore sits at the center of a much larger regional supply base. Singapore's central location in the region and excellent transportation facilities make it an ideal place to coordinate regional supply activities. For example, Seagate ships components and subassemblies by air freight every day from Penang, Malaysia, to support its just-in-time assembly plants in Singapore. Such an operation would be highly

TABLE 5-2. Structure of Singapore's Computer Hardware Industry, 1994

| Product | Output (US$ millions) | Value Added (US$ millions) | Employment (Number of People) |
|---|---|---|---|
| Computer systems | 5,900 | 1,350 | 8,500 |
| Data storage (disk drives, CD-ROM etc.) | 7,300 | 1,750 | 27,000 |
| Office Automation (printers, fax machines, cartridges) | 3,350 | 1,450 | 9,000 |
| Semiconductors | 5,450 | 1,200 | 16,000 |

Source: Economic Development Board, Electronics 2000 Industry Report (Singapore: EDB, 1995).

risky in a place with less reliable or more expensive airport and ground transport facilities.

*Software.* Singapore is known primarily for hardware production, but it has also found niche opportunities in software. A big advantage is the fact that 75% of the population is Chinese, yet the language of business and government is English. This gives Singapore a unique opportunity to function in the English-dominated industry, while developing software for the large Chinese language market. For instance, in 1995 Apple introduced the Apple Chinese Dictation Kit based on research done at the Apple-ISS Research Center, a joint venture with the Singapore government.

Like the hardware industry, the software industry is led by MNCs, including IBM, Apple, Lotus, Novell, Oracle, and Microsoft. Multinational consulting and systems integration firms have also established offices in Singapore to serve the regional market. The MNCs have upgraded their activities beyond marketing and product localization. However, domestic companies have also found opportunities in the software industry.

The largest private domestic software company is Computer Systems Advisors (CSA), which specializes in systems integration and custom programming. Creative Technology also produces software. It has developed a DOS-compatible Chinese language operating system and a word processing program

TABLE 5-3. Largest Domestic Computer Hardware Companies in Singapore, 1996

| Company | Electronics Revenue (US$ millions) |
|---|---|
| Creative Technology | 1,309 |
| IPC | 569 |
| Aztech Systems | 302 |
| Wearnes International | 141 |

Source: "Riding the Roller Coaster," Electronic Business Asia (June 1997): 42–45.

that it hopes to market in China. Another large company, Singapore Network Services, is a state-owned enterprise that has developed a number of government networks and has begun to commercialize its software and networking services. More local companies have been moving into the software industry, and a number have grown to more than 100 employees in size.

As Singapore faces increasing competition from its neighbors for low-value hardware assembly, the government is targeting the software industry as a new growth opportunity. The success of the local industry is encouraging, but a shortage of programmers and other professionals is making it difficult to support continued growth. Other countries such as India, China, and the Philippines have large pools of programmers to draw on, and their governments are also moving to promote software. Singapore's best bet is probably to become regional management center for software production, as it has done for hardware.

### Industrial Policy

Singapore's government practices a unique form of industrial policy, combining a conservative economist's dream of open trade and investment regimes with the same economist's nightmare of heavy government intervention in the market to guide the economy. After Singapore's separation from Malaysia in 1965, the government of Prime Minister Lee Kwan Yew was faced with high unemployment, poverty, and loss of open access to the Malaysian market. Singapore's economy had been based on its role as a key trading port and military base for the British Commonwealth. These roles had not led to what the government saw as a socially desirable form of economic development, and the situation seemed sure to worsen when the British military pulled out in 1971. Singapore's leaders felt that only industrialization would lead to sustainable development. With a local market of only 2.8 million people, Singapore's economic planners were spared the temptation to engage in import-substitution, as most developing countries were doing at the time, and decided to promote Singapore as an export platform. The government felt that Singapore lacked a strong base of entrepreneurs capable of achieving rapid industrialization, so it turned to multinational corporations for the necessary investment and technology to support export-oriented manufacturing.

The MNCs were lured to Singapore by the promise of low wages, peaceful labor relations, a good infrastructure, a stable political environment,[20] and financial incentives that heavily favored export production. While countries today clamor for foreign investment, in those days, such a friendly attitude towards MNCs was rare, and Singapore was able to attract a great deal of investment and quickly become an MNC export platform.

In spite of its open courting of foreign investment, however, the Singapore government was not willing to leave its economy in the hands of the private sector. As Dr. Goh Keng Swee, architect of Lee's economic strategy stated, "free wheeling capitalism will only perpetuate social insecurity, mass unemployment, glaring contrasts between rich and poor, and continued exploitation by a minority of Western and local capitalists."[21]

The government balanced the power of the MNCs by retaining control of key economic sectors such as land development, banking, air travel, and petroleum refining in state-owned enterprises, or "statutory boards" as they are called. Unlike most countries' state enterprises, however, Singapore's statutory boards are run on a truly commercial basis. They are expected to turn a profit and allowed to go bankrupt if they lose too much money. The statutory boards not only gave government the ability to retain control over an economy dominated by foreign capital, but they were also used to develop Singapore's infrastructure to perhaps the best in the world and to partner with MNCs in projects that would improve Singapore's technology or train workers. The government also mobilized large amounts of domestic capital to complement foreign investment through a forced savings program called the Central Provident Fund, and it invested in education to upgrade its workers' skills. This ability to accumulate financial and human capital was the key to Singapore's continuing economic success.

The government promoted industrialization by supporting strategic industries in which it felt Singapore could compete in international markets. It started with labor-intensive industries such as textiles, but it soon moved to include more capital-intensive industries such as petroleum refining. Electronics was another targeted industry. The emphasis shifted over time from simple components in the 1960s to consumer electronics in the 1970s and then to computers and peripherals in the 1980s. Employing an MNC-led development strategy, the tiny city-state grew into one of the world's largest producers and exporters of electronics products. The key elements of Singapore's computer industry policies included creating an attractive location for foreign investment, developing a world-class information infrastructure, developing human resources and technological capabilities, promoting domestic computer use, and linking computer use to the creation of a domestic software and services industry. The government's ability to execute its strategies successfully has required an ability to coordinate policies effectively among the various agencies involved in implementation and to avoid the bureaucratic competition that has plagued some of the other countries in the region.

*Creating and Upgrading an MNC Export Platform.*   In 1979, the government identified the computer industry as one of the "brain services" that would serve as a pillar of growth in the 1980s. The Economic Development Board began to seek out investment by MNCs in the industry. Its first big success was in attracting Seagate to manufacture disk drives, which launched Singapore into world leadership in disk drive production. The EDB was not satisfied with just attracting one investment, however. It followed up by targeting other disk drive companies, offering the attraction of a growing pool of workers with experience in the industry and the presence of suppliers that had come to Singapore to support Seagate. The EDB followed a similar process in PC production, attracting Apple in 1981, and later Compaq and others. It has also been successful in recruiting Hewlett-Packard, IBM, DEC, and others to produce PCs and peripherals.[22]

Singapore's open trade policies have given it an important advantage as a location for the distribution and production activities of multinational corporations. Many companies use Singapore for warehousing, repackaging, and distribution of products made elsewhere, since they can move goods through Singapore without paying import duties. Manufacturers also can import necessary components and intermediate goods duty free.

Singapore provides an attractive environment for foreign investment, with no limitations on capital movement or repatriation of profits. When the EDB began promoting Singapore as a production base to multinational computer and electronics companies in the early 1980s, it offered tax breaks and other incentives and worked closely with foreign companies to help them set up operations. In some cases, the EDB has taken an equity position in joint ventures with MNCs. For instance, EDB took a 26% share in a semiconductor foundry called TECH Semiconductor in partnership with Hewlett-Packard, Texas Instruments, and Canon. The efforts of the EDB have given Singapore an edge over other countries in attracting foreign investment, although other countries such as Thailand and Malaysia are now following its example in offering packages to attract investors.

On top of attracting new investment, the government has worked hard to encourage MNCs already in Singapore to upgrade their operations there. The EDB offers incentives to entice MNCs to transfer more advanced technologies to Singapore, and also to send Singaporean workers to company headquarters for training to implement the transfer of new product lines to Singapore. There is also a government-supported program called the Local Industry Upgrading Program (LIUP) to help domestic companies improve their technical capabilities. The program pays for an engineer from an MNC to work full-time, providing technical and managerial assistance to local firms that supply the engineer's company with parts or services.[23]

*Developing Human Resources and Information Infrastructure.*   Singapore undertook a number of initiatives to develop the communications infrastructure and human resources necessary to support the computer industry. Singapore Telecom invested heavily to provide high-quality voice and data communications services, and plans are in place for a completely digital network with fiber optics replacing all copper cable by 2005. The National Computer Board (NCB) developed a number of computer networks for both the public and private sector. The Teleview videotext system was installed in libraries, homes, and public buildings in the 1980s, but it is being replaced by Internet access.

The government has trained thousands of computer professionals to support its computerization programs, as well as to supply needed skills to the computer industry. The NCB supported a program to train 1,000 computer professionals per year during the 1980s, and it helped the National University of Singapore and Nanyang Technical University develop computer science and management information systems programs.[24] It also supported the training of production engineers and set up engineering research centers on flexible manufacturing and factory automation. At the lower grade levels, the government has put computers in classrooms of primary and secondary schools and is promoting the use of computer-aided instruction in the schools.

*Technology Development.*   MNCs operating in Singapore have steadily upgraded the level of technological sophistication of their manufacturing processes and product lines, and they have expanded the range of activities carried out in Singapore. The government has provided incentives to companies to conduct R&D and to locate regional headquarters in Singapore. It also has established partnerships with several MNCs and foreign governments to conduct R&D and training in computer technology. These include the Institute of Systems Science (ISS), a training center originally set up by the government in partnership with IBM to train business and government executives and managers about computer use. ISS continued to train managers, professionals, and technical staff until the late 1980s, when its mission was changed to R&D focused on Chinese language operating systems, middleware, and applications including multimedia. As part of its new mission, the ISS joined with Apple to form the Apple-ISS Research Center which has developed Chinese-language voice recognition software. The National Computer Board established an Information Technology Institute (ITI) to conduct research on software engineering, computers and communications, and knowledge systems. NCB also joined the Japanese government in establishing the Japan–Singapore Institute of Software Technology and the Japan–Singapore Artificial Intelligence Center.

The Singapore government did not have a formal science and technology policy structure until 1991, when it established the National Science and Technology Board (NSTB) and formulated a National Technology Plan. Most of the government's efforts are aimed at encouraging MNCs to conduct R&D themselves, or in partnership with government research institutions. Public R&D spending is just 37% of total R&D spending in Singapore. Despite government efforts to increase R&D by the private sector, Singapore's electronics industry has failed to invest heavily in R&D. The electronics sector invested just 0.9% of its revenues in R&D, compared to 2.41% for Taiwan's electronics industry.[25] This is one of the ramifications of relying on MNCs, who do most of their R&D in their home countries. The government's efforts to increase R&D in Singapore are now focusing more on domestic companies, especially those that are large enough to support investment in R&D.

*Promoting Computer Use.*   Unlike other governments in the region, the Singapore government has taken a two-pronged approach to computer industry policy, emphasizing production and use equally. Computer use throughout the economy has been supported as a way to improve productivity and bolster Singapore's position as a manufacturing, commercial and financial center. Government has taken the lead by computerizing its own agencies and those of state-owned enterprises such as Singapore Airlines and the Port Authority of Singapore, and by developing a number of interorganizational networks and on-line services. It has also promoted computer use by the private sector and mobilized public opinion in favor of computer use.

Computer use has grown rapidly throughout the economy, and Singapore is now a sophisticated user in many sectors, from manufacturing to shipping to finance. Singapore's total computer investment in 1995 was equal to 2.25% of its GDP, compared to 1.97% for Korea, 1.89% for Japan, 1.31% for Hong Kong and 0.80% for Taiwan.[26] Singapore also has more installed computers per capita than any country in Asia. The high levels of computer literacy in Singapore have increased its attractiveness to foreign investors and served to support the government's plans to make Singapore into a regional hub for information-intensive industries.

NCB carried out its computerization program in two phases. The first phase was the Civil Service Computerization Programme (CSCP), carried out between 1981 and 1986. Through the CSCP, the government took the lead in computerization, improving its own operations, stimulating demand for local products and acting as a role model for the private sector in adopting new technologies. Training in computer skills was also emphasized, through secondary- and university-level computer science programs, private training programs, and several joint programs with foreign institutes and corporations.

The second stage of Singapore's strategy was the National Information Technology Plan (NITP), adopted in 1986. NITP continued to focus on training and infrastructure, but it expanded the thrust toward national computerization into the private sector and encouraged local technology development. To promote computer use, financial incentives were offered for investment in hardware and software, including accelerated depreciation and elimination of sales taxes. A national campaign was undertaken to increase public awareness of the value of computer use, through events such as IT Month and IT Career Week. The government also established a number of national data networks such as Tradenet, MediNet, and LawNet.

The TradeNet project involved the key trade organizations, including Customs, the Port of Singapore, banks, shipping firms, and trading companies. Rather than wait for the private sector to computerize on its own, the government has virtually forced it to do so by requiring that all trade documents be submitted electronically. Singapore could do this because most of its 2,000 trading companies are relatively large, English-speaking firms that already had computer experience. In contrast, Hong Kong's efforts to promote EDI were hampered by the fact that most of its 35,000 trading companies are small, Chinese-speaking family operations with no computer experience.

*Linking Use to Production of Software and Services.*   Singapore's domestic market is not large enough to support much of a software and services industry by itself. However, Singapore has sophisticated users in a number of industries and business is conducted in English. Therefore, software and services developed for the local market should have good export potential. The government has tried to encourage export of products originally developed for local use, an example of which is the Tradenet EDI system.

The government originally developed Tradenet for the purpose of improving the efficiency of Singapore's port facilities by speeding up the turnaround time for goods passing through the Port of Singapore. Ships entering the harbor could send the necessary documentation ahead electronically for processing by Singapore Customs. Upon arrival, the documents would already be processed and the ship could unload and load cargo immediately. There was even specialized software developed to coordinate the unloading and loading process to save time.

The original Tradenet EDI software was purchased from IBM. However, once the system was in place, the Singaporean government established a state-owned enterprise, called Singapore Network Services (SNS), to operate the system. SNS then modified the EDI software and developed it into a commercial product that it now sells to customers in Singapore and abroad. SNS has developed EDI systems in the United States and Canada and has joint ventures in Malaysia, Philippines, China, Canada, and India. It has expanded beyond the trade sector to develop other government networks in Singapore, such as MediNet and LawNet. Using its experience operating government networks, SNS has sold its services to private clients such as Apple, Sony, and Seagate in Singapore.[27]

Tradenet is a case of government promoting computer use to improve national productivity, and then developing a commercial service based on that use. Singapore's government is the only one of the five Asian countries discussed in this book that has effectively linked domestic use to the development of commercial software and services in its IT policies. Moreover, Singapore is viewed as successful by policy-makers in Japan, Korea, and Taiwan, who are now developing strategies for multimedia and information infrastructure which consider the linkages between computer use and the production of information services, content, and software.

*Policy Coordination.*   An important element of Singapore's successful computer industry strategy was coordination of efforts among key government actors, especially the NCB and EDB. The NCB is a statutory board established in 1981 to implement the national computerization plan. NCB's board members included representatives of the Ministries of Finance and Education, the EDB, the Singapore Computer Society, the Singapore Federation of Computer Industry, and the National University of Singapore. Representing the key actors in production, use, education, and finance, and with the support of the political leadership, the NCB was able to act as an effective coordinator of IT policy. NCB's efforts to promote IT use and improve the information infrastructure complemented EDB's role in promoting production.

A potential conflict over policy turf arose with the development of the IT 2000 plan aimed at developing Singapore's national information infrastructure (NII). IT 2000 fell into a gray area between the jurisdiction of NCB and the Telecommunications Authority of Singapore (TAS). Rather than allow a destructive turf war to develop over NII, as happened in Japan and Korea, the Singapore government dealt with the issue at the highest levels. The solution was to leave TAS in charge of regulation of telecommunications and Internet providers and to reorganize NCB to separate its services and promotional activities. The part of NCB responsible for developing government information systems was spun-off into a state-owned corporation called National Computer Systems, which began competing with the private sector in the systems integration business in 1996. Meanwhile, the section of NCB responsible for NII was divided into eight industry application clusters, each of which works with relevant government agencies and private companies to promote NII applications within those industries.[28]

More broadly, a new high-level steering committee called the National IT Committee (NITC) was created to provide policy coordination across ministries and oversee the government's IT strategies. NITC is headed by the senior minister of state for defense (a powerful person in the Singapore government structure), with the deputy prime minister as advisor, and includes permanent secretaries of the key ministries (Information and the Arts, Communications, Trade and Industry, Finance, and Labor), and the chief executives of four statutory boards (NCB, EDB, Tourism Promotion Board, and the National Science and Technology Board), along with the chairman of Singapore Telecom and the vice-chancellors of two universities.

The ability of the Singapore government to avoid being paralyzed by bureaucratic conflict and develop a coordinated approach to IT policy has been critical to its success in responding to the rapidly changing environment of the computer industry. Singapore has avoided such conflict because IT policy has received the attention of government officials all the way up to the level of Prime Minister, and those officials have worked out and enforced solutions when conflict threatened.

*The Next Phase: Facing New Challenges.*    Singapore's drive to become a regional center for computer hardware production has been an extraordinary achievement, but past success is no guarantee of future victories. The ups and down of Japan and Korea in the computer industry illustrate this point vividly. Singapore has positioned itself well in the global production system, but it faces challenges just like any other country.

For one thing, the concentration of domestic production on a few segments of the industry creates risk. The disk drive industry has been investing for years in places like Malaysia and Thailand, and is now moving into China, the Philippines, and Vietnam to tap new sources of low-cost skilled labor. As these countries gain experience, they are coming closer to Singapore's capabilities in disk drive manufacturing while maintaining lower costs for labor, facilities, land, and compliance with environmental regulations. The short product cycles of the disk drive industry are already making obsolete Singapore's role as "engineering transfer station." Rather than ramping-up production in Singapore and then shifting assembly to Malaysia or Thailand, companies are going straight from design and prototyping in the United States to production in one Asian location, which might be Singapore or one of its neighbors. So far, Singapore has held on to a 45% share of the world's final disk drive assembly, but in time, MNCs might bypass Singapore and move more operations to other countries.

In addition to the risk of being bypassed, Singapore also faces the possibility that hard disk drives themselves might become obsolete. Disk drives are not the only storage media available for computers, and in time other storage technologies such as optical drives or DVD might match or surpass the price/performance of disk drives. Even industry leader Seagate has been investing heavily in software companies, at least in part to diversify away from depending entirely on disk drives for its revenue.

Another challenge for Singapore is to improve the competitiveness of its own entrepreneurs to reduce its dependence on MNCs, which still keep most high-value activities in their home countries. The low level of R&D in Singapore's electronics industry is evidence that MNCs are still not doing much product development there. Local companies are more likely to conduct higher value activities in Singapore and make Singapore more of a center of innovation in the future.

Probably the biggest challenge, however, is the simple fact that Singapore is a tiny country with limited land and labor, both of which are in very tight supply. Already, the country depends on immigrants for up to 20% of its workforce.[29] This includes large numbers of factory workers hired from Malaysia and other nearby countries in spite of a government levy of US$235 to US$321 a month per foreign worker. It also includes large numbers of engineers, mostly from China and India. At Aztech Systems, more than 40% of the engineering and R&D staff is foreign, a number that is not unusual in Singapore's electronics industry. SGS-Thomson employs workers in Singapore of eighteen different nationalities. Even at the government-funded Institute of Microelectronics, two-thirds of the staff consist of foreigners, with one-third from China and India.[30] The need for more engineers will only get more acute as new semiconductor plants are opened. An average wafer fab employs about 500 engineers[31] with specialized skills in wafer fabrication technology, which Singapore's universities are not producing. So SGS-Thomson, Chartered Semiconductor, and TECH Semiconductor are setting up a joint training program for this discipline.[32]

The challenge is to continue to move up to higher value activities in Singapore and shift lower value activities offshore, which means training more engineers and other professionals needed by those higher value activities. The government is fully aware of these challenges and is taking a number of steps to confront them. These include diversification of the local economy, supporting local entrepreneurs, and investing regionally in new production locations. A fourth initiative is the ongoing IT 2000 plan to further improve Singapore's national information infrastructure and develop new IT applications.

*Diversification: Creating New Industry Clusters.* The government has developed a diversification strategy influenced by the work of Michael Porter, who consulted with the Singapore government in developing a plan to create new industry clusters. The government is planning to create clusters in electronics, new media, broadcasting, telecommunications, and entertainment. True to its history, the EDB is pursuing investment from world leaders in each of these industries. Singapore has targeted specialized niches where it can leverage its existing capabilities and infrastructure to gain a competitive advantage in new industries.

As part of its Electronics 2000 plans, the government is focusing on diversification and on creating capabilities that are now lacking in Singapore, particularly R&D and production technologies for critical components. The EDB has been active for several years in trying to move Singapore's electronics industry upstream from assembly of computer hardware to semiconductor fabrication. The initial moves were the creation of Chartered Semiconductor and TECH Semiconductor. The government is now reclaiming land for ten new chipmaking facilities and will make the required water and power available. It has started a one-year course for engineers to learn skills necessary for semiconductor production so the needed personnel will be available when the plants come on line. It will also take an equity position in projects when it is necessary to attract outside investment.

In addition to moving upstream from computers into silicon, the government is also trying to move Singapore downstream into information services, entertainment, and new media. It has already succeeded in attracting Disney and HBO to do post production of movies in Singapore, including language dubbing for Asian markets and editing to meet the cultural sensitivity of countries in the region.[33]

*Supporting Local Companies.*   The historical attitude of the Singapore government toward its local entrepreneurs has been one of benign neglect.[34] Busy courting the MNCs, the government has done little to support local companies, and the few Singaporean companies that have succeeded in the computer business have done so with little help from the government.[35] While the government continues to put a great deal of energy into its relations with MNCs, it has recently begun to pay more attention to supporting local SMEs. An important part of the industry cluster strategy involves creating linkages between local companies and MNCs and upgrading the capabilities of the local companies. The Local Industry Upgrading Program is a first step in getting MNCs to help local companies improve their capabilities. Also, as part of the Cluster Development Fund, the government is supporting promising local enterprises in order to accelerate their development. Local leaders such as Creative Technologies and IPC are now participating in various R&D projects in partnership with the government in an effort to increase R&D in Singapore.

Another way to stimulate the private sector is to privatize state enterprises, a process that is underway in Singapore. Probably the most important recent case is the decision to spin off NCB's computer services functions into National Computer Services (NCS). NCS is being transferred to private owner-ship and will have to compete with other private companies for government computing services. It will also be free to compete for private sector business. The privatization of NCS has created a large new private domestic company in the computer services industry, but it will allow other private companies to have a shot at the government projects previously handled by NCB.

*Regionalization.*    Perhaps the most important element of Singapore's new in-formation industry strategy is the expansion of Singapore's role as a regional hub. This means moving beyond being mainly a regional center for electronics manufacturing to become a hub for telecommunications, broadcasting and entertainment.

The idea of regionalization goes back to Singapore's Growth Triangle strat-egy of 1991 for moving labor-intensive production to nearby Batam, Indonesia, and Johor, Malaysia, while doing higher value production in Singapore. The government is now expanding the concept to a much grander scale that in-volves virtually all of Southeast Asia, China, and India.

Rather than just serving as an intermediary for MNC investment and manufacturing in the region, the Singapore government is now making heavy investments in other countries with the idea of "cloning" the Singapore ex-perience in China and elsewhere. Outward investment from Singapore has run into the tens of billions of dollars, as shown in table 5-4.

Singaporean real estate development companies, encouraged and sup-ported by the government, are building six industrial parks in Asia. The largest is in Suzhou China, where the EDB and private companies are building a huge (70 square km;) industrial park. Others are in Wuxi, China; Batam and Bitan, Indonesia; Bangalore, India; and Ho Chi Minh City, Vietnam. While Singaporean manufacturers are invited to locate production in these parks, the main targets are multinationals that already have stakes in Singapore and

TABLE 5-4. Singapore's Cumulative
Investment in Asia[a]

| Country | Amount Invested (US$ billions) |
| --- | --- |
| China | 17.3 |
| Malaysia | 7.3 |
| Hong Kong | 4.6 |
| Indonesia | 3.5 |
| Thailand | 1.7 |
| Vietnam | 1.5 |

*Source:* Hiebert, *Far Eastern Economic Review* (April 25, 1996): 59.

[a]Approved investment

need lower cost production sites. In the words of EDB chairman Philip Yeo, "from the Singaporean government point of view, we've now become the partner of the multinational, not just in Singapore but also in the region."[36]

Another recent investment is a partnership with the Japanese trading company Mitsui and the Japan Associated Finance Company (JAFCO) to establish a venture capital fund to invest in midsize export-oriented and computer-related firms in India. Mitsui and JAFCO, a venture capital firm affiliated with Nomura Securities, each invested $3 million in the India Direct Fund while the Singapore government contributed $25 million.

The idea behind these investments is to make Singapore a managerial center for the entire region and to replicate Singapore's business environment so investors can take advantage of cheap labor and gain access to local markets while being insulated from the problems of the local environment. Part of this involves "managing the corruption," that is, dealing with the local red tape and paying the necessary bribes so that companies in the industrial parks can keep their hands clean and concentrate on manufacturing. Recreating Singapore has not been easy, and Singapore has had to dispatch Senior Minister Lee Kwan Yew and other top officials to China to keep the projects there on course. It has also had to pressure local companies and managers to move offshore to help implement its strategies. As Lee himself said, "Singapore is such a cozy place that managers and workers are happy to stay put."[37]

*IT 2000.*    The next stage of Singapore's computerization strategy is IT 2000, a comprehensive national information infrastructure (NII) project. The government is again taking the lead, providing services, upgrading the telecommunications network, and attempting to stimulate demand for new services. The IT 2000 plan was originally drawn up in 1991 as a strategy for creating a digital communications network that would link every business, school, government agency, and home in Singapore. IT 2000 preceded the information superhighways proposals later put forth by Vice President Al Gore in the United States, and the various NII proposals in other countries. In fact, Singapore was a leader in promoting the NII concept and is often mentioned as a model for other countries' NII plans. However, it wasn't long before the Singaporeans began to understand that the initial vision of a government-built NII was misdirected, and in 1995 the IT 2000 plan was revised to reflect rapid changes taking place in the global information industry, primarily the explosion of the Internet.

The original IT 2000 focused on creating the infrastructure to support new applications. However, the Internet came along and created a vehicle for developing valuable applications immediately instead of talking about the year 2000. In the words of NCB CEO Stephen Yeo, the idea now is not "building the NII, but evolving it."[38] The Internet has caught on rapidly with the general public, and the government licensed three service providers to support Internet use. Also, while the original IT 2000 plan emphasized building a digital, fiber-optic network connecting every home, business, and government agency in Singapore, the revised plan envisions a more flexible network including fiber, cable, and wireless technologies.

Many outsiders have questioned how Singapore's desire to take advantage of technologies such as the Internet can be reconciled with its historical concern for maintaining control over information flowing into the country. So far, the issue of censorship of the Internet has been muted. The Ministry of Information and Arts filters some information and service providers are expected to block certain pornographic sites, but the government knows that people can get around those barriers. Its position is that the Internet is a "big city" with good parts and seedy areas and that the red light district should be kept on the fringes of that city.

*Comments on Industrial Policy.* Not only has the government taken a comprehensive approach to computer policy, but it also has taken care to integrate the different elements of the strategy. The ability to develop a coordinated strategy for production, use, and infrastructure contrasts with the lack of coordination evident in Japan and Korea. The critical difference for Singapore has been support from the highest levels of government, particularly former Prime Minister Lee Kwan Yew and his economic advisors, who have guided Singapore's efforts to create an information economy.

The government has used IT as an important part of its continuing campaign to attract foreign companies to Singapore. Singapore has successfully promoted itself as the "Intelligent Island," that is, a superior location for manufacturing, trade, and financial service industries and a regional hub for Southeast Asia. This self-promotion sometimes irritates other countries in the region, and it is difficult to determine whether Singapore's public relations effort has a significant effect on the investment decisions of MNCs (versus direct financial incentives, for example). But there is no doubt that the focused efforts of the EDB to work closely with MNCs has been an important factor in Singapore's success.

Some skeptics argue that the Intelligent Island campaign is actually targeted for domestic consumption, with the goal of promoting national pride and identity. Others argue that Singapore cannot hope to become Asia's information hub when it restricts the flow of information through various forms of censorship. But apart from the hype and controversy, Singapore's government has created an excellent infrastructure, developed its human resources and technological capabilities, and attracted world-class computer makers and a deep network of suppliers and subcontractors. As a result, Singapore has become a major hub in the computer industry's global production system.

## Conclusions

Singapore's success in building its computer industry is a classic example of the triumph of government industrial policy, which forged tight linkages with the global production system. Singapore's industry structure is dominated by MNCs, with domestic companies being only a minor, supporting influence.

Singapore's rapid economic growth in the past three decades has been driven by foreign direct investment, and the computer industry has been no exception. The government of Singapore created a very attractive investment environment for MNCs, with low wages, peaceful labor relations, a stable political and economic environment, good infrastructure, and attractive tax incentives to foreign investors. Also, the government provided financing through state-owned development banks and joint ventures with state-owned enterprises when necessary. Its strategy involved not only attracting MNCs, but also providing them with incentives to upgrade the technological level of their local activities and to help local suppliers improve their capabilities.

As a result, Singapore has grown into a regional hub of computer hardware production, serving as a production and distribution base for a number of MNCs, whose activities support an extensive base of suppliers and subcontractors. In addition to promoting production, Singapore has promoted public and private sector use of IT, and it supported both production and use by upgrading its information infrastructure.

In coming years, Singapore will face different types of challenges as it expands its role in the computer industry. Singapore works well as a safe, stable enclave for managing high-tech production and trade. Its strategy of developing similar enclaves elsewhere in Asia is more difficult for a country accustomed to hosting MNCs in an environment that it controls but has less experience going out into foreign countries to do business. And while Singapore's plans to move upstream from computers into semiconductors fit well with its present political/economic model, it might be more difficult to move downstream into the entertainment and information services industries, which are uncomfortable with the type of control the Singapore government is accustomed to exerting. Singapore's continued success will thus depend on its ability to adapt to new environments while retaining the well-coordinated partnership between government and the private sector that has served it well for thirty years.

## Hong Kong

The computer industry exemplifies quite well the evolution of Hong Kong's economy as well as its industrial policies over the past fifteen years. In the 1980s, Hong Kong took advantage of its excellent infrastructure, friendly business environment, and a good base of supporting industries to become an early player in the global PC industry.

Hong Kong's domestic computer production reached US$2 billion in 1990 but then began to decline as the cost of manufacturing in Hong Kong rose rapidly and companies began to move production into China. However, Hong Kong has retained a vital position in the industry as a conduit between China and the rest of the world. For MNCs and other companies looking to tap

China's cheap labor and growing market, Hong Kong serves a valuable function as a bridge between Western (as well as Japanese) and Chinese business cultures. Hong Kong's businesspeople have close ties to China and know how to deal with the myriad complications involved in doing business there. At the same time, they operate in a very Western business environment in Hong Kong and understand how international businesses think and function. They provide financial services, distribution, marketing, and management for companies doing business in China. They also perform a special legal function for Taiwanese companies that are not permitted to invest directly in mainland China, and thus channel large amounts of investment and trade through Hong Kong (although the transition to Chinese rule in 1997 has put this role in question).

Hong Kong's excellent transportation and communications infrastructure and business environment enhance its position as the gateway to China. While the Hong Kong government has not subsidized the computer industry or pursued foreign investment in the industry, it maintains low corporate tax rates and has invested heavily in infrastructure development.

The rapid deindustrialization of Hong Kong was not without its costs, however. While the exodus to China created opportunities for managers, traders, stock brokers, and other professionals, it wiped out a half million jobs in Hong Kong. Most of these were held by older workers with limited skills and education who could not simply find jobs as investment bankers. Hong Kong has not developed new, more technology-intensive industries to replace the labor-intensive production that was leaving. However, some of the more skilled workers and managers were absorbed into new or expanded businesses that provide services such as trade, finance, marketing, and technical supervision for manufacturing operations in China.

While other East Asian governments aggressively promoted computer production, Hong Kong shunned industrial targeting in general. But in spite of its ideological aversion to intervening in the market, the Hong Kong government eased into a more active role as the territory faced the challenges of deindustrialization and greater competition from elsewhere in Asia. In particular, starting in the late 1980s the government began to take steps to promote high-tech industries. It has taken steps to upgrade the territory's technological capabilities and human resources, supported R&D, and assisted high-tech entrepreneurs with business incubation programs. The scale of these initiatives has been relatively small and their impacts limited so far, but they mark a new attitude toward industrial and technology policy. It is too early to tell what impacts the transition to Chinese rule might have on Hong Kong's industrial policies, but there has been some discussion of promoting the territory as a technology center supporting southern China's industrial base.

### History of Hong Kong's Computer Industry

Hong Kong has been involved in electronics production since the late 1950s when Sony began assembling radios there. The electronics industry was driven by foreign MNCs, which produced consumer items such as TVs, VCRs, and tape recorders, as well as components such as semiconductors, capacitors, and transformers.[39] In 1961, Fairchild Semiconductor set up a transistor and diode assembly plant, and by 1966 the company employed 4,500 workers in Hong Kong. Other chipmakers followed over the years, including National, Motorola, Teledyne, Philips, Hitachi, and Sanyo. Foreign investment was dominated by U.S. firms, which accounted for the largest share of total investment and employment.[40] One of the earliest and largest foreign investors is Motorola, which has been in Hong Kong since the early 1970s and now has its regional headquarters there. Motorola assembles and tests a wide variety of semiconductors in Hong Kong and also is one of the largest foreign investors in China.

While Hong Kong was led into the electronics industry by MNCs, local companies soon joined in. Unlike Singapore, Hong Kong had a large base of local entrepreneurs consisting mostly of refugees from Shanghai and elsewhere in China, who had fled communist rule in the 1950s. The refugees had been business owners and managers in China and brought capital, machinery, and entrepreneurial skills with them. They teamed up with Hong Kong's large trading companies, which provided them with additional capital and connections to export markets. These entrepreneurs initially went into the textile and toy businesses, but by the 1960s they saw opportunities in the electronics industry. Many had sent their children abroad to study management, finance, and engineering—skills that were vital to success in electronics.

Hong Kong's first electronics company, the Champagne Engineering Corporation, started as an assembler of Sony radios in 1959 and soon began producing its own radios. By 1961, there were twelve firms producing radios in Hong Kong. Hong Kong's workers gained experience as engineers and managers working for foreign MNCs, and as in Taiwan, many eventually left to start their own companies. The combination of cheap labor, a favorable business environment (with low taxes and few regulations), and strong entrepreneurial skills made Hong Kong the early leader among the NIEs in electronics. Over time, an industry cluster developed consisting of MNCs, local suppliers, and subcontractors. Production grew rapidly throughout the 1970s and 1980s as MNC investment continued and more local companies participated. By 1984, electronics accounted for 22.6% of Hong Kong's exports and employment in the electronics industry peaked at about 107,000 people.

Computer production began in Hong Kong in the early 1980s as the PC era arrived. Multinational computer companies invested in Hong Kong as a low-cost production site, sourced components there, and contracted with Hong Kong companies for OEM production. By 1990, Hong Kong was producing PCs, motherboards, add-on cards, modems, mice, disk drives, printers, monitors, and other peripherals and components. Thousands of small local companies also produced plastic casings, metal parts, and electronic components for the computer and electronics industries.

Hong Kong also was developing another role in the computer industry as a gateway to China. China's uneven liberalization process and desire to develop a domestic computer industry led it to adopt tariffs and other trade barriers. This created unique opportunities for Hong Kong companies to make money by circumventing the restrictions. Most PCs and peripherals produced in China are exported, in order to take advantage of China's export incentives (including tariff-free importation of components). But many go only as far as Hong Kong, from where they are shipped back across the border. Some are smuggled up the Pearl River, as so-called "water goods," while others are brought in by paying off customs agents. Some products such as printers are imported into Hong Kong from other countries, repackaged with goods such as printer supplies, and then shipped into China with documentation that understates the value of the shipment. Major multinational corporations generally eschew such practices, but even their products can find their way into China through intermediaries, sometimes before the products are even introduced officially. For example, Chinese distributor Legend Holdings planned a sales campaign for a new AST notebook PC line in 1995 only to find that machines smuggled in from Hong Kong had hit the streets before their campaign was launched.[41]

During the 1980s, the costs of operating in Hong Kong rose rapidly as wages increased and real estate costs soared. By 1992, hardware production in Hong Kong began to decline rapidly as production moved to China. According to government figures, the total output of Hong Kong's computer industry was US$1.6 billion in 1994 (down from US$2.1 billion in 1993) with value added of US$296 million (compared to US$329 million in 1993).[42] Much of the slack was taken up by production in southern China, as illustrated by the growth in production in nearby Shenzhen, China, home to a large special export zone (figure 5-2). Hong Kong continued to play a vital role in the industry by managing many of southern China's factories. In these cases, manufacturing is done in China while marketing, sourcing, quality control, and sometimes design and product development remain in Hong Kong. Often the Hong Kong business owns the factory in China; in other cases, it shifts to a pure trading role and contracts with Chinese-owned factories for production. MNCs have likewise moved production to the mainland, but many retain management functions in Hong Kong as well.

Two companies that illustrate the relationship of Hong Kong and southern China in the computer industry are VTech and the Legend Group. VTech is a Hong Kong-owned company that has succeeded by using Hong Kong as a base for marketing and management while moving its production to China. The Legend Group is a more complex case involving two closely linked companies, one in Hong Kong and one in China. The two cases illustrate how companies can exploit the capabilities and opportunities presented on both sides of the border.

*VTech.*   Hong Kong's most successful homegrown computer and electronics company is VTech, which was founded in 1977 by two former engineers of NCR in the United States.[43] VTech started by making video games and other consumer products on an OEM basis, and over time the company moved up

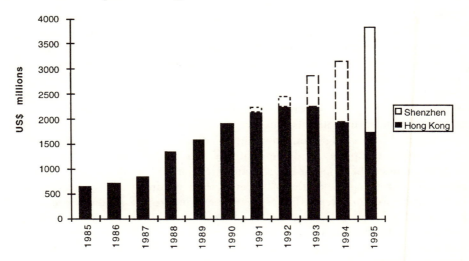

FIGURE 5-2. Computer Hardware Production in Hong Kong and Shenzhen, 1985–1995. *Source:* For Hong Kong: Reed, 1991–1997; For Shenzhen: Xinhua News Agency, (1996).

Note: Data for 1991–1994 in Shenzhen are authors' estimates (dashed lines).

to original design manufacturing. It has been successful in developing its own brand name products as well. Its product mix includes PCs, electronic toys, and telecoms equipment (mainly cordless phones and satellite receivers). In 1993, PCs accounted for 58% of sales, but electronic toys provided more than 80% of profits.

VTech was a leader in developing multiprocessing PCs when it released its Platinum dual 486-based PC in 1993, but demand for the Platinum never took off because Intel lowered the price of its Pentium chip, driving 486 systems out of the market. After suffering losses in the PC market, VTech decided to concentrate on niche markets where it could differentiate its products on features rather than battle industry leaders on price. VTech has developed novel products such as the Sound Learning Talking Keyboard to help small children to use PCs. The keyboard plugs into a PC's parallel port and is designed to work exclusively with VTech's Sound Learning software. Its large letter-shaped keys are arranged alphabetically rather than in the confusing "QWERTY" configuration. For grade-school-age children, there's the Precomputer Power Pad with a full alphanumeric keypad, LCD screen, and BASIC programming with the look and feel of a laptop. These products target a specific market that is not as crowded with competitors, and one in which VTech's strengths in electronic toys give it an advantage. More broadly, VTech is reducing its stake in the PC industry in favor of the electronic games and wireless communications markets. It is also moving into software and content, producing CD-ROMs for the education and entertainment market.

VTech is a very international company. It is listed on both the Hong Kong and London stock exchanges and its shares can be bought through an ADR program in New York. And while VTech does produce its own brand name products, it is also an OEM for companies such as AT&T, Alcatel, Nokia, and Philips. Most of its production is done in a 1.3 million square foot factory in Dongguan, China, but it conducts R&D in both Hong Kong and China. VTech invests heavily in R&D, with over 1,000 R&D staff located mostly in its Tai Po labs in Hong Kong's New Territories. This emphasis on R&D has enabled the company to introduce about seventy new products a year in recent years.[44]

VTech is unusual in the Hong Kong computer industry in several ways. One is its success in marketing its own brand name products as well as producing for others. Another is its high level of R&D and its emphasis on design and product innovation. The third is the relatively high degree of vertical integration in its manufacturing. In addition to utilizing China as a production base, it also taps China's engineering talent to design and produce its own motherboards and other components. As of 1993, VTech employed 150 engineers in its Dongguan factory. VTech's story is evidence that Hong Kong companies can move beyond managing cheap production in China, but so far there are few other companies that have done so.

*Legend Computer.*   Perhaps the best computer industry case illustrating the symbiotic relationship of Hong Kong and China is the Legend Group, which includes Hong Kong Legend and Beijing Legend.[45] Beijing Legend is a quasi-state-owned enterprise in China, affiliated with the Chinese Academy of Sciences. Originally called New Technology Development, Inc., the company was reorganized as Beijing Legend in 1989. Hong Kong Legend was formed in 1988 as a joint venture of Beijing Legend, DAW (a Hong Kong computer dealer), and China Technology Trade Ltd., a mainland company operating in Hong Kong. Hong Kong Legend went public in 1994, selling 27% of its shares on the Hong Kong market, while Beijing Legend and DAW kept 42% and 31%, respectively.

The rationale for the relationship between DAW and Beijing Legend was described by one analyst as "borrowing a boat to go to sea."[46] In this case Beijing Legend was borrowing a proverbial boat from DAW to gain access to foreign markets. Beijing Legend provided technical expertise from the Chinese Academy of Sciences, access to the China market, know-how in dealing with Chinese government officials, and low-cost production. DAW provided knowledge of international markets and connections with multinational companies such as IBM and 3Com, whose products it sold in foreign markets.

The joint venture started out just doing distribution, then moved into motherboard design and manufacturing in 1989. In 1991, Beijing Legend started making Legend brand PCs in China. In 1994, it used capital from the company's public offering to begin printed circuit board production. The management of the two companies is closely linked. Three of the five executive directors for Hong Kong Legend are from Beijing Legend, and the chairman of Hong Kong Legend is also the president of Beijing Legend.

Beijing Legend was the number two PC vendor in China, with 6.9% of the market in 1996. No other local vendor had more than 3% of the market. Hong Kong Legend supplies components to Beijing Legend in semi-knockdown form for reassembly in China. The finished PCs are all exported, then some are shipped back into China, where they are sold through Beijing Legend's distribution channels. Beijing Legend also sells Hewlett-Packard and Toshiba brand products through its distribution business, while Hong Kong Legend has its own distribution channels in China that sell AST and Kingston products.

Legend has used its overseas connections to develop close ties to the United States and other markets. The company operates a research center in Silicon Valley and operates twenty-seven branch units around the world. The company ranks third in the world in motherboard production and exports large numbers of motherboards and add-on cards. In fact, overseas sales of components make up the majority of the company's sales.[47]

The relationship between the two companies has gotten closer over time. As of July 1, 1997, Hong Kong Legend is longer treated as an offshore company in China, and the two ventures will likely merge more of their businesses. The China market offers opportunities for all kinds of hardware, as well as software and services, and much of the company's future growth will be on the mainland. But even as more of the business shifts to China, Hong Kong is expected to be a center for finance, marketing, and other business operations for the Legend group.

*Summary.*   Hong Kong became an early player in the PC industry by capitalizing on its entrepreneurial business culture, its excellent business environment and infrastructure, and its well-developed supply base for electronics components. The tight-knit networks of small, flexible firms with strong overseas ties helped the colony attract investment and participate in the global production system. Hong Kong was initially the home to hardware production by MNCs and by local companies supplying the MNCs. As the cost of doing business in Hong Kong soared and China opened up to foreign investment, a new division of labor emerged with production in China and management in Hong Kong. Hong Kong's managerial skills and its unique relationship to China have made it a vital link in the Asian production network.

### Industry Structure

Hong Kong's computer industry structure is a mix of small-and medium-sized local companies and foreign multinationals. The hardware industry consisted of 119 companies employing 9,280 workers in 1994. This was down from 213 companies with 21,495 workers in 1990, reflecting the rapid shift of production to China (table 5-5). The major products are motherboards, expansion cards, PCs, disk drives, printers, monitors, and keyboards. Most of Hong Kong's computer companies are small, labor-intensive assembly or subcon-

TABLE 5-5. Hong Kong's Computer Hardware and Components Industry

|      | Number of Companies | Number of Workers | Value added (US$ millions) |
|------|---------------------|-------------------|----------------------------|
| 1985 | 264 | 24,084 | 162 |
| 1986 | 236 | 18,319 | 187 |
| 1987 | 242 | 19,420 | 244 |
| 1988 | 327 | 30,143 | 440 |
| 1989 | 253 | 24,442 | 393 |
| 1990 | 213 | 21,495 | 512 |
| 1991 | 158 | 16,431 | 485 |
| 1992 | 152 | 12,146 | 484 |
| 1993 | 105 | 10,790 | 329 |
| 1994 | 119 | 9,280 | 298 |

Source: Hong Kong Census & Statistics Department, *Annual Survey of Industrial Production* (1995).

tractor operations. Hong Kong's electronics industry generally relies on imports of technology and key components from Japan and the United States.

*Computer Hardware.*    Hong Kong's hardware industry is part of a larger cluster that includes southern China. That cluster produces a wide range of systems, peripherals, and components, although most production involves assembly and manufacturing of mature products with limited design, product development, or use of advanced manufacturing processes. The division of labor between Hong Kong and China has shifted in recent years. Until recently, many companies maintained production lines in both places. China produced high-volume products for which speed and flexibility was not critical, while Hong Kong produced the smaller orders with a fast turnaround time. It was easier to hire people temporarily in Hong Kong to fill an order, while it was more difficult to assure on-time delivery from a factory in China. But China's capabilities have improved with experience, and most companies now do all their manufacturing in China and just retain business functions in Hong Kong.

The Hong Kong government estimates that Hong Kong companies now manage five million workers in southern China, a number greater than Hong Kong's entire workforce. Hong Kong's capabilities have driven the extraordinary economic growth and industrialization of the nearby regions of southern China, while the proximity of such a low-cost labor force and large market has sustained high growth in Hong Kong as it shifts from manufacturing to services.

The Hong Kong/South China region is attracting more production by U.S., Japanese, and Taiwanese companies that are looking for cheap labor and access to the China market. In spite of the difficulties of doing business in China, these companies feel the market potential and cost savings are simply too great to ignore. The city of Shenzhen hosts a fast-growing computer industry, with IBM, Compaq, Great Wall, and other computer makers producing about US$2 billion worth of computer hardware and software in 1995. This figure is higher by itself than Hong Kong's total computer production, and it is only part of the total production in Guangdong Province.[48]

An important aspect of Hong Kong's position as conduit to China has been what William Overholt refers to as the "airlock for China—an entry point for technology, capital, management skills, and ideas."[49] The key to this role is insulating foreign companies from the difficulties of dealing with China's complex, highly regulated economic system, and helping Chinese businesses establish linkages to the outside world. As China opens up its economy and its businesspeople get experience dealing with outsiders (and foreigners get more experience in China), this role may gradually become less important. But, as Overholt points out, Hong Kong investment dominates much of the production in China's special economic zones, and even as some MNCs by-pass Hong Kong, newcomers targeting China will likely look to Hong Kong's managers to serve as their intermediaries.

As an example, in 1994. NEC moved production of its low-end desktop PCs to its Hong Kong subsidiary. NEC builds the PCs in Shenzhen and ships them back to Japan, but they work through subcontractors in Hong Kong. Japanese engineers often work with those subcontractors rather than directly with the Chinese manufacturers.[50] NEC also sources components from its Hong Kong offices to supply its assembly operations in China.

Hong Kong also serves as a channel for investment into China. As one of the world's major financial centers and home to banks and other financial institutions with strong ties to China, Hong Kong is an ideal place to manage capital flows into and out of China. This role has been especially important for Taiwanese companies investing in China, since direct investment is still highly restricted. Taiwan's movement of labor-intensive manufacturing to China has largely been implemented by investments through Hong Kong affiliates or partners. There are many Taiwanese companies producing PCs, motherboards, and peripherals in China, but they keep a low profile. In the words of one supplier to the Taiwanese companies, "They stay under water. You never know they're there until they need help, and then they surface."

Hong Kong is also an important channel for communications and transportation into and out of China. The territory's natural harbor at the mouth of the Pearl River has made it a key entrepôt for trade into China ever since the British took control in the nineteenth century, and its excellent sea and air cargo facilities have helped it maintain that position. Hong Kong's telecommunications infrastructure is also outstanding, matching Singapore in quality but with lower cost service. Hundreds of MNCs use Hong Kong as a central switching point for communications into China.

While the Hong Kong/South China industry cluster embodies a powerful mix of management, infrastructure, and low-cost labor, it lacks a strong technology base. Little R&D is carried out and MNCs have been slow to move technology-intensive functions to the area. As a region, Hong Kong/South China lags behind Korea, Taiwan, and Singapore in technology development. Foreign companies are now moving to take advantage of China's large supply of engineers and computer scientists, but that might not work to benefit Hong Kong/South China, because most of the engineers are in Shanghai or Beijing where China's leading universities are located. Companies can locate in those areas and be closer to the largest Chinese markets and also more easily find the necessary technical personnel.

*Software.*   Like the other East Asian economies, Hong Kong has not done nearly as well in software as it has in hardware. Total revenue for the industry is estimated at US$323 million in 1994, with value added of US$141 million.[51] Hong Kong's software industry consisted of about 500 independent software vendors with about 8,500 employees as of 1994, according to a study by IDC and Dataquest for the Hong Kong Productivity Council.[52] The industry consists mostly of small companies. About forty-five companies in IDC's survey had revenues of more than HK$10 million (about US$1.28 million), and only ten had more than 100 employees. Most of the companies (62%) were independent Hong Kong companies, while 27% were foreign owned and 11% were affiliated with Hong Kong business groups. The Hong Kong–owned companies are generally underfinanced, relying on personal funds or family and friends for capital.

Hong Kong's software industry consists largely of entrepreneurs who move quickly from production to trading to any other opportunity that presents itself to make money. Small software companies scramble to survive by offering product development, localization of imported products, distribution, and support services. Among the independent software vendors, about 60% were actually involved in software development, while the rest were involved in trading, training, and other services. However, only 22% of these companies' revenues came from software made in Hong Kong, with the rest coming from imported products and various services. So far, few have been able to grow beyond this type of operation and develop successful commercial products. The reasons, according to the vendors polled, include high staff turnover, high rental costs for office space, shortages of experienced workers, lack of capital, and software piracy.[53]

Hong Kong's software industry is far removed from leading markets such as the United States, but the China market offers great potential for the future. As computer use grows in China, and if software piracy is reduced, Hong Kong's companies could use their proximity to and knowledge of China to target a major growth market. High rental costs and shortages of programmers are likely to push production to China; ultimately, Hong Kong might end up with a trading and managerial role in software as well as hardware.

*Computer Use.*   As a user of computer technology, Hong Kong ranks below Singapore, but ahead of Korea and Taiwan in average diffusion. But the average doesn't mean much in Hong Kong, where large financial institutions, trading companies, and MNC subsidiaries are world-class IT users, while thousands of small businesses still do their accounts with pen, paper, and handheld calculators. Fax machines and cellular phones are very popular with small businesses and individuals, but computers have not been readily adopted. This is partly because of the cost of computerizing, but also because of the difficulty of keyboard entry of Chinese characters. Smaller companies are expected finally to begin to computerize as voice and handwriting recognition becomes available and younger family members with computer experience enter the business.

### Industrial Policy

The Hong Kong government historically has avoided explicit policies to promote the computer industry. Until the late 1980s, the government limited its activities mainly to providing infrastructure, educating computer professionals, and improving its own information systems. While there are no specific tax incentives for the computer industry, Hong Kong's low corporate and personal tax rates act as an incentive to foreign investment in general.[54] The government had no formal IT policies before 1989 and tended to be a conservative user itself, mainly employing computers to reduce labor costs in established functions.[55] Starting in the 1990s, however, the government started taking steps to upgrade Hong Kong's technology base and improve its already strong information infrastructure.

*Developing Technology and Human Resources.* The government's most aggressive technology initiatives have involved support for research and development and technical education. One example was the establishment of the Hong Kong University of Science and Technology (HKUST) as a center for research and education in advanced technology. HKUST has a strong focus on information technology, including computer science, engineering, and management information systems. In addition, Hong Kong's two Polytechnic Institutes were upgraded to university status, reflecting a higher status for technical education. The government also invested HK$105 million[56] in a technology training program for employers to train staff in new technologies. To promote R&D, the government has funded research centers in telecommunications technology (initial investment of HK$84 million), rapid prototyping technology (HK$30 million), EMC engineering (HK$26 million), liquid crystal displays (HK$14 million) and textiles (HK$8.5 million). A Coordinated Applied Research and Development Scheme was launched in 1995, with an initial government investment of HK$50 million. The government has also provided HK$200 million in matching funds for Hong Kong companies to conduct R&D.[57]

Additionally, the government established the Hong Kong Industrial Technology Center Corporation (HKITCC), which provides support services to start-ups and small companies in high-technology industries. HKITCC's functions include business incubation, technology transfer services, and product design and development support services. The government provided land and a one-time grant of HK$250 million and a loan of HK$188 million for construction of a building to house seventy to eighty tenants and for operating costs. The Center hopes eventually to have a mix of start-ups, small- and medium-sized enterprises, a few multinationals doing product customization, and support companies such as banks and legal firms.

HKITCC has identified multimedia technology as an area of focus, building on Hong Kong's success in film production, broadcasting, video creation, and electronic toys. Other areas identified include networking, telecommunications, application software, and microelectronics design. HKITCC advocates three broad strategies for Hong Kong's high technology industries: (1) Focus on the development of knowledge-based industries; (2) Become a management center for the region by focusing on finance, R&D, design and marketing; and (3) Serve as brokeraging partners to channel foreign technology into China and to commercialize technologies developed in China.[58]

The Hong Kong government's industry and technology promotion efforts are small in scale compared to those of Korea, Singapore, and Taiwan, but they still represent an important break from the laissez faire attitude of the past. Concerns are being raised that service jobs will follow manufacturing jobs to the mainland, and that Hong Kong needs to develop technological capabilities as well as managerial skills to maintain its economic vitality. There is still a heated debate between those who think the government should do more and those opposed to virtually any intervention, but the balance seems to be tilting in favor of a more active government role than in the past.

*Promoting Computer Use.*    Responding to concern about the low level and poor quality of computer use in the public sector, the government upgraded its data processing agency to the department level, creating the Information Technology Services Department (ITSD) in 1989. A computer network linking government departments was completed in 1996.

In order to promote computer use in education, the government introduced computer courses in public schools and provided PCs to support those programs. The Department of Education also began to provide funds to secondary schools for computer rooms, software, and teacher training and developed a network linking different schools.

Hong Kong has also promoted computerization by developing a number of public networks. The most controversial has been Tradelink, an electronic data interchange (EDI) network established to handle trade documents. Tradelink was initially conceived by a consortium of trading companies as a means to improve the efficiency of Hong Kong's port facilities and to facilitate trade. The government initially refused to participate, saying EDI should be a private sector initiative. However, after Singapore's government created its Tradenet EDI system, the Hong Kong government agreed to a public/private partnership called Tradelink Electronic Document Services which would develop a Community Electronic Trading Service (CETS).[59] Implementation of Tradelink was delayed by an impasse between the government and IBM, which was to be the main contractor. Finally, in 1995, Hewlett-Packard replaced IBM as the systems integrator and provider of core hardware and software for CETS.[60] By this time, the Hong Kong government was already years behind

Singapore in applying EDI for trade documents, and major trading companies and multinationals in Hong Kong had developed their own EDI systems for their data communications needs.

*Information Infrastructure.* No place in Asia has a better or less expensive telecommunications infrastructure than Hong Kong. Without the publicity of Singapore's IT 2000 plan, Hong Kong Telecom has gone about building a 100% digital network and has been installing fiber-optic lines to buildings throughout the city. In the rapidly arriving network era of computing, this high-quality, low-cost infrastructure is a major asset for Hong Kong. The quality and cost should continue to improve as the government carries out its liberalization plan in order to create competition. Hong Kong Telecom's monopoly has been removed for local service and its international monopoly will be gone in 2006. Hong Kong's telecommunications costs are already lower than any of the NIEs or Japan (table 5-6).

Hong Kong's strategy for telecommunications is to promote competition in order to cut prices and improve services. The Office of Telecommunications Authority (OFTA), which regulates the industry, issued four licenses for domestic service providers to provide all fixed services in Hong Kong. Hong Kong Telephone Company (a subsidiary of Hong Kong Telecom) is one, joined by Hutchinson Communications (owned by property developer Hutchinson and international telecommunications provider Telstra), New T&T (owned by Wharf Holdings, which also provides cable TV service), and New World Telephone (owned by property developer New World Holdings and US West). In order to ensure a fair competitive environment, OFTA has developed rigorous interconnection rules for providers. If they cannot agree on terms, OFTA has the power to determine the terms of interconnection.

OFTA also has licensed four mobile providers: Hutchinson, Hong Kong Telecom CSL (a Hong Kong Telecom subsidiary), Pacific Link (partnered with Vodaphone), and Smart Tone (affiliated with property developer Sun Hung Kai). The battle over Hong Kong's wireless market is extending to the digital wireless market. OFTA has not mandated a particular technology standard, allowing companies to choose among competing wireless standards. Hong Kong's status as a leading user of wireless has spurred the development of a

TABLE 5-6. Cost of Three-Minute Call to United States (in 1994)

| | |
|---|---|
| Japan | $6.98 |
| Korea | $4.88 |
| Taiwan | $6.00 |
| Singapore | $5.81 |
| Hong Kong | $3.80 |

*Source:* EMF International, *World Competitiveness Report 1995* (1995).

local industry in wireless devices, and companies such as VTech have used Hong Kong as a base for developing products for international markets.

Hong Kong has not announced an official NII strategy, but OFTA did release a position paper saying Hong Kong should be promoted as a regional telecommunications hub. This means: (1) being a physical switching center; (2) being a center for software and content distribution, for example, publishers based in Hong Kong will use electronic publication for distribution; and (3) attracting more business to Hong Kong to take advantage of Hong Kong's information infrastructure.[61] Hong Kong has been quick to jump on the Internet, with nearly 100 Internet service providers operating in the territory as of early 1997 and a higher rate of Internet use than in the other three NIEs.

While each of the Asian NIEs (plus Malaysia) has set a goal of becoming a regional communications hub, Hong Kong is in the best position to do so, and it is already a switching hub for hundreds of MNCs' private networks. The only serious competitor to Hong Kong as a communications hub is Singapore, but Hong Kong's advantage is the presence of strong competition in the local market and its proximity to China.

*Policy Coordination.*   In contrast to Singapore's highly coordinated efforts to promote computer production and use, Hong Kong's policies have lacked any overall strategic direction. There is little effort to integrate policies for industry promotion, education, R&D, and computer use, nor is there any government body with the responsibility or authority to do so.

Hong Kong's policies toward the computer industry have been the result of the individual initiatives of different government agencies. Industry promotion has been carried out mainly by the Industry Department, government computerization is managed by ITSD, while telecommunications are regulated by OFTA. Several councils, such as the Vocational Training Council, the Hong Kong Productivity Council, and the Industry and Technology Development Council are also involved in various aspects of computer policy. But the lack of policy coordination has reduced the impact of even these limited efforts.

## Conclusions

Hong Kong's position in the computer industry is a result of its role as a gateway to China and its linkages to the global computer industry. Hong Kong's strengths and weaknesses in the computer industry are closely related to its industry structure, which now consists mainly of companies with manufacturing operations in Southern China. Hong Kong has lost much of its manufacturing base; it is now mainly a center for finance, trade, and distribution for the computer industry.

However, unlike Singapore—which likewise is moving towards a service-based economy—Hong Kong has not developed strong design and engineering capabilities, except in certain products such as wireless communications. There are only a few exceptions such as VTech, which has a strong R&D base in Hong Kong. R&D spending in Hong Kong equals just 0.1% of GDP,[62] compared to 1.9% for Korea, 1.7% for Taiwan, and 0.9% for Singapore.[63] Singapore is attempting to develop higher value manufacturing at home even as it moves labor-intensive production offshore, but Hong Kong is allowing most of its manufacturing to leave while just maintaining business functions at home. Hong Kong's failure to develop stronger technological capabilities is a reflection of the absence, until recently, of industrial policies to develop such capabilities.

The future of Hong Kong in computers depends partly on political and economic developments in Beijing now that Hong Kong is under Chinese control. Hong Kong's role as gateway between China and the world is partly dependent on its status as a Western-style economy with close ties to the Chinese market. If the Chinese government compromises Hong Kong's business environment, either through repression, corruption, greed, or by accident,[64] Hong Kong could face an outflow of capital, foreign companies, and of its own residents who hold foreign passports.

On the other hand, many in Hong Kong argue that Hong Kong will actually be better off now that the transfer is complete and the uncertainty is over. China has a huge stake in Hong Kong, both economically and politically, and is certainly aiming for a smooth transition. The notion of "one country, two systems" may end up, in the words of one China scholar "one country, one-and-a-half systems," with Hong Kong losing some of its unique characteristics. But this should not mean the demise of Hong Kong as an economic dynamo; there is simply no substitute for Hong Kong's capabilities, even if the business environment become more restrictive than in the past.

Whatever the future holds for Hong Kong in general, the Hong Kong/ South China computer industry will face continuing challenges. While the region has a good mix of cheap labor and engineering talent in China and managerial skills and infrastructure in Hong Kong, the industry is still concentrated in assembly of low-margin, decreasing returns hardware products. Instead of upgrading their technological capabilities, Hong Kong's producers have moved to China to retain their cost competitiveness in labor-intensive manufacturing. Hong Kong has kept the knowledge-based financial, commercial, and managerial functions, but its position in the industry will be more sustainable if it develops corresponding skills in technology.

Hong Kong's economic success is often cited as evidence of the superiority of laissez faire policies and is seen by some as disproving the notion that government intervention has been critical to the East Asian success in computers. Whether nonintervention is a viable strategy for competing in computers cannot be tested with just one case, especially such a unique case as Hong Kong. In any case, Hong Kong has never been as pure an example of laissez faire economics as its boosters claimed. It is, however, an outstanding example of an economy that has taken advantage of its unique position by creating a favorable business climate and infrastructure to support the efforts of its entrepreneurial population.

# 6

# Findings from the East Asian Experience

The previous three chapters have shown how Japan and the Asian NIEs have succeeded in building competitive computer industries. Each country's history is unique and helps answer questions such as the following: What are the forces that have made so many U.S. PC makers turn to Taiwanese companies to design and build their computers? Why did all the major disk drive makers set up production in Singapore? How did Korea become a world leader in DRAMs yet fail to make a mark in PCs or peripherals? Why does Japan control so many key components technologies yet remain weak in systems and software? How has Hong Kong been able to maintain a critical managerial function for southern China's computer manufacturing base even as its own production has shrunk?

The focus of this chapter, however, is on more general questions that can be answered by comparing the experiences of companies and countries. For instance: What are the key factors that determine company and country success in the computer industry? What is the relationship between company and country success? And is there an East Asian model of industrial policy that helps explain the strengths and weaknesses of the five countries? The answers to these questions are complex, but we have been able to draw some broad conclusions from the history of the global computer industry and the experiences of the East Asian countries:

- Companies that have succeeded in the computer industry are highly focused on specific industry segments that fit their own capabilities. They are able either to define new markets or to capitalize on opportunities within markets created by others. The most successful companies are fast and flexible in their decision-making, enabling them to respond to rapidly changing market and technology environments.

- Successful countries are marked by focused companies within diversified national industry structures and have strong linkages to the global production system. They respond to the changing global environment through a dynamic process of learning and adapting that continually enhances national capabilities.
- These success factors are not just the result of individual business or government actions, but also from effective coordination between business and government strategy. When government policy is aligned with market forces and business strategies, industrial policy can be very effective. When government policy-makers ignore market forces and business strategies, their efforts are either ineffective or counterproductive.
- There is an East Asian model for computer industry policy. That model is linked to more general explanations of East Asian economic development, and it helps explain both the strengths and weaknesses of the Asian computer industry. Key features of the model are: emphasis on building and enhancing national capabilities; an outward orientation aimed at promoting exports and attracting technology transfer; strong policy coordination within the government and between the government and the private sector; and, an emphasis on production and investment over consumption.

To elaborate on these conclusions, we return to the model first presented in chapter 1, and use it to organize the discussion of our findings in terms of five key elements. These are as follows: (1) the global production system of the computer industry; (2) the national industry structure; (3) the size and sophistication of the domestic computer market; (4) national capabilities for computer production and use, and (5) government industrial policy (figure 6-1).

The important elements of this framework are not just the contents of the five boxes shown in the figure, but also the interactions among the five factors. Particularly important are: linkage of companies and countries to the global production system of the computer industry; promotion of a diversified national portfolio of focused companies; creation of a sophisticated domestic user base and access to a large user market, whether domestic or international; development by government and industry of national capabilities in human resources, infrastructure, technology, and management; and coordination of industrial policy to support the industry and the market. Also, it is important to note that this model is not static; the model has a time element to it, because these interactions are repeated over time, and the impacts of each interaction reverberate throughout the whole system.

The findings are discussed here moving from the left to the right sides of figure 6-1. We start with the global production system and East Asia, and then move to industry structure, industrial policy, the domestic market, and na-

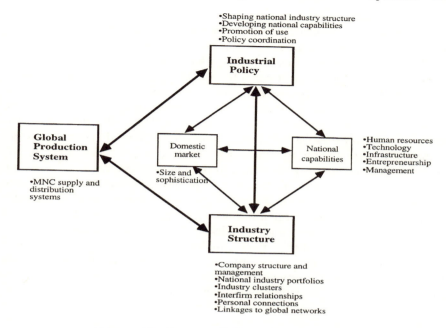

•Shaping national industry structure
•Developing national capabilities
•Promotion of use
•Policy coordination

**Industrial Policy**

**Global Production System**

•MNC supply and distribution systems

Domestic market

•Size and sophistication

National capabilities

•Human resources
•Technology
•Infrastructure
•Entrepreneurship
•Management

**Industry Structure**

•Company structure and management
•National industry portfolios
•Industry clusters
•Interfirm relationships
•Personal connections
•Linkages to global networks

FIGURE 6-1. Computer Industry Success Factors

tional capabilities. We conclude with our findings about the dynamics of competition and the East Asian model for computer industry competitiveness.

## The Global Production System and East Asia

The East Asian experience is first and foremost a story about companies and countries successfully competing in the global computer industry, beginning with mainframes in Japan and extending to PCs, components, and peripherals throughout the region. At the same time, those companies' and countries' heavy emphasis on hardware and their failure to capitalize on opportunities in software, services, and use have helped keep them out of the most profitable increasing returns segments of the industry.

The most common road to success in the hardware industry was through linkages of companies and countries to the global production systems controlled by U.S. multinationals. The opportunities for developing such linkages mainly occurred in the PC era. The mainframe and minicomputer industries were characterized by firms that optimized resources within a company and a country. By contrast, the PC industry is characterized by firms that optimize resources on a global basis with much less regard to company or country boundaries. IBM led the way in globalizing the PC industry. Faced with the need to develop a new low-cost PC quickly, IBM turned to firms that could supply the necessary components and peripherals on time and at the best price. Many of these turned out to be Asian companies that had gained experience producing components for the consumer electronics industry.

After IBM had created its own supply base for the PC, other firms piggy-backed on IBM's initial investments to exploit and expand the Asian production network. Compaq, Apple, Dell, and others succeeded by concentrating on design, assembly, and marketing, while sourcing components, peripherals, and even complete systems from Asian suppliers. This willingness to tap capabilities wherever they existed created opportunities for Asian companies and countries to participate in the computer industry.

While barriers to entry were high in the mature mainframe industry, the PC revolution made it possible for new companies and countries to participate in the global production system—and even become leaders in some industry segments. The East Asian region became the leading center for PC hardware production, in spite of the continuing leadership of U.S. companies.

Even more important than the technology behind the PC was the layered and highly segmented structure of the PC industry that created opportunities for East Asia. Different segments of the industry favor different industry structures and capabilities, creating opportunities for a variety of companies and countries. A few segments (e.g., microprocessors and operating systems) are dominated by a near-monopoly producer, such as Intel and Microsoft, that control critical architectural standards. Other segments (e.g., flat-panels, hard disk drives, printers) have settled into oligopoly market structures, with a few firms controlling most of the market. There is still room for newcomers to enter these markets, such as Samsung's entry into flat-panel displays, but large investment requirements and technology hurdles keep the number of companies small.

Even in oligopolistic industries there have been opportunities for countries to participate as production platforms for industry leaders. In the disk drive industry, for instance, Singapore was able to attract leading multinationals and develop strong local manufacturing and engineering capabilities. As the MNCs moved lower value-added production to Malaysia and Thailand, Singapore retained its position in higher value-added engineering activities, as well as a critical role in managing production throughout the region.

Some segments of the hardware industry have yet to consolidate and so still retain a wide open competitive structure. In hardware, these include PC systems, motherboards, and various other components, subcomponents, and peripherals. The flexible structure of the PC industry has continued to create opportunities for companies that are faster and more responsive than their competitors, particularly in meeting the demands of ever shorter product cycles.[1] These segments provided opportunities for Taiwan's vast network of small companies to develop linkages with foreign MNCs as suppliers, OEMs, and subcontractors. The Hong Kong/South China region has likewise thrived on these segments of the industry, while Japan and Korea have struggled to compete.

The other segments of the industry that remain highly competitive are software and services, where start-ups and specialists still can find numerous opportunities beyond the reach of Microsoft's ever-growing empire. However, East Asian companies have had little success in software and services, and their countries have not attracted much MNC investment for software production.

It is our conclusion that the East Asian countries have succeeded in those industry segments where competitive demands matched their own industry structure and capabilities. The nature of the competitive environment for each market segment has helped define the position of different countries in the computer industry. But what exactly are the characteristics of national industry structure that are important in determining a country's strengths and weaknesses, and how do the East Asian countries compare on those characteristics?

## National Industry Structure

A country's industry structure consists of its domestically owned firms, as well as foreign companies producing, selling, or sourcing in that country. An industry structure is more than the sum of its parts, however. The strengths and weaknesses of a national industry structure also depend on the total portfolio of companies, their relationships to each other and the complementarities that develop among them.

### Company Structure and Management

Focus, flexibility, and speed are the keys to company success in the PC industry. As a result, the PC industry has tended to favor smaller firms over the giants that dominate the mainframe industry. Smaller companies tend to be more focused than larger ones. They are not saddled with sunk costs from previous large investments, and thus they can change direction quickly to respond to new opportunities. They also generally are hungrier than large companies, because they are usually managed by the owner, who has a heavy personal stake in the success or failure of the company. Such companies tend to be more aggressive in pursuit of new market opportunities and are more willing and able to bend the rules when necessary to get something done quickly. Large companies are often saddled with bureaucratic decision-making and multiple layers of management that make it difficult to move quickly.

These generalizations are not always true, however. More important than sheer size is corporate culture and management style. For instance, Hewlett-Packard is a very large company (more than US$30 billion in revenues), but it is managed in a very decentralized structure. Individual units operate almost as separate companies and are encouraged to maximize their own profits even if it means competing with other HP units. As an example, the company marketed its ink-jet printer technology aggressively, even though it knew it would take sales away from its laser printer business. Indeed, while many large older firms have struggled or collapsed in the PC era, giants such as Toshiba and Hewlett-Packard have thrived in different segments of the PC industry. And Microsoft, a $10 billion company, was able to refocus much of its corporate strategy to target the Internet in a matter of months. For Microsoft, such flexibility is a result of having one clear leader and an entire organization ready to follow that leader.

While sheer size has often been a disadvantage in the PC industry, it does have its advantages in certain commodity components markets. Large companies can raise capital and mobilize internal resources to make large investments in R&D as well as plant and equipment needed to compete in high-volume products such as DRAMs and LCDs. Diversified companies such as the Japanese and Korean electronics giants can also use revenues and profits from existing businesses to subsidize losses encountered while developing a new business.

While diversified electronics companies have done well in high-volume components, most of the computer industry is dominated by more focused companies, whose success and survival depend on competing in computers. The U.S. computer industry consists almost entirely of computer-only firms, as does Taiwan's industry. Singapore's domestic leaders are all independent firms whose focus is on the computer industry, and most of the multinationals producing computer hardware in Singapore are U.S. computer makers. On the other hand, most of Japan's and Korea's leading computer producers are large electronics conglomerates, for whom computers make up only part of their revenues (table 6-1). In the past, those conglomerates could subsidize their computer businesses with profits from consumer electronics or components, but now they are finding that consumer electronics has gone from a cash cow to a cash drain. Commodity semiconductor production goes from profitable to unprofitable over the course of business cycles in the industry. Also, as the size of the computer industry has increased, it becomes more costly to subsidize a large but unprofitable computer operation.

There are some exceptions to the rule that computer-only firms are most successful in computers. For instance, computers make up only 20% of Toshiba's revenues, yet Toshiba is the leading notebook computer maker in the world. Toshiba has been able to focus its energies on a segment of the market in which its capabilities in precision manufacturing and miniaturization gave it an advantage. Likewise, television makers such as Samsung and Tatung have done well in the related computer monitor industry.

For the most part, however, companies with broadly diversified product lines find it difficult to keep up in the demanding computer business. In the PC era, each segment of the industry has simply become too large and too competitive for anything less than a total commitment to winning in that business; a company can only make such a commitment to a limited number of businesses. Ultimately, the potential benefits of diversification are usually not enough to compensate for the loss of focus on individual market segments.

TABLE 6-1. Top Computer Companies in the U.S. and Asia

| Company | 1996 Computer Revenues (US$ millions) | 1996 Company Revenues (US$ millions) | Computer Revenues as % of Company Revenues |
|---|---|---|---|
| U.S. | | | |
| IBM | 75,497 | 75,497 | 100 |
| Hewlett-Packard | 31,398 | 39,427 | 80 |
| Compaq | 18,109 | 18,109 | 100 |
| EDS | 14,441 | 14,441 | 100 |
| DEC | 13,610 | 13,610 | 100 |
| Microsoft | 9,435 | 9,435 | 100 |
| Japan | | | |
| Fujitsu | 29,717 | 47,170 | 63 |
| Hitachi | 15,242 | 68,735 | 23 |
| NEC | 15,092 | 44,766 | 34 |
| Toshiba | 14,050 | 58,300 | 24 |
| Canon | 6,907 | 10,430 | 51 |
| Matsushita | 6,410 | 64,102 | 10 |
| Korea | | | |
| Samsung Electronics[a] | 1,890 | 19,832 | 9 |
| Samsung Display Devices | n.a. | 3,074 | n.a. |
| Trigem | 1,070 | 1,070 | 100 |
| LG Electronics[a] | 425 (1935)[b] | 9,373 (10,256) | 5 |
| Hyundai Electronics[a] | 230 | 3,957 | 6 |
| Daewoo Telecom[a] | 180 | 1,053 | 17 |
| Taiwan | | | |
| Acer | 5,860 | 5,884 | 99 |
| Inventec | 1,585 | 1,585 | 100 |
| Mitac | 1,371 | 1,371 | 100 |
| FIC | 1,100 | 1,100 | 100 |
| Tatung | 935 | 4,450 | 21 |
| Compal | 719 | 719 | 100 |
| Singapore | | | |
| Creative Technology | 1,309 | 1,309 | 100 |
| IPC | 568 | 568 | 100 |
| Aztech Systems | 302 | 302 | 100 |
| Hong Kong | | | |
| VTech | n.a. | 321 | n.a. |
| Legend | 478 | 478 | 100 |

Sources: Electronic Business Asia (June 15, 1997); Datamation, (June 15, 1997); Korean computer revenues provided by company officials.

[a]Data do not include peripherals. Includes systems and applications.

[b]Data include peripherals and components as well as systems and applications. Communication from K. S. Park, LG IBM PC Co.

A national production system is characterized by more than just the quality of individual companies. There is no doubt that decades of U.S. leadership can be attributed largely to the performance of companies like IBM, DEC, Microsoft, and Intel. It is also true that Japan's ability to become a leading producer of computer hardware has much to do with the strength of companies such as Fujitsu, Hitachi, Toshiba, and NEC. This is not the whole story, however. National competitiveness is also a result of the mix of companies in a country's industry portfolio, the presence of industry clusters, the networks of relationships among firms and individuals, and a country's linkages to the global production system.

## National Industry Portfolios: Focus Within Diversity

While more focused *companies* are generally more successful, *countries* benefit from having a diversified portfolio of companies producing a wide range of products. Some countries specialize in a few computer products, such as Korea with DRAM and Singapore with disk drives and PCs, while others (such as Taiwan) produce a wide range of systems, peripherals, and components. A country that specializes in a few products and depends on a few companies will reap large benefits when demand for its key products are growing rapidly, or when its leading companies are doing well. However, a broader based industry is less vulnerable to downturns in any market segment or poor performance by one or a few companies. The DRAM price collapse of 1996 caused serious problems not only to companies such as Samsung, but also to the entire Korean economy as the value of its chip exports fell. Likewise, if Singapore were to lose its leading position in disk drives, it could cause serious problems. Partly for this reason, the Singapore government is pushing hard to develop other industries such as semiconductors, software, and entertainment. By contrast, Taiwan's broadly diversified computer industry is less vulnerable to a downturn in one or two industry segments.

Concentration of a country's industry in a few companies can be as dangerous as concentration in a few products. The U.S. computer industry has seen the decline of IBM, DEC, and Apple, and the disappearance or near destruction of companies such as Data General, Prime, and Wang—yet the slack has been taken up by the constant flow of new companies and continued success of other older companies. But when Japan's big computer makers all slumped in the early 1990s, there was no one else to take up the slack.

Countries also benefit from having a broad mix of large and small companies at different levels of the value chain, from components to systems to software and services. Japan has a good combination of large-and medium-sized hardware producers that control many key technologies. With a few exceptions, it lacks the independent smaller companies that would provide the entrepreneurial energy that Japan needs, especially in the software industry. Korea's industry structure is even more top-heavy, with a few horizontally diversified companies competing in DRAMs, LCDs, and monitors—even as they also build cars, ships, bridges, and VCRs. Korea has very few technologically sophisticated smaller companies either in upstream components and equipment industries, or in software or PC systems.

Taiwan has a better company mix, with small, medium, and large companies, although there are no giants on the Japanese or Korean scale. The small companies fill market niches and create a broad and deep supply base, while larger companies serve as major suppliers to multinational vendors; in one case, Acer, has become an international brand leader as well. Taiwan's move upstream into memory chips and LCDs has been partly the result of computer companies like Acer and Tatung expanding their computer product base, but those companies have been joined by larger companies from outside the electronics industry that have diversified into semiconductors. Singapore's industry structure consists of major MNCs that produce in Singapore and a large number of smaller suppliers that support the MNCs. There are only a few midsized local firms, such as Creative and IPC, that have developed products for international markets. Hong Kong's computer industry consists of a few MNCs and many small-and medium-sized local companies that manufacture in China for both the China market and for export.

## Industry Clusters

A key to achieving a sustainable competitive position in computer production is the creation of industry clusters consisting of large numbers of companies with complementary skills. Michael Porter, in his influential book *The Competitive Advantage of Nations*,[2] focused on industry clusters as a source of national competitiveness, pointing to such diverse cases as the Italian ceramic tile industry and the Silicon Valley electronics industry. Industry clusters embody a range of specialized capabilities that give a geographic region a competitive advantage. Those capabilities can also enable a country to sustain its leadership even when it loses an initial competitive advantage, such as cheap labor. Japan's strong supply base for electronics includes a number of companies that have near-monopoly positions in key upstream components, materials, and equipment. Singapore's dense network of suppliers and its strong process engineering capabilities have helped it retain its lead in the disk drive industry in the face of competition from lower cost locations nearby. And Taiwan's PC industry is supported by an extraordinary cluster of companies producing components and subassemblies.

The computer industry consists of a number of horizontal industry segments, each of which may develop local industry clusters. When more than one segment is located in a country or region, a broader industry cluster can develop, as is the case with Silicon Valley, which produces computers, semiconductors, semiconductor equipment, networking equipment, disk drives, printers, and software. The computer industry also benefits from proximity to other segments of the broader electronics industry. For example, the consumer electronics industry contributed high-volume manufacturing methods and graphics display capabilities, and the telecommunications industry supplied networking technologies. The presence of a strong supplier network is a key part of the national infrastructure to support electronics production in all segments.[3]

In contrast to hardware and packaged software, the information services industry has clustered near major centers of computer use, usually in or near large urban areas. However, the services segment is becoming less dependent on location as programmers and consultants increasingly travel or telecommute to serve more distant clients. This even includes programmers in India and other countries providing programming services for U.S. companies.

The notion of industry clusters is extremely valuable in understanding the evolution of computer production in the United States and in East Asia. At various times, some analysts have forecast the decline of Silicon Valley, brought about by Japanese competition, high wages, movement of production offshore, or overregulation. So far, Silicon Valley companies have moved many activities to other locations, both in the United States and abroad, but the Valley remains the undisputed center of technology creation for the computer industry.

Asia has a number of important industry clusters in the electronics and computer industries. Taiwan's dense cluster of electronics components suppliers has been critical to its ability to design, prototype, test, and manufacture new products faster than anyone in the world. Japan has broad and deep clusters of components and equipment suppliers for the computer, semiconductor, and consumer electronics industries. Singapore's disk drive cluster has been discussed in detail, and the Singaporean government is now trying to create new industry clusters in other sectors. Hong Kong has developed a large base of components suppliers and contract manufacturers in southern China. On the other hand, Korea's supply base is limited, especially in computers. Korean PC makers import most of their components from Japan, the United States, and, to some extent, Taiwan. And in spite of the Korean *chaebols'* remarkable performance in DRAMs, they must still import most of the key components, materials, and equipment to produce semiconductors.

### Interfirm Relationships in the National Industry Structure

The global computer industry is built on a complex variety of relationships with companies interacting as buyers, sellers, competitors, and strategic partners. The most successful companies have flexible relationships with other firms that adapt over time to new conditions. Companies need to be able to interact in different ways under different circumstances. For instance, IBM develops applications for Microsoft's operating systems, yet it competes with Microsoft in the operating system market and cooperates with Microsoft in development of certain PC standards. Such interactions in the U.S. industry are carried out through arms-length commercial transactions, informal cooperative relationships, or formal alliances and joint ventures. Many relationships are based on personal relationships that permeate Silicon Valley and are maintained even when people change companies. This fluid, network structure has been important to supporting valuable cooperation within a highly competitive environment. National industry structures likewise benefit from flexibility rather than rigid, hierarchical relationships.

Japan's industry is organized within the hierarchy of the *keiretsu* system, but there are many looser relationships that transcend the *keiretsu*. Japanese business groups include vertically integrated supply chains as well as broader families of diversified companies organized around a common bank and trading company. These groups overlap; for instance, NEC is part of the large Sumitomo group, but also has its own supply chain of components and equipment makers. Companies tend to interact closely with other group members, but many still sell to customers outside their own group and even outside Japan. This allows them to sell to a broader market and thus lower production costs, while still giving some advantage to their group members by serving their needs first. The top tier of suppliers in the Japanese industry are multinational companies and technology leaders in their own right. There are also a number of independent companies such as Sony, Canon, and Kyocera that have thrived outside the *keiretsu* system and are involved in various relationships with both Japanese and foreign firms. At the bottom of the production pyramid are many smaller suppliers that depend on one major customer for most of their business. The Japanese industry structure is reasonably flexible, but it produces few spin-offs and leaves limited room for entrepreneurship.

Korea's industry structure is often compared to Japan's, but it is actually more rigidly hierarchical. Companies are organized vertically within the *chaebol* structure, and major *chaebol* members are often run by family members of the *chaebol* founder. Smaller companies are subservient to the lead company and do little business outside their own group. They rarely develop into international competitors or technology leaders the way that Japanese suppliers have done. There is also a shortage of independent companies that have grown into strong competitors in their own right, because the *chaebol* control distribution channels and independent companies cannot easily raise capital.

Taiwan's computer industry has a network structure that bears a strong resemblance to Silicon Valley. People move regularly among companies, and relationships among people are probably more durable than relationships among companies. Relationships between firms are loose and shifting with no rigid vertical hierarchy of companies, although larger companies do act as nodes around which smaller companies organize their production. The larger companies are either part of business groups (such as Tatung and Formosa Plastics) that have expanded into computers, or successful computer companies (such as Acer and Mitac). Those companies are the sources of many spin-off companies, which often retain ties to the parent company.

Interfirm relations within Singapore are centered around the production systems of the big MNCs, but suppliers are not generally linked to one particular MNC. Local companies mostly work as contract manufacturers and suppliers for the MNCs or for bigger local producers such as Creative Technology or IPC. Singapore's manufacturers and suppliers are part of larger regional production networks of MNCs, which reach into Thailand, Malaysia, Indonesia, and increasingly into China and India, but are still coordinated from Singapore.

Hong Kong has shifted most of its manufacturing base to southern China, but it retains its managerial role as well as serving as a conduit for trade and investment. There are only a few large firms in the Hong Kong/South China computer industry, such as Legend and IBM/Great Wall, but there are thousands of small companies that feed the MNC production networks. There are also many Taiwanese companies doing labor-intensive production that is not economical to do in Taiwan. Production networks are generally decentralized with family and personal relationships forming an important basis for interfirm linkages. The role of Hong Kong is also unusual in that many commercial transactions are done for the purpose of circumventing China's regulatory and tariff structure, using various means such as disassembly and reassembly, re-exports, and outright smuggling.

### Personal and Social Networks

Personal relationships and social networks are important to success in the computer industry and are most effective when they transcend national boundaries. While Western economic theory is based on the notions of pure profit maximization and professional corporate management, personal relationships are often significant factors underlying business decisions.

This is more especially true in East Asia, where personal relationships and social networks carry great weight. For instance, in Japan, personal networks are often based on alumni networks of universities, which are particularly tight among people of the same graduating class. The most elite network is that of Tokyo University alumni, who dominate the upper echelons of government and industry. These networks have helped "Japan, Inc." coordinate policy between government and industry, and the networks create an invisible but powerful barrier to outsiders. Korea's personal networks are based on family and correspond to the *chaebol* system. Top positions in *chaebol*-affiliated companies generally go to offspring and relatives of the founder, although some *chaebol* have turned more to professional managers in recent years.

The Chinese networks of Taiwan, Hong Kong, and Singapore are based on family first, with other affiliations based on ties to a common ancestral city in China and on alumni networks. The key difference between the Chinese networks and those of Japan and Korea is the international nature of the Chinese networks. Chinese engineers in Silicon Valley are valuable resources to be nurtured and tapped when needed, and family ties are the basis of many investment decisions around Asia and the world. While it is difficult to measure or prove such an effect, it is clear that the global nature of the Chinese networks has been a major factor in the integration of Taiwan, Hong Kong, and to a lesser extent, Singapore into the global computer industry.

Linkages to the Global Production System

A country is more effectively integrated when it has multiple linkages to the global network. This is best when many local companies have ties to many multinationals or sell directly in foreign markets. Strong linkages to the global production system offer a number of rewards to national industries. The most obvious is access to foreign markets, either through the distribution channels of MNCs or through direct exports to local distributors. Nearly as important is the market information that flows back through those linkages. In a fast-changing industry like the PC industry, it is critical to have timely information on market trends in lead markets. A third benefit is the flow of technology to local producers through interaction with MNCs. These benefits to the local industry are of greatest value when they flow through multiple channels, rather than being limited to links between a few large companies.

There are many ways to establish linkages to global production networks, markets, and technology sources. One is through attracting and working with MNCs. While many governments have worried about the detrimental effects of MNCs on local economies, the experience of the computer industry suggests that their presence is not only positive, but necessary. MNCs bring in capital and technology that would be expensive to develop locally, and they provide a ready-made channel to global markets. They also force local companies to achieve world class capabilities in order to compete with or sell to the MNCs. Japan put shackles on IBM in the 1960s and 1970s to protect local producers, but it kept IBM around as a competitive yardstick for its local companies. Without IBM's competition, Fujitsu, Hitachi, and NEC probably would have competed with each other but never achieved the high level of technological capabilities that they did. Further evidence of the value of foreign competition is the fact that Japan never produced reasonably priced PCs to world standards until Compaq, IBM, Apple, and Microsoft shook up the local market.

This finding about the value of MNCs contradicts the beliefs of many governments and development economists that infant industries require protection from foreign competition until domestic companies are strong enough to compete on their own. There are numerous examples of countries, including Brazil, India, France, and Mexico, that have tried unsuccessfully to nurture their computer industries behind various forms of protection. Countries such as Singapore and Taiwan (as well as Ireland and Israel) have succeeded by integrating themselves into the MNCs' production networks.

Japan's overseas connections are limited by the vertical integration of the *keiretsu* system, which funnels trade, technology, and information through the lead company in the production chain. For end products such as systems, printers, and monitors, Japan's links to the global production system are mainly through the big computer vendors that sell to foreign markets and OEM customers. A few companies, such as Toshiba and Canon, have developed their own brand name marketing channels overseas; others, such as

NEC, Fujitsu, and Hitachi, are now planning to market their own brands more aggressively. In components and production equipment, Japanese companies have more extensive links to foreign customers; for instance, Japanese chipmakers cooperate with Intel to design chips that support Intel's microprocessors, and Japan's semiconductor equipment makers have close relationships with all the major foreign chipmakers.

Korea's ties to the global network are even more restricted, with most interactions flowing through a few large *chaebol*. The *chaebol* mostly sell components and peripherals to foreign systems makers, and they have some OEM relationships with those companies as well. Few Korean computer exports carry Korean brand names, because the *chaebol* lack strong international marketing capabilities and distribution systems, especially in computer markets. Korean firms have also been developing new linkages to international markets and production networks with investments in companies such as AST, Maxtor, and Zenith. These investments have been in declining companies, but the Koreans hope to turn those companies around and gain access to markets and technologies. With the exception of Trigem, few non-*chaebol* companies have the resources to target foreign markets on their own, and Trigem only does so as an OEM.

By contrast, Taiwan's production network can be seen as an extension of the global production networks of the PC industry, with multiple ties to the world's leading MNCs. Rather than channeling their trade through a few large companies as Japan and Korea do, Taiwan has many companies with direct relationships to MNCs as OEMs, subcontractors, and suppliers. Many Taiwanese companies do business with several MNCs, and most MNCs have ties with a number of Taiwanese companies, creating multiple channels through which information and technology can flow and giving Taiwan's companies a broad perspective on the international market.

Singapore's national production system is linked to the global production system directly through the internal structures of the many MNCs located in Singapore. These MNCs organize a regional supply network from Singapore and then market the products through their own global marketing and distribution channels. As the MNCs have decided (with government persuasion) to expand and upgrade their activities in Singapore, the flow of information and technology to Singapore has accelerated. Most local companies are suppliers to MNCs, but a few, like IPC and Creative Technology, have developed their own marketing capabilities in foreign markets.

Hong Kong's computer industry is linked to the global production system mostly through MNCs that operate in Hong Kong or that buy from Hong Kong companies. The linkages mostly take the form of management of financial flows in and out of China, coordination of logistics, and oversight of labor-intensive manufacturing operations. They do not involve as much technology flow as seen in Singapore, because MNCs have made little effort to move technology-intensive operations to Hong Kong or China.

Figure 6-2 summarizes these national industry structures in East Asia and the nature of their linkages to international markets and the global production

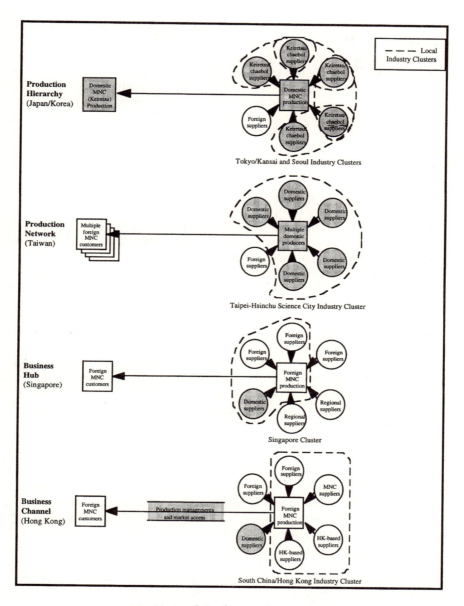

**Production Hierarchy (Japan/Korea)**

Keiretsu chaebol suppliers

Keiretsu chaebol suppliers

Keiretsu chaebol suppliers

Domestic MNC production

Keiretsu chaebol suppliers

Foreign suppliers

Keiretsu chaebol suppliers

Domestic MNC (Keiretsu) Production

Local Industry Clusters

Tokyo/Kansai and Seoul Industry Clusters

**Production Network (Taiwan)**

Domestic suppliers

Domestic suppliers

Domestic suppliers

Multiple domestic producers

Foreign suppliers

Domestic suppliers

Domestic suppliers

Multiple foreign MNC customers

Taipei-Hsinchu Science City Industry Cluster

**Business Hub (Singapore)**

Foreign suppliers

Foreign suppliers

Foreign suppliers

Foreign MNC production

Domestic suppliers

Regional suppliers

Regional suppliers

Foreign MNC customers

Singapore Cluster

**Business Channel (Hong Kong)**

Foreign suppliers

Foreign suppliers

MNC suppliers

Foreign MNC production

Domestic suppliers

HK-based suppliers

HK-based suppliers

Production management and market access

Foreign MNC customers

South China/Hong Kong Industry Cluster

FIGURE 6-2. National Production Systems in East Asia

system. We characterize Japan and Korea as production hierarchies, with national industries organized in a pyramid structure and most interaction with the outside world being funneled through the companies at the top of the pyramid. Taiwan is characterized as a production network, with both internal and external relations organized in a network structure of companies and individuals. Singapore has evolved into a business hub, serving as a center for the regional production networks of many multinational corporations. Hong Kong is a business channel between China and the outside world, providing skills in management, finance, and trade, as well as specialized knowledge of China's business environment.

### Impacts of Industry Structure on Production

The differences among national industry structures helps explain the specialization of different countries in the computer industry. Japan and Korea have structures that are good for supporting high-volume manufacturing of commodity products; cash and know-how can be shifted around within the group to support large investments and capitalize on process technologies developed for other products. Since there is little job mobility in each country, and companies work with the same suppliers over and over, knowledge rarely leaks outside and organizations develop institutional capabilities that can be continually tapped.

However, such hierarchical structures are much less effective in producing innovative new products or processes that require new skills and perspectives. While Silicon Valley companies try to tap the best source available for any technology, process, or product, regardless of where it is, the *keiretsu* and *chaebol* tend to restrict themselves to their own supply channels. They are willing to acquire outside technology, but they do not benefit from a wide variety of interactions with different companies and individuals that would help provide a broader perspective and new ways of doing things. The other problem with the *keiretsu* and *chaebol* systems is the need to support the "family" of suppliers. This relationship has its advantages, such as the trust that develops from such long-term relationships or the ability to squeeze suppliers in hard times rather than lay off workers in the parent company. Such relationships become costly to support, however, when less expensive, faster suppliers are available outside the family. While U.S. PC companies were sourcing low-cost parts from Asia and using Taiwanese OEMs for much of their manufacturing, Japanese computer makers stuck with their traditional suppliers, even when they moved their own production offshore. Only in the mid-1990s—when it was faced with a competitive challenge in its own market—did the Japanese PC industry start turning to non-Japanese suppliers for a large share of components and manufacturing.

The Taiwanese network structure is very good at getting products to the market quickly. It has also been good at nurturing entrepreneurship, as people move around and start new companies. This constant churning gives companies a steady flow of new ideas and perspectives. Smaller companies cannot depend on one large customer to keep them busy, so they are always looking for new niches to fill, and even larger companies move quickly into new product areas. The nature of this system has its drawbacks, however, especially in commodity products that require large investments. Taiwanese companies rely on a fast follower strategy with Japanese producers of monitors, CRTs, DRAMs, and LCDs, licensing Japanese technology one generation removed from the market lead. This saves the cost of heavy R&D investments, but it also means that Taiwan's companies never earn the large profits that accrue in the first months of a new product generation.

Singapore's MNC-dominated industry structure means that the country is strong in the industry segments where those MNCs are involved. For now, that includes disk drives, PCs, printers, and, increasingly, semiconductors and software. The MNC connection is highly effective in linking Singapore to the global production system, and the presence of leading MNCs has strengthened the capabilities of local suppliers. The disadvantage is the risk that those companies will go elsewhere, but the development of a strong local supply base and good infrastructure has kept them in Singapore so far. The government's incentives to the MNCs to upgrade their activities in Singapore have helped strengthen their commitments to Singapore as well.

Hong Kong's ability to manage a complex set of interfirm relationships across the border has enabled many companies to tap the low-wage workforce on the mainland to carry out labor-intensive manufacturing activities. The use of cheap labor in China has been a disadvantage in terms of developing more technologically sophisticated, higher value-added production. There is very little product design or R&D, and most engineering is process oriented. Unlike Taiwan, Hong Kong's small companies have rarely grown into larger companies that can support a local production network. While Korea's excessive vertical integration is a problem for its competitiveness in computers, Hong Kong's nearly flat network of small manufacturers is also limited in its ability to move beyond simple assembly operations.

The virtues of a flexible, network-type industry structure would seem to be equally applicable in the software industry—in the United States, this has been the case. Certainly, the hierarchical structure of Japan's software industry has hobbled innovation and slowed the growth of a packaged software industry. What is surprising on the surface is that Taiwan and Hong Kong have not done especially well in software either, in spite of more flexible industry structures. In these cases, a different set of problems has arisen. Small software companies might be able to develop innovative products, but they lack the resources to commercialize them successfully. In the hardware industry, a company can make cables one day and keyboards the next in order to keep a stream of income, but software companies need to stay with a product to justify a user's investment in the program. Software products often are not commercially viable until several generations have passed and users feel they can invest, having the confidence that the program will continue to be upgraded and supported in the future. Lacking strong venture capital markets or wealthy "angels" to finance several years of operations, Asian software companies often do not survive long enough to develop successful products.

The bigger problems faced by all of the East Asian countries in software go beyond industry structure; these include lack of English language capabilities and poor intellectual property protection. Equally important is the small size of domestic markets (outside Japan), lack of user sophistication, and the low value placed on software and services by domestic customers.

## Role of the Domestic Market

Computer companies gain a competitive advantage from close proximity to sophisticated users and access to large markets, whether domestic or foreign. The rapid adoption of personal computer technology in the United States market helped U.S. hardware and software firms achieve their leading position in the PC industry. Although most hardware (and some software) companies produce for a global market, there are still benefits to being close to the end user. Producers can rely on domestic revenues to support investments in R&D and production capacity, and to underwrite the costs of entering export markets. Even more important, producers benefit from close interaction with advanced users, whose input is invaluable in developing and improving both hardware and software products.

Among the East Asian countries, only Japan has a large domestic computer market, and Japan has been far behind the United States in adoption of PC technologies. The isolation of Japan's domestic PC market from global standards put Japanese computer makers at a disadvantage in global markets, because products developed for the domestic market could not be exported. In fact, Japan's most successful global player has been Toshiba, which was doing so poorly in the domestic market that it concentrated on making portable PCs for export based on the global Wintel standard. The NIEs have targeted export markets, working closely with the MNCs to understand their needs and integrate themselves into their global production systems. Only Japan has built a computer industry that mainly serves the domestic market. Korean companies make PCs for both the domestic market and for export, while Korea's DRAM and monitor production is mostly exported. Taiwan and Singapore, by contrast, have become major exporters of PCs and peripherals while still depending on imports for much of their domestic IT demand. None of the NIEs has used its domestic market as a base for developing many products for export. Instead, most successful Asian companies have focused on producing for global markets, or for the global production network.

### Software and Services: Production Close to Use

Producing for the global production network has worked well in hardware, but it has been less successful in developing software and services industries

Success in software and services depends on close interaction with sophisticated end users, because the global production network is much less developed for software than for hardware. Software companies may go to India or China for inexpensive programmers, but product development takes place close to lead users. Lead users do not have to be in big markets, however. Even small countries such as Hong Kong, New Zealand, and Israel have highly sophisticated users in industries such as banking, agriculture, and defense. Local companies have developed software for these sectors that was eventually commercialized and sold internationally.[4] The domestic market is even more important for information services such as systems integration, custom programming, network services, and outsourcing, which require an intimate understanding of individual customers' businesses that comes only with close interaction with the customer.

To succeed in software and services requires adopting a national strategy that focuses on both production and use—what Rob Schware[5] refers to as a "walking on two legs" strategy. In East Asia, the slow adoption of computer technology has been accompanied by a corresponding underdevelopment of software and services industries.

In addition to the effects of the domestic market on production, it is worth also considering the level of computer use as it affects productivity and competitiveness of individual companies and national economies. Table 6-2 presents some indicators of computer use in East Asia. Among the NIEs, Singapore is the most advanced user of computer technology in the region in terms of both installed base and level of investment. Singapore has been the only country in the region to emphasize production and use equally in its computer policies. Singapore has also been the most successful in applying computer

TABLE 6-2. Computer Use in the Pacific Rim

| Country | Investment (Investment in Computer[a] as % of GDP, 1995[b]) | Growth (Growth Rate in Computer Investment, 1985–1995) | Installed Base (Number of Computers per 1,000 People, 1995[c]) | Software (Software Production as % of GDP, 1995[d]) |
|---|---|---|---|---|
| United States | 3.23 | 9.6 | 365 | .86 |
| Japan | 1.89 | 9.5 | 145 | .15 |
| Singapore | 2.25 | 12.2 | 189 | .84 |
| Hong Kong | 1.31 | 17.1 | 171 | .04 |
| Korea | 1.97 | 17.8 | 78 | .13 |
| Taiwan | 0.80 | 8.3 | 98 | .12 |

[a]Hardward, software, and services.

[b]IDC, data provided to authors.

[c]Karen Petska-Juliussen and Egil Juliussen, *The 8th Annual Computer Industry Almanac* (Glenbrook, Nev.: Computer Industry Almanac, 1996).

[d]See table 4-2.

technologies to improve government services and upgrade the country's infrastructure. The other countries have lagged in adopting information technologies, although Korea and Hong Kong have been catching up from initially low levels.

As other countries look to East Asia's experience in computers, they should not be so impressed with the Asian production network that they overlook the underdevelopment of the domestic market in most countries. Computer use has benefits that span the entire economy, and promotion of production at the expense of use is a bad bargain, no matter how impressive the production numbers. Also, as we enter the network era of computing, user and producer skills will increasingly overlap, and one key to success in production will be a very strong customer orientation. The absence of a knowledgeable user base will become more of a competitive disadvantage in software, services, and information content, industries in which the East Asian countries are already weak.

All of the East Asian governments have promoted hardware more aggressively than software, which partly explains their poor performance in software. However, it is not likely that traditional industry promotion strategies would work well with software in any case. Rather, government policy can shape the software and information services industries by promoting domestic use, supporting venture capital and over-the-counter stock markets, and protecting intellectual property rights. With software and services being the most rapidly growing segments of the computer industry, the Asian countries are so far missing out on a great market opportunity. This opportunity will become even more attractive as local and regional IT markets grow rapidly in the future.

## National Capabilities

The single most important factor for long-term competitiveness at the national and company level is the development of superior capabilities. At the national level, these include skilled workers, good infrastructure, and the ability to assimilate and develop technology. Company capabilities include entrepreneurial skills, innovation, product and process technologies, and management skills.

### Human Resources

The creation of the Asian production network for computers has been closely linked to the availability of engineers and other skilled professionals in the region. While cheap factory labor may have been a factor in the early shift of production to Asia, the presence of skilled engineering talent was more important in the long run. It was those engineering skills that enabled the Asian network to move rapidly from assembly of simple products to engineering and manufacturing of sophisticated products. The Asian countries have produced large numbers of scientists and engineers, especially at the bachelor's degree level. In 1992, Asia produced nearly as many bachelor's degrees in science and engineering as Europe and North America combined. Granted Asia has about four times the population of the Europe and North America, and thus is producing a lower level proportionately. Still, the sheer numbers of technical people in Asia have helped fuel its drive in high-tech industries such as computers. And while Asia's graduate programs are far behind those of the United States and Europe, Asian countries have tapped the U.S. university system to provide training to large numbers of people (table 6-3).

While Asia as a region has trained large numbers of scientists and engineers, there are significant differences among the countries in the region in both training and management of human resources. These differences help explain some of the differences in the countries' performance in the computer industry.

Each of the five countries in this study has emphasized training of technical professionals as part of their high-technology promotion efforts. Japan has the highest ratio of scientists and engineers to its population, rivaling the United States, followed by Korea, Singapore, and Taiwan (table 6-4). Japan and the three NIEs for which we have data have all surpassed the United States in the share of its population holding science and engineering degrees, with Korea in the lead. Japan produces the largest number of advanced degrees, in number and in proportion to its population. But unlike Japan, Korea and Taiwan have sent large numbers of students to earn doctoral degrees in the United States, giving them not only access to the U.S. university system, but also a chance to develop a network of contacts in the United States. Most of the 40,700 Japanese students in U.S. universities in 1992 were undergraduates, and only 11% were studying science and engineering. By contrast, most of the students from China, Taiwan, and Korea were graduate students, and the number studying science and engineering ranged from 36% (Korea) to 65% (China).[6]

The difference is obvious to anyone doing interviews in these countries. Most top Japanese executives, academics, and officials have advanced degrees from leading Japanese universities, while their counterparts in Korea and Taiwan will usually hold a degree from a U.S. university. Singaporean and Hong

TABLE 6-3. Human Resources in Science and Engineering by Region

| Region | First University Degrees in S&E, 1992 | Doctoral Degrees in S&E, 1992 | Foreign S&E Students Enrolled in U.S. Universities, 1991–1992 |
|---|---|---|---|
| Asia | 523,651 | 11,223 | 126,665 |
| Europe | 299,057 | 25,089 | 20,625 |
| North America | 242,877 | 19,449 | n.a. |
| Latin America | n.a. | n.a. | 17,669 |

Source: National Science Foundation, *Science and Engineering Indicators, 1996* (Washington, D.C.: NSF, 1996).

TABLE 6-4. Human Resources of the United States and East Asian Countries

| Country | Scientists & Engineers in R&D per 10,000 Workers, 1990[a] | % of 24-Year-Olds with Science & Engineering Degrees, 1992[b] | Masters and Ph.D.s Earned in Science & Engineering, 1990[a] | Ph.D.s Earned in Science & Engineering in U.S. Universities, 1992[b] |
|---|---|---|---|---|
| United States | 75.6 | 4.6 | 66,508 | 16,336 (1993)[c] |
| Japan | 74.9 | 6.2 | 36,549 | 171 |
| Korea | 48.8 | 6.7 | 7,070 | 1,458 |
| Taiwan | 27.1 | 5.9 | 4,011 | 1,422 |
| Singapore | 37.2 | 4.8 | 200 | n.a. |
| Hong Kong | n.a. | n.a. | n.a. | n.a. |
| China | 5.6 | 1.2 | 20,787 | 2,079 |

Sources:

[a]National Science Foundation, *Human Resources for Science and Technology: The Asian Region* (Washington, D.C.: NSF, 1993).

[b]NSF, 1996.

[c]U.S. citizens and permanent residents.

Kong leaders are more likely to have degrees from the United Kingdom, owing to their former colonial ties. These differences cannot help but have an impact on the "global-ness" in outlook among the business, government, and academic institutions in these countries.

Beyond the broad numbers, there are important differences among the countries in both the quantity and quality of computer professionals. The number of math and computer science degrees produced in each country is dwarfed by the production of engineers. Japan's output of bachelor's degrees in math and computer science trails even that of Korea and is barely ahead of Taiwan. Compared to the United States, all of the Asian countries' output of computer scientists is tiny, whether at the bachelor's, master's, or Ph.D. level. While Japan and China actually produced more engineers with bachelor's degrees from 1982 to 1990 than the United States, the United States produced more than twice as many computer science degrees as all the other countries combined (table 6-5).

The number of software professionals was more closely proportional to population, but the definitions and quality vary across countries. Japan, for instance, has a large number of software professionals, but most of them do not have university degrees in computer science. Rather than treat software development as a desirable profession, there is a tendency to shunt less talented workers into the data processing departments of large companies where they end up as programmers. More generally, training processes that are geared to the lowest common denominator, as well as seniority-based promotion, tend to discourage initiative and limit the upward mobility of talented people.

Similar problems can be found in the large Korean *chaebol*, which have large pools of technical people, but generally push the best people into hard-

TABLE 6-5. Engineering and Computer Professionals in Asia and the United States

| Country | Bachelor's Degrees in Engineering, 1982–1990[a] | Bachelor's Degrees in Math & Computer Science, 1982–1990[a] | Masters and Ph.D.s in Math & Computer Science, 1990[a] | Number of Software Professionals[b] |
|---|---|---|---|---|
| United States | 646,906 | 424,091[c] | 14,032 | 1,744,616 |
| Japan | 677,258 | 30,258 | 827 | 850,000 |
| Korea | 219,486 | 32,550 | 596 | 295,798 |
| Taiwan | 69,851 | 18,941 | 465 | 121,800 |
| Singapore | 7,445 | n.a. | n.a. | 9,772 |
| Hong Kong[d] | 49,864[e] | 48,456[e] | n.a. | 14,954 |
| China | 875,206 | 90,921 | n.a. | 993,650 |

Sources:

[a]NSF (1993).

[b]Capers Jones, *Software Productivity and Quality Today—The Worldwide Perspective* (Carlsbad, Calif.: Information Systems Management Group, 1993). Data updated in 1995 in correspondence to authors.

[c]NSF (1996).

[d]Source for all Hong Kong data: Hong Kong Census and Statistics Department.

[e]Number is total persons with bachelor's degree as of 1996, not comparable to figures from other countries.

ware, giving short shrift to software. Also, the *chaebol* are able to hire most of the best talent in Korea, leaving smaller companies unable to attract enough high-caliber workers. Another major problem in Korea is the poor quality of graduate education, a problem only partially alleviated by sending students to the United States for graduate school. Finally, Korean companies have found it difficult to capitalize on the international outlook that could be offered by employees who have studied or worked abroad. Even when Korean companies send workers abroad specifically to expand their horizons, their management culture makes it difficult for senior managers to accept the views of subordinates when they conflict with their own views.[7] In all, Korea does a good job in developing engineers and technicians, but is less successful in developing more advanced skills or taking advantage of younger people who have those skills.

Taiwan has successfully used the U.S. university system to provide graduate education to its students, and uses U.S. companies to provide high-tech industry experience. In many cases, Taiwanese companies are able to hire people with high levels of education and experience from the United States, often by offering the opportunity to start their own companies in the future. Even those who remain in the United States are considered valuable sources of information to the Taiwanese industry, and they may eventually be lured back to work in Taiwan. However, there is a significant cost to having so many of the country's best and brightest working abroad, because many will never return.

Singapore has a talented pool of manufacturing professionals with specialized knowledge of disk drive production and a few other sectors of the computer industry, but it has a serious labor shortage that has forced it to depend heavily on immigration for engineers and other technical workers. The government has targeted graduate education for greater attention, and the country is benefiting from a second generation effect, whereby the children of many laborers are now getting university degrees. Both factors promise to upgrade Singapore's human resource base in the future. Still, Singapore's population is simply too small to support continued expansion of the high-technology sector, and allowing more immigration threatens the government's ability to maintain social and political stability. One answer is to encourage offshore investment and retain the highest value jobs in Singapore, but the trick might be to convince Singaporeans to leave their comfortable life on the island and venture into more challenging environments.

Hong Kong has lagged behind the other countries in this group in developing its human resources for high-technology industries. In the 1990s, however, the government moved aggressively to catch up, by upgrading existing university and polytechnic programs and by creating the Hong Kong University of Science and Technology. The post-1997 situation will be critical, however, as many of the colony's best educated people have obtained citizenship or landed immigrant status in other countries and will likely leave if they find the political situation becoming difficult. On the other hand, those who spent time overseas have developed networks of business contacts around the Pacific and enhanced their own value. Also, as Hong Kong's industry becomes intertwined with China, it is able to take advantage of the large numbers of Chinese engineers, computer scientists, and other technical personnel (see tables 6-4 and 6-5). While other countries are also moving into China, Hong Kong is in the best position to capitalize on this resource.

In summary, there are at least two problems that the five countries have in common. One is the weakness of graduate studies in their universities and the need to send students overseas for a quality graduate education. The other is the general inability to train and manage software professionals to produce innovative, internationally competitive software. Each country puts out many more electronics engineers than computer scientists. This is certainly driven by the better job prospects in the electronics industry, but it also perpetuates the Asian focus on hardware. As a result, much of the Asian computer industry is focused on hardware engineering and manufacturing, and it has failed to seriously challenge U.S. leadership in the innovation-intensive segments of the computer industry.

Each country has responded to encourage innovation and develop "soft" skills with initiatives to encourage creative thinking throughout the education process. Change is not coming easily—especially within entrenched educational bureaucracies—and will take time to implement. In the meantime, China, India, Russia, the Philippines, and other countries offer abundant, low-cost programming talent that is increasingly attracting the attention of the global computer industry.

## Technology

Companies compete by developing two types of technological capabilities: product and process technologies. Product technology is the ability to design new products or improve existing products. Process technology is the knowledge required to manufacture a product in volume at acceptable quality levels.

An example of product technology would be Intel's design of a new microprocessor generation. A less obvious example would be a Taiwanese company designing, then manufacturing, a new notebook computer for an American PC maker. Product technology is not just "know-how," but is also tied to the concept of "know-what"—it is necessary to know what the market needs in order to develop successful new products. Among the Asian countries, Japanese companies have by far the strongest product technologies, ranging from notebook computers to LCDs, laser printers, and a variety of components and production equipment. Korean companies' strengths in product technology are mostly in commodity chips, monitors, and LCDs. Taiwan has good product technologies in a range of components and peripherals, as well as systems. Singapore's MNCs are leaders in disk drive, PC, and printer technologies, and its local companies are standard setters in sound cards. Hong Kong has only developed product technologies for specialized products such as electronic games and some wireless communications devices.

While product technology is often thought of in terms of developing new products or making technological leaps in existing products, much product technology involves steady, incremental progress in existing product lines. The Japanese have been especially good at such incremental improvements (or *kaizen*, as it is called in Japan) and have been strongest in competing after product standards are established. Most U.S. companies tended to focus more on big leaps and were hampered by an unwillingness to look outside their own organizations for ways to improve their products.[8] Japanese companies have also applied a "trickle up" process, in which a new technology is introduced in a consumer item in order to gain manufacturing experience; after the manufacturing process is mastered, the technology in introduced into more advanced products.[9] This was the case in Sharp's development of LCD technology, which it originally used in pocket calculators, then steadily introduced into a series of more advanced products, including televisions, notebook computers, and camcorders.[10] Other Japanese companies have likewise developed core technologies for one product and then applied those technologies to a diverse range of products, as in the case of Canon's diversification from cameras to copiers to semiconductor steppers, all of which are based on core technologies in optoelectronics.

Companies often protect their product technologies through patents or copyrights, but the value of many intellectual property rights are of limited duration in the computer industry, as new product generations make old products obsolete. Other core technology, such as source code for software, may continue to be employed in succeeding product generations and can retain its value. Process technologies are not as easily protected through legal means, but they are often embedded in the companies that develop them, as they become part of institutional memory of those companies.

Process technology is the knowledge of how to make something. There is a significant amount of engineering involved in taking a product from prototype to large-scale manufacturing. Japanese manufacturers gained competitive advantages over foreign competitors in many industries through advances in the manufacturing process such as just-in-time, lean manufacturing, and quality control circles. Other companies have imitated those processes and developed new techniques such as computer-assisted manufacturing to further improve the manufacturing system. Korea has achieved high yields in DRAM production by developing process technologies, while Taiwan has specialized in flexible production techniques. Singapore's disk drive industry is exceptionally good at ramping up production of new generation products and transferring older generations offshore.

The initial success of the five countries in computers largely resulted from the ability to acquire and assimilate technology from abroad. Continued growth has been supported by the ability to develop technology locally. The most basic level of technological capability is the ability to evaluate new technologies to decide which ones to license or acquire. The next level is adapting technology for local use, such as localizing software or modifying equipment. Beyond these technology adoption capabilities is the ability to develop new technologies, or design new products using existing technologies. Firms conduct their own R&D, but these efforts are complemented by the presence of university research centers and other public research institutions. In the United States, for example, a great deal of R&D is conducted by university researchers and eventually commercialized through licensing or creation of venture companies.

Among the East Asian countries, Japan is by far the biggest spender on R&D, spending about US$63 billion in 1993, or 2.7% of GDP (table 6-6). Korea, in second place, spends just one-tenth of Japan's level, and Taiwan,

TABLE 6-6.   R&D Spending in the United States and Asia

| Country | R&D as % of GDP,1993 | Computer Industry R&D as % of Industry Revenues |
|---|---|---|
| United States | 2.6[a] | 13.2 (1990–1993)[a] |
| Japan | 2.7[a] | 7.5[b] |
| Korea | 2.6[c] | 3.7 (1991–1993)[d] |
| Taiwan | 1.8 (1995)[e] | 4.6[f] |
| Singapore | 1.2[g] | n.a. |
| Hong Kong | 0.1[h] | n.a. |

*Sources:*
[a]NSF (1996).
[b]*OECD Economics at a Glance* (Paris: OECD, 1996).
[c]Asian Technology Information Program, "Update on Status of Science and Technology in Korea" (Tokyo: ATIP Reports, 1997).
[d]Korea Institute for Industrial Economics and Trade, data provided to authors.
[e]Directorate General of Budget Accounting and Statistics, 1997 (www.dgbasey.gov.tw).
[f]Ministry of Economic Affairs, provided by Market Intelligence Center, Institute for Information Industries.
[g]EMF, *World Competitiveness Report* (Geneva: EMF, 1996).
[h]David Kahaner and Julian Wu, "General Remarks About Hong Kong" (Tokyo: Asian Technology Information Program, 1995). Note that government statisticians place Hong Kong's R&D at less than 1% of GDP.

Singapore, and Hong Kong spend even less. Korea has boosted its R&D spending to 2.6% of GDP, but its entire R&D investment for all industries and technologies is not much larger than that of the corporate R&D budgets of IBM or Siemens. Only Japan really has the resources to compete in a wide range of high-tech industries, and only Japan has relied heavily on R&D as a basis of competition. Even Japanese companies would benefit from focusing on a few key technologies in which they are already leaders, or have good prospects to become leaders.

Korean and Taiwan have historically relied on a "fast follower" approach to technology, licensing technologies just behind the leading edge from Japanese or U.S. companies. Given their limited resources, they needed to concentrate their efforts on technologies in which they could realistically compete and avoid direct competition with leading MNCs as much as possible. Korean companies have begun to compete more directly with the Japanese in products such as DRAMs but have also become more active in strategic alliances with some U.S. and Japanese companies. A problem for Korea has been the government's across-the-board funding of research in numerous fields, putting a little money into everything, rather than focusing on a few key technologies. The government has also funded development of technologies that have never gained acceptance outside the domestic market, such as the Ticom minicomputer. Korea's limited capital and human resource base make it imperative that it narrow its focus in the future.

Taiwan's companies have long cooperated with MNCs, finding ways to add value to technologies originally developed abroad, while developing some new technologies in government-affiliated labs and institutions. Key technologies for the computer, communications, and semiconductor industries have been developed in public institutions, then often spun-off to private companies for commercialization. The Taiwan government has made some mistakes of its own, but by working with industry and concentrating on filling the gaps in the private sector's capabilities, it has generally had a good track record in technology policy.

Singapore has taken the strategic approach of cooperating with MNCs in R&D partnerships aimed at specific technologies such as Chinese character recognition. Domestic companies are too small to do much R&D, so the government has taken a direct role in many of these technology partnerships. Given its limited resources, Singapore has done very well in developing process technologies, and has had some successes in product technologies. Hong Kong was a late starter in R&D and still spends less than 1% of its GDP on R&D, according to informed estimates by government statisticians. Its recent policy initiatives have been aimed at training the scientists and engineers and providing some incentives needed to bolster its technological abilities.

The key to success for each of the NIEs has been in finding ways of leveraging their own R&D efforts to capitalize on the much larger investments being made by MNCs. This has helped the countries to upgrade their own technological capabilities and enhance their positions in the MNCs' production networks.

### Infrastructure

Participation in a global production system depends on the presence of a strong supporting infrastructure that includes port facilities, telecommunications, land, water, and even amenities such as good hotels and local transportation. Companies utilize lean manufacturing techniques that require the ability to get components to the right place at the right time at a reasonable cost. This cannot be done without good air and sea port facilities and efficient processing of customs and other documents. The computer industry is also closely linked to telecommunications on both the user and producer sides. Computers only begin to achieve their potential in improving productivity when they are linked together in networks; only then do they enable people to work together and share information in new ways and improve the functioning of organizations. Therefore the presence of a good telecommunications network is important to the development of a sophisticated user base needed to support software and services production. The computer hardware industry benefits from good telecommunications networks; companies can be connected to the electronic data interchange (EDI) networks of the major MNCs and use the Internet and other networks as communications tools. As MNCs locate product design and engineering functions around the world, it is critical to be able to send large amounts of information electronically to link these operations.

Among the East Asian countries, Hong Kong and Singapore clearly have the best transportation and telecommunications networks. These two have the advantage of being small islands with good natural ports, but they also have invested in world class facilities and streamlined the processing of documents through trade related EDI systems. They have both invested heavily in their telecoms infrastructures and have low rates for local and international service. Japan's telecoms infrastructure is well developed, but service is very expensive. Meanwhile, bureaucratic infighting within the government has hobbled efforts to improve the system. Korea and Taiwan have both moved to reform their telecoms sectors, introducing competition to some segments of the market, but changes have been incremental.

### Entrepreneurship and Innovation

Entrepreneurship and innovation are critical assets for firms and countries in the computer industry. Differences in these assets have been an important factor in determining the relative competitiveness of East Asian countries in computers. Some countries seem to be full of entrepreneurs and innovators, in both small and large companies. Other countries either have lower levels of entrepreneurship and innovation, or they fail to reward such capabilities and stifle innovators who are possible competitors to established firms. The highly entrepreneurial Taiwanese computer industry manufactures a wide range of products for niche markets that are ignored by their Japanese and Korean competitors. Indigenous entrepreneurs such as Japan's Nintendo and

Singapore's Creative Technology have developed and dominated new market segments, even in countries with industries that are dominated by multinational giants.

The presence of entrepreneurial and innovative people is a difficult phenomenon to explain. Some people credit cultural factors, such as American "rugged individualism" or the oft-quoted Chinese proverb that "It's better to be the head of a chicken than the tail of an ox." Others point to policy factors, such as government policies that favor either large or small business. Other factors might include the presence of venture capital markets and over-the-counter stock markets to support start-up businesses. In some countries, bankruptcy laws protect the personal assets of entrepreneurs, while in other countries the laws can lead to prison for bankruptcy. There is no research we are aware of that convincingly explains the level of entrepreneurial activity in a country. Some would argue that smaller companies are more entrepreneurial and innovative, but this notion is at least partially refuted by the success of large companies such as Hewlett-Packard and Sony in developing new, innovative products. Also, start-ups such as Microsoft and Sun have managed to maintain their entrepreneurial culture even after growing into multibillion dollar companies.

We argue that at the national level these differences are largely determined by differences in national industry structures and government policies. Japan and Korea have industry structures dominated by large, vertically integrated business groups that limit newcomers' access to capital and distribution channels. Those groups also tend to be risk averse and do not promote entrepreneurship (or "intrapreneurship") within their ranks. Singapore's focus on attracting MNCs has put its own entrepreneurs at a disadvantage, because the MNCs have monopolized human and other resources. In contrast, Taiwan's many small-and medium-sized enterprises have had to survive by being entrepreneurial, and larger companies often reward successful managers by helping them set up their own businesses. In Taiwan, government incentives have also favored smaller companies; in Japan and Korea, such incentives have gone mostly to large domestic companies, and in Singapore, they have gone to MNCs.

### Management

Management is critical to company success, and the presence of many skilled, experienced managers in a country provides a foundation for national competitiveness. Management includes all the capabilities needed to successfully run a company in the dynamic, globally organized computer industry. These capabilities include financial and human resources management, and the ability to coordinate the efforts of R&D, marketing, and manufacturing to get the right product to the market at the right time. Such skills also include the ability to manage in an international environment. Management capabilities are largely developed through experience, but can also be enhanced through education. In the United States, that education is often in the form of an

MBA or advanced engineering degree, while in Japan it is usually in a company training program. When the training is in-house, it is more likely to focus on company-specific knowledge, while university programs provide a more general set of skills and knowledge.

A specialized management skill that is critical to success in the PC industry is logistics. Acer's fast-food model of PC production is based on getting the right components to the right place at the right time. Other Taiwanese OEMs are now performing the logistics function for their customers. Interestingly, one of the new competitors in manufacturing logistics is DHL, which has used its skills in logistics management in the courier business to manage the PC manufacturing process for some vendors.

Marketing is another critical management function, even in a technology-intensive industry such as computers. Firms must search out market opportunities, set up distribution channels, provide support services, and possibly advertise to build brand recognition. The capabilities required vary according to the channel chosen. Selling through an original equipment manufacturer under that company's brand name is probably the easiest method, while marketing one's own brand name products requires the greatest investment and the widest range of capabilities. On the other hand, brand name recognition is a valuable asset and own-brand sales offer the largest profit potential. Companies like IBM, Compaq, and Hewlett Packard are able to charge a price premium because of brand recognition and well-established sales and distribution channels. Among the East Asian computer companies, only a few—such as Toshiba, Acer, and Creative Technology—have been able to establish any brand recognition outside their home markets. Marketing is probably even more important in the packaged software industry, and the East Asian industry has had little success in developing a strong market presence outside of the video game market.

A vital element of marketing is market intelligence. Being able to forecast demand is absolutely critical in an industry where being three months late with a product, or not having sufficient inventory to meet demand, can mean missing out completely. Poor forecasting has caused well-publicized problems for companies such as Apple and IBM in meeting market demand. Even components suppliers and subcontractors need to have their own market intelligence capabilities to anticipate the needs of their OEM customers. The market intelligence efforts of companies and government institutions in Taiwan and Singapore have been important factors in those countries' success in the computer industry.

Another important management skill is the ability to manage in different national environments and to deal effectively with legal and cultural issues. Many companies have stumbled trying to operate in China, for instance, including the worldly (and Chinese) Acer. Hong Kong managers have been effective managing in China, increasing their value to the industry. Sometimes this involves dealing with unruly workers or making the necessary payments to officials. Singapore is trying to specialize in managing in China (in the Suzhou industrial park that the Singapore government is building), but it is finding that recreating the Singapore model inside China is a bit tricky. This is not to say that China is a unique case. Every country presents its own managerial problems, as many Japanese companies discovered when they invested in the United States. Matsushita's problems dealing with the Hollywood culture in its MCA acquisition are just another example of the difficulties involved managing across borders, despite the rhetoric often heard about "borderless economies." In the global production network, these skills are highly valuable.

Table 6-7 summarizes the key points in the foregoing discussion about each country's industry structure, national capabilities, and its role in the global computer industry.

## Industrial Policy

It is clear from the country studies that national production systems and capabilities do not develop simply as a result of market forces, but instead are heavily influenced by government industrial policy. Industrial policy changes the incentives of private companies and individuals, changes the competitive environment of firms, and may help or hinder the creation of national capabilities.

For the purposes of this analysis, we are mostly interested in sectoral policies that target the computer industry, but we also take into account the effects of more generic policies that affect the computer industry or create capabilities relevant to the industry. The power and resources available to the state vary by country, depending on the structure of the political system, prevailing ideologies, and the government's ability to act independently of interest group pressures. This is important to remember when comparing countries, because governments must make policies within different constraints, and a policy that is successful in one place might not be feasible in another. Industrial policy can involve a wide range of tools. A government can regulate the industry, create state-owned enterprises, nationalize existing companies, use its own procurement process, offer subsidies to the private sector, or invest directly in R&D.[11]

The most important areas of computer industry policy are those that: (1) shape the national industry structure and develop global linkages; (2) create national capabilities; or (3) influence the nature of the domestic market. Just as important as the particular policies in each area, however, is whether these policies are coordinated across the government and whether there is coordination between government and the private sector.

### Shaping National Industry Structure

Computer industry policy in each country tended to reinforce existing industry structures. This is advantageous when a country's industry structure is well suited to a large and growing segment of the industry and global economy,

TABLE 6-7. Industry Structure, National Capabilities, and Role in Global Computer Industry

| Country | Industry Structure | National Capabilities | Role in Global Computer Industry |
|---|---|---|---|
| Japan | Large diversified *keiretsu*, large- and medium-sized independents and small suppliers. Vertical and horizontal linkages within *keiretsu*, looser relations across groups and with independents. | Manufacturing, process technologies, key upstream components technologies, strong distributions channels at home and (in some cases) abroad. Skilled workforce. Financial strength of large firms. | Major producer of mainframes, notebook computers, peripherals, semiconductors, and other components, materials and manufacturing equipment. Linked to global industry via distribution channels of major firms, strategic alliances, and investment in foreign companies. |
| Korea | Large *chaebol* and affiliated suppliers. Strong vertical linkages controlled by lead member of *chaebol*. Family ties within *chaebol*. Weak SME sector. | Manufacturing, process technologies, financial strength of large firms. Educated, hardworking labor force and good engineering skills. | Produce DRAMs, monitors, and flat-panel displays for global markets; PCs for domestic market. Linked through distribution channels of *chaebol*, OEM relations with MNCs, investments in foreign companies. |
| Taiwan | A few medium/large independents and affiliates of larger groups. Many SMEs. Loose, network relationships. Family and other personal relationships are important. | Engineering and design skills, speed to market, entrepreneurial energy, access to technology, and market information via overseas Taiwanese; deep and broad supply base. | Supplier and manufacturer for the global PC industry. Full range of desktops, notebooks, peripherals, and components. Linked to global markets by close OEM/ODM and supplier relations with leading MNCs and through personal networks. |
| Singapore | Subsidiaries of major MNCs and foreign suppliers. A few local independents and many local suppliers to MNCs. Close ties to regional supply and production network. | Excellent infrastructure, good business environment, cluster of suppliers, specialized skills in engineering and manufacturing for disk drive industry. | Manufacturing base for MNCs in PC, semiconductor, and disk drive industry. Supply MNCs with some components. Regional production and operations hub for many MNCs. |
| Hong Kong | Local and MNC computer makers with management in HK and production in China. Local suppliers and subcontractors with loose network relations. Close ties with both MNCs and Chinese manufacturers. | Location, strategic position to China, managerial skills, financial markets, transportation, and communication infrastructure. | Manager for manufacturing base in southern China. Channel for foreign investment into China. Transportation and communication hub for MNCs and Chinese firms. |

but it is detrimental when government policy props up an industry structure that is becoming outmoded.

Japan's industrial policies capitalized on the strengths of the *keiretsu* system to compete with IBM in mainframes and develop high-volume components production. Domestic competition was strong, but it was managed by MITI so as to prevent "excessive" competition and duplication of investment. Japan's industrial policy has been less active in the PC era, but government regulations have become detrimental to the growth of the industry. In particular, the Ministry of Finance crippled the growth of smaller, innovative companies by limiting the flow of initial public offerings onto the stock market. Also, MPT's regulation of the telecommunications industry has slowed the development of data networks and adoption of the Internet.

The Korean government has similarly shaped and reinforced the national computer industry by directing subsidies toward a few large electronics firms and making no effort to restrict the market power of the *chaebol*. The *chaebol* do compete vigorously with each other, but their control over distribution and access to capital enable them to drive out competition from smaller companies. While the government has tried to promote SMEs, it has actually reinforced the *chaebol* system by directing most subsidies to SMEs that are affiliated with *chaebol* groups, rather than independent companies.

Taiwan's industrial policies have filled in the gaps in capabilities of the SMEs rather than trying to subsidize a few large companies only. Government subsidies benefit many companies, and many companies are invited to participate in R&D consortia. Also, Taiwan's lenient bankruptcy laws encourage entrepreneurship by limiting the costs of failure. Such policies have reinforced the decentralized structure of the Taiwanese industry while helping overcome the disadvantages faced by small companies. However, when a bigger company such as Acer ran into financial trouble, the government helped rescue it, in order to save jobs and preserve a national leader.

Singapore's computer policies continued the MNC-led pattern of development that earlier government policies had already established. These policies were successful largely because of the quality of MNCs that came to Singapore and the supporting industries that sprung up around them. Even today, Singapore continues to court new MNC investment—but it is also supporting local companies more actively. On the surface, Hong Kong appears to maintain an evenhanded approach to small and large companies, but it is clear that the big local companies are heard when they voice their concerns and needs. In general, though, Hong Kong's computer industry is pretty much what the market has made it.

The character of national industry structures has been heavily influenced by trade and foreign investment policies, which can either promote or discourage links with the global economy. For instance, Japan's restrictions on IBM's activities kept IBM from dominating the Japanese market and created the opening for Japanese companies to get into the computer industry, but they also supported a Japan-centric point of view in the industry. There are continuing complaints by U.S. companies about unfavorable treatment in the

Japanese market (for instance in supercomputers), but in general the Japanese computer industry has become more open to foreign companies in the past decade. The presence of informal barriers such as distribution channels and high land prices now keeps foreign companies from having free access to Japan.

The Korean government has also restricted foreign investment in strategic industries, and the Korean computer industry still has limited MNC participation. Korea's restrictions on foreign companies are being challenged by the United States and Europe, as Korea prepares to enter the OECD and starts to comply with World Trade Organization rules. As a result, the local industry structure might have a more foreign flavor in the future, although informal barriers also still remain in Korea.

At the other end of the spectrum, the Singaporean government has not only welcomed foreign investment, but it has based its entire computer industry strategy around attracting leading MNCs to locate in Singapore. MNCs are treated as business clients, with government officials acting as account executives to work closely with the MNCs and keep them happy. Hong Kong has not been so aggressive in courting MNCs, but it has an open investment policy and provides a low-tax, pro-business environment that is attractive to foreign investors.

Taiwan has been in the middle, courting some MNC investments while restricting others; for the most part, Taiwan is neutral toward trade and investment in the computer industry. More important to Taiwan's success has been its efforts to promote exports, particularly through the Institute for Information Industries, which conducts extensive market research for the computer industry. Good market intelligence is one of the most important requirements of doing business internationally, and Taiwan's government has provided this service in a manner that the private sector could not afford to do on its own.

The differences in external trade and investment policies have had a critical impact on how each country has participated in the global computer industry. By restricting MNC participation, Japan and Korea have isolated themselves from some of the dynamism of the PC industry, and they have been limited mostly to selling standardized components and peripherals to foreign vendors. Taiwan, by working with the MNCs, has integrated itself into the design and engineering process of new product generations, while Singapore has developed critical manufacturing capabilities for the PC and disk drive industries. Hong Kong has interacted with MNCs to play a vital role in the management of China's manufacturing sector.

### Developing Capabilities

Education has been the most effective and pervasive instrument for developing national capabilities in East Asia. The East Asia governments have made general education a high priority, and they have also instituted programs to provide training in specific skills needed by industry. The creation of large pools of science and engineering talent have been critical to East Asia's ascendance in electronics and computers. This success is a tribute to the high quality of math and science education in the primary and secondary school systems of each country.

Beyond secondary education, the East Asian countries have a less impressive record. University students are often not challenged academically, and there are limited opportunities for graduate-level education. To compensate for the mixed quality of graduate education in their own universities, Taiwan and Korea have taken advantage of the U.S. university system to provide this training. While there is a resultant "brain drain" due to people staying in the United States to work, both countries have been able to tap the expertise of their citizens working for U.S. companies. The Taiwanese government in particular has taken an active role in recruiting people back from the United States to work in its own research labs and set up the industrial park at Hsinchu in part to attract overseas Taiwanese to return to Taiwan. In the future, however, the Asian countries will suffer competitively if they do not upgrade their graduate education and research programs.

A more fundamental weakness in the Asian educational system is the heavy emphasis on memorization and standardized testing, which is effective for training followers, but not very good for developing creative thinkers and innovators. East Asia's continuing weaknesses in software and other innovation-driven industries is at least partly a result of educational systems that reward memorization rather than problem solving. Each of the five countries has recognized the problem and is at least rhetorically committed to reforming its educational system. But such reform involves fundamental changes in the entire educational process, and such change will not be easy to accomplish.

In addition to education, government support for R&D has been an important force in upgrading the technological capabilities in the five countries. R&D policy has been most successful when it works in partnership with the private sector to develop commercially viable technologies. The Asian governments have invested in computer-related R&D through various public research institutions, such as Japan's ETL; Korea's ETRI and KAIST; Taiwan's ITRI and its affiliates, ERSO and CCL; and Singapore's ISS, ITI, and NSTB. Each of these governments also has provided incentives for private sector R&D through grants, tax incentives, and other mechanisms. Japan, Korea, and Taiwan have coordinated R&D consortia involving government labs and private companies, while Taiwan and Singapore have set up research partnerships with individual companies. Hong Kong's government has been less active in promoting R&D, only recently offering some grants for private sector R&D. Hong Kong's lack of technological capabilities can be blamed at least partly on the government's inaction in this area. At the same time, the top-down approaches to R&D taken by Japan and Korea have proven ineffective in the PC era, because government R&D has gone toward developing mainframe or minicomputer technology or has targeted technologies with little commercial relevance. Taiwan's government R&D has been more effective in developing technologies for the PC industry, despite recent complaints that ITRI is competing too much with the private sector.

The best government efforts have been those that complement and cooperate with the private sector and are flexible and responsive to changing conditions. Also, by working with MNCs, governments can encourage the transfer of knowledge and skills to local people. For instance, Singapore and Taiwan have set up joint research centers with IBM, Apple, Siemens, and other MNCs, staffed by local personnel. Not only do those centers develop technologies that can be used locally, but they also provide invaluable experience for the local people to learn how technology leaders organize and conduct R&D. R&D consortia among domestic companies provide no such benefits, but rather they reinforce the insulated, nationalistic orientation that already is a problem for many companies, particularly Japan and Korea.

Perhaps the biggest failure of all the Asian countries has been the lack of support for university research. Unlike U.S. universities, which draw some of the best researchers and receive strong government support, university labs in Asia are generally far inferior to those in the private sector. University research, unlike corporate R&D, is more likely to produce new ideas unfettered by the need to create commercial products. In fact, university research has been the source of many new technologies and products for the computer industry. For example, the Mosaic web browser was created at the University of Illinois, and most of the team that developed Mosaic was later hired by Netscape. Other university researchers in the United States have created new companies to commercialize their research, providing an important source of energy and innovation for the computer industry that is generally lacking in Asia.

### Shaping the Domestic Market

Policies that promote competition in the domestic market have been most effective, including competition among domestic companies and with foreign companies. Policies that protect domestic industries from global competition have been counterproductive. This is clear from the case of Korea's ban on PC imports and from Japan's more informal market barriers that kept prices high and usage low for many years. This lesson is reinforced outside East Asia by the failures of protectionist policies in India and Brazil to develop strong national computer industries, even as they slowed adoption of computer technologies.

Domestic computer investment can be stimulated by tax breaks, depreciation allowances, or other financial incentives for investing in computers. It can be depressed by application of tariffs, sales taxes, or other levies that raise the price of computers, or by nontariff barriers such as closed distribution systems. Governments can influence how computers are employed to improve productivity throughout the economy. They can also stimulate the domestic market through their own use of computers, investing heavily in new technologies and serving as an example to the private sector. This has been the case in Singapore, but nowhere else in Asia. Governments can stimulate private sector investment by building computer networks and putting information and services on-line. In Singapore, the government not only created an electronic data interchange (EDI) network to handle trade documentation, but it also required that all trading companies use the system to process trade documents.

### Policy Coordination

While competition is vital in the private sector, coordination is necessary to good policy-making. Policy-making is also best when input is sought from the private sector and other outside experts, and when decisions are made to achieve national goals without being derailed by bureaucratic competition or favored treatment to large companies. In general, we would argue that industrial policy will be most effective when it is coordinated by one government body (or at most two) with the authority to command cooperation from the various agencies and institutions who will carry out the strategy.

Each of the five countries has employed some mechanism for consulting with the private sector as part of its policy-making process. Japan's policy-makers have long conferred with industry leaders before making policy. This consultation is often informal, but it can also be carried out through various committees formed to advise government ministries. Korea has likewise consulted with its business leaders, but policy has been more top-down in the past. Now that big business has grown so powerful in Korea, government is forced to tailor industrial policies more to fit the wishes of the *chaebol*. One element lacking in both Japan's and Korea's policy process is an explicit way of getting input from international sources. While MITI maintains listening posts overseas in the form of the Japan External Trade Organization (JETRO), it does not generally bring foreigners into the policy consultation process.[12]

By contrast, Taiwan's government has long had a formal committee called the Science and Technology Advisory Group, under K. T. Li, consisting entirely of foreigners and overseas Taiwanese who advise the government on technology policy. Members of this group are top executives in U.S. and European companies who offer a different perspective than can be provided from within the tight-knit Taiwanese science and technology community.[13] The Singaporean and Hong Kong governments also confer regularly with foreign businesspeople as part of the policy formulation process—not surprising given the role of MNCs and foreign investment in their economies.

On the issue of policy coordination, both Japan and Korea have gone from a relatively unified command structure for industrial policy to an environment with highly fractious bureaucratic infighting and a lack of cooperation from the private sector. Japan's MITI and Korea's Ministry of Trade and Industry used to have clear positions as pilot agencies for industrial policy. But by the 1980s, computer policy began to be blurred with communications as digital communications became a major issue. This brought Japan's Ministry of Posts and Telecommunications and Korea's Ministry of Communications into the picture and led to often paralyzing battles for bureaucratic turf. Korea appears to have settled the issue to some degree by creating the new Ministry of Information and Communications, which has authority over all communications policy (including digital), while leaving the Ministry of Trade, Industry, and Energy to deal with hardware issues.

Taiwan's computer policies have been coordinated under the Ministry of Economic Affairs (MOEA), which is the parent of IDB, III, and ITRI. The strong leadership of K. T. Li has also been an important factor in providing policy coordination. The one area of policy that remains outside MOEA's reach is telecommunications, and this remains a major problem for Taiwan. Singapore, of course, has one of the clearest chains of command for industrial policy in the world. In the words of Stan Shih, "Only in Singapore is the government run like a business."[14] In Singapore, industry promotion is the domain of the Economic Development Board (EDB), while computer use falls under the National Computer Board (NCB) and telecommunications policy under the Telecommunications Authority. These three agencies must work together and resolve their differences—or those differences will be resolved at the highest levels of government. By contrast, Hong Kong's policies are loosely coordinated at best. Industry promotion falls under the Industry Department, while government computerization is the responsibility of the Information Technology Services Department, and telecommunications are regulated by the Office of Telecommunications Authority.

The impact of these different policy-making environments has been clear in the ultimate policy direction of each country. Japan and Korea have had somewhat inward-looking computer industry policies (and when they have looked outward, they have more often seen threats than opportunities). The nature of the policy-making process just reinforces the trend. It also reinforces the favored treatment given to the largest companies, which are the only ones with real input into the process. Taiwan, Singapore, and Hong Kong have been much more outward-looking. This is not surprising given their smaller size and greater dependence on trade, but consulting with outsiders provides a clearer understanding of the global environment.

The ability of Singapore and Taiwan to coordinate industrial policy is evident in the effectiveness of those policies and the lack of duplication of effort, especially in Singapore. While Japan and Korea had similar success in other industries, neither has been able to put together coherent policies to respond to the PC revolution—and in fact some of their policies have been counterproductive. Hong Kong's laissez faire ideology and decentralized government kept it from developing much of a policy for the industry until the 1990s, when it introduced various initiatives to upgrade its technical skills and industry capabilities. The entire Hong Kong/South China region is now experiencing higher wages, and it needs to coordinate its efforts regionally to upgrade its technology base.

## Industrial Policy and Outcomes

Table 6-8 summarizes the key points regarding each country's industrial policies related to the computer industry. In each case, computer industry policy has followed the general patterns for industry development established earlier in other industries.

## Competitiveness: A Dynamic Process

Success or failure in the computer industry is not a result of static conditions or one-time decisions. Rather it is the outcome of an dynamic process of ongoing interaction among government policy, business decisions, technology advances, and changes in the market. These interactions can create agglomerations of capabilities and establish path dependencies that determine success or failure. The global production system has evolved through a complex pattern of such interactions over time, and each country's role in the industry has been determined by its own dynamic evolution within that system.

The development of industry clusters in places such as Taipei, Singapore, or metropolitan Tokyo is not simply the result of some initial comparative advantages that made those places better than any other place to build PCs, disk drives, or LCDs. The patterns that have emerged have instead been driven by the interaction of MNC production decisions, national capabilities, local markets, industrial policy, and the structure of national production systems.

Analyzing the specialization patterns of the computer industries in Singapore and Taiwan, Poh-Kam Wong focuses on the dynamic interaction of three factors: entrepreneurial innovation, state intervention, and agglomeration of comparative advantage.[15] For instance, the entrepreneurial decisions in the 1970s by foreign electronics companies, including floppy disk drive maker Tandon, to locate in Singapore helped that country develop capabilities in mechanical engineering and to create a supply base of metal parts and electrical components. When the EDB began targeting the computer industry, it first targeted disk drives and was able to persuade Tom Mitchell and Alan Shugart to locate Seagate's assembly operations in Singapore. Seagate was followed to Singapore by some of its suppliers, further improving Singapore's supply base, and Singapore's workers gained experience and skills in disk drive production.

This agglomeration of capabilities encouraged EDB to pursue other disk drive makers; over time, a virtuous cycle kicked in, with more suppliers coming to Singapore, followed by more drive makers, and Singapore's workers gaining higher levels of specialized technical skills. This process was path dependent, in that decisions made over time were dependent on earlier choices by companies and the government. The result of the process was the creation of an industry cluster focused on disk drives, which propelled Singapore to world leadership in disk drive production. The capabilities of this cluster have locked

TABLE 6-8. Computer Industry Policies in East Asia

| Country | Shaping National Industry Structure | Developing Capabilities | Shaping Domestic Market | Policy Coordination |
|---|---|---|---|---|
| Japan | Subsidies concentrated on a few large companies. Barriers to imports and MNC investment in early years. | Science and engineering education. R&D in govt. labs, subsidies to private firms, consortia. Forced foreign companies to transfer technology. | Trade barriers before 1976. Informal barriers remain, local firms favored in govt. procurement. Low levels of govt. use. | MITI was key agency in 60s and 70s. Bureaucratic conflicts and duplication of effort between MITI and NTT in 70s; turf battles between MITI and MPT in 80s and 90s. |
| Korea | Subsidies to large *chaebol*. SME grants often went to *chaebol* members. Barriers to trade and investment. | Strong science and engineering education. R&D in govt. labs and public/private consortia. Taeduk Science Park built to centralize technology efforts. | Import ban, 1982–1987. Tariffs on motherboards and some peripherals. Govt. use is low. Favors local companies and supports TICOM use in govt. networks. | MTI was lead agency in 80s, but MOC challenged in 90s. New balance of power favors MIC (former MOC). |
| Taiwan | Subsidies and services benefit small and large companies equally. Generally open to trade and investment. | Good education in engineering, computer science. Hsinchu built as high-tech center. Support to exporters through MIC. Government-sponsored R&D at ITRI and R&D incentives to private sector. | Open to imports. Low levels of govt. use. III gets govt. contracts, hurting local services industry. Developing applications for small business. | Policy is coordinated under MOEA, implemented by ITRI, IDB, and III. Telecoms policy is separate and not coordinated with computer policy. |
| Singapore | Pursued foreign investment, offering incentives and assistance to MNCs to locate and upgrade activities. Limited support for domestic companies. | Upgraded computer sci. education, trained users. Joint R&D efforts with MNCs. Build excellent telecoms, port, and other infrastructure. | IT use treated as key to national competitiveness. Open market. Heavy govt. use, and promotion of private sector use. Built many networks. | Policy coordinated from Prime Minister's office down. EDB leads on production, NCB on use, Telecoms Authority on telecoms. |
| Hong Kong | Open to trade and investment. Large and small companies treated equally. | Built excellent port and telecoms infrastructure. Liberalized telecoms market. Created HKUST, upgraded other univs. Support start-ups at HKITCC. | Open market. Slow govt. adoption of IT. Trade-link bogged down. Developing new networks to promote use. | Little coordination. Industry Department, ITSD and OFTA work independently on production, use, and telecoms policies. |

in Singapore's position as a critical cog in the production process, even after rising wages made Singapore an unlikely location for such a labor-intensive industry as disk drives.

The success of Taiwan's PC industry is likewise best seen as a dynamic process that involved entrepreneurship, industrial policy, and path dependent agglomeration. Companies such as Acer and Mitac were highly entrepreneurial companies that sought and found opportunities within the newly emerging PC industry in the early 1980s. They were supported by a strong supplier network that had evolved from earlier MNC investments, local entrepreneurial efforts, and government initiatives. Once Taiwan began targeting the PC industry (thanks largely to K. T. Li's entrepreneurial initiatives within the government bureaucracy), industrial policies were introduced that were critical to supporting the efforts of the private sector. Over time, Taiwan developed capabilities in flexible manufacturing, systems engineering, market responsiveness, and logistics that were unmatched anywhere in the world. This agglomeration of capabilities has made it almost impossible for a PC maker to succeed without a strong presence in Taiwan.

Sometimes a country is not able to lock in its position in an industry segment, as with Korea in PCs. While Korea's output and exports of PCs grew on a pace to match those of Taiwan in the 1980s, Korea did not attract as many MNCs and did not develop a supplier base of the depth and breadth of Taiwan's. Why did Korea fail to continue to build on its early success in PCs? It appears that the evolution of Korea's PC industry was short-circuited by the government's decision to raise barriers to imports and foreign investment, and by the lack of independent entrepreneurs to develop capabilities beyond the immediate needs of the *chaebol*. The *chaebol* continued to buy components from Japan, at times ignoring local companies outside their own group. The *chaebol* also failed to develop close ties to MNCs at the design and engineering level and therefore were not ready for the major market shifts that came in the late 1980s. Since then, Korea has struggled to regain competitiveness in PCs, but it must fight against the locked-in positions of Singapore and Taiwan in many segments of the industry.

Japan likewise got onto an unfortunate path in the PC industry with the victory of the NEC standard in its domestic market. This isolated most of Japan's PC industry from the global industry dominated by the IBM/Wintel standard. Only in the mid-1990s has most of the Japanese industry shifted to the global standard; even now, NEC is producing its PC-98 series for Japan while making standard Wintel machines for export. On the other hand, Japan's success in consumer electronics gave it an early leg up in many components and materials for the PC, a position it has solidified and locked in over time. The evolution of Canon from cameras to photocopiers and fax machines to steppers and laser printers is itself a form of path dependency, because technology strengths in an earlier product line give the company a strong position to compete in newer products.

## An East Asian Model for Competing in Computers

We have argued that the continuous interaction of government policy, national industry structure, and the global production system has put each country in its present position in the global industry. After sifting through the many similarities and differences among the five countries, it is natural to ask whether there is an East Asian model for the computer industry. In other words, is the rise of East Asia to a leading position in the global computer industry due to some common characteristics of structure and policy, or is it just an accident of geographical proximity? Are the similarities just superficial, or do they point to a common underlying model of industry development?

We would argue that there is a common model and that our findings on the computer industry link to the more general literature on East Asian economic development. Furthermore, within the elements of the East Asian model, we can explain much of the success and failure of the individual East Asian countries, as well as their general success relative to other regions of the world.

There are four features that are emphasized in many attempts to develop a general East Asian economic development model: (1) building and enhancing national capabilities; (2) an outward orientation aimed at promoting exports and technology transfer; (3) strong policy coordination within government and between government and the private sector; and (4) emphasis on production over consumption.

The emphasis on building and enhancing national capabilities, including human resources, infrastructure, technology, and managerial skills, has been uniformly critical to East Asia's success in computers. Other countries (such as Mexico, India, and Brazil) have attracted foreign MNCs or have developed local industries to supply their own protected markets, but they have failed to develop capabilities needed to support global competitiveness in computers. By contrast, each of the East Asian countries has continuously tried to upgrade its capabilities, in order to produce more sophisticated products with more local input and value added. This common focus has helped the East Asians remain competitive even as rising wages drove labor-intensive production offshore. On the other hand, when the East Asians have been less successful, it has often been due to gaps in specific capabilities. For instance, Korea has developed strong skills in semiconductor engineering, but it can not compete with Taiwan in PC engineering skills. More generally, none of the East Asian countries has developed software skills anywhere near the quality of their hardware skills, a fact that is reflected in the near absence of a competitive software industry in those countries.

The second aspect of the East Asian model has taken on different characteristics across the countries, with resulting different outcomes. The outward-oriented model employed by Japan and Korea has been based on using a domestic profit sanctuary, protected by formal or informal trade and investment barriers, to subsidize exports. However, this approach has only served to leave Japan and Korea relegated to a peripheral position with weak linkages to the global production system. Only the external shock provided by IBM, Compaq, and Microsoft has jolted the Japanese companies to become serious about international markets and to tap into the capabilities of the Asian supply network. On the other hand, Taiwan, Singapore, and Hong Kong have had much more open policies toward trade and investment, and they have becoming deeply integrated into the global industry.

The third element of the East Asian model is the importance of policy coordination, both within government and between government and industry. The most successful policies have occurred when government consults closely with both local and international business people, and when government policy is coordinated and policy jurisdictions are well defined. The model of such policy coordination was Japan's MITI, whose guidance of the Japanese economy was imitated by economic pilot agencies in Korea, Taiwan, and Singapore. By the advent of the PC era, however, both Japan and Korea faced vigorous bureaucratic infighting, and policy-makers seemed to become less attuned to the needs of the private sector. The result has been a number of disjointed policy initiatives that have often seemed to completely ignore the dramatic changes happening in the international computer industry. By contrast, Singapore and Taiwan have been better able to coordinate their policies internally, although Taiwan's coordination is somewhat looser. Even more important, policy-makers in Singapore and Taiwan have consulted with business leaders and other experts at home and abroad to monitor the global market environment, and their policies have been generally more attuned to the demands of the market.

A final aspect of the East Asian model has been the promotion of production over consumption, a strategy often contrasted with the high priority given to the consumer in the United States. While the wisdom of the East Asian strategy can be debated in other industries, there is no question that it has been detrimental in computers. Other than Singapore, which has explicitly promoted computerization, the Asian countries have been slow to exploit the economic benefits of computer use throughout the economy. The other four countries are now investing heavily in computers to try to catch up, but they remain behind the United States and other countries that have much more experience in applying information technology in business, government, and education.

The secondary effect of promoting hardware production over use is the lost opportunities for developing software and services industries related to use. The price of such lost opportunities becomes ever clearer as almost every type of hardware becomes a commodity and East Asian companies continue to work harder for less profit. Meanwhile the fastest growing and most profitable segments of the computer industry remain firmly in the hands of U.S. companies, which benefit from their proximity to the largest, most sophisticated computer market in the world. The implications of these findings will become even more important in the knowledge-intensive economy of the twenty-first century.

# 7

# Lessons for Companies and Countries

Hindsight is 20/20, and it is easy to weave a series of ad hoc decisions and coincidental events into a theory of grand strategies and master plans. It is also tempting to imitate the successful strategies of another, not realizing that those strategies succeeded under a particular set of circumstances that no longer hold. The East Asian computer industry flourished within a competitive environment that has already changed dramatically and will be very different in the future. The industry itself continues to change rapidly, with new technologies, new markets, and new industry structures developing as the network era arrives. Still, that does not mean that we cannot learn from the past. So before we look at the emerging network era and its implications, we look first at what durable lessons the PC era offers for companies competing in computers. Second, if there is an East Asian model, then what does it say for countries that would like to apply the model's lessons to their own situations? Finally, how do the interests of companies and countries interact, and what have been the impacts of globalization on national interests?

## Competing in Computers: Companies

For companies, success can be measured in a number of ways. Profitability, return on investment, increase in shareholder value, growth, market share—all of these are indicators of a company's competitiveness. However, they are only byproducts of underlying competitiveness that is based on fundamental assets and capabilities.

In order to frame our discussion of company competitiveness, we return to the distinction presented in chapter 2 between two broad categories of activities in which companies compete: (1) the diminishing returns manufacturing business that includes PCs and most of the hardware associated with them; and (2) the increasing returns businesses of microprocessors, operating systems, packaged software, and information content.[1] The nature of competition and the strategies for success differ for each world and companies must organize and manage their businesses accordingly.

### Competing in Decreasing Returns Markets

In diminishing returns markets, product categories are already well defined and competition is based on getting the right amount of the right product to market at the right time at the lowest cost. Some components (such as memory chips) call for long production runs of standardized products, thanks to longer, more predictable product life cycles. However, most products in the computer industry have short life cycles, and falling behind in development or miscalculating demand can be disastrous. Furthermore, demand is differentiated based on product characteristics; having the wrong mix of features can lead to products gathering dust on the shelves or in warehouses. In some market segments, such as PCs and printers, there is some room for developing brand name recognition, based on customer perceptions of quality, reliability, or service and support. However, in today's market, a company's brand reputation rarely allows it to charge much of a price premium and will not sway customers to buy a product with the wrong features.

The most important characteristic of decreasing returns markets is that competition starts anew every day. Customers face little or no costs switching from one vendor to another, so each buying decision is based on the combination of price, performance, and features available at the time of purchase. This is true for companies selling to end users, as well as for suppliers selling to other producers. A business might have thousands of Compaq computers and be quite satisfied with them, but if Dell offers them a better deal, Compaq had better match it or face losing the sale. Likewise, PC makers might use Seagate disk drives in one model and turn to Quantum for the replacement model if Quantum can offer better features or a better price. In a business with little customer lock-in, there is precious little margin for error.

*Competitive Success Factors.*   In the decreasing returns world, successful business strategy typically hinges upon the following factors:

- *Cost.* With prices set by the market, companies' margins are determined mostly on the cost side. In true commodities such as DRAMs, the key to reducing costs lies in learning curve efficiencies associated with high-volume production. High volumes not only lead to reduced marginal costs, but they also to lower average costs because heavy R&D and capital investments are amortized over larger numbers of units. However, in most segments of the computer industry, product cycles are too short and technology change too rapid to achieve such long production runs of standardized products. Instead, most cost reduction comes from continuous process improvements at every stage of the production process, from procurement to manufacturing to logistics.

- *Speed to market.* In each new product generation, there is a brief period, often measured in months, in which higher margins can be sustained. Companies that hit the market in volume at the right time can take advantage of these margins and stay profitable. Those that are continually late are unprofitable, no matter what production volumes they can achieve. Eventually, such companies have to cut back on R&D, causing them to fall further behind the leading edge in new technologies. In this environment, companies must balance the need to minimize costs with the demands of getting to market on time. Companies that can keep up with the product cycle and control costs will ultimately be the winners.

- *Technology.* Staying at the leading edge in product technology provides the opportunity to earn those brief profit margins, while improving process technologies can help lower costs and improve speed to market. Market leaders need to focus on both types of technologies, while fast followers must emphasize process technology and have strong engineering skills to adopt new technologies developed by others. Equally important is the ability to leverage core technology strengths in one product into related products, such as transferring skills in optoelectronics from cameras to copiers to semiconductor steppers.

*Strategies and Capabilities.*   How does a company minimize costs while getting products to market on time and master the necessary technologies to stay competitive? And what are the critical capabilities a company needs to carry out these strategies? There are several strategies and characteristics that have marked successful firms in these segments of the industry:

- *Cooperation with market leaders.* This is essential for getting necessary information on technological and standards directions. Hardware makers need to work with Intel to get to market on time with the latest product generations, and components makers need to work with PC leaders such as Compaq to get new components qualified for new product generations. Notebook makers need to work with flat-panel display companies to incorporate new display generations into their products. A few companies achieve this coordination through vertical integration, as Toshiba does in notebook PCs, but even Toshiba works closely with Intel.

- *Alliances in design, manufacturing, R&D, and marketing.* No company can do everything on its own in today's computer industry, and competing in commodity markets requires large investments of capital and corporate energy. Companies can leverage their own capabilities and reduce their risks through effective alliances. There are hundreds of such alliances crossing the Pacific Rim today, as companies try to extend their reach and capabilities. Unfortunately, alliances are rarely as successful in practice as they look on paper, due to conflicting incentives, incompatible corporate cultures, changing market conditions, and a host of other reasons. The ability to choose alliance partners, structure the relationships, and manage them effectively is a key to success in an era when R&D and capital costs can run into the billions of dollars.

- *Close monitoring of lead markets.* The PC industry has placed a premium on close linkages with a company's immediate customer, for example, end users for PC makers, PC makers for disk drive makers, or disk drive makers for recording head makers. It is still important to have close linkages with one's immediate customer, but it is increasingly important that companies even further up the value chain have strong market intelligence capabilities in end user markets, so they can anticipate market trends. In many cases, this requires setting up production or product design in the United States, as many Asian companies have done, to be close to the leading market.

- *Management of the engineering and manufacturing process.* This includes purchasing, quality control, logistics, and production planning for manufacturing. It involves decisions about factory layout, production flow, and shipping, as well as longer term decisions about where to locate factories and make-or-buy decisions throughout the production chain. Management of the engineering process, from product design to prototyping to volume ramp-up needs to be closely coordinated with the manufacturing process, through effective communication and streamlining of decision making. Technical solutions such as electronic data interchange and groupware programs are increasingly important, but the key in both manufacturing and engineering management is the human element, which requires good management systems, proper incentives to managers and workers, team-building, and the ability to attract and maintain good people.

- *Capital.* Different segments of the hardware industry require different types of capital, and companies must focus on segments that match their capital resources as well as other capabilities. For instance, DRAM production requires large amounts of patient capital in order to continue to invest heavily even in downturns in the business cycle. Trying to compete with the Japanese in low-margin memory chips nearly destroyed Intel before it shifted all its energies to the microprocessor business. Texas Instruments has stayed in the DRAM business, but it has used joint ventures in order to reduce its exposure to downturns (and avoid the wrath of Wall Street) while still expanding capacity.

Competing in Increasing Returns Markets

The processing of knowledge is an increasing returns business wherein competition is winner-take-all (or most), and management is a series of quests for the next winning product, standard, or platform. Success in this world depends on a very different set of factors. Companies cannot win just by executing better than their competitors; they must also win on strategic decisions based on less tangible factors such as vision, intuition, and gamesmanship.

Competition involves choosing which markets to enter as well as executing entry with skill. Management in this environment is not production oriented but mission oriented. Organization structure is flat because the deliverers of the next product for the company need to be organized in small teams that report directly to top management, having a sense of direction and free rein to pursue it. Every time the mission changes—which will be often—the company needs to change and adapt. Leadership means watching for the next technological generation that is coming, figuring out what shape it will take, and positioning the company to take advantage of it.

*Competitive Success Factors*

- *Identifying major shifts in technology.* Some examples are the shift from mainframes to PCs, or PCs to network computing. Major technology shifts create a discontinuity in the market and an opportunity to control new standards and tap the gold mine of increasing returns in a new market. Those controlling existing standards will try to define the new paradigm in terms of the old. IBM, Fujitsu, and others initially treated the PC as a smart terminal for the mainframe, and Microsoft and Intel have treated the Internet as a network to connect Wintel-standard PCs. Newcomers will try to redefine the market around a new set of technology standards, as DEC did in minicomputers; Apple, Microsoft, Intel, and others did in PCs; and as Sun, Oracle, Netscape, and others are trying to do in the network era. Those who are able to anticipate and recognize major shifts in technology and move to define new technology standards will be the biggest winners in any standards-based competition.
- *Defining products and creating markets.* Companies that define new products and services and create markets for them gain an initial advantage over competitors that must follow a standard set by others. It is not just being the first to market that is critical; the key is to be the first to set the dominant design standard that others must follow. Apple set key design standards for PCs, then for graphical user interfaces and parlayed its lead into two decades of success. Netscape created the market for web browsers and controlled most of the market before Microsoft and others could respond.

- *Establishing the dominant standard.* Standards setters have the opportunity to lock-in customers around their product and may lock customers in for future product generations as well. However, the fear of lock-out means that competitors will move much more quickly to respond. The company that sets initial design standards does not always maintain control of the market that it creates. Apple's failure to sustain the Macintosh as the dominant graphical user interface in the face of competition from Microsoft's Windows is one example of an early leader losing out to a latecomer. In fact, with the exception of DOS (which it did not develop), Microsoft has never been the initial leader in any standards competition. Instead it has let others create the market and define a dominant design, then it has come in with its own product that eventually becomes the dominant standard, partly by leveraging its control over operating systems standards. Companies are now well aware of the value of controlling a dominant standard (or at least preventing a competitor from establishing its own proprietary standard) and will respond quickly to new standards competition.
- *Supporting an open standard* is an alternative strategy to prevent being at the mercy of a proprietary standard holder. Standards such as TCP/IP for the Internet, or GSM for digital wireless, are set by standards bodies and not controlled by any company. Even when there are competing proprietary standards, companies often favor the one that is more open. For instance, much of the enthusiasm for the network computer and the Java programming language is that they are based on standards not controlled by Microsoft or Intel.

*Strategies and Capabilities.*   What strategies are likely to succeed in such competitions, and how can companies organize themselves to compete in the increasing returns world of standards competition? First, there a few strategic approaches that have proven successful and others that are being tried in the network era.

- *Product design and strategic marketing.* The first key is to get the right combination of product features at the right price to create a market and establish a dominant design. The trick is not so much speed as it is timing. There have been numerous attempts to develop handheld computer/communicators, or PDAs, but they simply did not offer sufficient value to entice customers to part with $500 to $1,000. Finally, U.S. Robotics scored a big hit with its Palm Pilot product, by finding the right combination of features at the right price ($300). On the other hand, users paid much more for notebook computers because they retained full PC functions and could be used as a true portable substitute for the desktop computer.

One strategy that is being employed in the network era is discounting heavily to build up an installed base. Netscape initially offered its browser free and controlled more than 80% of the browser market within a very short time. Recognizing the threat, Microsoft responded quickly with its own free browser, which it also bundled with its Windows operating systems, gaining a 40% market share by 1998.

- *Developing complementary assets/network externalities.* Standards-based products do not stand alone, especially not in the network era.[2] They depend on the existence of other products and other technologies that support and enhance them. IBM's success in developing a broad base of complementarities around its open PC standard is the classic case. The global hardware production system, the huge number of software developers creating applications for the IBM PC, the extensive distribution network and, ultimately, the large installed customer base gave the IBM PC an unassailable position as the global PC standard. Unfortunately for IBM, it lost control of its own standard, but Microsoft and Intel have continued to expand the range of complementary assets supporting the IBM (now Wintel) standard. The importance of complementary assets is well understood now, and companies are competing vigorously to gain support for their standards in the network era, whether they are browsers, programming languages, e-mail systems, groupware, search engines, on-line transaction systems, or network computers. The winners will be those that develop products and technologies that appeal to customers, then develop the complementary assets necessary to establish them as standards.

Companies compete not simply by locking in a product on their own, but also by building formal and informal alliances of companies organized around the base technology. The key to success in knowledge-based design, therefore, is management of the cross-company mutual feedback. This can be done by establishing mutually beneficial and reinforcing linkages with other companies. Success or failure is often decided not just by a single company, but also by the success or failure of the web to which it belongs. NEC built its dominant position in Japan's PC industry by creating a web of software developers and distribution channels committed to its architecture, but it lost that position when a powerful set of competitors rallied around the competing DOS/V standard that was compatible with the global Wintel standard. Apple's unwillingness to license its Macintosh operating system until very late in the game left it as a niche player that was ultimately squeezed out by the Wintel standard. Apple's Power PC alliance with IBM and Motorola failed to challenge Wintel when it failed to gain the support of outside companies, or even of IBM's PC company.

While there are many ways in which firms can sustain and enhance relationships with other firms in the industry, perhaps the most effective is by leveraging user bases. This means transferring a user base built up on one product to neighboring products. For example, Microsoft levered its DOS user base onto Windows 3.1, Windows 95, Windows NT, and finally Internet Explorer by offering inexpensive upgrades and bundling applications with the operating system. Other companies producing hardware and software for the Wintel platform were also able to carry their own users forward to new generations of that platform. By contrast, Apple offered no upgrade path from the Apple II to the Macintosh, and lost an opportunity to convert the large installed base of Apple II users in the educational market into Macintosh users.

The interdependence of companies within a web means that rather than attempting to take over all products in the ecology, dominant players in a web need to allow dependent players to lock in their dependent products by piggybacking on the web's success. By ceding some of the profits, the dominant players ensure that all participants remain committed to the alliance. This strategy applies equally to subcontractors in production networks, independent retailers in distribution networks, and independent developers in software networks. The exception to this rule might appear to be Microsoft, which competes aggressively in many applications markets against its partners in the Wintel platform; even Microsoft, however, might be paying a price for this "infinite greed"[3] as competitors rally to establish non-Microsoft standards in network computing. One PC company president commented ruefully to the authors that "We're all killing ourselves to make money for Microsoft and Intel." Only time will tell if the accumulated resentment will come back to haunt the two companies as it did IBM in an earlier era.

- *Learning how to adapt and position for technology waves.* Successful companies adapt to generational change in the short term and position themselves for revolutionary change in the longer term. Generational change, which is illustrated by the move from 286-, 386-, 486-, and Pentium-based computers, is upward compatible and does not eliminate older generations. However, even generational change is unpredictable in its timing and particular requirements. In order to adapt to changing markets and still have the discipline to meet the critical requirements of time to market, David Yoffie recommends that companies develop processes that are iterative and mission focused.[4] That is, they must start with a broad vision and allow new information to be incorporated into product design while focusing on tight integration of the entire project to meet deadlines.

In the longer term, the ability to profit under increasing returns requires the ability to see what's coming in the next technology cycle and to position oneself for it. Technology comes in successive waves; therefore, those who have lost out on one wave can position for the next (if they have the resources to survive long enough). Conversely, those who have made a killing on one cycle cannot become complacent. As Intel's Andrew Grove puts it, "Only the paranoid survive." In more positive terms, Grove argues that companies must learn to recognize and respond to strategic inflection points that herald fundamental changes in an industry.[5]

The only way to have the vision to perceive and respond to opportunities in new markets and technologies is to adopt an organizational structure and culture that promote learning. People from top to bottom must be alert to sources of information both inside and outside the organization. It is vital to listen to workers, customers, suppliers, market researchers, as well as less traditional sources of information. Such information must be actively sought, and those at the top need to listen to as many sources as possible and avoid being isolated behind protective secretaries and receptionists. CEOs such as Lou Gerstner of IBM and Stan Shih of Taiwan's Acer spend much of their time meeting with CEOs of customers, suppliers, and strategic partners, while Bill Gates takes time off each year just to read new books and Andy Grove teaches a course at Stanford. Such exposure to a broad range of ideas is critical to being attuned to challenges and opportunities.

- *Leaving losing markets and focusing on core strengths.* Intel left the DRAM market when it could not withstand the Japanese onslaught, but the company has made enormous profits in microprocessors. America Online, CompuServe, and Prodigy have ceded dominance of the networking market to the Internet, but instead of exiting completely, they have become adjuncts of the Internet by supplying access and specialized services.[6] By contrast, IBM has refused to give up on its OS/2 operating system, even as its own PC company sells most of its machines bundled with Windows. The big Japanese and Korean conglomerates seem incapable of bowing out of any major product line, either because of the need to maintain employment or from fear of ceding ground to their domestic competitors. Thus, valuable corporate resources are expended in old, losing markets rather than being redeployed to maintain areas of existing strength and develop new markets.
- *"To boldly go."* Finally, firms that wish to compete in the increasing returns world must have leaders with the vision to recognize big trends and strategic inflection points, and the courage to respond with big moves. Bill Gates's recognition of the importance of the Internet and his decision in 1995 to recast Microsoft as an Internet company came only months after he had downplayed the importance of the Internet. Such a change of heart requires not only an open mind, but also a willingness to make big gambles with an entire company's future. In fact, the history of the computer indus-

try has been defined largely by a few such gambles, such as Thomas Watson, Jr.'s decision to gamble IBM's future on the System/360, and IBM's decision to build the original IBM PC. That history is also littered with many unsuccessful gambles, so no one should underestimate the risks that go with the high potential returns of this type of competition.

## Summary

The distinction between increasing and decreasing returns markets in the computer industry is useful because it helps to identify the nature of competition in two different worlds and the strategies and capabilities needed for success. While the division is a valuable one to help managers conceptualize their business and its demands, the two worlds are not so neatly divided in reality.[7] Many companies are involved in both types of activities. For instance, Intel is a classic example of a company operating in the increasing returns business, yet it still runs factories, purchases parts, and equipment and ships products just like any commodity DRAM maker. In fact, much of Intel's success in protecting its dominant position comes from its strengths in manufacturing and process engineering, which have helped it cut costs and be able to price its new product generations competitively.

Also, we have identified several hybrid markets such as PCs, printers, and information services, in which companies have been able to apply increasing returns strategies to what appear to be decreasing returns market segments. For instance, companies such as Dell have used innovative marketing, distribution, and logistics to differentiate themselves in the commodity PC industry.

One lesson from this analysis is that execution always matters, even in innovation-driven, increasing returns businesses. Another lesson is that there are many opportunities for innovation, even in decreasing returns businesses, and such innovation often separates the winners from the losers more than size or deep pockets. While each world has its own competitive characteristics and places a premium on different capabilities, success factors from one world can also be valuable in the other.

## Country Competitiveness

National success in computers is usually thought of in terms of production, value added, exports, or employment. These are all important indicators of a country's competitiveness, but a more fundamental determinant of long-term success is its role in the global production system. A country that hosts a broad, deep portfolio of companies—with high-quality linkages to the global industry—and develops strong capabilities for computer production can become an indispensable part of the global production network.

National competitiveness can be achieved in a number of ways, for instance: (a) when a country controls key standards or technologies that everyone must have access to; (b) when a country has become integrated into the design, manufacturing, supply, and distribution systems of major global companies; (c) when a country has developed unique capabilities in one or more segments of the industry; or (d) when domestic companies develop successful global brands of their own.

Japan is indispensable to the global computer production system because of its control over critical technologies and its role as the leading supplier of many components and peripherals. Japan has seen its near monopoly challenged in DRAMs and LCDs by Korean competitors, but it is still the leading producer of both of those components, as well as CD-ROM drives, floppy disk drives, and large monitors. Japan also has strong brand names in peripherals, such as Canon and Epson in printers, and Sony and NEC in monitors. Japanese companies are also leading suppliers of critical components such as laser engines for printers and cathode ray tubes for monitors. Further upstream, Japanese companies have near monopolies in critical subcomponents, materials, and production equipment. On the other hand, Japan's position is much weaker at the systems level, where only Toshiba has established a strong brand name outside the domestic market. Therefore, it is quite possible to produce a PC without any Japanese involvement at the systems level, but it is nearly impossible to produce one without Japanese parts and technology.

Taiwan has become an indispensable part of the global production system because of its tight integration into the design, engineering, manufacturing, logistical, and distribution processes of the PC industry. Today, nearly every major PC maker has strong links to Taiwan. Taiwan's capabilities in board design, systems engineering, flexible manufacturing, and speed to market cannot be matched anywhere in the world. Taiwan is also the leading producer of a variety of peripherals and components, and it is quickly expanding its semiconductor capacity. Taiwan's position is one of interdependence, because it still depends on outside sources of technology and equipment, but the PC industry depends heavily on Taiwan's capabilities to get products to market on time and at a low cost.

Korea has not established such a critical position in the computer industry; it controls no critical technologies and is not deeply integrated into the production systems of the leading computer makers. Korea is a major producer of DRAMs and LCDs but does not have a majority of the world's production in either category. On the other hand, Korea's success in DRAMs did have an important benefit for the global PC industry, because it precluded the possibility of collusion or cartelization of the DRAM market by Japanese companies. Its push into LCDs should have a similar effect on the flat-panel display market. Korean companies can make nearly all the components that go into a PC but are weak in motherboard design and system engineering when compared with Taiwan. The companies also lack the flexibility and speed of the Taiwanese companies; as a result, Korean firms have only achieved limited success beyond commodity components and monitors.

Singapore has gained a key role in the global production system as a high-quality production platform for disk drives, PCs, and some peripherals. Many MNCs organize a regional supply network from Singapore and then market the products through their own global marketing and distribution channels. Singapore's skills are critical to the disk drive industry, and the country's infrastructure and capabilities make it a vital part of the production networks of companies such as Apple, Compaq, and Hewlett-Packard. It is also developing new linkages in other related industries such as semiconductors and entertainment, hoping to expand its role as a regional business hub.

Hong Kong is indispensable in its role as the bridge to China. Many MNCs coordinate production and marketing in China through their own offices in Hong Kong, or through local partners there. Hong Kong's functions mostly take the form of managing financial flows in and out of China, coordination of logistics, and oversight of labor-intensive manufacturing operations. They do not involve the type of technology flows and advanced manufacturing management that is seen in Singapore. Hong Kong does face some competition as a managerial center from Shanghai, but for now, no one can provide the functions that Hong Kong does in managing access to China.

## Country and Company Performance

Using the framework of increasing and decreasing returns, figures 7-1 and 7-2 summarize the present competitive situation in the computer industry. Figure 7-1 shows the country location of company headquarters by market segment, while figure 7-2 shows the location of production activities by country within the global value chain.

The message of the two figures is quite simple. While U.S. companies dominate in the increasing returns segments of the market, Japanese, Taiwanese, and Korean companies compete in decreasing returns segments; U.S. and Japanese companies dominate the hybrid segments. Activities tend to be located geographically in order to take advantage of local capabilities. Increasing returns activities such as R&D, product design and engineering, and software development are concentrated in the United States and Japan in order to take advantage of those countries' technological capabilities, human resources, and large domestic markets. Capital-intensive activities such as DRAM and LCD production are mostly located in Japan and Korea, where companies can raise large sums of capital and have access to necessary engineering skills. Activities that rely on speed and flexibility, such as PC, motherboard, and hard drive production, are mostly done in Taiwan and Singapore, which have the skills and strong supplier bases to get products from design to volume production very quickly. Labor-intensive activities generally take place in Southeast Asia and China, where large pools of low-cost, well-educated workers are available (and in the case of Hong Kong/South China, strong managerial capabilities).

This picture is is changing rapidly. The East Asian NIEs are steadily moving up the value-added scale to carry out more R&D, design and engineering, while the emerging NIEs such as Malaysia, Thailand, Indonesia, and China attempt to go beyond labor-intensive activities and develop their own tech-

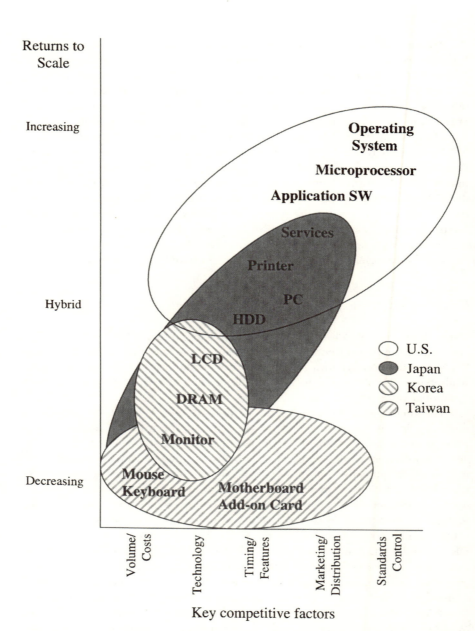

Returns to
Scale

Increasing

**Operating
System**

**Microprocessor**

**Application SW**

Services

Printer

PC

HDD

Hybrid

LCD

DRAM

Monitor

○ U.S.

● Japan

◇ Korea

◇ Taiwan

Mouse
Keyboard

Motherboard
Add-on Card

Decreasing

Volume/
Costs

Technology

Timing/
Features

Marketing/
Distribution

Standards
Control

Key competitive factors

FIGURE 7-1. Company Competitiveness

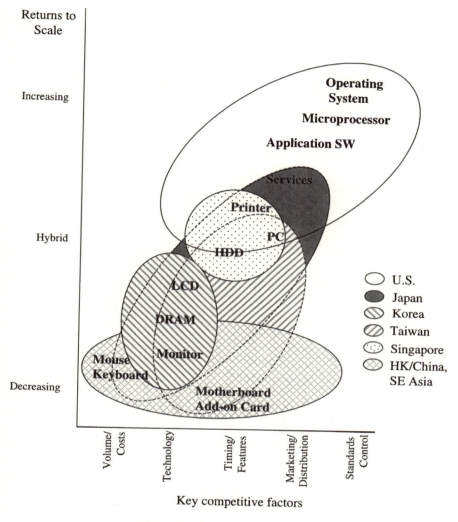

FIGURE 7-2. Country Competitiveness: Location of Activities

nological capabilities. This process has put enormous pressure on everyone involved, particularly in the hardware industry. Japan finds itself losing market share in DRAMs, monitors, LCDs, and other hardware markets to well-financed Korean companies. Taiwanese companies, with the support of the Taiwanese government, are also moving into some of those market segments, often in partnerships with U.S., European, and Japanese companies. Battles over market share are fierce, and profit margins are driven to almost nil, just as the theory of decreasing returns would predict.

The recent turmoil in Asian economies will exacerbate these problems. The impact will depend upon how long the Asian crisis will last. If Asian governments react quickly and effectively to shore up their financial systems and restore confidence in their economies, the whole episode could turn out to be a temporary, if painful, interruption in their decades-long economic boom. If on the other hand, the Asian governments try to avoid any painful restructuring, they may find themselves once again following Japan's lead, this time into prolonged economic stagnation.

As other countries look at these East Asian experiences in the computer industry, they should consider what it is that has given these countries such an important position in the industry. The common elements of East Asia's strength are all found in the decreasing returns side of the computer industry, where all five countries compete vigorously. They should also examine where East Asia has been left out, notably in the increasing returns businesses that are still mostly controlled by U.S. companies. In fact, it is not the East Asian countries, but India, that appears to have the best prospects in the software industry. The keys to success and failure, as we have argued earlier, are found in the mixture of industrial policy, industry structure, linkages to the global production system, and the creation of national capabilities. The question is what countries can do to develop a mix of government and business strategies that is likely to be effective. This leads us to another question brought up in chapter 1:

What are the implications of the East Asian experience for the United States and other countries trying to reap the benefits of the computer boom and avoid being left behind in the global competition for jobs, exports, and technology?

The answer to this question depends on a country's present position in the global production system, and the capabilities on which it can build. For the United States, the question is how to maintain leadership and ensure that the leadership of U.S. companies translates into benefits for the U.S. economy and workers. For Japan and the other East Asian countries discussed in this book, the question is how to preserve their existing areas of leadership against the inevitable onslaught of competition from newer, low-cost Asian producers, and how to make inroads into segments of the industry where they have as yet not been successful. For developing countries, the question is how to find and exploit opportunities in the global production system and how to develop the necessary capabilities to expand and enhance their position.

## The United States: Preserving Leadership

For the United States, the biggest issue is how to defend that country's position as the leading innovator and controller of most of the standards in the computer industry, while moving aggressively into new markets and technologies to project that leadership into the future. A related issue is how to ensure that the success of U.S. companies continues to benefit the U.S. economy proportionately.

This leadership appears to be safe in industry segments in which U.S. companies control the architectural standards or where marketing skills and access to the lead market are important to success. These categories would include microprocessors, operating systems, PC systems, workstations, packaged software, and information content. The situation is less secure in industries that are driven by technological leadership with weaker customer lock-in, such as disk drives, printers, and network hardware. In some high-volume components, such as DRAMs and LCDs, the U.S. position already ranges from weak to moribund.

In terms of projecting leadership into the future, U.S. companies are driving the evolution of the industry into the network era through the efforts of entrepreneurial companies such as Netscape, 3Com, Cisco, and established companies such as Microsoft, Sun, Hewlett-Packard, and IBM. These companies are battling to set standards for the new era with little or no competition from abroad. The other key U.S. advantage is the dynamism of the domestic market, which has embraced the Internet and gone on-line in much larger numbers than that of any other country.

Perhaps the biggest problem for the United States is not how to support U.S. computer companies, which seem to be quite capable of competing around the world, but rather how to ensure that the U.S. benefits more from the success of those companies. In particular, it is disturbing that so many U.S. citizens lack the skills to perform the high-quality jobs that are being created by the computer industry. There is no question that immigration brings valuable human resources and helps U.S. competitiveness, but the failure of the U.S. education system to train a significant share of its population for information age jobs should be a source of serious national concern.

The United States generally seems to abhor the notion of industrial policy, yet government policy has been an important factor in the growth of the computer industry. The biggest early user of computers was the U.S. government, including the military, and government procurement helped drive development of new technologies. Also, the antitrust actions taken against IBM helped create the independent software, services, and peripherals industries in the United States. And almost by accident, the military's attempt to develop a secure data communication system has grown into the Internet, in one of the most successful applications of industrial policy in history. The question for the United States is not so much whether government policy has had an impact in the past, but what beneficial steps the government can take in the future.

Some of the most useful things the government could do are more general in scope but would have strong indirect effects on the computer industry. These include improvements in science, engineering, and mathematics education at all levels and measures to increase the national savings rate and lower the cost of capital. Most policy-makers and analysts agree on the need for such generic policies to improve overall competitiveness, although little has been done after years of rhetoric on these issues.

When the subject of more targeted industrial or technology policies arises, the agreement dissolves. For instance, there is a major controversy over whether the U.S. government should try to challenge Japan's leadership in certain "critical technologies" such as LCDs, semiconductor etching equipment (steppers), and DRAMs. The government is already supporting the U.S. Display Consortium for flat-panel display development, and a large share of Sematech's funding has gone toward catching up in stepper technology. An earlier initiative in memory chips, US Memories, fell apart in the late 1980s because it failed to get support from the computer industry. The collapse of US Memories and the failure of Sematech to make a dent in Japan's lead in the stepper market suggest that efforts to promote strategic industries are risky. However, Sematech's success in improving manufacturing processes and upgrading the U.S. semiconductor equipment industry provides hope for those who support such targeted intervention.

Our conclusion is that government targeting can make a difference in viable but struggling industries by encouraging companies to make otherwise marginal investments. This was the case with Sematech. In well-established industries in which the U.S. is virtually absent, however, it is difficult to catch up—and even large government subsidies are unlikely to make a difference. Concerns have been expressed about American dependence on Japan for defense-related technologies such as flat-panel displays, but the emergence of Korean and other suppliers has eased those fears. It is unrealistic and unnecessary for the United States to compete in every single segment of the computer industry. Government money would be better spent on education, infrastructure, and smaller scale, more diversified R&D that is more likely to help sustain U.S. strength in innovation-driven segments of the industry.

Finally, the fact is that the United States is still a major base for much high-value hardware manufacturing, in spite of the shift of production to Asia. Therefore, government funds can be well spent training the human resources needed by manufacturers, and developing process technologies to enhance U.S. manufacturing capabilities.

### Japan: Regaining the Edge

Japan wants to protect its lead in hardware against challenges by Korea, Taiwan, and others; it is also very concerned about U.S. dominance in software and U.S. control of most computer industry standards.

Japan's position in many hardware markets seems to be well defended by very capable Japanese companies that need little help from the government. In emerging hardware markets such as ATM switches, set-top boxes, flash memory, and DVD, Japanese companies are either leaders or competitors. The government's concern now is that these companies are moving too much production offshore and hollowing out Japan's manufacturing base. This fear was heightened when the yen rose to its peak of 80 per dollar in 1995, but eased somewhat as the dollar rebounded in 1996. Beyond trying to maintain a weaker yen, the Japanese government cannot do very much to keep manufacturers from going offshore, especially because offshore production helps ease Japan's politically troublesome trade surpluses.

Another concern in Japan is the gap with the United States in IT use. After the United States announced its information superhighways initiative in 1993, MPT, MITI, and NTT quickly announced their visions for Japan's national information infrastructure (NII), all emphasizing the great danger of falling further behind the United States in this suddenly critical race. Since then, the panic has subsided, but the government is spending hundreds of millions of dollars on various NII test projects, albeit with virtually no cooperation among the two ministries and NTT.[8] At the same time, the boom in PC sales and the rapid spread of the Internet in Japan have closed the gap in computerization, but Japan still lags the United States in PC penetration and networking of computers. This problem has much to do with the remaining NTT monopoly and the high prices of telecommunications services in Japan, issues that the Japanese government has been unable to address effectively for more than a decade.

Japan's other big concern is an old one—software. For twenty years, Japan chafed under IBM's control of the mainframe architecture, which left the Japanese mainframe makers subservient to IBM's standards. In the PC era, Microsoft has taken IBM's place as the new software tyrant, controlling the operating system and taking the largest share of the Japanese applications market as well. In the early stages of the new network era, it is U.S. companies such as Netscape, Microsoft, Sun, and IBM that are vying to define the standards for software on the net. The Japanese government has tried a number of initiatives to break the U.S. lock on software, but to little avail, and its prospects for doing so in the future do not look good.

Japanese companies have shown they can compete in global markets for video game software, and in the domestic market for certain business applications such as word processors. The potential exists for Japan to have a more vibrant software industry even without controlling the key standards, but the industry is now hamstrung by lack of capital and poor protection of intellectual property. Probably the best things the government could do for the software industry would be to crack down on piracy, make it easier for companies to raise capital, and promote computer use in Japan. Those moves, and the deregulation of telecommunications, do not fit the "Japanese model" of industrial targeting, but in the present environment they are likely to be more effective than new subsidies or R&D consortia.

## The Asian NIEs: Staying Ahead of the Pack

Each of the East Asian newly industrialized economies (NIEs) has carved out its own place in the computer industry's production network, with surprising little competition among the four economies. While there is strong competition in a few products such as monitors and PCs, for the most part Singapore has disk drives, Korea has DRAMs, Taiwan has most other components and peripherals, and Hong Kong has China. This division of labor is not secure, however, as Taiwan and Singapore move aggressively into semiconductors, and more important, as the developing countries of Southeast Asia, China, and elsewhere target many of the NIEs' strongholds. Those countries are now mostly doing labor-intensive assembly tasks, but as they gain experience they are moving into more advanced manufacturing. With large pools of science and engineering talent, China, the Philippines, Vietnam, and India are positioned to compete with the NIEs in many areas of hardware production.

The common problem of the NIEs is not how to create jobs, because they all are facing labor shortages. Instead, the NIEs need to move labor-intensive production offshore, while creating and retaining higher value activities at home. However, the NIEs do not control the marketing and distribution side of the production chain, and they must depend on MNC marketing channels. They also are not competitive in leading edge technologies or in product design, limiting their opportunities to move upscale in the industry.

To stay competitive, the NIEs are beginning to develop their own regional production networks, where they provide management, technology, and marketing skills. This can be seen at the company level in Acer's moves into DRAM production on the one hand and into software and content on the other. At the national level, Singapore's government is consciously working to move the country both upstream into silicon and downstream into services and content, with the aim of developing high value-added industries.

These moves will not be easy, because they do not build directly on the NIEs' strengths in manufacturing and process technology, but instead require them to develop new strengths in product innovation, marketing, and other "soft" skills. They also put the NIEs into direct competition with U.S. and Japanese companies in industries that those companies are not ready to relinquish. Japanese companies have been willing to transfer mature technologies to Korea and Taiwan, but they may become less cooperative if they face competition in leading edge hardware products, where the highest profits are. The NIEs may also find that they are already at a disadvantage in many software products compared to China and India, which have larger and lower cost pools of software engineers, programmers, and other software professionals.

To summarize, the NIEs are being squeezed between the developing countries and industrial leaders in the computer industry. They are already competing in the most crowded segments of the market, and those segments are getting more crowded all the time. To move into less crowded, more profitable segments will require the creation of new capabilities to compete in these industries.

While the NIEs must fight hard to retain their positions in the global production structure, they also can find opportunities in local and regional markets for software and services. These markets are underdeveloped in the NIEs themselves and in Asia in general. Domestic software and services markets could be expanded through government computerization and network development, and by getting government agencies out of competition with the private sector. Products developed for the domestic market will have better export potential if efforts to curb pirating in the region begin to have an effect. So far, the NIEs themselves have often been lax about intellectual property protection; if they want to develop their software industries, however, they need to do a better job at home and encourage their neighbors to do the same. If the NIEs are going to move into the software side of the industry, they need to develop a new mindset about software and services and begin to value them and be willing to pay for them.

### Developing Countries: Finding a Place at the Table

Developing countries such as Thailand, Malaysia, China, Indonesia, and the Philippines already are active participants in the global production system. They are mostly providing cheap labor for simple assembly but are increasingly being tapped for their engineering skills and improving manufacturing capabilities. China, India, and the Philippines also provide low-cost programmers to the software industry. Those countries, and others that wish to become players in the computer industry, can learn a lot from the experiences of the East Asian countries.

The first implication of the East Asian experience is the importance of integration into global production system. This has been illustrated and discussed in detail in previous chapters and needs little elaboration. In the past, many developing countries tried to develop computer industries through protectionist measures such as high tariffs, market reserves for local companies, and restrictions on foreign investments. This has been a special temptation for large countries (such as China, India, Brazil, and Mexico) that felt their domestic markets could support a national industry. The outcome in each case was that local firms settled for earning easy profits in the protected market and failed to upgrade their technical capabilities or venture out into competitive international markets. Users in those countries suffered from high prices and poor quality products, hurting the entire economy. As a result, most developing countries have either completely or partially liberalized their computer markets and in most cases have begun to pursue rather than discourage foreign investment.

The second implication is the importance of developing national capabilities, mainly human resources and infrastructure, that can serve as a basis for attracting investment and moving beyond simple assembly functions to higher value added activities. Cheap labor is only useful at the low end of the value-added curve, and even assembly workers need to have some level of literacy and job skills to work in the computer industry. By training engineers and other technical people, a country can follow the lead of Korea, Taiwan, and Singapore up the value chain in the industry. Most developing countries have poor infrastructures in general and lack the resources to deploy high-quality transportation and communications throughout the country. However, they can concentrate resources on specific geographical locations (such as industrial parks) to provide high-quality infrastructure for high-tech companies.

This is already happening in places such as Bangalore (India) and Guadalajara, (Mexico), which are following the examples of Hsinchu (Taiwan) and Taedok (Korea) as high-tech clusters supported by good infrastructures and proximity to university and government research institutions.

A third implication is the importance of looking for opportunities in the entire computer industry, rather than just in hardware. Hardware production offers more immediate, visible signs of success; that is, a factory is built, jobs are created, goods are exported, and politicians take the credit. Software companies are more likely to operate out of a nondescript buildings, producing a product that is nearly invisible; there are no trucks pulling out of loading docks full of widgets to be shipped around the world. However, the playing field is less crowded in software and services, and local companies can target domestic market niches and avoid competing directly with global giants. In many cases, local firms can work with those giants to customize their products for local markets. Also, the software industry is now developing its own global production system and tapping developing countries, such as China and India, that have low-cost, skilled programmers. Even small countries, such as Barbados, Costa Rica, and Jamaica, are finding opportunities in data entry, call centers, and other low-end services.[9] These activities do not require large investments and can be carried out virtually anywhere there is a satellite link, obviating the need for a strong physical infrastructure.

In addition to software and services, the other opportunity that most of the Asian countries have missed is in computer use. We have made this point in the context of Japan and the NIEs, but it is especially important to developing countries that can garner great benefits from the application of computer technology. Even very poor agricultural regions can benefit from crop price information and technical support, and this may only require a phone line and a PC with a modem for access to national or international markets. Computerization of banks, government agencies, customs offices, and other key institutions can greatly enhance the productivity of developing countries as well. As computer use develops, local software and services industries gain opportunities to develop, but the use itself should be the first consideration. Among the NIEs, Singapore provides a good model for effective computer use, especially in government, while other examples would include Hong Kong's banks and Korea's manufacturers. Developing countries can study these cases, as well as less successful examples, to learn valuable lessons.

At a more general level, all countries could benefit from greater emphasis on computer use and on production close to use, whether in software, services, or content. The information services sector in particular offers exciting opportunities for newly industrializing and developing countries. As a link between producers and users, information services can greatly improve the effectiveness and productivity of computer use within a country and can also become an important industry in its own right. The interaction of service providers and user organizations develops capabilities on both sides—capabilities that benefit the entire economy.

As shown in figure 7-3, the information services industry is in a unique position with regard to computer production and use. Hardware and packaged software tend to be developed as standardized products that are purchased in discrete, arm's-length market transactions. Their development and production involve limited interaction with users, mostly in the form of market research and product testing (e.g., beta testing). In contrast, services involve close, two-way interaction between providers and users. Also, many hardware and software purchasing decisions are made or influenced by service providers, such as systems integrators and outsourcing companies. Such professionals provide a link between buyers and sellers of hardware and packaged software. For these reasons, we place the information services industry at the junction of production and use.

## Country versus Company Competitiveness

Countries are rightfully concerned about the degree to which they benefit from company capabilities, because companies can move activities to another location and take their assets with them. This concern is at the heart of the U.S. debate about company versus country competitiveness, as discussed in chapter 1. On one side, the United States is the home to computer companies with extraordinary competitive assets, yet those companies increasingly produce, sell, and even design their products offshore. It is reasonable to question

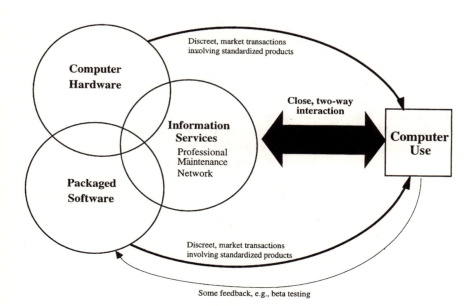

FIGURE 7-3. Information Services as Link Between Production and Use

how much the U.S. benefits from being the headquarters for Seagate, for instance, when more than 75% of Seagate's employees are in Asia. On the other hand, Singapore is the site of much of Seagate's production, but Singapore likewise might wonder what the risks are of Seagate bypassing Singapore for lower cost locations.

These issues are complex, and the answers depend largely on how a particular country defines its national interest in the computer industry. National interests can be measured by the number of jobs created by the industry, the quality of those jobs, total output or value added, trade balances, or creation of valuable technology. The issue of company versus country capabilities turns mainly on the extent to which national capabilities benefit the economy or society as a whole, as opposed to just benefiting a particular company.

As a general rule, the extent to which company capabilities benefit a country depends on the nature of a company's activities in that country. It is likely that indigenous companies are more valuable than foreign MNCs, because domestic companies generally carry out a wider range of activities in their home country and most profits go to local investors. For instance, the capabilities of IBM, Intel, Seagate, and Microsoft benefit the United States more than other countries in which those companies do business, because most of their headquarters functions, R&D, and high-value production remains in the United States.

The degree to which a host country benefits from the capabilities of foreign MNCs varies greatly. If an MNC makes products for export, the country benefits from the marketing and distribution channels of that company. If the MNC sources from local suppliers, the benefit is greater, because it helps local companies develop linkages with global markets and forces them to achieve international standards for quality and price. As MNCs conduct more technology-and engineering-intensive activities such as R&D and initial production ramp-up, there is more technology transfer and local workers gain more valuable skills. Singapore has benefited greatly from the presence of MNCs, which have steadily upgraded their activities there. Taiwan has also benefited from serving as a supplier and contractor to a wide range of MNCs, even though there is much less actual MNC presence in Taiwan.

Countries benefit from MNC capabilities through the mechanism of spin-offs and job mobility. Taiwan's PC industry is full of owners, top managers, and engineers who got their start with IBM, Texas Instruments, AT&T, and other MNCs. Hewlett-Packard has had a number of spin-offs in Singapore and Intel has had many spin-offs in Malaysia. This leakage of people and knowledge suggests that, over time, company capabilities tend to become country capabilities, especially when companies can be persuaded to expand and upgrade their presence in a country.

### Country versus Company in the Hard Disk Drive Industry

To look at the question of country versus company success in a specific industry segment, we turn to the hard disk drive industry. A group of researchers at the University of California, San Diego, has gathered data on the location of different activities in the disk drive industry.[10] Their data (table 7-1) show that country success in the disk drive industry appears very different depending on what measure one uses. For instance, based on nationality of the firm that does final assembly, U.S. firms have about 85% of the global market. However, based on the geographical location of final assembly, the U.S. share was only 4% in 1995 (and about 1% in 1996), while Southeast Asia accounted for 64% of world production. The United States has about 20% of world employment in the disk drive industry, while Southeast Asia accounts for 41% (Singapore, Thailand, and Malaysia have about 12% each), yet 42% of the industry's wages are paid in the United States. Looking just at American companies, 29% of employment and 62% of wages paid remain in the United States.

For those concerned about the benefits to the United States from such a global industry, these figures should be reassuring. They show that while labor-intensive jobs have long since gone offshore, the United States remains the largest employer in the industry. The data also show that the jobs remaining in the United States pay more than twice the average for the industry (20% of the employees earn 42% of the wages), and that the United States accounts for a large share of the value added in the production chain. As a high-wage country, the United States has little chance to compete in labor-intensive activities (such as manual subassembly), but it has been able to retain its leadership in R&D, product design, capital-intensive manufacturing of key components (e.g., semiconductors, heads, media and production equipment), marketing, and management.

For lower wage countries in Southeast Asia, this division of labor also makes sense, because these nations benefit from the creation of jobs and are able to develop skills and capabilities associated with disk drive production. For instance, when U.S. disk drive makers came to Singapore, their initial contribution to the local economy was the creation of low-paying assembly jobs. In time, they hired and trained Singaporean engineers, transferring knowledge and skills to the local workforce. Singapore also developed a strong supplier base that made it an attractive site for other drive makers. Singapore is now going further to create the managerial skills needed to act as a business hub and regional headquarters for the MNCs. Malaysia and Thailand are going through a similar process of skill development, as companies such as Seagate and Western Digital move higher value production to those countries. This upgrading is important to a developing country, since one of the objectives of economic development is to increase wages. If a country is to remain competitive in the computer industry as wages rise, it needs to improve the skills and the productivity of its workers.

One irony in the disk drive story is that until recently Japanese companies followed a strategy that some Americans wish that U.S. companies would do— that is, keep most of their production at home. Yet, partly because they failed to take advantage of the capabilities developing in Southeast Asia, the Japanese disk drive makers were relegated to a market share of less than 15%. So

TABLE 7-1. Global Distribution of the Hard Disk Industry, 1995

| | Company Nationality (market share) | Location of Final Assembly (% of total) | Employment (thousands) | Employment (% of total) | Wages Paid (share of total) |
|---|---|---|---|---|---|
| United States | 88.4 | 4.6 | 58,532 | 20 | 42.2 |
| Japan | 9.4 | 15.5 | 19,234 | 7 | 23.9 |
| Singapore | 0 | 45.0 | 33,051 | 12 | |
| Malaysia | 0 | 9.6 | 35,790 | 12 | |
| Thailand | 0 | 7.8 | 37,219 | 13 | |
| SE Asia subtotal[a] | 0 | 64 | 117,388 | 41 | 12.9 |
| China | 0 | 2.2 | 28,740 | 10 | |
| Other | 2.2 | 15.3 | 74,635 | 26 | 21 |
| Total | 100 | 100 | 287,059 | 100 | 100 |

Source: Peter Gourevitch, Roger E. Bohn, and David McKendrick, "Who Is Us? The Nationality of Production in the Hard Disk Drive Industry," The Data Storage Industry Globalization Project (La Jolla, Calif.: Graduate School of International Relations and Pacific Studies, University of California, San Diego, 1997).

[a]Includes Singapore, Malaysia, Thailand, Philippines, and Indonesia.

even though they kept a higher share of employment in their home country, Japan's total employment in the industry was less than 20,000 in 1995, compared with more than 58,000 in the United States.

## Conclusions

In conclusion, we would argue that companies must work for the good of their owners, workers, and customers, focusing on their own capabilities and taking advantage of other capabilities they need wherever they can find them. Their challenge is to use the global production system to get the best products to the market on time and at the lowest cost. The challenge for countries is to develop capabilities that are needed by the global production system, taking into account each country's existing capabilities and the strengths and weaknesses of local companies and industry structures.

Company success can be measured by standard indicators such as profitability, growth, market share, and technological leadership. The proper measures of country success depend on the country's circumstances. For some, total employment is critical, while for others it will be value added or wages paid. It would be wrong for Thailand to measure its success in disk drives by looking at the market share of Thai-owned companies, just as it would be wrong for the United States to gauge its position based on the share of final assembly located in the United States. Countries need to set realistic objectives and identify meaningful indicators to measure their success.

While company and country success can conflict at times, this need not be the case. The key to developing policies that align company and country objectives is to involve the private sector (producers and users) in the policy-making process and to develop operational definitions and measures to serve as a basis for policy choices. Especially important is the availability of common data sets for production and use at both company and country levels. There are private data sources, such as IDC and Dataquest, and some international reports such as the OECD's annual *Information Technology Outlook* volumes.[11] But there are no comprehensive, commonly accepted sources of data on which business and government policies can base decisions. Developing such measures will be critical in order to develop company and country strategies for the emerging network era, in which the industry's complexity promises to increase far beyond even that of the PC era.

# 8

# Competing in Computers in the Network Era

Network computing is based on the convergence of computing, communications, and multimedia content. The concept has been the basis of visionary treatises on the information society as far back as the 1960s,[1] but the actual convergence always seemed just around the corner until the 1990s, when the Internet exploded onto the scene—the global network of networks that evolved from the U.S. Defense Department's ARPANET (created in 1973). However, use of the Internet had never spread much beyond the research and academic communities until the arrival of the World Wide Web in the early 1990s. The hyperlinked Web, combined with graphical Web browsers such as Mosaic and Netscape Navigator, made it easy to navigate the Internet. Users clicked on a word or symbol and were quickly connected to a computer that could be located anywhere in the world. The Web also made it possible to embed words, pictures, sound, and video in a document, creating a true convergence of computing, communications, and content. Dependence on low-speed communications networks meant that using the Web could try one's patience, but companies, organizations, and individuals still poured onto the net with content ranging from annual reports to family photos. Meanwhile, electronic mail became an important, easy-to-use, and low-cost form of communication, allowing people to send and receive messages at their convenience and attach data files to their messages.

If the PC revolution caught many companies off guard during its decade-long march to overthrow the mainframe regime, the network era has been even more startling in its speed and impact on computer companies. By mid-1995, Microsoft was launching its Microsoft Network as a proprietary online service. Other online companies such as America Online argued that Microsoft would have an unfair competitive advantage by virtue of bundling Microsoft Network with the company's Windows 95 operating system. By the end of that year, however, Internet fever had caught on so fast that Microsoft was scrambling to refocus its entire company on the Internet, partly to prevent

Netscape from establishing a new dominant standard with its Navigator browser. By mid-1996, Netscape was accusing Microsoft of using anticompetitive practices to promote its Internet Explorer browser. While the fear of Microsoft remained a constant, the battleground shifted completely in less than a year from proprietary online services to the more open, nonproprietary Internet. In his book, *Only the Paranoid Survive*, Intel CEO Andrew Grove stated that the Internet had the feeling of a "strategic inflection point" that would fundamentally alter the competitive environment in the computer industry.

Countries have likewise had to revise their national information infrastructure (NII) plans because of the Internet. When Vice-President Al Gore announced the U.S. NII plan in 1993, countries across the Atlantic and Pacific were panicked by the perceived competitive advantage that the United States would gain from building an "information superhighway." They responded with their own NII visions, focused on building ubiquitous broadband fiber-optic networks with applications such as interactive TV and video-on-demand. But by 1995, even Singapore, the first country to develop a comprehensive NII plan, was revising its IT 2000 plans to take advantage of immediate opportunities created by the Internet. Other countries, such as Japan and Korea, had to revise their plans before they even began to be implemented.[2]

## The Network Era

Three things are new about the network era. First, it represents a new paradigm in which the network rather than the computer becomes the focus of the computing world—as illustrated by the slogan "The network is the computer" originally coined by Sun Microsystems. One upshot of this is that it will matter less what type of hardware is used to connect to the network, because all kinds of computers can talk to each other using Internet protocols. The mainframe computer, long considered a doomed paradigm, will coexist comfortably with the PC; the PC, in turn, will remain a viable part of network computing. At the corporate level, network computing means that many of the attributes we have come to associate with the mainframe or the PC—such as processing power and data storage—are moving from the desktop onto the network. Central servers will do more of the work that is now done on PCs, and applications that are currently loaded from PC hard drives will move to more central locations on corporate networks. If it achieves its promise, the network computer (NC) will have enough processing power and data storage capacity to bring applications that reside in the corporate networks down to the local level, allowing users complete control of these applications.

The network paradigm goes far beyond corporate computing, however, and extends to national and even global information infrastructures, as illustrated by the Internet. The Internet makes it possible for anyone with a computer connected to the Internet to communicate with anyone else with a connected computer anywhere in the world regardless of time or distance. This easy access greatly extends the possibilities for collaboration, integration of business operations, and direct access to niche markets.

Second, software rather than hardware is the primary component of the network era. The hardware components consist of the computers and the conduits on which digital information travels from one point to another. The rest of the network consists of software and information layered on one another, as shown in table 8-1. As the primary technology is shifting under network computing, the value-added is also shifting from the computer per se to the network. While the focal point for value-added in the PC era was the operating system and its applications, the focus of value-added in the network era is the Web browser and its applications. The Web browser embodies in a tightly integrated package the three-way convergence of information, communications, and computing that is so often talked about in the network era. The Web browser has come to be a new platform for *information* and *applications*, and the *interface* for accessing and exploiting the Internet. As Brian Kahin puts it, the Web browser is the "platform on which the expanding resources, functionality, and bandwidth of the Internet is being implemented."[3]

Figure 8-1 shows how the Web browser is at the center of the Internet, and by extension, the network era. The current battle between Microsoft and Netscape is over whose browser will be the new platform for the Internet and the network era. Each company has come to the battle from different positions. Microsoft grew out of the computing zone (right-hand side of figure 8-1), developed a monopoly in operating systems, and extended it to applications. Microsoft's current drive is to extend its software monopoly to servers and the browser (oval in figure). In contrast, Netscape grew out of the Internet zone (left-hand side, circle) and dominated browsers (at one point, having 85% of the market). It is currently vulnerable to Microsoft's actions unless it is

TABLE 8-1. Layers in PC and Network Computing

| Layers | PC Computing | Network Computing |
|---|---|---|
| Information and services | Files on disk drive. | On-line databases, multimedia content, Web pages, usenet, listserves. |
| Software | Stand-alone applications, office suite; operating systems, development tools. | E-mail, groupware, information packaging and streaming, electronic commerce; browsers, search engines, intelligent agents, development tools |
| Hardware | Computers, local area networks, data communications. | Information appliances, servers, routers, hubs, bridges, switches, cable, satellites, and telecommunications networks. |

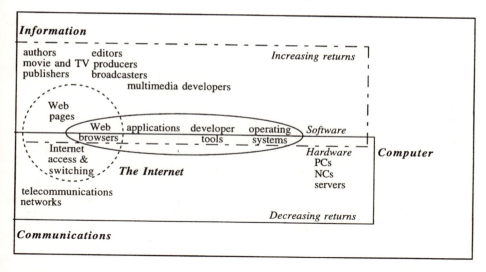

FIGURE 8-1. The Internet and Convergence in Network Computing. *Source:* Adapted from Brian Kahin, "The Internet Business and Policy Landscape," in *The Internet as Paradigm*, (Queenstown, MD: The Institute for Information Studies, 1997): 53.

able to extend its server and electronic commerce software, and get other software companies to develop applications for its platform.[4]

Third, the network era is creating new opportunities for businesses in computer hardware, software, and information. It is also creating new opportunities for access to markets on a global basis. Figure 8-1 also shows the areas within the computer, communications, and information landscape where different kinds of business opportunities will exist. The hardware components of the computer and communications infrastructure (bottom left, and right center of figure) are vast and involve large investments, but these are largely commodity businesses with decreasing returns to scale—even the new businesses in network computers and information appliances.

In contrast, software and content (middle and upper left of figure) involve new areas of creativity and innovation with many opportunities for businesses to enjoy increasing returns. The increasing returns businesses in the PC era were concentrated primarily in microprocessors, operating systems, and applications for PCs. In the network era, the new opportunities for increasing returns will be concentrated around the Internet including Web browsers, applications, and content.

As the foregoing suggests, the increasing returns business opportunities of the network era are in production-close-to-use. Value is created by producing applications, information, or services that businesses and consumers want. To achieve increasing returns, a producer must develop a new platform or adopt an existing one, develop products for that platform, and then encourage others to develop applications also, thereby increasing the value from use. The greater the number of applications the greater the value to users, and the greater the number of users the greater the returns on investments.

The final outcomes of the changes taking place as the network era unfolds are almost impossible to predict—like trying to predict the weather for a sail across the Pacific based on traveling a few miles outside San Francisco Bay. However, it is human nature to imagine what the future might bring, and for companies and countries it is necessary to make plans based on the best forecasts available. So based on our analysis of the history of the computer industry and interpretation of current trends, we step into the breach and offer our analysis of the implications of the network era. To start, we return to the format used in analyzing the central computing and PC eras, and look at the new technologies, new user markets, new industry players, new industry structures, new business strategies, and global production system that are evolving with the network era (table 8-2).

### New Technology

The new network era technology is computer networking, including local and wide area networks and the Internet. Hardware technologies include routers, bridges, hubs, servers, and modems used to build the networks and all sorts of information appliances ranging from PCs to palmtops. Software technologies include: Internet protocols; Web server software; browsers and associated applications such as search engines, intelligent agents, and groupware; and software languages and development tool kits for creating websites, applications, and content (table 8-2).

The underlying communications technology is the public switched network of the telephone companies on which the Internet and private networks ride. The long distance portion of the public network is fiber-optic and sufficient for voice, data, and video, but the local loop to businesses and households has inadequate bandwidth. The high cost of installing fiber for the local loop—along with reticence of the telephone and cable companies to make the needed investments—has opened the door to other communications technologies including wireless telephony and low orbiting satellites. So far there is no clear winner among these technologies, and so the bandwidth for the "Last Mile" is more or less static, rather than increasing dramatically as had been expected with telecommunications deregulation.[5] This lack of adequate bandwidth in the public switched network is constraining the continued rapid penetration of network computing nationally and globally.

The Internet is most emblematic of the network era; it is a heterogeneous network of networks that in 1996 comprised over 100,000 computer networks in 100 countries.[6] The technologies of the Internet have become so popular that they are being used in building corporate intranets and extranets, which number more than three times those of the Internet.[7] The Internet is unlike previous technologies in a number of ways:

- it is open rather than proprietary, based on a set of open communications standards that facilitate interchange of content between networks;
- it enables anyone with access to the Internet to reach out to any other computer in the world that also has access—without belonging to the same network;
- operation and control of the Internet is decentralized throughout the network;
- intelligence is distributed throughout the network;
- access is usually based on a flat fee, rather than based on usage;
- its low cost, ease of access, and ease of use have led to exponential growth;
- overall, it tends to resist control by a single company or government.

These features have led to the Internet's phenomenal growth and overwhelmed a number of proprietary technologies controlled by individual companies.[8] Since 1990, the number of users has doubled every year up to an estimated 100 million people worldwide in 1998.[9] Traffic on the Internet is growing even faster, doubling every six months. Table 8-3 shows Internet use in the United States and Asia Pacific.

### New User Markets

Just as the PC era brought individual users and new uses of computing (word processing, spreadsheets) into the market, so the network era is defining new users in the form of corporate and social "communities" and new uses of computing in the form of the World Wide Web, the Internet, and private networks (table 8-2). Some of these involve established markets whereas, others involve new market niches. Table 8-4 identifies different kinds of markets in hardware, software, and information products and services.

The computing hardware needs of business users and consumers are being met by an ever-wider array of computing devices. Just as the PC earlier challenged the mainframe, so now the network computer and other information appliances are challenging the PC as the "one size fits all" computing solution. This trend is reflected in the growth of new computer options such as the network computer, palmtop devices, and WebTV. The growth in the number of computer options is due to network computing, which enables companies to provide businesses and consumers with access to computer resources from large servers carrying vast stores of data over large-scale, speedy networks. Thus the market for network hardware will continue to grow and diversify.

There will also be new markets in software. There are only a few hundred network-based end user applications available today, so there are opportunities for creating many more applications and for tools to make application development easy and quick.[10] Key business applications will be for enterprise in-

TABLE 8-2. Network Era Compared to Central Computing and PC Eras

| Central Computing Era | PC Era | Network Era |
|---|---|---|
| **Technology** Vacuum tube to transistors, integrated circuits | Smaller, cheaper, more reliable integrated circuits | Computer networks; hubs, routers, network computers; server software, browsers, search engines. |
| **User markets** Business users globally, departmental users | Individual users alone, or in groups and markets that are global because of common requirements of individual users. | Social and business networks; function-oriented markets; health, entertainment, business, education, government, shopping, finance, entertainment. |
| **Industry players** First movers in the mainframe industry were U.S. firms: IBM, Honeywell, Unisys, Control Data. Followed in Europe by "national champions" ICL, Siemens-Nixdorf, and Groupe Bull, and in Japan by Fujitsu, Hitachi, and NEC. New players in the computer industry focused on minis: DEC, Packard, Prime, Data General, Tandem, and Wang. IBM joined the pack. | New companies and new countries: Intel, Microsoft, Apple, Novell, and Compaq in U.S.; Toshiba and NEC in Japan; Acer, FIC, Mitac, and Tatung in Taiwan; IPC, Wearnes, Aztec, and Creative in Singapore. | Established computer, telecommunications, consumer electronics, and media firms. New entrants that create new value in content (Lexis–Nexis) or at the boundaries of converging technologies (Netscape, Pointcast). |
| **Industry structure** Concentrated, oligopolistic industry, comprised of a few large companies. IBM the dominant computer company worldwide. Distributed, competitive industry, comprised of many medium-sized firms in minicomputers. Leaders were new entrants DEC and Hewlett-Packard, and later IBM. | Distributed, highly competitive industry, comprised of SMEs horizontally segmented, using network economies and making chips, computer systems, peripherals, or software. IBM leadership replaced by Intel and Microsoft. | Concentration in commodity production. Distributed, highly competitive industry in new market segments. Alliances between the firm and its suppliers and customers and producers of complementary products. |
| **Business strategy** Competition between *companies* using proprietary systems to lock-in customers and lock-out competitors. Entry into niche markets | Competition between *platforms* using functions and features to differentiate products with Intel/DOS emerging as dominant platform. Competi- | Competiton within the Internet model for information services. Price competiton among commodity hardware manufacturers. Standards |

TABLE 8-2. (*continued*)

| | | |
|---|---|---|
| not penetrated by main frames with move-up to larger systems; worldwide competition between companies using proprietary systems to lock-in customers and lock-out competitors. | tion among companies for market share in horizontal segments. | competition in software markets. Wide open field for new product innovators in software and content. |
| Global production system Company- and country-based production systems with global distribution. Mainframe companies large and vertically integrated for economies of scale and make complete systems bundled with software. Minicomputer companies are medium-sized and make complete systems; large third-party supplier industry. | Global division of labor for production with R&D, design, marketing by U.S. firms; manufacturing and logistics by Asian firms. | Production split between commodity and innovative products, between thin margins and high margins, between commodity hardware producer countries of Asia and software and content in the United States. |

tegration, value chain management with suppliers and customers, industry-wide integration such as banking and retail networks and, of course, electronic commerce. Approximately eighty percent of electronic commerce development currently focuses on business-to-business transactions and is putting into place standards and an infrastructure that will also serve business-to-consumer transactions in the future.[11] Applications are being deployed that enable businesses to do customer service (order entry, processing, and fulfillment) over the Internet rather than through telephone-based bullpens, and to add new features such as product configuration, order pricing, or loan payment simulation. Government, education, and health care represent other markets for application development.

Finally, there will be markets in information services for firms that can assist companies to choose migration paths to new network technologies and build Web pages, intranets, and extranets between companies and their business partners. There will also be content-related opportunities that fall within the traditional purview of the computer industry. Since the network era will make more information available than ever before, a central problem will be to sift through information for relevance and manage the information to create knowledge-based opportunities. Thus, there will be a huge need for efficient and effective search engines to find really relevant data, intelligent agents to continually scan and search the Internet for updates to that data, and data mining and analytic tools to develop meaning from the data.

TABLE 8-3.  Internet Use in the United States and Asia-Pacific

| Country | Internet Hosts (1997) | Hosts/1,000 People | Number of Internet Users (1997a) | Users/1,000 People |
|---|---|---|---|---|
| United States | 11,829,141 | 45.8 | 54,680,000 | 212.0 |
| Japan | 955,688 | 7.7 | 7,970,000 | 64.0 |
| Australia | 707,611 | 40.2 | 3,350,000 | 190.3 |
| New Zealand | 155,678 | 44.5 | 210,000 | 60.0 |
| Korea | 123,370 | 2.8 | 155,000 | 3.5 |
| Taiwan | 40,706 | 1.9 | 590,000 | 27.6 |
| Singapore | 60,674 | 21.7 | 150,000 | 53.6 |
| Hong Kong | 48,660 | 8.4 | 200,000 | 34.5 |
| Malaysia | 40,533 | 2.1 | 90,000 | 4.7 |
| Indonesia | 10,861 | 0.06 | 60,000 | 0.3 |
| Thailand | 12,794 | 0.22 | 80,000 | 1.4 |
| Philippines | 4,309 | 0.07 | 40,000 | 0.6 |
| India | 4,794 | 0.005 | 40,000 | 0.04 |
| China | 25,594 | 0.02 | 70,000 | 0.06 |

*Sources:* Hosts: Network Wizards, Internet Domain Survey, July 1997 (www.nw.com); Users: For United States, Georgia Tech Research Corporation, 1997 (www.gc.maricopa.edu); for Japan, *Far Eastern Economic Review* (June 13, 1996): 71; for all other users, International Data Group, *IDG China Market News Updates* (www.idgchina.com) (July 8, 1997), table citing the source as The New Century Group.

[a]1996 for New Zealand, Korea, Taiwan, Singapore, Hong Kong, Malaysia, Indonesia, Thailand, Philippines, India, China.

The Internet, information appliances, simpler software, and new information products will bring about wider and deeper penetration of the technology—to newly industrializing and developing countries; to small- and medium-sized enterprises; and to beginning users. They will also deepen penetration within existing markets and encourage greater use in all markets. But the real demand, where companies and countries stand to gain from the opportunities, will come from the technology's role in making the Internet truly more and more useful for households, organizations, and commercial markets.

### New Industry Players

Some analysts such as David Moschella[12] argue that the key players in the network era will not be computer companies but telecommunications companies and the governments that regulate them. This conclusion is based on the fact that the telecommunications industry controls the critical resource for the network era—bandwidth. Moschella states that control over this resource will return power to the nation-state, since the telecommunications industry remains the domain of one or a few domestic providers in every country. And, in fact, despite a trend toward liberalization around the world, telecommunications remains a highly regulated industry.

TABLE 8-4. New Markets in Network Computing

| Products and Services | Increasing Returns Markets | Hybrid Markets | Decreasing Returns Markets |
|---|---|---|---|
| Information and services | Information packaging and streaming (Pointcast) Electronic marketplaces, auctions and clearing houses (Travelbids, Winebid.com) | On-line merchants (Amazon.com) On-line services (AOL, Prodigy, CompuServe) On-line databases (Lexis–Nexis, Reuters, NY Times) | Website design Intranet design Network integration Consulting Customizing packages Custom applications |
| Software | Operating systems Office suites Browers (Netscape Navigator, MS Internet Explorer) Groupware (Lotus Notes) Electronic commerce software Database software Network software (Cisco) | Niche applications Software languages (Java, Active-X] Development tools Applets Search engines Intelligent agents | |
| Hardware | PC microprocessors Smart network hardware (hubs, routers, switches) | Servers "Smart" information appliances | PCs Components Peripherals "Dumb" information appliances |

This argument describes the present state of the network era, but it is not a situation the computer industry is willing to accept passively. Rather than sit and wait for the slow-moving telephone and cable companies to invest in increased bandwidth, the computer industry is looking for ways either to accelerate the process or to circumvent it altogether. Bill Gates is a main investor in Teledesic Corporation, which plans an "Internet-in-the-Sky" network of low-orbiting satellites, presenting an alternative to both telephone and cable companies in the future. Meanwhile, Microsoft has invested $1 billion in cable TV company Comcast, which presents an alternative to telephone companies in the present. Such efforts are aimed at presenting competition to the entrenched providers in the hopes of stimulating action to eliminate bandwidth bottlenecks and, if they do not respond, to go around them in the future.

Outside the United States, however, Moschella's analysis is more compelling. Even Microsoft and Intel lack the resources and influence to clear bottlenecks in bandwidth around the world. However, when predicting the key country players, the winners will be those that open their markets, encourage competition, and give incentives for investment, rather than those that allow telecommunications monopolists to stifle the growth of networks. Dynamic new companies will spring up in those countries where diffusion of network technologies is broadest and sophisticated users drive the development of new software and information products and services. New entrants will create value in applications and in content, at the boundaries of converging technologies or in network-based services (table 8-2).

### New Industry Structure

While the network era will define new user markets and new uses of the technology, it will also create new industry structures. If the centralized era was marked by vertical integration and the PC era by horizontal specialization, the network era currently presents a more amorphous and complex industry structure characterized by a blurring of the divisions among industries through diversification, vertical integration, mergers and acquisitions, and strategic alliances. Despite all the activity, when the smoke clears, the broader information industry is likely to look more like the horizontal structure of the PC industry than the vertically integrated structures of telecommunications, broadcasting, and publishing. As illustrated in table 8-5, there will be horizontal segments for hardware, software, network services, and information. Of these four segments, network services is entirely new with the network era, whereas the others have new elements within them.

TABLE 8-5. Network Era Industry Structure, ca. 1997

| Industry Segment | Products and Services in the Industry Segment | | | Key Factors in Industry Competition |
|---|---|---|---|---|
| Information | Finance, education real estate, travel, databases, gambling, shopping, games, News, magazines, books Music, movies | | | Responsive to markets; Design innovation; Fast, flexible |
| Network services | Intranets, extra-nets and private networks | Internet and private online services | Electronic commerce networks | |
| Software | Operating systems, business and end user applications | Browsers, search engines, email, groupware | Intelligent agents | |
| Hardware | Components, network hardware; long distance and local telephone | Servers, PC, NetPC, NC; wireless and satellite networks | Information appliances; broadcasting and cable TV networks | Scale and scope; Quality at low cost; Process innovation |

Even though the fortunes of individual computer companies will rise and fall in the network era, the computer industry landscape is pretty well defined. The most important changes in the network era will happen beyond the boundaries of the computer industry in the form of mergers, acquisitions, and strategic alliances. Telephone companies are consolidating to create global giants through strategic alliances (Sprint/France Telecom/Deutsche Telekom and AT&T's 12 World Partners), mergers such as MCI and WorldCom, and acquisitions such as SBC's purchase of Pacific Telesis. Moschella[13] predicts that these giants and the local telephone companies (Regional Bell Operating Companies, or RBOCs) will swallow up the current entrepreneurial Internet Service Providers (ISPs). Time Warner's acquisition of TCI, Disney's acquisition of ABC, and the News Corp./Fox empire of Rupert Murdoch have crossed the lines between communications, publishing, broadcast TV, and entertainment content. Links to the computer industry have been slower to develop, but experiments such as the Microsoft/NBC channel, Microsoft's involvement in the Dreamworks SKG movie studio, and Microsoft's purchase of WebTV are moves in that direction. Thus, the shape of the information industry is moving in different directions at the same time and will take time to sort out.

## New Business Strategy

Early on, the network era was characterized by two competing business strategies for information service providers: (1) the private, closed network strategy, which puts control at the center of large conglomerates that "push" content on users; and (2) the public, open strategy, which devolves and distributes control throughout the system ultimately responding to the "pull" of end users. The public, open strategy is clearly the current winner, because trials with Interactive TV and other push approaches have been remarkable for their lack of success while Internet ventures are booming. The Internet is also clearly winning over the proprietary services of Prodigy, CompuServe, and America Online, which have had to evolve into value-added Internet providers, offering specialized service in addition to standard Internet access.

It is likely, however, that both the proprietary and public networks will move toward a common business model for delivering technology and services to end users—the information utility. Under this model, customers use a PC or information appliance to access the network and a monthly subscription is charged for the service. The hardware might be purchased, leased, or even given away as part of a service contract. Service providers make money from these subscriptions, and possibly from advertising and other revenues. For users, it means little or no up-front cost, and the ability to control monthly charges based on the level of service they choose. For providers, it means "recurring revenues" that are not dependent on constant technology change, software upgrades, or more PC users coming along. But it does require more usage, the provision of content and services that engender usage, and the development of billing systems that ensure the proper distribution of revenues to providers. Thus, for example, the content provider, network service provider, and the browser/search providers would receive a unit and/or percentage charge on each transaction. Microsoft's effort to ensure that its browser and Windows are at the heart of every transaction is aimed at achieving such a steady and growing revenue stream. As usage increases so do revenues, far beyond what could be achieved by simply selling more copies of Windows.

The utility model is already standard for telephone, cellular phone, and cable TV service throughout the world and therefore is well understood and accepted by business and household consumers. This model is also implicit in the global trends toward corporate outsourcing of computer and telecommunications services and the recent trend toward leasing PCs to avoid obsolescence. Several telephone companies are already developing plans to offer information appliances for a monthly fee, and television makers have plans to include set-top boxes or WebTV devices inside TV sets. Access to the Internet via corporate networks or on-line services generally involves a flat fee without charges for use. However, this has increased congestion on the Internet tremendously. It is likely, therefore, that "usage" charges will be enacted across the Internet to deal with congestion, and the "free" Internet will gradually disappear. The nature of competition among information utility providers will be decided by nation-states, with domestic providers, and by global telecommunications companies engaged in alliances with these providers.

The traditional business model for hardware and software companies— the vertically integrated firm engaged in all phases of design, production, and marketing and selling branded products through its own distribution networks with all revenues and profits accruing to the firm—is being replaced. The PC era introduced a new business model oriented around software platforms rather than firms. For computer hardware companies, this shift meant that they no longer needed to make everything themselves, and created what Andrew S. Rappaport and Shmuel Halevi[14] called the "computerless computer company" that outsourced manufacturing and logistics to take advantage of the global production network while retaining design, marketing, and business management as core competencies. The shift also increased the number of software companies, but it made them highly dependent upon a platform leader as new business alliances were formed among companies committed to a particular software platform such as IBM's OS/2, Apple's Mac OS, and Microsoft's DOS/Windows. Although revenues and profits still accrued to individual firms, their returns depended upon the market share enjoyed by a particular platform as much as their share of the particular market segment in which they competed (e.g., graphics packages or geographic information systems).

The network era is increasing the importance of product platforms and introducing the Internet itself as a new platform for computer companies to do business. The business model has shifted from that of a single company selling its own products or services to a company that is part of a larger business network that cross-markets a platform and sells complementary products that add value and help to "grow" the market share of the platform, which in turn, benefits all participants. The aim of the participants is to have the adopted platform be dominant in the market, perhaps creating a virtual monopoly that ensures increasing returns for some participants in the business network.

The battle over what hardware and software will be the "gateway" to the Internet illustrates the dynamics of this new business strategy. Oracle, IBM, Sun, and others champion the network computer (NC) running Java software as a low-cost device ($500 or less) that would link end users to the Internet and/or corporate servers. Users would download Java software as needed, and tap into databases, video libraries, or other types of content residing on those servers. The NC would not only be less expensive to buy, but it would also cost much less than the PC over its life cycle because of lower software, training, and support costs. Microsoft and Intel have argued that the PC running Windows will continue to be the only realistic alternative for accessing the Internet. However, less than a year after Oracle began touting the NC concept, Microsoft and Intel announced their own Network PC, a low-cost, centrally administered PC that would lower administrative costs for business PCs. They are now even acknowledging a limited role for the NC.[15]

The NC is just one example of a broader concept called the low-cost information appliance that could be used in the home, in the office, or on the road for a variety of purposes from e-mail to Internet access to storing addresses, recipes, and digital photos. Products fitting this description are already on the market and more are on the way. The information appliance industry is at a stage similar to the earliest PCs in the late 1970s: it is a relatively simple, low-cost technology; the market is not yet developed so the right vision can make the market; standards exist for hardware interfaces, software interfaces, and programming languages (Java) that reduce the risk of pioneering the technology;[16] and the dominant players in the PC industry are in a state of denial about the potential of these appliances. Consequently, there are new business opportunities in design and marketing, production, distribution, and sales and support. There also are opportunities at all levels of the technology from microprocessor to the complete hardware package, and from operating systems to end user applications. The information appliance industry is wide open, with the hardware advantage going to the Asia-Pacific region and the software advantage belonging to the United States, but each segment offers opportunities for new entrants.

While the utility model will apply increasingly to the network services industry and the platform model to computer hardware and software, this says nothing about the kinds of business models that will succeed for corporate users in the network era. Most user companies are focusing on developing intranets, extranets, and electronic commerce on a business-to-business basis, planning eventually to migrate them to the consumer market. These intranets and extranets generally focus on achieving greater efficiency in operations and communications. In some cases, network computing is being used to remake the core functions of firms from product development to inbound logistics, production, marketing and sales, distribution, and service and support. It is also remaking their relations with suppliers and customers. In the process, these firms are being made both more efficient and more responsive to market change and more interdependent with their suppliers and customers through mutually beneficial alliances.

The true significance of the network era is that value is moving away from stand-alone hardware and software and onto the network. Whether the "Wintel" standard is toppled means a lot to the fortunes of Microsoft, Intel, and others who have strong competitive positions in the present PC industry. But it is much less important than what network computing means more broadly for the information technology industry. The key will be how the network creates value and how that value can be appropriated by producers, business users, and consumers. For the information industries, this will determine which companies are winners and losers in the next round of competition. For countries, there are great potential benefits from creating and using networks as well as from producing hardware, software, content, and services for the network. The current battle for Web browsers and servers occurring in the United States will probably set the global standard, with U.S. companies dominating the market. But there will be much open competition on many other fronts. A key question is: Which companies and which countries will seize the opportunities and reap the benefits?

## Implications for Companies

As companies face the new round of competition that will mark the network era, they will need to address several issues. These boil down to choice of type of business, strategic management of technology, organization of teams and business partners, and using the Internet as a business platform.

### Choice of Type of Business

*Companies must make basic choices about what kind of business they want to be and can be: increasing or decreasing returns businesses.* A recent *Wall Street Journal* article about a software company called Analytical Graphics, Inc., provides a significant perspective on theses choices.[17] The company has developed the Satellite Tool Kit, a packaged application that turns volumes of satellite tracking data into a 2-D view of any satellite in orbit. Although the market is small and specialized, government agencies, contractors, and commercial operators purchase the product to help schedule downlinks, site ground stations, and design satellites. In response to demand, the company subsequently developed add-ons and upgrades, including 3-D animation. All together these products accounted for 75% of the company's $7 million revenues in 1996, which were expected to double in 1997. Every first-time sale came at great cost to the company, consuming 51% of the $10,000 sales price for trade shows, magazine ads, regional sales offices, and sales calls. The way to increase sales was to cut prices but company officials felt that even at $10 a copy people might not give up their current tools for the Satellite Tool Kit. Moreover, a new competitor had recently introduced a low-priced 3-D satellite animation tool that could threaten its market. So, Analytical Graphics decided to give the software away free, inundating the market in the hopes of becoming the industry standard and relying on future add-ons as the sole source of revenue. It produced 75,000 copies and distributed them in trade magazines; it also began free Web downloads. It will take months (or even years) to see whether the scheme pays off; if it does, the returns will be great. As the writer of the *Wall Street Journal* article put it, "When a niche product becomes standard, the winner takes all." This case illustrates that increasing returns businesses are not for the faint-hearted; the risks are large because the potential returns are also large. Analytical Graphics is making a bold move and risking the future of the company by giving away its basic software in order to increase its market share and therefore the demand for its high-return add-on products. One could argue, however, that the really risky thing is not doing it at all and losing out to a new entrant.

The case also suggests that the paths companies can take are increasingly becoming binary choices. The first path, which is illustrated by Analytical Graphics' move, is based on exploiting the ubiquity of networks and establishing one's product as the standard for a given layer (the "Software" layer in table 8-1). Success depends upon generating excitement about the product in user markets, developing add-ons, getting others to develop complementary products, and securing favorable reviews in the press and elsewhere. This can help to elicit investment capital to enable the company to assemble a critical mass of customers, new products, and more developers of complementary products. This path offers increasing returns for the investment if the product captures significant market share. But this path is also a never-ending challenge because the company must run a lean operation, never stumble, keep generating add-on products and bringing along its customers and complementary developers, and start another round with the next generation of products.

The second path of decreasing returns, which Analytical Graphics might have stayed on, caters to a defined clientele, combines software with consulting, and develops stable, long-term relationships with the customer base. In this path, products tend to have relatively lower unit-volumes, relatively higher prices, and a direct sales force. As an investment, this path is predictable and prudent and is based as much on selling people's time as on selling products per se. It is a more reliable though still competitive strategy. The danger is that new entrants with great products can undermine the company's position. The key issue for a company, therefore, is knowing what kind of risk it is willing to take and what products or services it can produce for what markets.[18] This is where strategic management of technology enters.

## Strategic Management of Technology

*The experience of previous computing eras clearly indicates that company success increasingly depends on generating a continuous stream of successful new products in very short product cycles over an extended period. This requires* strategic product management to create a family of products that share a common platform and address a related set of market applications.[19] IBM's System/360 was the first such hardware family in the computer industry. The System/360 was a big gamble for IBM at the time because it involved putting all of IBM's eggs in one basket, but the System/360 is probably the single most successful family of computers in the history of computing.[20] It was followed by other notable product families such as the DEC PDP/VAX mini-computers, the original IBM PC, the Intel microprocessors, and the Microsoft DOS/Windows/NT operating systems.

Companies desiring to be in the increasing returns business in the network era must be leaders of a platform.[21] Their challenge is to create a platform from which they can develop a stream of derivative products, get others to develop complementary products, and develop the next platform while bringing the first one to market. Product leadership requires a complete rethinking of products, with the goal of defining the critical common core around which a platform and derivative products can be built. Companies in decreasing returns businesses will be technology followers. Their challenge is to pick the right platform, develop complementary products for it, and get their products to market in parallel with changes in the platform by the leader. For example, developers of applications for Windows 98 must get their next products ready to ship when Microsoft's upgrade ships. The key is to be fast, flexible, and responsive to changes by the platform leader.

Both increasing and decreasing returns businesses need to understand the power of platforms if they are to be successful—even though each relates to platforms differently. A platform traditionally refers to a set of components and their interfaces with one another and the outside. A PC is a set of mechanical, electronic, and metal components with a standard interface between these components and to the outside (software, networks). Product platforms must have four key features: scalability, standardization, openness, and complementary assets. Scalability means the ability to increase size and complexity without the need for redesign of core and related components. Standardization means that the components and their interfaces are standard so that derivative products can be easily created. Openness means that the specifications for the components and/or their interfaces are public so that others can create complementary assets (products or services). In the network era, scalable and standard "platforms" increase the ability to create derivative products over an extended time period, and open architectures enable others to develop complementary assets that increase the value of the platform to users.

The power of platforms stems from the fact that a well-designed platform provides the basis for creating derivative products, for continually renewing those products, and for creating the next generation of products without starting from scratch.[22] The commonality of technologies and markets for the underlying platform in turn can lead to economies in manufacturing, distribution, and service. Netscape's Web browser and server make up such a platform. Derivative products include its communicator, search engine, electronic commerce applications, and development tools. Netscape also provides linkages to other companies' search engines, information packaging and streaming applications, and electronic commerce applications. Netscape gave its Web browser free to individual users in order to build demand for its Web server, which it sells to corporate users for a hefty price. The larger the installed base of corporate users and developers for Netscape's Web browser and applications, the greater the value of its Web browser/server platform.

### Organizational Management

*In the network era, companies will need to deal with both the internal management of teams to create new products and services and bring them to market successfully, and the external management of the business ecology in which the firm operates.* For example, one description of the software firms of the future is as follows:

> Software development will change with this change in the infrastructure [the Internet]. Rather than a single software development entity making a single "system," hundreds of firms will be contributing smaller, Internet compatible "applets" that may be seamlessly combined by integrators and users within a distributed computing environment. The software firms of the future will have the potential of seeing its program modules used in hundreds of different applications, many of which it will not control. Instead, the design, development, and integration of software will be controlled in aggregate by masses of developers with shared interests.[23]

This scenario illustrates how organizational architectures follow product architectures. Big, vertically integrated companies ruled the mainframe era, whereas smaller, more focused and flexible firms were the PC leaders. The type of organization that will succeed in the network era is still not clearly defined, but it is sure to look more like companies in the PC industry than in the mainframe or telecommunications industry. Its hallmarks will be speed, flexibility, responsiveness to the market, and decentralization of decision-making. This generalized picture will vary according to whether a company is competing in increasing or decreasing returns businesses. Decreasing returns businesses will require ever greater ability to respond quickly to markets; to operate more efficiently through outsourcing; to make innovations in design, marketing, branding and distribution; and to tightly integrate their operations with suppliers and customers. For such companies the network will be a tool to support such innovation. But fundamentals such as cost, quality, performance, and features will still be important, and high-volume production might still require more traditional organizational structures, at least for manufacturing.

Companies in increasing returns businesses face a bewildering array of opportunities and threats and must do away with traditional structures. The network era moves at such a rapid pace that companies must be able to make and execute decisions extremely quickly just to keep up with new technologies and market opportunities to say nothing of driving those changes. Companies must be organized to support teams that are responsible for new products and services from beginning to end. For any new platform, there will be a team responsible for common components and interfaces and other teams responsible for derivative products. Teams need to be small for speed, but supported by nonbureaucratic core functions such as purchasing, marketing, pricing, and distribution. Team managers need to meet and coordinate frequently, to define the boundaries and interfaces and synchronize the work. Product teams will need to interact closely with end users and with developers of complementary assets in order to ensure their products work well together.

*Companies will also need to influence their external business ecology in the network era.* Successful platforms will involve a product (hardware, software, information) built around a compatibility standard plus complementary producers and corporate users that form an "economic network" of suppliers and buyers. What will differentiate one platform from another is the specific compatibility standard(s) around which they form, such as UNIX or Windows NT for operating systems and Microsoft Internet Explorer or Netscape Communicator for the Internet. Companies that seek increasing returns need to create a "business ecology" along with the design of a new platform, whereas those in decreasing returns need only join a winning business group. The larger the business ecology the greater the market the members can reach and the greater the returns to all members of the ecology, although the platform/ecology leader should receive the greatest returns. Companies therefore must not only have a plan for their own product or service, but they must also have a plan to create and help out the larger business ecology on which their plans depend for success. This larger ecology is likely to include business partners that create complementary products and services; suppliers and distributors; and customers that provide valuable information about desired product features.

*The top management of companies will need to interact closely with key customers and business partners in order to create and maintain coalitions.* Partnerships traditionally have been made between firms on the basis of complementary capabilities, such as technology or financing. These considerations will continue to be important, but the most important consideration will be how the alliance reinforces the product platform. For example, Microsoft is trying to extend its dominance in software from the PC era to the network era by building Internet capabilities into all of its software, and creating new software such as Windows CE for information appliances. Around 4,000 independent developers that create applications for Windows are aligned with Microsoft's efforts. In contrast, Sun, IBM, Oracle, and others have aligned to create a viable alternative to Microsoft's monopoly by creating the NC, the Java language, and Java applications that are uniquely geared for network computing. Creating and evolving these larger ecologies requires that heads of companies be able to spot where various markets are going, create a network of business partners to serve the markets, coevolve the partnership with them, and continually look for other partners that can enhance the network.

Finding and keeping such leaders will be a most challenging task, as illustrated by Apple's succession of CEOs and declining business fortunes.

### Use of the Internet as a Business Platform

The power of the Internet as a business platform is that it provides different forms of leverage for increasing and decreasing returns businesses. For hardware companies, the Internet provides new options for more efficient production, marketing, distribution, and customer service. For software and information product and services companies, the Internet can provide the firms' core "manufacturing" capabilities, as well as provide new options for greater efficiency. In hardware, product and process innovation follow upon one another and use different technologies. The Internet cannot be used to build innovative hardware products per se; it can only contribute to improving businesses processes through support of practices such as concurrent design, integrated logistics, or direct distribution. Consequently, the prospects for increasing returns for physical products as a result of network computing are limited.

In contrast, the Internet provides great potential for increasing returns in software and information because the product and the production process can be intertwined, with considerable opportunity for leverage and network economies. Analytical Graphics, Inc., discussed earlier, illustrates the power from linkage between product platforms and the Internet as a business platform. The company is using the Internet to distribute free copies of its Satellite Tool Kit in order to increase market share and to make money from selling add-ons. Although the market for its product is small and specialized, the Internet enables the company to have global reach overnight at nearly zero production and distribution cost. It also enables the company to have a low-cost relationship with its customer base through publication of new product announcements, an electronic help-desk, customer feedback, and newsgroups.

The use of the Internet for both "manufacturing" and distribution can be seen most clearly with information products such as books (or magazines or journals). Presently, books are created by one process and marketed and distributed by another. Innovating companies such as Amazon.com achieve economies in marketing and distribution by using the Internet, but they must rely upon traditional publishers and physical distribution for their products. While Amazon.com can make a business through marketing and distribution on the Internet, the possibilities for increasing returns to scale are limited. However, using the Internet for the process of creation, marketing, and distribution of information products, and developing a relationship with the customer for follow-up derivative products, provides new opportunities for increasing returns. Imagine the following scenario:[24]

A book publisher creates a Web site on the Internet through which authors submit manuscripts. Editors pick up these manuscripts, review them, attach their comments and store everything in a shared archive. The publisher and editors meet electronically over the manuscripts, having reviewed relevant material from the archive, decide on which will be published, and communicate their comments and instructions for final manuscript preparation to the authors. Once the final manuscript is accepted for publication, the editors work directly on text and graphic files submitted by the authors, communicating with one another as required to shape the manuscript for "publication."

Marketing and promotion is also conducted through the Internet. Notables are contacted for testimonials, given the Web address where they can find the manuscript, and asked to e-mail their comment for quotation in promotion. Book reviews are solicited and/or placed in journals and magazines. The appropriate electronic mailing lists are accessed and culled for targeted promotion, perhaps changing the promotional message slightly as appropriate, and promotional flyers which contain an Internet address that can be clicked for direct ordering are constructed and distributed electronically. As the order is being placed, the customer is informed where they might find reviews on the book or a chat room on the book. They are also informed about books on similar or related topics and how they might easily and quickly preview them.

In addition to such standard publication of the entire book, chapters of the book are repackaged as monographs, as part of "custom" book publishing for classroom use, or as part of an information service which includes material from other books handled by the publisher, or by other publishers. Where there is market demand, the book is translated into other languages using automatic translation supplemented by a highly skilled native language editor, the promotional messages adjusted for cultural sensitivity, and the content supplemented by text, graphics, video, or other material as required.

This publishing company has no physical inventory of books; only electronic ones. It also has no offices and no physical address; only a Web address on a server on the Internet through which it is able to reach whatever markets it chooses to target.

This scenario illustrates how the Internet provides the technology for marketing, distribution, and service of products. More important, the scenario shows how the Internet provides the technology for "manufacture" of information products. These technologies for manufacturing already exist, as do applications for electronic commerce. So the scenario is not futuristic; it is possible now.

Because these possibilities are new, companies must learn about what the network era means for them and their customers through experimentation in their own companies. In particular, they must experiment with intranets, extranets,[25] and the Internet to find out how they can use this new medium in their own business, so they can develop products and services for corporate users and so they can leverage the power of the Internet for their business. If a company is not a sophisticated user of the technology, it will not know how to be a producer. Even hardware makers need to be users in order to understand the market. Therefore, businesses must develop a critical mass of experienced, sophisticated developers and business users. The greater the number of sophisticated users in their business ecology, the greater the chance that some users will come up with new products or new ideas for products that can be commercialized. In rolling out 3,000 JavaStations at Sun Microsystems headquarters in Silicon Valley in July 1997, President Scott McNealy is reported to have told his engineers, computer scientists, and other staff that they needed to be the first users of this new technology if they expected Sun's customers to use it, and they needed to use it so they could come up with new applications for customers. What is true for Sun is also true for other companies. If they do not want to be disadvantaged in the network era, they must embrace the technology and learn how to invent new products and services and use them in their own companies as they offer them to others.

## Asia's Role in the Network Era

The network era will clearly present new opportunities for companies and countries in the global computer industry, but the key question is for whom? Will the convergence of computing, communications, and consumer electronics fit the unique capabilities of Asian countries and lead to an Asian era in computers? Can Asian companies and countries develop world leadership in new technologies to compete with the United States, or will Asia continue to be largely a workshop and supplier for U.S. multinationals? Will the network era be one mainly of cooperation or competition between the United States and Asia?

Asia's role in the network era will be even more complex than its role in the global production system of the PC era. Not only will the Asian countries compete in the full spectrum of hardware markets, but Asia will also be a large and dynamic market and will likely find opportunities in software and services. For the U.S. computer industry, the expanding role of Asia as a market and producer will present both opportunities and possible new threats.

### Asia-Pacific Computer Market

Between 1985 and 1995, the Asia-Pacific computer market grew from 17% of world demand to 32%, surpassing Europe and closing in on North America. Given its large population and rapid economic growth, the Asia-Pacific market is likely to be the largest in the world by the early twenty-first century. Table 8-6 shows the size and growth rates of the three major regional computer markets (including hardware, software, and services).

Japan (table 8-7) is by far the largest market in the region because of its size, wealth, and capacity to absorb the technology, but informal barriers still make it a problematic market for outsiders. As a result, many companies are bypassing Japan to focus on the emerging Asian markets, including China, India, Indonesia, Thailand, South Korea, and Malaysia. These markets are much smaller than Japan now, but they have great long-term potential.

These countries are likely to be especially important markets for some of the new products being developed for the network era. If information appli-

TABLE 8-6. Computer Market by World Regions, 1995

| Region/Country | Market Size (US$ billions) | As % of Total | Annual Growth Rate (%), 1990–1995 |
|---|---|---|---|
| North America | 187.3 | 39 | 9 |
| Europe | 139.2 | 29 | 5 |
| Asia Pacific | 153.5 | 32 | 15 |
| Total | 480.0 | 100% | 9% |

*Source:* McKinsey & Company, *The 1996 Report on the Computer Industry* (New York: McKinsey & Company, 1996).

ances are successful in the marketplace, it is likely to be in emerging markets with low PC penetration. In such markets, cost and ease of use will be vital to expanding use beyond a small segment of the population with the wealth and skills to buy and use PCs. Therefore, the Asia-Pacific region could be a driving market for information appliances. The United States is already heavily invested in PCs, but much of Asia is just starting computer use, so switching costs are low. Also, the United States has many experienced users who would not want to give up their familiar PCs, whereas Asia has many novices who could benefit from information appliances to access the Internet and other networks.

In order to achieve the predicted diffusion of the Internet to more than 1 billion users, a cheaper, simpler technology than the PC is needed. PC users

TABLE 8-7. Asia-Pacific Computer Markets by Country

| Country | Total Computer Spending, 1995[a] ($US millions) | Growth in Computer Spending, 1985–1995 (%) | Total Computer Spending to GDP, 1995 (%) |
|---|---|---|---|
| Japan | 96,590 | 9.5 | 1.89 |
| Australia | 9,630 | 10.4 | 2.75 |
| New Zealand | 1,599 | 11.4 | 2.81 |
| S. Korea | 8,952 | 17.8 | 1.97 |
| Taiwan | 2,119 | 8.3 | 0.84 |
| Hong Kong | 1,887 | 17.1 | 1.31 |
| Singapore | 1,880 | 12.2 | 2.24 |
| Malaysia | 1,365 | 16.0 | 1.62 |
| Indonesia | 1,118 | 23.4 | 0.58 |
| Philippines | 573 | 27.0 | 0.79 |
| Thailand | 1,326 | 17.0 | 0.80 |
| China | 4,540 | 32.7 | 0.65 |
| India | 2,298 | 31.4 | 0.75 |

*Source:* IDC, "Revenue Paid to Vendors for Systems, Software and Services, 1985–1995" (Framingham, Mass.: IDC, 1997).

[a]Hardware, software, and services

represent only about 5% of the world's population; even in the United States, only about 40% of households have a computer. And while the majority of U.S. businesses and households can at least afford a PC, this is not the case for Asia or much of the rest of the world. Table 8-8 shows that worldwide there are more than 220 million households with income between US$15,000 and US$35,000 that could likely afford a sub-$500 information appliance but could probably not afford a $2,000 PC. By comparison, there are only 165 million households earning more than US$35,000 that can afford a PC. Only in the United States does the market potential for PCs surpass that of information appliances. The potential of the Asian market becomes more obvious by projecting to the year 2001, when the number of Asia-Pacific households that can afford an information appliance more than doubles to 132 million. The combination of economic growth and expansion of telecommunications services should create tremendous demand in the region for low-cost hardware to connect to the Internet and other information services.

In addition to its potential as a hardware market, Asia also presents a large potential market for software, services, and content customized for local languages and cultures—in particular, the huge Chinese-language market. That market would include software and content related to Chinese culture, history, business, food, music, movies, games, and other forms of entertainment and education. The market could also include special hardware and software for speech and handwriting recognition to replace the cumbersome process of keyboard entry of Chinese and other Asian languages.

The network era represents an opportunity for countries to use their home markets to develop competitive industries by promoting use and production-close-to-use. The opportunity must be recognized and seized by governments, regulators, and software and service companies in order to reap the benefits.

The key policy issue for Asian governments that will determine whether the region's potential is realized is whether national networks are open, competitive, and allow a free flow of information. To the extent that regulators choose open, competitive networks and allow access to the global Internet, they will increase the value and reduce the cost of using the network and

TABLE 8-8. Household Income (millions of households)

| Region/Country | $500 NC ($15,000–35,000) | | $2,000 PC (above $35,000) | |
|---|---|---|---|---|
| | 1996 | 2001 | 1996 | 2001 |
| United States | 28 | 30 | 59 | 66 |
| Europe | 68 | 64 | 46 | 60 |
| Asia-Pacific | 54 | 132 | 33 | 59 |
| Rest of world | 73 | 106 | 27 | 52 |
| Total | 223 | 332 | 165 | 237 |

Source: Paul Seever, Global Business Opportunities, based on income distribution data from the World Bank and economic growth forecasts by the World Bank and private economists.

create opportunities for domestic producers. If local markets are slow to develop, countries will not be able to succeed in the emerging markets for Internet-based software, information, and services.

In summary, in the network era, the Asia-Pacific region could be a leading market for low-cost hardware and for regional software, information, and services if governments in the region promote competition for telecommunications, the Internet, and new information services in order to promote computer use.

### Asia-Pacific Computer Production

The PC revolution has already turned Asia into a major production center for the global computer industry. Production of computer hardware, software, and services grew at an annual rate of more than 9% between 1990 and 1995 worldwide, led by Asia-Pacific companies with a 12% growth rate (table 8-9). The flow of investment into Asia that marked the PC era has continued, as multinational corporations relocate activities to gain access to markets and lower their costs of production. There has been a steady shift in hardware production from North America and Japan to the Asian NIEs and, more recently, to China and Southeast Asia.

All this activity is centered around hardware, and therein lies the key issue for Asia and the United States. Can any Asian country, or group of countries, escape the boundaries of commodity manufacturing with its decreasing returns and instead participate in the increasing returns segments of the market? So far, the answer has been negative at the microprocessor, software, and PC system levels, because U.S. firms have continued to set and control standards and skim off more of the profit in this industry. Another question is whether future hardware platforms will have similar opportunities for increasing returns business, such as that now enjoyed by Intel. If the information appliance gains acceptance, it is likely to be based on low-cost chips and other commodity components in which U.S. companies have no competitive advantage, and the balance of power could shift toward Asia's low-cost manufacturers. Such a development would not hurt the U.S. software industry, but it could be a major challenge for important segments of the hardware industry.

TABLE 8-9. Computer Production by Company Headquarters, 1995

| Region/Country | Production by Vendor HQ (US$ billions) | As % of Total | Annual Growth Rate (%), 1990–1995 |
|---|---|---|---|
| North America | 321.6 | 67 | 10 |
| Europe | 48.0 | 10 | 1 |
| Asia Pacific | 110.4 | 23 | 12 |
| Total | 480.0 | 100% | 9 |

*Source:* McKinsey & Company (1996).

Competitive Scenarios

We see two possible scenarios that would present serious threats to the U.S. industry: (1) the Japanese computer makers will rejuvenate their companies and their products and storm global markets, and (2) China and its circle of neighbors will ascend to leadership in Asia and a competitive position in the global market.

*The Japanese Juggernaut Rejuvenated.*    The prospect of Japan taking over the global computer industry faded in the early 1990s but has been raised again toward the end of the decade. For instance, a recent cover story in *Electronic Business Asia* screamed "Japan Hatches PC War Plan."[26] The essence of the story was that Japanese companies have adopted the Wintel platform, reorganized their operations, launched new products, formed alliances to boost their presence in the global market, and are positioned to storm the U.S. and Asian markets. It argues that a pitched battle is therefore on the horizon between Japan and rest of the world, with the prospect that the long-feared Japanese takeover of the global computer market will actually occur by 2005.

The rationale for this argument is based on the realization by Japanese companies of the strategic importance of the PC.[27] First, the PC is at the heart of the client-server architecture that is replacing the mainframe in corporate computing, and the PC is also the key platform for the Internet and multimedia. Second, the PC is the key to succeeding beyond the Japanese market. Third, achieving high volumes in PC production will enable the Japanese manufacturers to realize economies of scale in the production of key PC components that they produce (liquid crystal displays, large-capacity/small-format hard disks, battery technology, specialized motherboards and chipsets, slim-line CD-ROM and DVD drives, high-end monitors, and printers).

In addition, the Japanese have come to realize that they must be competitive in the critical U.S. market. NEC, which feels it "must aim for more than 10% of the world market"[28] in PCs, sees success in the United States as the key to success in Asia on the grounds that "what is successful in the U.S. will be successful in Asia."[29] Toshiba, the most successful notebook PC company in the world, sees expansion into desktops in the U.S. market as a key to gaining market share globally and to regaining a significant presence in the Japanese market. Fujitsu, Hitachi, and Sony have also entered the U.S. market with new lines of PCs, all claiming that success in the United States is a key to long-term competitiveness in computers and, more generally, in electronics.

The bloodbath has already started, but mostly in Japan so far. Although Compaq launched the initial price wars in Japan in 1992, Fujitsu went one better in 1995 by reportedly selling its feature-laden PCs well below cost in order to gain market share. It succeeded, going from around 9% to 22% of the Japanese market at the end of 1996. Reaction among other computer makers has been strong, with NEC saying "Fujitsu pursued a violent strategy last year, just to get into the market," and Toshiba labeling Fujitsu's "silly price competition" in pursuit of market share as unfair.[30] So far, the Japanese computer makers are fighting each other and U.S. companies in the Japanese PC market, but what about their prospects in the rest of the world?

Nobody counts the Japanese computer and electronics companies out. They have unequaled product development and manufacturing know-how; they are the world leaders in miniaturization; they can achieve control over quality and logistics through vertical integration; they have deep pockets to buy their way into markets through acquisitions and protracted price wars; they have confidence from their past takeover of global markets in consumer electronics; and they have targeted the PC industry like never before because of its strategic importance. But, are the Japanese once again fighting the last computer war? They passed IBM in mainframe production in 1992, about ten years after the PC era started. The Japanese computer companies might pass the United States in PC production too, but they might miss out on the network era just as they missed the PC era.

It is particularly indicative that no major Japanese computer company is restructuring around the Internet, despite the claims of companies such as NEC to be "computer and communications" companies. And it is unlikely that they will be able to do so anytime soon, because the large Japanese companies feel they do not have the required flexibility. As put by the President of Hitachi, "For us to get out of a business would involve firing people, and that cannot be done easily in Japan. . . . We are in Japan, and we have to do things the way things are done here. . . . Our key words now are globalization, new products and businesses, and speed."[31] Thus, unable to shrink or otherwise restructure dramatically, the Japanese strategy is to grow.

In short, the vertically integrated, top-down, bureaucratic Japanese companies excel at production of commodity products for well-defined and steadily growing markets. Therefore, Japan can be expected to be a dominant competitor in making hardware—a business with steady growth, but diminishing returns. But while they have restructured for more efficient commodity manufacturing, they have yet to restructure for knowledge-based, increasing returns businesses in the network era.

Indeed, the formidable strengths of Japan's companies are likely to be weaknesses in the network era where the biggest payoffs are not in hardware but in software, networking, and content, and where increasing returns accrue to innovators that are focused, responsive, and fast to market with new products and services that users want. Here Japan's computer makers have major disadvantages at home and abroad. At home, despite impressive recent growth due to pent-up demand, the continued growth of Japan's computer market is constrained by high telecommunications and Internet costs. Moreover, the global industrial strategy of the computer makers is not in tune with the network era. The large Japanese firms seek growth by extending their grip on an ever-growing range of technologies from silicon to systems. Vertical integration is still believed to be a basis for competitive advantage. As put by several Japanese executives:

Up to now you could do business by completely outsourcing. . . . But it's questionable if that will be the case in the future (Fujitsu). The consumer electronics market went through a similar phase in the postwar years, when there were literally hundreds of television makers in Japan and the U.S. Only a few of them survived. The key to those who survived was the development of in-house technologies, a condition that will increasingly apply to the PC industry (Toshiba). NEC's vertical integration synergy is going to come from semiconductors, communications, and PCs. Companies like Compaq which only know computers have an inherent weakness (NEC).[32]

This view has an obvious appeal for the Japanese. If they are to compete successfully in the PC industry, they must develop some advantage over U.S. PC makers that outsource most of their production and concentrate on design and marketing. Given that the microprocessor and operating system are controlled by Intel and Microsoft, the Japanese firms can achieve advantage only in volume manufacturing and ability to produce complementary technologies that other PC makers must purchase. Their scale enables them to achieve quality at low cost, and their vertical integration may enable them to milk their own technology to maximum advantage. Because of their strengths in commodity manufacturing, they represent a very serious threat to the U.S. hardware industry, especially if product life cycles begin to slow down to the point where the manufacturing skills of Japan's computer and electronics companies can truly assert themselves.

More broadly, however, the emphasis on mass production and vertical integration reflects a fundamental failure of Japanese computer makers to understand network economies and increasing returns businesses. They remain locked into organizations, strategies, and businesses with diminishing returns and have yet to overcome weaknesses in software. They also have shown little innovation in marketing and still have limited distribution channels and weak brand image outside Japan. For the Japanese juggernaut to move beyond hardware and tap the greater potential of the network era, a change in perspective and strategy is still needed.

*China Circle Ascendant.*    Both the Internet and information appliances present a strategic opportunity for the so-called "China Circle," which includes mainland China, Hong Kong, Taiwan, and the Chinese business community in other Asian countries. China is an ideal market for low-cost information appliances, as are its Asian neighbors and many developing countries throughout the world. Whereas the developed countries' computerization began in the central computing era, and the NIEs in the PC era, China's efforts and those of other developing countries coincide with the network era. Since there were only about five million PCs in China as of 1996, the switching costs to another platform would be low. Even at US$1,500 apiece, PCs are expensive by China's standards and the market is limited, whereas the potential for US$300–$500 information appliances is probably twice that of PCs, given China's income distribution and business structure. China is building the modern telecommunications networks needed to support widespread diffusion of the network computer and the simple, easy-to-use information appliances fit well with the level of computer experience in the country.

On the production side, China has a vast pool of programmers (around one million) to develop applications, services, and content for the Chinese language market, and an even larger pool of low-cost labor that can be marshaled to build information appliances. China's vast market potential also gives it the leverage needed to attract technology, foreign investment, skilled designers, and experienced entrepreneurs to produce for export as well as its own market. But China cannot do it alone.

Hong Kong, Taiwan, and Singapore can provide the key resources China needs. Hong Kong's entrepreneurs know how to do business with China and the West and provide linkages between China and the rest of the world. Hong Kong also manages production for foreign multinationals, Taiwanese subsidiaries, and mainland companies in nearby Guandong Province. These roles could be expanded post-1997 to other parts of China. Taiwan has skills in R&D, design, and production; strong linkages to foreign multinationals; market intelligence in leading and emerging markets; and the managerial capabilities to coordinate production across the China Circle. Taiwan may already be the single largest investor in China via Hong Kong, and rapprochement between the two governments could unleash a powerful force of complementary capabilities. Singapore can attract foreign multinationals to locate key production facilities in China through the development of industrial parks, such as the one being developed in Suzhou. If successful, such production cocoons can help MNCs gain access to China's market and capabilities without learning all the nuances of doing business there.

The computer industries of Malaysia and Thailand represent additional assets, because they are dominated by Chinese entrepreneurs, engineers, and scientists who retain family and business ties with China. They too could become part of the China Circle that would eventually encompass Indonesia and the Philippines as well as smaller countries of East Asia. Cultural and linguistic ties, as well as family and business networks, have created linkages among the countries in the China circle. The business organizations—which tend to be decentralized, freewheeling, and highly adaptive—and the management practices of entrepreneurs are similar among the countries of the China Circle.

Some of this potential is already being realized as trade and investment grows among the China Circle countries, but in China itself there is no coordination of policies to promote the process. Instead, each province competes to attract investment and develop its own information industries, while various agencies of the central government compete with each other over policy turf. If China's government can provide leadership and coordinate efforts to exploit the Internet and the network computer, to create strong industry clusters, and to cooperate with Hong Kong, Taiwan, and Singapore, the China Circle could become a leader in this new segment of the computer industry. It could also be a serious competitor to the United States, at least in the Asian markets.

The major obstacles to the China Circle scenario are more political than economic. While there are strong incentives for China to manage a smooth transition in Hong Kong, there are questions as to whether Beijing will allow Hong Kong to retain its freewheeling Western flavor and maintain the integrity of the legal system and civil service. And while China and Taiwan have reason to seek a peaceful settlement, their political and economic systems are so different that it is difficult to imagine how they will do so. A further obstacle to success in the network era could be China's tendency to control the network from the top. The combination of overregulation, censorship, and barriers to information flows could leave China isolated from the Internet and the global information economy.

The implications of the China Circle scenario are that production of computer hardware would shift even more to Asia than in the past, and that a vibrant software and services industry would develop around local language and culture. The key question is whether such a China Circle would cooperate or compete with the United States and Japan. Japan's history in the region and its closed in-house business model have set it apart in the past. But Japanese foreign policy has begun to promote "Asia for Asians," touting Japan's Korean and Chinese ancestry, and continues to pour foreign aid into the region. Also, Japanese companies are increasingly developing alliances with Taiwanese manufacturers in everything from semiconductors to PCs to monitors. A problem for cooperation between Japan and the China Circle is that both are fundamentally hardware makers, competing directly in an increasing number of industry segments; therefore, the success of one will often come at the expense of the other. Still, there is plenty of room for cooperation; Japanese companies can increasingly turn to Asia for labor-intensive production and as a market for consumer goods, and Japan can in return provide capital and technology that the Asian countries need.

The relationship between the United States and the China Circle is less competitive, because the United States specializes in the increasing returns businesses that do not compete directly with the China Circle's core businesses. Conflict is more likely to arise over issues such as intellectual property rights and general trade disputes. Previous disagreements over intellectual property rights between the United States and China have strained relations between the two countries. If China can make hardware and sell it in the United States, but most U.S. software is pirated in China and elsewhere in the China Circle, the notion of complementary specialization is no longer so attractive to the United States.

## The New Global Production System

The geographical contours of the network era production system are still evolving, but the role of the Asian countries will be determined by several factors.

- *Where are the growing markets?* The computer industry depends upon growth to keep the global production system going. The big emerging markets of Asia such as China, India, and Indonesia have billions of potential new users—although it will be years before most of them are in a position to be users, either at home or on the job. Another source of growth will come from innovation in use and production-close-to-use that meets the needs of users not served by present products and services. The network era is precipitating innovations that will attract such new users, particularly in the emerging markets of Asia. The growth of those markets will naturally push more production into the region to take advantage of the opportunities created.

- *Will Asia become a lead market?* Asia will become a large market, but probably not a *lead market*—one that sets the trends. The United States is and will continue to be the lead market in the world, and therefore computer makers from countries with ambitions to be competitors in the global computer market will have to locate production and product development in the United States. Few Asian companies outside Japan, Korea, and Taiwan have the capabilities to do this, and even those are focused mostly on hardware opportunities. There is a good possibility of the China Circle becoming a lead market for low-cost hardware devices and for Chinese-language software and content. It is not likely to become a leader, however, in creating and adopting new categories of products and services with global appeal, partly because of language differences and partly because the government of mainland China continues to put restrictions on trade, investment, and the free flow of information and ideas.

- *Who defines new applications and markets, hence controlling standards for increasing returns markets?* The keys to controlling standards are close interaction with the lead market and a strong focus on defining and winning standards battles. The U.S. firms have the advantage of being in the leading market and understanding its nuances in ways that foreign firms cannot easily match. These U.S. firms also control existing technology standards in microprocessors and software and are highly motivated to protect those standards and expand their control into new market segments. The constant competition between start-ups and existing standard bearers has moved U.S. companies such as Netscape, Sun, Oracle, and Microsoft to set new Internet standards before Asian contenders were even able to join the fray. Japanese companies do control some hardware standards (such as DVD) that will become more important in the convergence of computers and consumer electronics. But nearly all the key platform standards are based on software and are being set by U.S. companies.

- *What will be the nature of technical innovation and product cycles?* Will innovation slow such that the industry becomes commoditized? Product cycles and technical innovation vary in different segments of the computer industry and will continue to vary with the convergence of computers and communications in the network era. In those segments characterized by frequent innovation and short product cycles, advantage will accrue to companies in the United States, Taiwan, and Singapore by virtue of their responsiveness to the market and flexible management. Products with incremental change and extended product cycles favor Japanese and Korean companies, although much of the low-end production will be done outside those countries. This distinction is quite clear in most existing hardware categories, but it is not clear whether new forms of hardware will be simple standard products designed to access the Internet and other networks, or whether there will be a wide variety of products with different features and capabilities.

- *Who will best manage production globally?* The computer industry will continue to become more global in the network era. The production system will have more participants from around the world as more countries demand participation for domestic firms in exchange for market access. Individual companies will themselves go global by locating near lead markets and by sourcing parts, components, manufacturing, logistics, distribution, marketing, and design from others. The most successful companies will be those that manage on a truly global basis, meaning that they optimize production to use the best capabilities wherever they exist and tailor core products and services to meet local market conditions. If the Japanese and Koreans become more globally oriented in PCs, servers, and information appliances, they will challenge U.S. companies even more in hardware. Taiwan and Singapore are already tightly integrated into the global production network and will be strategic partners to United States and other firms in the network era. If China can "borrow enough boats" from Hong Kong, its role will continue to expand, often in competition with other Asian countries.

    Regardless of country, however, the concept of managing globally is much newer to companies in telecommunications and information services, so the network era will present a real challenge for them. Countries that promote competition and allow foreign investment in their communications sectors—and whose telecommunications companies are able to create effective alliances across borders—will be winners in the network era. So far, only Hong Kong and Singapore have an international orientation in telecommunications, with Hong Kong Telecoms being especially global due to its ties to Cable and Wireless of the United Kingdom.

What then will the global production system look like in ten or fifteen years? The most likely scenario is a continuation of the status quo, but with some elements of Japanese resurgence and a greater role for the China Circle.

The status quo will continue in terms of the distribution of increasing and decreasing returns business. As in the PC era, the United States will remain dominant in increasing returns businesses, which in the network era will include microprocessors, network hardware, software, information services, and information content. Japan and its Asian neighbors will still be the leaders in most decreasing returns hardware businesses. Japan's resurgence will not overwhelm the U.S. computer industry, but Japanese companies will almost certainly gain market share in PCs, printers, hard drives, and other hardware products where the United States now leads. Japan will also compete with the United States in the design and production of information appliances. Korea will compete vigorously with Japan in high-volume manufacturing of commodity components as well as in information appliances and peripherals such as DVDs. But Japan's resurgence will hurt Korea more than any other country unless Korea moves beyond trying to beat Japan while still depending on Japanese technology.

Taiwan and Singapore will continue to play important roles in production of all kinds of computer hardware and will further expand their activities in semiconductors and software. They will also shift more labor-intensive production into China and elsewhere in Asia, expanding the overall importance of the China Circle. Hong Kong must rely on its position vis à vis China to maintain its role in the computer industry, even if it is able to upgrade its technical abilities. Ultimately, the future of Taiwan, Singapore, and Hong Kong is closely tied to the fortunes of China. If the political and economic environment is friendly, the China Circle scenario presents a great opportunity for all four economies. If political conflicts arise within China, or if new tensions arise between China and Taiwan, the prognosis is poor for all members of the China Circle.

Ultimately, all the Asian competitors will be fighting with each other in hardware and will no doubt take some of the hardware business away from the United States. But as the DRAM industry has shown, when everyone is fighting over the same business, there is a tendency to build excess capacity and drive prices down, even when demand is soaring. In the past, there was a division of labor within Asia, with each country specializing in certain segments of the industry. But now, the NIEs are directly challenging Japan and competing more with each other, and even China and the ASEAN countries want to move up into higher value products. The resulting competition will likely lead to a shakeout of many industry segments and a return to a more stable division of labor, with countries exploiting the competitive strengths of their industry structures and national capabilities.

## Implications for Asian Countries

While the network era is creating a new policy environment for countries, the lessons learned in the PC era will continue to be important for countries. Creating and expanding high-quality linkages to global markets and the global production system will be more important than ever, as will improving national capabilities through investment in education and R&D. However, the network era will put a higher premium on using computer technology and make it more difficult to succeed simply through strength in manufacturing and technology. Four additional factors will become considerably more important as the scope of competition expands to include communications and content as well as computing.

*First, it will be more difficult to separate production from use.* The Japanese succeeded in consumer electronics partly because their own consumers were very demanding, so Japanese companies created innovative products to meet local demand. These products were equally successful in global markets. Neither the Japanese nor any other Asian companies have done the same in computers, especially not in software or services. In the PC era East Asian countries have done well as producers of hardware for export while being slow to use the technology themselves. In order to participate in the network-based software, services, and content industries, countries (like companies) must be advanced users of the network. Even in traditional hardware industries, countries will find that use of information technologies will be a key to competitiveness in the future, as global production networks are coordinated through advanced information systems to support design, procurement, logistics, and distribution.

*Second, competition in domestic markets must be encouraged to promote innovation and movement into new market segments.* The giants that make DRAMs and flat-panel displays are not likely to experiment with innovative Internet-based products and services; if they do, they are not likely to be successful. These new markets require flexible organizations, not bureaucratic, top-down companies that stifle creativity. Creative people willing to take risks can be found in any country, but in countries such as Japan and Korea, they often find it impossible to raise capital or develop distribution channels. As long as a few large conglomerates control capital markets and distribution networks, innovation and entrepreneurship will be stifled. Governments did much to create those giants, and only governments have the ability to rein in their power and create space for smaller companies to grow. If they fail to do so, Japan and Korea in particular will likely never become significant innovators or create new markets.

*Third, telecommunications is critical in the network era.* A recent study of member countries by the Organization for Economic Cooperation and Development (OECD) shows that countries saddled with overpriced service and monopolistic competitive environments are already behind in Internet and network adoption[33] (table 8-3). Among the countries in this study, only Singapore and Hong Kong have introduced some limited competition and offer low-cost telecommunications service. Widespread, low-cost Internet access is critical to competing in the network era, and that access depends on a competitive telecommunications market. Deregulation of telecommunications will be perhaps the most important government policy decision that will determine national competitiveness in the network era. It may be true, as David Moschella argues, that nations will gain some leverage for a time through control over domestic telecommunications markets.[34] In the end, however, the countries with the most competitive, dynamic telecommunications markets will flourish in the network era by leading in adoption of new technologies, products, and services and setting new standards.

*Fourth, governments can play a positive role in promoting use of the technology.* Government action to promote greater use is warranted by the fact that the real benefits of use in the network era accrue only when there is a critical mass of institutional (business, government, education) and household users. Corporate users benefit most when they can be connected to large user markets, and individual users benefit most when they can be connected to those with whom they need/desire to communicate, exchange information, or execute transactions. In addition to promoting competition in telecommunications, government can set an example through its own use of the technology and can provide incentives and remove barriers to private sector use.

Each country in the region, as well as the United States, must contend with these facts of life. Our prescription for each country varies, however, according to its present position. Some countries need to focus on developing basic capabilities and creating linkages to the global industry, while others need to shake up existing industry structures and cut back excessive regulation. A brief synopsis of recommendations follows:

### Japan and Korea

- Deregulate telecommunications and increase competition.
- Use antitrust laws to break down *keiretsu* or *chaebol* control over the distribution system.
- Deregulate and stimulate the venture capital and initial public offering markets to direct capital to entrepreneurs.
- Invest in government computerization and promote use throughout the economy.
- Revamp the educational system to encourage creativity, emphasize software skills, and promote computer use.
- Remove formal or informal barriers to trade and foreign investment.
- Invest in basic research to complement heavy applied R&D by industry and reinforce strengths in hardware.

### Taiwan

- Deregulate telecommunications and introduce competition in basic service.
- Continue to invest in R&D and education, but focus more on software.
- Invest in government computerization and promote use throughout the economy.

### Singapore

- Diversify around existing strengths in disk drives, PCs, and semi-conductors.
- Improve the educational system at all levels.
- Encourage entrepreneurship and provide incentives to local companies as well as foreign MNCs.
- Loosen reins on information flow to succeed as a regional business and information hub.

### Hong Kong

- Invest in R&D and technological education.
- Retain favorable business environment to support continued role as gateway to China after the transition to Chinese rule.
- Invest in government computerization and promote use throughout the economy.

### China

- Deregulate and increase competition in telecommunications.
- Improve legal structures and business environment.
- Encourage imports and foreign investment.
- Invest in science and engineering education to gain further strength in human resources.
- Maintain favorable relations with other Asian countries and with United States to support leadership role in computer industry.
- Invest in government computerization and promote use throughout the economy.

### Other Developing Countries

- Invest in human resources for computer use and production.
- Promote domestic use of computers.
- Invest in telecommunications infrastructure and encourage competition as markets develop, especially in specialized services such as Internet access.
- Develop linkages with the global industry and markets by encouraging investment, technology transfer, and trade.
- Support exports by providing market intelligence and other services to domestic companies.

## Implications for the United States

There are three major implications of the findings in this book for U.S. companies and for government agencies and policy-makers concerned about U.S.

competitiveness in the global computer industry. The first is that the Asia-Pacific region is a tremendous market whose potential is yet to be realized and whose exploitation requires new strategies by U.S. companies and the U.S. government.

- The Asia market for all types of computer hardware, software, and services has grown faster than the North American or European markets for a decade and will become the world's largest in the twenty-first century. Interested U.S. companies must move into these markets with clearly defined and focused strategies. However, there is a question about the extent to which U.S. companies will be able to participate in the Asian market. While the countries of APEC agreed in 1996 to eliminate tariffs on IT products by the year 2000, many nontariff barriers will remain. Some of these involve various government requirements for technology transfer, exports, and local sourcing, and limits on the geographic and business scope of U.S. firms.[35] Others involve the very structure of Asian economies, in the form of closed distribution channels, *keiretsu* and *chaebol* relationships, and even high land prices that make it costly to set up business.
- Companies need to consider each country's market potential separately, because the realizable market potential often is at odds with popular perceptions. For example, Vietnam has been touted as having large potential, but careful analysis shows that its potential is far less than that of other countries like Indonesia, South Korea, or Taiwan. Similarly, China might be the biggest potential market in the world, but it is also one of the "meanest" in the sense that doing business involves numerous difficulties and high risk.[36] Companies need to consider informal barriers to penetrating each market, and these differ from country to country. Success requires developing effective channels, setting up sales and service partnering with domestic companies, and hiring and training local managers familiar with the market. In China, it will also require setting up production, exporting a substantial portion of production, transferring technology, and upgrading local skills. The U.S. firms involved must be patient and understand that return on investments in the region will take time to be realized. But they should also have a clear strategy to make these investments profitable within a reasonable time frame. Some losses can be justified as the price of an "education" in Asian business, but companies must be ready to make changes if they continue to lose money.
- The U.S. government can assist U.S. computer companies in important ways. It should promote adoption and implementation of intellectual property laws. It should monitor and enforce existing trade agreements and take action to eliminate informal barriers as well. History shows that the latter are often more difficult to sur-

mount than formal tariffs and quotas, because they are less transparent and are implemented in more arbitrary ways. The Clinton
administration has made trade policy a major focus of its foreign
policy and has achieved some success in increasing market access,
but it and future administrations need to maintain that focus even
in the face of conflicting policy demands. Of particular importance
in the network era is opening up telecommunications markets,
which in most countries are still the domain of state-owned or regulated monopolies. The Federal Communications Commission has
been working to reduce the prices charged by foreign carriers to
connect calls from the United States and has promoted competition
in general. The ability of U.S. companies to market network-
oriented products and services around the world will depend on
breaking down national barriers in the telecommunications sector.

The second major implication of our findings for the United States is that,
despite their remarkable successes in a short period of time, no East Asian
country has risen to become a major competitor to the U.S. computer industry
except Japan—and whereas Japan succeeded in mainframes it has stumbled
badly in PCs. In general, then, the findings might be considered good news
for the U.S. computer industry.[37] These findings indicate that:

- The Japanese threat to U.S. leadership that was feared in the 1980s
  has been turned back, at least for now.[38]
- There are no new Japans emerging among the East Asian countries.
  The concern that Korea would become another Japan was clearly
  overstated, and the China Circle has yet to produce companies that
  can compete head-on with U.S. firms.
- Since protectionist policies have been shown to hurt one's consumers and businesses more than they help, markets for computing
  products and services are likely to become more open. There will
  be exceptions, but the trend in recent years is toward more open
  computer and communications markets.
- None of the East Asian countries have much of a chance of gaining
  architectural control of a major technology standard, or becoming
  a leader in software or services outside their own markets.
- The U.S. computer industry can continue to rely on East Asia as a
  production base and a reliable, cost-efficient supplier of parts, components, peripherals, and OEM systems.
- While Asian countries will be competitors to the United States for
  jobs and investment, they will also provide a large, rapidly growing
  market for U.S.-made systems, software, services, and entertainment content.

The third major implication of the findings is that all this good news might
let the U.S. computer industry takes its eyes off Asia as a source of competition. This would be a serious mistake. The history of the computer industry

is full of failures and blunders by individual companies that resulted from arrogance, complacency, and parochial thinking of corporate leaders. It is also marked by the misguided policies of governments committed to protecting domestic firms and promoting national champions rather than encouraging domestic competition, and generally trying to isolate themselves from the global industry. Although the United States continues to be very successful in the global computer industry, serious competitive threats to hardware manufacturing could come from the Asia-Pacific region.

Therefore, U.S. companies need to avoid complacency with regard to Japanese competitors, and they also need to stay engaged in the Japanese market. The trend toward bypassing Japan to concentrate on the rest of Asia is a dangerous strategy. Not only does it mean passing up on the world's second largest market, but it also means that U.S. companies can lose touch with important technology developments in many areas in which Japan is the world leader. The U.S. government likewise should not become so obsessed with the growing trade deficit with China that it ignores Japan. Much of the progress made by U.S. companies in Japan can be traced to efforts of the U.S. Trade Representative office, and continued progress will require ongoing vigilance.

The China Circle scenario poses another competitive threat to the U.S. computer industry. This threat is potentially equal to or greater than the Japanese threat, but it comes from a different source—the Chinese government. In order to promote production in China, the government maintains import tariffs and requires that foreign firms produce in China and export much of their production if they want to sell in China. Even more important, the Chinese government controls large segments of the economy and is directly involved in most of the major procurement decisions for large investments throughout the country. Those decisions sometimes appear to be made on political grounds as well as price or technology considerations. There is also the problem of intellectual property protection and lack of solid legal structures to enforce contracts and other agreements.

So U.S. companies and the U.S. government are in a difficult position with regard to China. They agree on the need to push for enforcement of intellectual property rights, to lower trade barriers and to foster a good business environment. But when the U.S. government has put pressure on China over issues such as intellectual property, China has threatened to retaliate against U.S. companies, trying to create a wedge between government and business. In addition, the U.S. government has other political and security issues to consider in dealing with China, and those concerns often become involved in economic decisions such as renewal of China's most-favored nation status. Meanwhile, other countries have allowed the United States to carry the ball in pressuring China to open its markets, while their companies do not have to fear possible retaliation from the Chinese government.

The entire China Circle scenario can turn into a negative for the United States if political disagreements put U.S. companies at a disadvantage in the China market. Repeated acrimonious trade disputes have only raised tensions and then made the United States look weak when it has backed down at the last minute or had to make further threats to enforce existing agreements. Quiet persuasion might be more useful in helping China's decision-makers see some of the potential benefits from reducing trade barriers and protecting intellectual property, such as developing a domestic software industry and realizing the benefits of computer use. At the same time, it would be helpful for both the U.S. government and U.S. businesses to maintain a realistic view of the potential of the Chinese market. China will not be the world's largest computer market for a long time, and companies should not be willing to make reckless concessions to get into that market. Nor should the U.S. government allow fear of retaliation against U.S. companies weaken its resolve when important issues are at stake.

## Conclusion: Asia's Computer Challenge

The phrase "Asia's Computer Challenge" carries two interpretations for the network era and beyond. The first is Asia's challenge to the United States in the computer industry. The message of this book in this regard is that Asia presents a continuing challenge to the U.S. industry. By creating a decentralized, horizontally segmented industry structure, the PC revolution opened the door for Asian countries to compete successfully in large segments of the industry. For the most part, the relationship has been complementary, with Asia taking over the decreasing returns work while U.S. companies focused on the increasing returns side of the business. But Asia competes directly with U.S. companies in a number of segments and will compete in emerging hardware products such as information appliances. So while Asia is a valuable partner and a large market for U.S. companies, it remains a threat as well. In the long run, Asia may become a leading market as it continues to grow and gain experience as a user, and Asian companies are likely to challenge the United States even in the increasing returns side of the industry.

The other interpretation of Asia's computer challenge refers to the challenges facing the Asian countries themselves. If Asia is unable to move beyond hardware and develop competitive software, services, and content industries, it will be relegated to the large but brutally competitive decreasing returns segments of the industry. Asia will enjoy continued job growth, but its companies will find it difficult to eke out profits and will be subject to the boom–bust cycles of commodity markets. The key to getting out of this trap is a fundamental reversal of the perspective that values production over use, hardware over software, and tangibles over intangibles. Asian governments are starting to move in this direction, as evidenced by the emphasis on NII initiatives and support for small business in many countries. Some Asian companies are likewise shifting their focus toward software and services. But, with a few exceptions, change is incremental and lagging behind the accelerated pace of "Internet time." Without more radical change, much of Asia faces the prospect of missing out on the vast potential of the network era.

# Appendix

TABLE A-1. Computer Hardware Production, 1985–1995 (in current US dollars, millions)

|      | Hong Kong | Singapore | Korea | Taiwan | Japan | United States |
|------|-----------|-----------|-------|--------|-------|---------------|
| 1985 | $660   | $1,194  | $579   | $989    | $18,318 | $47,122 |
| 1986 | $704   | $1,914  | $880   | $1,739  | $30,083 | $43,685 |
| 1987 | $853   | $2,928  | $1,459 | $2,890  | $39,952 | $47,635 |
| 1988 | $1,341 | $4,503  | $2,431 | $4,001  | $52,391 | $48,504 |
| 1989 | $1,593 | $5,368  | $3,180 | $5,046  | $54,587 | $49,296 |
| 1990 | $1,930 | $6,974  | $3,073 | $5,886  | $53,241 | $48,559 |
| 1991 | $2,145 | $7,977  | $3,499 | $6,106  | $59,563 | $47,965 |
| 1992 | $2,264 | $10,123 | $3,647 | $7,849  | $56,598 | $50,866 |
| 1993 | $2,264 | $12,346 | $4,212 | $10,003 | $58,757 | $52,176 |
| 1994 | $1,953 | $16,536 | $4,893 | $12,020 | $66,654 | $62,544 |
| 1995 | $2,167 | $21,127 | $6,795 | $16,111 | $73,475 | $77,835 |

*Source:* Reed, *Yearbook of World Electronics Data* (Oxford: Reed Electronics Research, 1991–1997).

TABLE A-2. Computer Hardware Production as % of GDP, 1985–1995

|      | Hong Kong | Singapore | Korea | Taiwan | Japan | United States |
|------|-----------|-----------|-------|--------|-------|---------------|
| 1985 | 1.89 | 6.75  | .61  | 1.60 | 1.37 | 1.17 |
| 1986 | 1.76 | 10.80 | .81  | 2.28 | 1.52 | 1.03 |
| 1987 | 1.73 | 14.50 | 1.07 | 2.80 | 1.66 | 1.06 |
| 1988 | 2.30 | 18.21 | 1.33 | 3.25 | 1.79 | 1.00 |
| 1989 | 2.37 | 18.41 | 1.43 | 3.38 | 1.88 | 0.95 |
| 1990 | 2.58 | 19.08 | 1.21 | 3.64 | 1.80 | 0.88 |
| 1991 | 2.50 | 18.89 | 1.19 | 3.41 | 1.75 | 0.85 |
| 1992 | 2.25 | 20.46 | 1.18 | 3.68 | 1.52 | 0.86 |
| 1993 | 1.95 | 21.55 | 1.27 | 4.39 | 1.37 | 0.83 |
| 1994 | 1.49 | 23.83 | 1.29 | 4.94 | 1.42 | 0.94 |
| 1995 | 1.51 | 25.29 | 1.49 | 6.12 | 1.44 | 1.12 |

*Source:* Reed (1991–1997).

TABLE A-3.  Total Electronics Production, 1985–1995 (in current US dollars, millions)

| | Hong Kong | Singapore | Korea | Taiwan | Japan | United States |
|---|---|---|---|---|---|---|
| 1985 | $3,639 | $4,032 | $6,415 | $5,776 | $88,858 | $177,571 |
| 1986 | $4,320 | $5,089 | $9,234 | $7,522 | $124,030 | $175,048 |
| 1987 | $5,301 | $7,565 | $13,639 | $10,702 | $149,766 | $187,586 |
| 1988 | $6,730 | $10,823 | $18,581 | $12,629 | $187,508 | $195,352 |
| 1989 | $7,536 | $12,511 | $22,451 | $15,090 | $184,804 | $200,459 |
| 1990 | $8,290 | $14,995 | $22,858 | $15,532 | $184,283 | $204,494 |
| 1991 | $8,429 | $16,710 | $25,268 | $16,517 | $207,378 | $206,009 |
| 1992 | $8,499 | $20,244 | $26,143 | $18,785 | $196,047 | $213,105 |
| 1993 | $8,949 | $23,557 | $28,803 | $21,156 | $212,045 | $218,065 |
| 1994 | $9,012 | $31,551 | $36,202 | $23,199 | $234,227 | $246,453 |
| 1995 | $9,597 | $39,825 | $49,368 | $29,416 | $267,109 | $285,097 |

*Source:* Reed (1991–1997).

TABLE A-4.  Electronics Production as % of GDP, 1985–1995

| | Hong Kong | Singapore | Korea | Taiwan | Japan | United States |
|---|---|---|---|---|---|---|
| 1985 | 10.44 | 22.79 | 6.80 | 9.32 | 6.63 | 4.42 |
| 1986 | 10.78 | 28.70 | 8.50 | 9.88 | 6.25 | 4.14 |
| 1987 | 10.75 | 37.46 | 10.01 | 10.38 | 6.21 | 4.17 |
| 1988 | 11.54 | 43.78 | 10.20 | 10.25 | 6.42 | 4.02 |
| 1989 | 11.22 | 42.92 | 10.10 | 10.12 | 6.38 | 3.85 |
| 1990 | 11.10 | 41.01 | 9.01 | 9.62 | 6.21 | 3.73 |
| 1991 | 9.83 | 39.58 | 8.59 | 9.21 | 6.10 | 3.64 |
| 1992 | 8.44 | 40.92 | 8.49 | 8.80 | 5.28 | 3.59 |
| 1993 | 7.71 | 41.11 | 8.66 | 9.29 | 4.95 | 3.48 |
| 1994 | 6.85 | 45.46 | 9.51 | 9.53 | 5.00 | 3.71 |
| 1995 | 6.67 | 47.67 | 10.83 | 11.18 | 5.23 | 4.10 |

*Source:* Reed (1991–1997).

TABLE A-5.  Total IT Spending, 1985–1995 (in current US dollars, millions)

| | Hong Kong | Singapore | Korea | Taiwan | Japan | United States |
|---|---|---|---|---|---|---|
| 1985 | $386 | $380 | $1,543 | $634 | $15,419 | $89,670 |
| 1986 | $442 | $433 | $1,749 | $735 | $25,537 | $97,700 |
| 1987 | $505 | $444 | $1,823 | $845 | $35,794 | $106,735 |
| 1988 | $565 | $494 | $2,372 | $1,031 | $46,419 | $115,850 |
| 1989 | $642 | $598 | $2,990 | $1,221 | $49,072 | $123,845 |
| 1990 | $627 | $885 | $3,555 | $1,444 | $63,116 | $131,920 |
| 1991 | $679 | $944 | $3,905 | $1,573 | $70,325 | $138,240 |
| 1992 | $854 | $962 | $4,887 | $1,742 | $70,153 | $153,141 |
| 1993 | $1,453 | $1,191 | $5,321 | $1,675 | $74,954 | $174,535 |
| 1994 | $1,735 | $1,363 | $6,374 | $1,956 | $78,307 | $193,152 |
| 1995 | $1,887 | $1,880 | $8,952 | $2,119 | $96,590 | $224,298 |

*Source:* IDC, "Revenue Paid to Vendors for Systems, Software and Services, 1985–1995" (Framingham, Mass.: IDC, 1997).

TABLE A-6. Total IT Spending as Percent of GDP, 1985–1995

|  | Hong Kong | Singapore | Korea | Taiwan | Japan | United States |
|---|---|---|---|---|---|---|
| 1985 | 1.11 | 2.15 | 1.64 | 1.02 | 1.15 | 2.23 |
| 1986 | 1.10 | 2.44 | 1.61 | 0.97 | 1.28 | 2.31 |
| 1987 | 1.02 | 2.19 | 1.34 | 0.82 | 1.48 | 2.37 |
| 1988 | 0.97 | 2.00 | 1.30 | 0.84 | 1.59 | 2.39 |
| 1989 | 0.96 | 2.05 | 1.35 | 0.83 | 1.69 | 2.38 |
| 1990 | 0.84 | 2.43 | 1.40 | 0.89 | 2.13 | 2.40 |
| 1991 | 0.79 | 2.23 | 1.33 | 0.88 | 2.06 | 2.44 |
| 1992 | 0.85 | 1.94 | 1.59 | 0.82 | 1.88 | 2.58 |
| 1993 | 1.25 | 2.07 | 1.60 | 0.76 | 1.75 | 2.79 |
| 1994 | 1.32 | 1.96 | 1.67 | 0.80 | 1.67 | 2.90 |
| 1995 | 1.31 | 2.25 | 1.97 | 0.84 | 1.89 | 3.23 |

*Source:* IDC, 1997.

TABLE A-7. Number of Internet Hosts

|  | Hong Kong | Singapore | Korea | Taiwan | Japan | United States |
|---|---|---|---|---|---|---|
| Total number of Internet hosts |  |  |  |  |  |  |
| 1995 | 12,437 | 5,252 | 18,049 | 14,618 | 96,632 | 3,178,266 |
| 1996 | 17,693 | 22,769 | 29,306 | 25,273 | 269,327 | 6,053,402 |
| 1997 | 48,660 | 60,674 | 123,370 | 40,706 | 955,688 | 11,829,141 |
| Number of Internet hosts per 1000 population |  |  |  |  |  |  |
| 1995 | 2.1 | 1.8 | 0.4 | 0.7 | 0.8 | 12.2 |
| 1996 | 2.9 | 7.8 | 0.7 | 1.2 | 2.2 | 23.2 |
| 1997 | 8.4 | 21.7 | 2.8 | 1.9 | 7.7 | 45.8 |

*Source:* Based on data from Network Wizards, "Internet Domain Survey" (January 1995, 1996, 1997), www.nw.com.

TABLE A-8. Number of Software Professionals

|  | Hong Kong | Singapore | Korea | Taiwan | Japan | United States |
|---|---|---|---|---|---|---|
| Programmers | 12,500 | 15,000 | 236,500 | 116,000 | 850,000 | 1,693,20 |
| Managers | 1,900 | 2,400 | 35,475 | 17,400 | 127,500 | 253,98 |
| Total Software Professionals | 14,400 | 17,400 | 271,995 | 133,400 | 977,500 | 1,947,18 |

*Source:* Capers Jones, *Software Productivity and Quality Today—The Worldwide Perspective* (Carlsbad, Calif.: Information Systems Management Group, 1993). Data updated in 1995 in correspondence to authors.

TABLE A-9.  Software Piracy Rates, 1994–1996

|  | Hong Kong | Singapore | Korea | Taiwan | Japan | United States |
|---|---|---|---|---|---|---|
| Software piracy rates (%) | | | | | | |
| 1994 | 62 | 61 | 75 | 72 | 66 | 31 |
| 1995 | 62 | 53 | 76 | 70 | 55 | 26 |
| 1996 | 64 | 59 | 70 | 66 | 41 | 27 |

*Source:* Business Software Alliance (BSA), "1996 BSA/SPA Piracy Study Results" (1996), www.bsa.org/piracy/ 96TABLES.HTM.

TABLE A-10.  General Indicators

|  | Hong Kong | Singapore | Korea | Taiwan[b] | Japan | United States |
|---|---|---|---|---|---|---|
| Population[a] | 6,189,800 | 2,986,500 | 44,851,000 | 21,471,000 | 125,213,000 | 263,119,008 |
| GDP per capita (PPP basis, US$)[a] | 21670 | 20470 | 9810 | n.a. | 21090 | 24750 |
| Average GDP growth, 1985–1995[a] | 5.96 | 7.38 | 8.68 | 7.67 | 3.10 | 2.59 |
| Percent of GDP in argiculture[c] | 0.16 | 0.15 | 7.07 | 3.55 | 2.12 | 1.74 |
| Percent of GDP in manufacturing[c] | 13.64 | 33.30 | 41.09 | 36.25 | 35.45 | 23.23 |
| Percent of GDP in services[c] | 77.80 | 66.73 | 42.23 | 60.20 | 56.54 | 64.31 |
| Phone lines per 100 population[d] | 51.96 | 45.45 | 42.60 | 40.25 | 47.91 | 60.14 |
| Mean years of education[e] | 7.00 | 3.90 | 8.80 | n.a. | 10.70 | 12.30 |

*Sources:*

[a]International Monetary Fund (IMF), *International Financial Statistics Yearbook* (Washington, D.C.: IMF, 1996).

[b]Republic of China, *Taiwan Statistical Data Book, 1995* (Taipei: Council for Economic Planning and Development, 1995).

[c]United Nations, National Accounts Section, Statistical Office, *United Nations National Accounts Database* (New York: United Nations, 1996).

[d]International Telecommunications Union (ITU), *ITU Statistical Yearbook 1994* (Geneva, Switzerland: ITU, 1995), on diskette.

[e]From *Human Development Report 1993* by United Nations Development Programme. Used by permission of Oxford University Press, Inc.

# Notes

Chapter 1

1. Paul Krugman, "Competitiveness: A Dangerous Obsession," *Foreign Affairs* 73 (March–April 1994): 28–35.

2. For a good review and analysis of various points of view on national competitiveness, see David P. Rapkin and Jonathan R. Strand, "Is International Competitiveness a Meaningful Concept?" in C. Roe Goddard, John T. Passe-Smith, and John G. Conklin (eds.), *International Political Economy: State-Market Relations in the Changing Global Order* (Boulder, Colo.: Lynne Rienner, 1996): 109–129.

3. Robert B. Reich, "Who Is Us?" *Harvard Business Review* (January–February 1991): 53–59.

4. Laura D'Andrea Tyson, "They Are Not Us: Why American Ownership Still Matters," *American Prospect* (winter 1991): 37–49.

5. Shintaro Ishihara, *The Japan That Can Say No: Why Japan Will Be First Among Equals* (New York: Simon and Schuster, 1991).

6. Andrew Pollack, "Breaking Out of Japan's Orbit," *New York Times* (January 30, 1996).

7. U.S. Department of Commerce/International Trade Administration, *U.S. Industry and Trade Outlook*, 1998 (New York: McGraw-Hill, 1998).

8. Several analysts, such as Stephen S. Roach and Martin N. Baily, argued that computer investment was not having a measurable impact on productivity, based on historical evidence from the United States. Stephen S. Roach, *White-Collar Productivity: A Glimmer of Hope?* (New York: Morgan Stanley, 1988); Martin N. Baily, "What Has Happened to Productivity Growth?" *Science* 234 (October 1986): 443–451. More recently, however, research by Erik Brynjolfsson and Loren Hitt and by Frank R. Lichtenberg has found evidence that computer investment has high rates of return at the company level, while Kenneth L. Kraemer and Jason Dedrick found a strong correlation between computer investment and productivity growth in twelve Asia-Pacific countries. Erik Brynjolfsson and Loren Hitt, "Paradox Lost? Firm-level Evidence on the Returns to Information Systems Spending," *Management Science*, 42 (April 1996): 541–558; Frank R. Lichtenberg, *The Output Contributions of Computer Equipment and Personnel: A Firm-Level Analysis*, Working Paper No. 4540 (Cambridge, Mass.: National Bureau of Economic Research, 1993); Kenneth L. Kraemer and Jason Dedrick, "Payoffs

From Investment in Information Technology: Lessons from the Asia-Pacific Region," *World Development*, 22 (1994): 1921–1931.

9. Michael J. Boskin and Lawrence J. Lau, "Contributions of R&D to Economic Growth," in Bruce L. R. Smith and Claude E. Barfield (eds.), *Technology, R&D, and the Economy* (Washington, D.C.: Brookings Institution and American Enterprise Institute, 1996): 75–113.

10. Ibid.

11. David B. Yoffie, "Introduction," in David B. Yoffie (ed.), *Beyond Free Trade: Firms, Governments, and Global Competition* (Boston: Harvard Business School, 1996): 9.

12. Poh-Kam Wong, "Competing in the Global Electronics Industry: A Comparative Analysis of the Strategy of Taiwan and Singapore," International Conference on the Experience of Industrial Development in Taiwan, National Central University, Taiwan (May 19, 1995).

13. World Bank, *The East-Asian Miracle: Economic Growth and Public Policy* (New York: Oxford University Press, 1993).

14. For examples of revisionist thought on industrial policy, see Chalmers Johnson, *MITI and the Japanese Miracle* (Stanford, Calif.: Stanford University Press, 1982); Alice H. Amsden, *Asia's Next Giant: South Korea and Late Industrialization* (New York: Oxford University Press, 1989); Marie Anchordoguy, *Computers, Inc.: Japan's Challenge to IBM* (Cambridge: Harvard University Press, 1989); Robert Wade, *Governing the Market: Economic Theory and the Role of Government in East Asian Industrialization* (Princeton, N.J.: Princeton University Press, 1990).

15. The notion of increasing returns actually goes back as far as Adam Smith's *Wealth of Nations* and has reappeared as a subject of discussion over time by various economists. The 1980s saw a revival of interest, as exemplified by the work of economists such as Nicholas Kaldor, Paul David, Paul Romer, and W. Brian Arthur. For a collection of works on increasing returns starting with Smith, see James M. Buchanan and Yoon J. Yong (eds.), *The Return to Increasing Returns* (Ann Arbor: University of Michigan Press, 1994). For a discussion of increasing returns and decreasing returns in the computer industry, see W. Brian Arthur, "Increasing Returns and the New World of Business," *Harvard Business Review* (July–August 1996): 100–109. Arthur presents formal models of path-dependent, increasing-returns economic systems in his collection, *Increasing Returns and Path Dependence in the Economy* (Ann Arbor: University of Michigan Press, 1994).

16. "Computers: Japan Comes On Strong," *Business Week* (October 23, 1989): 104–112.

17. U.S. Department of Commerce, *U.S. Global Trade Outlook 1995–2000: Toward the 21st Century* (Washington D.C.: U.S. Department of Commerce, International Trade Administration, 1995). The problem with data on software trade is that customs records count only the value of the physical media (e.g., disks or CD-ROMs) on which the software is transferred, not the value of the program itself. The real value of the software exports is mostly in licensing fees paid to U.S. software vendors from customers abroad, but this is not separated out in government data on royalty payments.

Chapter 2

1. Michael Borrus, "Left for Dead: Asian Production Networks and the Revival of US Electronics," in Barry Naughton (ed.), *The China Circle: Economics and Elec-*

*tronics in the PRC, Hong Kong, and Taiwan* (Washington, D.C.: Brookings Institution, 1997).

2. David B. Yoffie, *Strategic Management in Information Technology*, (Englewood Cliffs, N.J.: Prentice Hall, 1994); Richard L. Nolan and David C. Croson, *Creative Destruction* (Cambridge: Harvard Business School Press, 1995); David C. Moschella, *Waves of Power: Dynamics of Global Technology Leadership, 1964–2010* (New York: AMACOM, 1997).

3. Anchordoguy (1989): 107.

4. See Franklin M. Fisher, James W. McKie, and Richard B. Mancke, *IBM and the U.S. Data Processing Industry* (New York: Praeger; 1983), especially chapter 1 for excellent documentation of these practices.

5. Bundling is "the offering of a number of elements that are considered to be interrelated and necessary from a customer's point of view, in the computer field, under a single pricing plan, without detailing the pricing of component elements themselves" (ibid.: 172).

6. The company had to train sales and service personnel and provide programming support for each system. The process was costly and chaotic. Economies of scale in engineering and manufacturing were reduced. These were not simple problems to solve because both the engineers who designed the systems and the customers who used them were committed to them.

7. Fisher, McKie, and Mancke (1983): 141.

8. However, for years IBM had been doing billions of dollars of business in computer services through its subsidiary, ISSC.

9. Thomas J. Watson, Jr., *Father, Son, and Co.: My Life at IBM and Beyond* (New York: Bantam, 1990).

10. W. Edward Steinmueller, "The U.S. Software Industry: An Analysis and Interpretive History," in David Mowery (ed.), *The International Computer Software Industry* (New York: Oxford University Press, 1996).

11. Similarly, in the 1950s and 1960s, companies offering computer systems (Burroughs, GE, Honeywell, RCA, Sperry Univac, SDS, and DEC) often did not manufacture their own components and peripherals, but purchased them from companies producing computer components and peripherals on an OEM basis. Ampex, Collins Radio, Potter, Data Products, Magnetic Memories, CalComp, Bryant, Telex, and CDC were OEMs that specifically made their products to attach to the computers of several different companies. The OEMs also sold their products to leasing companies who in turn marketed them to customers. Both SDS and DEC were able to enter minicomputer manufacturing because they were able to use OEMs for components and peripherals thereby reducing R&D and start-up costs. DEC itself became an OEM when it sold peripherals or configured systems for another vendor who differentiated its product from DEC's by the specific configuration of CPU, peripherals, or application software.

In 1960, peripherals represented 20 cents of every hardware dollar but by 1970 they represented 50 cents. As peripherals became an area of increasing user demand and profitability, the systems manufacturers began to produce peripherals in-house and the OEMs began selling their products direct to customers and to other system manufacturers who desired plug-compatibility with IBM [Fisher, McKie, and Mancke (1983): 286–289].

12. McKinsey & Company, *The 1995 Report on the Computer Industry* (New York: McKinsey & Company, 1995): 2–5.

13. Steinmueller (1996).

14. According to Steinmueller (1996) there is disagreement over whether fear of antitrust litigation led to IBM's decision to unbundle. Fisher, McKie, and Mancke (1983) argue that there is no direct evidence of a relation between IBM's unbundling decision and the Justice Department's antitrust action.

15. Avron Barr and Shirley Tessler, Presentation at the Fifth Annual Stanford Computer Industry Project Conference (September 19, 1996).

16. Mirek J. Stevenson, " '71 . . . The Year EDP Goes Multinational," *Datamation*, 17 (March 15, 1971): 36.

17. Select Committee on Science and Technology, *The Prospects for the United Kingdom Computer Industry in the 1970s*, vols. 1–3 (London: Her Majesty's Stationery Office, October 1971).

18. John Tagliabue, "Why European Computer Makers Flop," *New York Times*, (October 7, 1996).

19. For detailed descriptions of Japan's computer industry strategies, see Anchordoguy (1989) and Martin Fransman, *The Market and Beyond: Cooperation and Competition in Information Technology in the Japanese System* (Cambridge: Cambridge University Press, 1990).

20. NTT was government owned and under the control of the Ministry of Posts and Telecommunications until 1985, when it was partially privatized.

21. However, while Fujitsu's systems could run IBM software, IBM machines could not run Fujitsu's proprietary software.

22. Anchordoguy (1989): 110–111.

23. Benjamin Gomes-Casseres, "Computers: Alliances and Industry Evolution," in Yoffie (1993).

24. Richard N. Langlois, "External Economies and Economic Progress: The Case of the Microcomputer Industry," *Business History Review*, 66 (spring 1992): 1–50.

25. James Chposky and Ted Leonsis, *Blue Magic: The People, Power, and Politics Behind the IBM Personal Computer* (New York: Facts on File, 1988).

26. Charles H. Ferguson and Charles R. Morris, *Computer Wars: The Fall of IBM and the Future of Global Technology* (New York: Times Books, 1994): 52.

27. Ferguson and Morris (1994): 53.

28. Ibid.

29. The greater the number of applications developed for a particular operating system, the greater the sales for that system and the greater the chances that it would become the dominant software platform. Moreover, by tying developers to the operating system, a vast production network was created with strong incentives for developers to continually improve and expand their products. In order to increase their returns, application developers prefer to write for a dominant platform rather than for several competing platforms. The challenge for developers of operating systems, therefore, was to convince application developers that their system was, or soon would be, the dominant one.

30. In the microprocessor segment, the main competition was between Intel with its x86 and Pentium chips and Motorola with its 680xx and PowerPC chips. In the computer platform segment, the key competition was between IBM, the numerous makers of IBM compatibles, and Apple Computer. In the system software segment, the main competition was among Microsoft's DOS/Windows, IBM's OS/2, Apple's MacOS, and the various providers of UNIX operating systems.

31. W. Brian Arthur, *Increasing Returns and Path Dependence in the Economy*, (Ann Arbor: University of Michigan Press (1994): 100.

32. A U.S. Justice Department investigation discouraged Microsoft from acquiring Intuit in 1995.

33. Robert N. Noyce and Marcian E. Hoff, Jr., "A History of Microprocessor Development at Intel," *IEEE Micro*, 1 (February 1981): 8–21.

34. IBM was the first computer company to optimize resources for production on a global basis and did so as early as 1970. IBM assigned product development and manufacturing responsibilities to individual development laboratories and production facilities on a worldwide basis. Each laboratory specialized in a particular technology and carried the development responsibility for a product or technology for the entire company. Each IBM plant was given the charter to manufacture specific products both for the local market and for the export market. This worldwide assignment of development and production responsibility for each group of products into a single laboratory and plant concentrated development and production efficiencies for each group of products; it also eliminated many coordination problems experienced by firms with multiple manufacturing facilities in different markets. By assigning technology and production responsibility on a lab and plant basis, IBM was better able to adapt to available local resources and local environments in each country. IBM was able to cross national boundaries with technologies and products that had been planned and designed for the world market. IBM staffed its laboratories and plants with people from each country, and each country's export market often turned into imports in the United States for domestic use. In many countries IBM was not only a major employer but also a major exporter; therefore, the company was welcomed, or at least tolerated, rather than being resented as a competitor in the local market.

35. For example, estimates place the overall foreign content of U.S. computer hardware at 30% in 1992 compared to about 10% in 1986. United States International Trade Commission (USITC), *Global Competitiveness of U.S. Advanced-Technology Industries: Computers* (Washington, D.C.: USITC, 1993): 2–6.

36. U.S. imports of computer components and peripherals are so large that by 1991 the United States began registering deficits in its overall computer trade despite a positive U.S. trade balance in finished computers (ibid.).

37. Between 1990 and 1995, annual growth rates of Asian computer demand averaged 15%, compared to 9% for North America. Markets outside North America totaled 61% of global demand in 1995. McKinsey & Company, *The 1996 Report on the Computer Industry* (New York: McKinsey & Company, 1996).

38. Emily Thornton, "Logging Onto Asia," *Far Eastern Economic Review* (November 9, 1995).

39. As put by Langlois (1992), the mainframe and minicomputer industry had followed the traditional model of industrial organization articulated from Schumpeter down to Chandler and Lazonick. In this model, large-scale, vertically integrated firms derive integrated economies of scale from volume production and marketing and become the dominant players in an oligopolistic market. The visible hand of management replaces the invisible hand of the market where and when new technology and expanded markets permit unprecedented high volume and speed of materials through the process of production and distribution. The innovation of this model is the creation of capabilities within the firm that yield the potential for massive economies of large-scale production and distribution—the so-called dynamic capabilities theory of business organization.

Chapter 3

1. "Computers: Japan Comes on Strong" (1989).

2. "Japan Computer Lead Seen," *New York Times* (May 2, 1990).

3. A former IBM executive told the authors that in the 1980s, IBM was "almost obsessed" with the Japanese while underestimating the challenge from U.S. competitors in the PC industry. When he argued in a meeting that IBM's mainframe market forecasts looked too optimistic, he was told that IBM "was not going to get caught like the television industry." During the 1980s, IBM invested heavily in production capacity to be prepared for growth that never came as the market shifted from mainframes to PCs.

4. For a detailed analysis of the evolution of Japan's PC industry, see Joel West and Jason Dedrick, "The Rise and Fall of the PC-98 Regime: How Architectural Revolution Toppled the Dominant PC Standard in Japan" (Irvine, Calif.: University of California, Center for Research on Information Technology and Organizations (CRITO), 1997). Also, see Jon Choy, *Japan's Personal Computer Market: Awash in American Tsunami*, Japan Economic Institute (JEI) Report No. 6A (Washington, D.C.: JEI, 1994). For a history of NEC's PC business, see Martin Fransman, *Japan's Computer and Communications Industry* (New York: Oxford University Press, 1995).

5. The problems presented in dealing with the Japanese language are explained well in Choy (1994).

6. Japanese PC makers used front-end processors with complex dictionaries to handle phonetic input of *kanji* characters.

7. "Japanese Software: More Than Just Fun and Games?" *Electronics Business Asia* 4 (April 1993): 30–41.

8. Choy (1994).

9. Ibid.

10. Mike Galbraith, "NEC Taking No Part in Japan Price War," *Asia Computer Weekly*, 14 (1992): 1.

11. "Searching for a New Bullet," [Interview with Tadahiro Sekimoto] *Electronics Business Asia*, 5 (August 1994): 47–51.

12. Quoted in "Computer Makers Look Abroad For Parts: Competition from U.S. Makes All-Japan PCs Too Costly for Market," *The Nikkei Weekly* (September 20, 1993): 8.

13. "NEC Fends Off Foes with Cheap PC," *Japan Times Weekly International Edition* (January 30–February 5, 1995).

14. Robert Poe, "Can Fujitsu Reinvent Itself?" *Electronic Business Asia*, 4 (January 1993): 34–41.

15. Barbara Darrow, "Japan Inc.'s Rising Sun," *Infoworld* (January 28, 1991): 45.

16. Interview with Jerry Goetsch, Toshiba America Electronics Corporation.

17. Larry Holyoke, "How Toshiba's Laptops Retook the Heights," *Business Week*, (January 16, 1995): 83.

18. Ibid.

19. Ibid.

20. Jack Robertson, "Japanese Share of U.S. Notebook Market Rising," *Electronic Buyers News* (March 14, 1997).

21. Gary McWilliams, Emily Thornton, and Paul M. Eng, "If at First You Falter, Reboot," *Business Week* (June 30, 1997): 81–82.

22. IDC, data provided to authors.

23. Japan Electronics Industries Development Association (JEIDA), "Statistical Survey on Software Export/Import, 1995 Results" (Tokyo: JEIDA, 1996).

24. Organization for Economic Cooperation and Development (OECD), *Information Technology Outlook: 1994* (Paris: OECD, 1994).

25. JEIDA (1996).

26. Mochio Umeda, "Failing to Change: The Plight of the Japanese Computer Industry," *Prism* (second quarter, 1994).

27. Scott Callon, *Divided Sun: MITI and the Breakdown of Japanese High-Tech Industrial Policy* (Stanford, Calif.: Stanford University Press, 1996).

28. Ibid. This point was reinforced in interviews with market analysts in Tokyo with both U.S. and Japanese securities companies.

29. Ibid.

30. As has often been noted, lifetime employment only applies to male employees of major companies. Labor flexibility was provided by heavy use of temporary workers, subcontracting of work to firms that could be squeezed in times of slow demand, and the employment of young women who would only work a few years until marriage.

31. Lewis Y. Young, "Betting on Chips to Prop Up Consumer Declines," *Electronic Business Asia*, 6 (March 1995): 37–39.

32. Robert Poe, "Winds of Opportunity: Change in Japan Blows Business Asia's Way," *Electronic Business Asia*, 5 (April 1994): 40–47.

33. Some notable exceptions to this rule are Toshiba, Sony, and Honda. However, the fact that these companies are so often cited suggests how few exceptions to the rule there are.

34. Interviews with Toshiba America Information Systems managers.

35. Dieter Ernst, "Carriers Of Regionalization: The East Asian Production Networks of Japanese Electronics Firms," Berkeley Roundtable on the International Economy (BRIE) Working Paper 73 (Berkeley, Calif.: BRIE, University of California, 1994).

36. Noriko Takezaki, "Balancing Price with Quality: Japanese PC Makers Have Second Thoughts About Foreign Procurement," *Computing Japan* (March 1997): 18.

37. For example, a manufacturer could gain an advantage over its competitors by employing proprietary CAD/CAM software that would be expensive for its competitors to copy.

38. Michael A. Cusumano, *Japan's Software Factories* (New York: Oxford University Press, 1991).

39. Tetsushi Nakahara, "The Industrial Organization and Information Structure of the Software Industry: A U.S.–Japan Comparison" (Stanford, Calif.: Center for Economic Policy Research, 1993), 346.

40. Yasunori Baba, Shinji Takai, and Yuji Mizuta, "The User-Driven Evolution of the Japanese Software Industry: The Case of Customized Software for Mainframes," in David Mowery (ed.), *The International Computer Software Industry: Structure and Evolution* (New York: Oxford University Press, 1996): 104–130.

41. IBM, the world's largest software producer, makes most of its software revenue from mainframe operating systems and applications. It has failed to develop any big commercial successes of its own in the PC software market. But companies like Microsoft, Novell, Adobe, and Lotus (now owned by IBM) have more than filled the void in the United States.

42. Baba Takai, and Mizuta (1996).

43. William F. Finan and Jeffrey Frey, *Understanding the Growth Crisis in Japan's Electronics Industry* [English manuscript of book published in Japanese], (Tokyo: Nikkei, 1995).

44. Network economies are best seen in the case of the telephone. One telephone is a useless device. Two telephones connected by a wire create a communications channel with limited usefulness. Millions of telephones connected by a network of wires and switches represent a system with tremendous economic value. The same is true of PCs. While a single PC can be a valuable tool, its usefulness is limited. However, a networked PC can provide access to a wide array of services, from electronic mail to electronic document interchange to a wide range of Internet services.

45. Still, a distressingly high number of bugs always seems to make it through in each new product generation, thanks to the tremendous time-to-market pressures in the software industry.

46. Data on human resources from: National Science Foundation (NSF), *Human Resources for Science & Technology: The Asian Region* (Washington, D.C.: NSF, 1993) and NSF, *Science and Engineering Indicators 1996* (Washington, D.C.: NSF, 1996).

47. Nakahara (1993).

48. NSF (1993 and 1996).

49. Chalmers Johnson, "MITI, MPT, and the Telecom Wars," in Chalmers Johnson, Laura D'Andrea Tyson, and John Zysman (eds.), *Politics and Productivity: The Real Story of Why Japan Works* (Cambridge, Mass.: Ballinger, 1989): 177–240.

50. Joel West, "Utopianism and National Competitiveness in Technology Rhetoric: The Case of Japan's Information Infrastructure," *The Information Society*, 12 (1996): 251–272.

51. Japan Information Processing Development Center (JIPDEC), *Informatization White Paper* (Tokyo: JIPDEC, 1993).

52. Anchordoguy (1989).

53. Baba et al. (1996).

54. Ibid.

55. Callon (1996).

56. Ibid.

57. Anchordoguy (1989).

58. The plans for the Fifth Generation project were developed from 1979 to 1982 by a committee established by JIPDEC consisting of government, university, and industrial researchers, Japan Information Processing Development Center (JIPDEC), *Japan Computer Quarterly* (Tokyo: JIPDEC, 1993), 93.

59. Authors' interview with MITI official (1994).

60. Tom Cottrell, "Fragmented Standards and the Development of Japan's Microcomputer Software Industry," *Research Policy*, 23 (1994): 143–174.

61. The issue of software decompilation and its treatment under Japanese law is described in detail by Joel West, "Software Rights and Japan's Shift to an Information Society: Evidence from the 1993–1994 Copyright Revision Process," *Asian Survey*, 35 (1995).

62. Ibid.

63. JIPDEC (1993).

64. Interview with MITI official (1994).

65. Anchordoguy (1989); Martin Fransman, *The Market and Beyond* (Cambridge: Cambridge University Press, 1990); Fumio Kodama, *Emerging Patterns of Innovation: Sources of Japan's Technological Edge* (Boston: Harvard Business School Press, 1995).

66. This point is argued by Johnson (1989) and by Steven Vogel, *Freer Markets, More Rules: The Paradoxical Politics of Regulatory Reform in the Advanced Industrial Countries*, (Ithaca, N.Y.: Cornell University Press, 1996).

67. For detailed analysis of Japan's NII initiatives, see Joel West, Jason Dedrick, and Kenneth L. Kraemer, "Back to the Future: Japan's NII Plans," in Brian Kahin and Ernest J. Wilson III (eds.), *National Information Infrastructure Initiatives: Visions and Policy Design* (Cambridge: MIT Press, 1996): 61–111.

68. Authors' interview (August 1996).

## Chapter 4

1. Amsden, (1989).

2. "Sliding Scales," *The Economist* (November 2, 1996): 77.

3. See, for example, Ira C. Magaziner and Mark Patinkin, "Fast Heat: How Korea Won the Microwave War," *Harvard Business Review* (January–February 1989): 83–93.

4. MTI is now called the Ministry of Trade, Industry, and Energy, or MOTIE.

5. Linsu Kim, *Imitation to Innovation: The Dynamics of Korea's Technological Learning* (Boston: Harvard Business School Press, 1997): 139.

6. Dieter Ernst, *What are the Limits to the Korean Model? The Korean Electronics Industry Under Pressure* (Berkeley, Calif.: Berkeley Roundtable on the International Economy, 1994).

7. Electronics Industries Association of Korea (EIAK), *'95 Statistics of Electronics Industries* (Seoul: EIAK, 1996).

8. Reed, *Yearbook of World Electronics Data* (Oxford Reed Electronics Research 1994).

9. Much of this discussion is based on Kim (1997): 149–170. Additional insights were provided by Jae-ho Yeom of Korea University Sung-gul Hong, of Koduncia University of the Korea Institute for Economics and Trade and Seong-Taek Park in interviews with the authors.

10. Kim (1997): 151.

11. Kenneth Flamm, *Mismanaged Trade: Strategic Policy and the Semiconductor Industry* (Washington, D.C.: Brookings Institution Press, 1996): 177.

12. Kim (1997): 162.

13. This point was made to the authors by Seong-Taek Park of the Korea Institute for Economics and Trade.

14. Kim (1997): 170.

15. Ernst (1994).

16. "Shooting Stars, Comeback Kids & Also-rans," *Electronic Business Asia* 7 (July 1996): 44–45.

17. Dataquest, "Worldwide PC Market Grew 24% in 1995," (January 29, 1996), press release on Dataquest web page, www.dataquest.com.

18. Interview (January 1997).

19. Jon Skillings and Rob Guth, "Asia-Pacific PC Market Leaps 32 Percent in 1996," *IDG China Market News Updates* (1997), www.idgchin.com.

20. Karen Petska-Juliussen and Egil Juliussen, *The 8th Annual Computer Industry Almanac* (Glenbrook, Nev.: Computer Industry Almanac Inc., 1996).

21. Axmi Nakarmi and Robert Neff, "Samsung's Radical Shakeup," *Business Week* (February 28, 1994): 74–76.

22. Ibid.

23. Ernst (1994).

24. "Chaebols Told to Behave Nicely," *Electronics Business Asia* 4 (June 1993): 17–18.

25. Drew Wilson, "Locals Rule Home Market," *Electronic Business Asia*, 8 (May 1997): 28.

26. Ernst (1994).

27. Jason Dedrick, Kenneth L. Kraemer, and Dae-Won Choi, "Korean Technology Policy at a Crossroads: The Case of Information Technology," *Journal of Asian Business*, 11 (1995): 1–34.

28. Specifically, imports of PCs and peripherals were subject to certification that the product could not be produced domestically.

29. Dedrick, Kraemer, and Choi (1995): 9.

30. It also tends to shut out independent domestic producers, limiting the potential market of smaller competitors.

31. Korean semiconductor companies, by contrast, have entered into a number of joint development and production agreements with major U.S. and Japanese companies.

32. Kim (1997): 54–55.

33. Ibid.: 50.

34. Elsevier, *Yearbook of World Electronics Data* (Oxford: Elsevier Advanced Technology, 1993).

35. Kim (1997): 51.

36. Kim Nak-Hieon, "MIC Unveils Ambitious National Software Policy," *Electronics*, 68 (February 27, 1995).

37. For a detailed review of the KII initiative, see Kuk-Hwan Jeong and John Leslie King, "Korea's National Information Infrastructure: Vision and Issues," in Kahin and Wilson (1996): 112–149.

38. Ibid.: 144.

39. For a detailed history of Taiwan's electronics industry, see Wade (1990) and Michael Hobday, *Innovation in East Asia, The Challenge to Japan* (Aldershot: Edward Elgar, 1995).

40. Republic of China, *Statistical Yearbook of the Republic of China* (Taiwan: Directorate-General of Budget, Accounting and Statistics, Executive Yuan, 1991).

41. Market Intelligence Center/Institute for the Information Industry, *Taiwan's Personal Computer Industry Report: Hardware/Software Strategies and Trends* (Taipei: MIC, 1991). Note that domestic company production includes OEM production of foreign brand name products.

42. Interview with industry analyst.

43. Wong, (1995).

44. Kenneth L. Kraemer, Jason Dedrick, Chin-Yeong Hwang, Tze-Chen Tu, and Chee-Sing Yap, "Entrepreneurship, Flexibility, and Policy Coordination: Taiwan's Information Technology Industry," *The Information Society*, 12 1996.

45. Market Intelligence Center officials and others in Taiwan doubt that Intel's output was actually ten million units. They argue that five million is a more believable figure.

46. Shih has been profiled in magazines such as *Fortune* and has won various international awards as an outstanding executive.

47. Louis Kraar, "Acer's Edge: PC to Go," *Fortune* (October 30, 1995).

48. Shih's offer was symbolic, given his family's position as Acer's largest shareholder, but it was important in reestablishing his leadership and in taking responsibility for Acer's difficulties.

49. Interview with George Hsu, Chief of Staff, Chairman's Office, Acer.

50. For instance, if the CPU were purchased from Intel and shipped to Taiwan to be placed on the board, then shipped back to the U.S. market, it would have already gone down in price by the time the PC reached the distributor. Acer saves that cost difference by adding on the chips at the last moment.

51. Kraar (1995).

52. In addition to "client-server," "fast food model," and "global brand, local touch," there is "approaching the city from the country," and Shih's use of the Chinese proverb, "It is better to be the head of a chicken than the tail of an ox," to explain the philosophy behind Acer's creation of independent business units.

53. Market Intelligence Center/Institute for the Information Industry, "Taiwan's Information Services Industry and Market," *Asia IT Report* (April 1996): 1–11.

54. Like many such statements, it was actually made by a Chinese observer.

55. Hirokazu Kajiwara, "Taiwan's Electronics Industry: From an Import Substitution and Export Oriented Industry to a Highly Advanced Industry," in Ryuichiro Inoue, Hirohisa Kohama, and Shujiro Urata (eds.), *Industrial Policy in East Asia* (Tokyo: Japan External Trade Organization, 1993): 165–191.

56. Coopers & Lybrand, "Information Technology Sector Development: A Workshop for MIMOS" (Kuala Lumpur, Malaysia: 1995).

57. For instance, Taiwan's land reforms of the 1950s took land from large landholders and gave it to tenant farmers. Landholders were paid in shares of former state-owned industries, encouraging them to move from agriculture to industry. Also, many subsidies were provided to SMEs, giving investors an incentive to start new ventures and to spin-off new companies when they developed additional business activities. Finally, the government developed strategic industries through the use of state-owned enterprises, rather than subsidizing private industry as Japan and Korea had done. Thus, private firms in Taiwan did not move into heavy industries such as steel and petrochemicals that required large investments and large scale production.

58. Brian Levy and Wen-Jeng Kuo, "The Strategic Orientation of Firms and the Performance of Korea and Taiwan in Frontier Industries: Lessons from Comparative Case Studies of Keyboard and Personal Computer Assembly," *World Development*, 19 (1991): 363–374.

59. Scott Callon, "Different Paths: The Rise of Taiwan and Singapore in the Global Personal Computer Industry," Japan Development Bank, JDB Discussion Paper Series, no. 9494 (1994).

60. Callon (1994).

61. Coopers & Lybrand (1995).

62. Kajiwara (1993).

63. P. Wang, "Information Systems Management Issues in the Republic of China for the 1990s," *Information and Management*, 26 (1994): 341–352.

64. Ibid.

65. Evidently nationalism only goes so far, as it is said that many of these engineers end up going back to the United States after failing to readjust to Taiwan's crowded conditions and hectic lifestyle. One company official said that only 30%–40% of the returnees stay in Taiwan.

66. According to Coopers & Lybrand (1995) an average project manager in Taiwan makes just US$22,667 per year, compared to US$47,938 in Singapore. There are smaller gaps for analysts and programmers.

## Chapter 5

1. Actually the Hong Kong government quietly intervenes in the economy more than its supporters would admit. For instance, the government owns all land in Hong Kong and uses its power over land use as a means of influencing economic development. Also, note that this discussion of Hong Kong refers to the situation before the 1997 transition to Chinese rule.

2. With the exception of some floppy disk production by Tandon.

3. Background on the early development of Singapore's electronics industry is from Toh Mun Heng, "Partnership with Multinational Corporations," in Linda Low, Toh Mun Heng, Soon Teck Wong, Tan Kong Yan, and Helen Hughes (eds.), *Challenge and Response: Thirty Years of the Economic Development Board* (Singapore: Times Academic Press, 1993): 121–156.

4. Interview with David T. Mitchell (August 1996).

5. Seagate also approached the Taiwanese government at this time about locating some production in Taiwan; the government, however, was not interested, because it felt that hard disk drives were not appropriate for PCs. This mistake has helped virtually shut Taiwan out of the disk drive industry. See Callon (1994).

6. Dael Climo, "Labor Crunch," *Electronic Business Asia*, 6 (August 1995): 32–38.

7. Michael Bordenaro, "What does Seagate/Conner Hold for Asia's Factories?" *Electronic Business Asia*, 7 (April 1996): 54–56.

8. Callon (1994).

9. Wong (1995).

10. Borrus (1997).

11. In 1997, as its global market share plummeted, Apple cut back its activities in Singapore as part of a corporate restructuring that included outsourcing much of its production.

12. Reed, *Yearbook of World Electronics Data* (Oxford: Reed Electronics Research, 1996).

13. National Computer Board (NCB), *The Singapore IT Industry Survey Report* (Singapore: NCB, 1994).

14. Much of the following discussion is from Hung Kei Tang, "The Ascent of Creative Technology: A Case Study of Technology Entrepreneurship," in Neo Boon Siong (ed.), *Exploiting Information Technology for Business Competitiveness: Cases and Insights from Singapore-based Organizations*, (Reading, Mass.: Addison Wesley, 1996).

15. Dael Climo, "Another Global Player Pulls Back," *Electronic Business Asia*, 7 (April 1996): 17.

16. Singapore Trade Development Board (1995).

17. Borrus (1997).

18. Industry executive interview (1995).

19. "Contract Manufacturing Directory," *Electronic Business Asia*, 6 (August 1995): 54–55.

20. Lee's People's Action Party had effectively neutralized the major opposition parties and gained unchallenged political power.

21. Lim Chong-Yah and Associates, *Policy Options for the Singapore Economy* (Singapore: McGraw-Hill, 1988).

22. See Edgar H. Schein, *Strategic Pragmatism: The Culture of Singapore's Economic Development Board* (Cambridge: MIT Press, 1996) for examples of EDB's role

in developing Singapore's industrial base, its strategies for attracting foreign investment, and its internal workings and organizational culture.

23. Wong (1995).

24. Vijay Gurbaxani, Kenneth L. Kraemer, John L. King, Sheryl Jarman, Jason Dedrick, K. S. Raman, and Chee-Sing Yap, "Government as Driving Force Toward the Information Society: National Computer Policy in Singapore," *Information Society*, 7 (1991): 155–185.

25. Wong (1995).

26. IDC, calculated from data provided to authors.

27. Interview with Kah-Kwen Chen, Deputy Managing Director, SNS, October 1995.

28. Poh-Kam Wong, "Implementing the NII Vision: Singapore," in Kahin and Wilson (1997): 24–60. The industry clusters include: construction, digital library, education, health care, manufacturing and distribution, new media and Internet, public services, and tourism and leisure.

29. Murray Hiebert, "It's a Jungle Out There," *Far Eastern Economic Review*, (April 25, 1996): 58–61.

30. Climo (1995).

31. Interview with Kenneth James, *Business Times* (1995).

32. Climo (1995).

33. Economic Development Board (EDB), *Singapore: Film, Video, and Music Industries* (Singapore: EDB, 1995).

34. One could argue that by allowing most of the economy to be dominated by MNCs and state-owned enterprises, the government actually squeezed local companies out of many markets.

35. Although the government's Trade Development Board did help Creative Technology secure supplies of a key FM synthesizer chip from a Japanese supplier that was reluctant to sell to Creative.

36. Hiebert (1996).

37. Ibid.

38. Interview with Stephen Yeo, NCB (October 27, 1995).

39. Jeffrey Henderson, "Hong Kong: The Making of a Regional Core," in Henderson (ed.), *The Globalisation of High Technology Production: Society, Space, and Semiconductors in the Restructuring of the Modern World* (London: Routledge, 1989): 77–117.

40. Ibid.: 93.

41. David P. Hamilton, "PC Makers Find China is a Chaotic Market," *The Wall Street Journal* (April 8, 1996), online edition.

42. Hong Kong Census and Statistics Department, report prepared for authors (1995). These figures include computers and peripherals, but not components such as LCDs and printed circuit boards. The figure for total output is very close to the figures in Reed (various years) which are used for comparisons with other countries.

43. Background on VTech from Hobday (1995): 168–169.

44. Mike Levin, "VTech: Tough Lessons in Going Global," *Electronic Business Asia*, 5 (January 1994): 38–42.

45. Much of the following draws on an interview with Legend officials in January 1997.

46. Interview with Saiman Hui, IDC (August 1996).

47. "From Legend to Reality," *Business China* (January 8, 1996): 4–6.

48. Xinhua News Agency, "High-tech Industry Prospering in Shenzhen" (June 11, 1996). Shenzhen accounts for 40% of total high-tech output in Guangdong Province, but no figures are given for its share of computer production.

49. William Overholt, *The Rise of China: How Economic Reform is Creating a New Superpower* (New York: W. W. Norton and Company, 1995): 214.

50. Interview with semiconductor industry executive (1995).

51. Hong Kong Census and Statistics Department, Report prepared for authors (1995).

52. Hong Kong Productivity Council, *Consultancy Study on Hong Kong's Software Industry* (Hong Kong: Industry Department, 1995).

53. Ibid.

54. Kenneth L. Kraemer, Jason Dedrick, and Sheryl Jarman, "Supporting the Free Market: Information Technology Policy in Hong Kong," *The Information Society*, 10 (1994): 223–246.

55. Colin C. Greenfield and Eliza Lee, "Government Information Technology Policy in Hong Kong," *Informatization and the Public Sector*, 2 (1992): 125–132.

56. Exchange rate for the study period is HK$7.8=US$1.

57. David Kahaner and Julian Wu, "General Remarks About Hong Kong" (Tokyo: Asian Technology Information Program, 1995).

58. Author correspondence from James Liu, Chief Executive Officer, HKITCC.

59. Kraemer, Dedrick, and Jarman (1994).

60. Joy Tang, "Tradelink Picks HP for EDI Network Project," *Asia Computer Weekly*, 16 (1995): 3.

61. Interview with Anthony Wong, OFTA (1995).

62. Kahaner and Wu (1995). Officials of the Hong Kong Government Industry Department dispute this figure, pointing to a survey estimating that Hong Kong's private sector invests 1.4% of its revenues in R&D, compared to 6.7% for Korea, 0.93% for Taiwan, and 1.02% for Singapore. However, the large gap between Korea and the other NIEs is inconsistent with other data sources, making these figures suspect.

63. National Science Foundation (1993), for Korea, Taiwan, and Singapore. No data for Hong Kong.

64. As one article puts it, "Given the desire of mainland officials to cut themselves a slice of this lucrative pie, Hong Kong may die the death of a thousand ten-percents." *Public Affairs Report* (January 1995): 3.


## Chapter 6

1. Ralph Gomory argues that a vital component of competitiveness in high-technology industries is the "cyclic development" process, which requires turning out products again and again with incremental improvements in the product cycle. Ralph Gomory, "From the 'Ladder of Science' to the Product Development Cycle," *Harvard Business Review* (November–December 1989): 99–105.

2. Michael Porter, *The Competitive Advantage of Nations* (New York: Free Press, 1990).

3. Arnold Miller, "Building a Modern Electronics Industry," in Bjorn Wellenius, Arnold Miller, and Carl J. Dahlman (eds.), *Developing the Electronics Industry* (Washington, D.C.: World Bank, 1993).

4. Jason Dedrick, Seymour Goodman, and Kenneth L. Kraemer, "Little Engines that Could: Computing in Small Energetic Countries," *Communications of the ACM*, 38 (1995): 21–26.

5. Robert Schware, "Software Industry Entry Strategies for Developing Countries: A 'Walking on Two Legs' Proposition," *World Development*, 20 (1992): 143–164.

6. National Science Foundation (1996): 2–24.

7. From interviews with Korean executives.

8. Gomory (1989).

9. Fumio Kodama, *Emerging Patterns of Innovation: Sources of Japan's Technological Edge* (Boston: Harvard Business School Press, 1995). Also, Lewis Branscomb, "Policy for Science and Engineering in 1989: A Public Agenda for Economic Renewal," *Business in the Contemporary World*, 2 (1989).

10. See Kodama (1995) for a history of Sharp's LCD products.

11. Jason Dedrick and Kenneth L. Kraemer, "National Technology Policy and Computer Production in Asia-Pacific Countries," *The Information Society*, 11 (1995): 29–58.

12. MITI and MPT have invited the president of IBM Japan to sit on key committees discussing deregulation and national information infrastructure policies, but this person is a Japanese national and does not offer a true outsider's viewpoint.

13. Wade (1990).

14. Callon (1994).

15. Wong (1995).

## Chapter 7

1. Arthur, (1996).

2. See, for example, David B. Yoffie, "Competing in the Age of Digital Convergence," *California Management Review*, 38 (1996): 31–53; and Charles R. Morris and Charles H. Ferguson, "How Architecture Wins Technology Wars," *Harvard Business Review*, 71 (March–April 1993): 86–96.

3. .Bill Gates is said to have described a competitor's hesitation as a case of "finite greed." *The Economist*, "Squeeze, Gently" (November 30, 1996): 65–66.

4. Yoffie (1996).

5. Andrew S. Grove, *Only the Paranoid Survive: How to Exploit the Crisis Points that Challenge Every Company and Career* (New York: Doubleday, 1996).

6. Arthur (1996): 107.

7. Arthur (1996): 103.

8. West, Dedrick, and Kraemer (1996).

9. See Dedrick, Goodman, Kraemer (1995); and Robert Schware, *Prospects for Information Service Exports from the English-Speaking Caribbean* (Washington, D.C.: World Bank, 1996).

10. Peter Gourevitch, Roger E. Bohn, and David McKendrick, "Who is Us? The Nationality of Production in the Hard Disk Drive Industry," The Data Storage Industry Globalization Project (La Jolla, Calif.: Graduate School of International Relations and Pacific Studies, University of California, San Diego, 1997).

11. Organisation for Economic Cooperation and Development (OECD), *Information Technology Outlook* (Paris: OECD, various years).

## Chapter 8

1. Daniel Bell, *The Coming of Post-industrial Society; A Venture in Social Forecasting* (New York, Basic Books, 1973) and Yoneji Masuda, *The Information Society as Post-industrial Society* (Bethesda, Md.: World Futures Society, 1980).

2. See Kahin and Wilson (1997). For a cross-country comparison of U.S., Asian, and European plans, see *Information Infrastructure and Policy*, 5, nos. 1 and 2 (1996).

3. Brian Kahin, "The Internet Business and Policy Landscape," in *The Internet as Paradigm* (Queenstown, Md.: The Institute for Information Studies, 1997): 47–69.

4. Ibid.

5. As a result, both the computer industry and user organizations are developing various kinds of work-arounds to deal with bandwidth limitations. Industry solutions include bandwidth rationing, asynchronous communication, and backcasting, and use of faster components such as routers, servers, and modems. User organizations are using intranets, to keep activity off the crowded Internet, and developing new extra-nets—private networks among firms in an industry or a supply chain.

6. Anthony M. Rutkowski, "The Internet: An Abstraction in Chaos," in *The Internet as Paradigm* (1997): 1–22.

7. Ibid.

8. There are numerous examples of how the Internet has won out over proprietary technologies. The idea of interactive TV, with limited features offered by cable TV or telecommunications companies, is being superseded by the Internet TV concept, which combines broadcast TV with Internet access to material related to the broadcasting. Several U.S. regional telephone companies and cable TV companies have delayed or dropped plans to offer interactive TV, but AT&T and MCI now offer Internet access, and some cable TV companies are slowly gearing up to offer fast Internet access through cable modems. Meanwhile, providers of online services such as America Online, CompuServe, Prodigy, Lexis-Nexis, Dow Jones, and Reuters have had to offer Internet access as part of their proprietary services in order to survive. Microsoft had to redesign its Microsoft Network service to facilitate Internet access so it will not be left behind. Microsoft it is engaged directly in an all-out battle with Netscape to make Microsoft Internet Explorer (which it gives away free) the preferred browser for the Internet. In the business software market, the proprietary Lotus Notes groupware application was redesigned to become Internet-friendly and Microsoft's Office suite has been redesigned to include Internet features that make it easier to create and access Web pages.

9. Our estimate is based on triangulation of multiple sources.

10. Rutkowski (1997) says that there are "literally thousands of abstractions in the form of applications and services that run on top of the Internet and intranets;" but the number of end user applications to date is much more limited. Also see David Bollier, *The Networked Society: How New Technologies are Transforming Markets, Organizations, and Social Relationships* (Washington, D.C.: The Aspen Institute, 1997).

11. Bollier (1997): 6.

12. Moschella, (1997).

13. Ibid.

14. Andrew S. Rappaport and Shmuel Halevi, "The Computerless Computer Company," *Harvard Business Review*, 69: 69–80.

15. The PC versus NC issue has turned into a "choose-up-sides" debate reminiscent of the mainframe versus PC debates held fifteen years ago. Back then, a group of youngsters such as Gates, Jobs, and Wozniak were challenging their elders, who insisted that the PC was a mere toy with inadequate processing power and storage, which would never replace the mainframe and minicomputer as a real business tool. Now, those not-so-youngsters argue that the NC is an underpowered toy, with inadequate processing power and storage, which will never replace the PC as a real business tool. The subtext of this debate is the desire of many in the computer industry to

overturn the Microsoft/Intel regime, just as the PC ended IBM's rule. However, the speed with which Microsoft has recast itself as an Internet company suggests that it will not be caught napping.

16. Information appliances are considered low-cost consumer devices that perform limited or specialized computing functions, such as entertainment or Internet access. Network computers are devices for the business market that rely on either local or remote servers for software and data storage. These product forms came into existence in 1997 in the form of WebTV, Diba's information devices, and Oracle's network computer architecture. The dominant designs have yet to be established. The discussion in this section does not turn on the success of any particular hardware or software format, but on the notion that the network is replacing the PC as the center of value and intelligence, just as PCs replaced the mainframe.

17. Thomas Petzinger, Jr., "Analytical Graphics Waits for Windfall from a Freebie," *Wall Street Journal*" (July 25, 1997): B1.

18. This distinction has been made by Eric Schmidt, among others. See Bollier (1997).

19. Marc H. Meyer and Alvin P. Lehnerd, *The Power of Product Platforms: Building Value and Cost Leadership* (New York: Basic Books, 1997).

20. The System/360 was componentized, which meant that the core central processor and peripherals could be mixed and matched as needed. The central processor was scalable from small to very large, which meant that the design met the needs of a range of business users and allowed them to grow without major changes in their systems. The operating system was standard across central processors, which meant it was economical for developers to write applications for the System/360. The peripherals were plug-compatible, which meant that peripherals made by other firms could also be attached. The common components shared across a whole range of systems lowered the costs of design, manufacture, and support for IBM, while the common operating system and plug-compatible peripherals enabled other vendors to participate in the market and help grow it. See detailed discussion in chapter 2.

21. For example, beginning in the 1980s Hewlett-Packard developed an ink-jet printer design and process-engineering techniques that gave it a prominent position in the global market. The core technology was the disposable ink-jet head which was combined with mechanical, electrical, and software components to create a printer platform. The utility of these products was further enhanced by designing the external interfaces to work with all types and brands of PCs. Over the years, Hewlett-Packard developed the head to handle multiple pens and also to handle black-and-white and color. Together, these improvements resulted in three successive generations of product platforms and derivative products which lowered costs and/or addressed new markets. In fact, Hewlett-Packard's ink-jet printers created a whole new wave of demand for desktop printing in both consumer and business markets. See Meyer and Lehnerd (1997).

22. We cannot go into detail on the power of platforms here, but we point to several references. The first is the excellent article by Morris and Ferguson (1993). The second is the book by Meyer and Lehnerd (1997), which focuses on hardware, software, and information products. The third is an article on information products by Marc H. Meyer and Michael H. Zack, "The Design and Development of Information Products," *Sloan Management Review*, 37 (spring 1996): 29–48.

23. Meyer and Zack (1996).

24. This scenario draws from one for online journals in Meyer and Zack (1996).

25. An intranet refers to a network entirely within a company with no access from the outside; a "firewall" is built to protect the internal network from penetration. An extranet refers to a similar network among business partners such as a manufacturer and its suppliers and corporate customers. Both intranets and extranets tend to be built using the technologies of the Internet, which is why it is frequently said that all some companies will have to do in the future is to remove the firewall and be "on the Internet."

26. Dennis Normile, "Japan Hatches PC War Plan," *Electronic Business Asia*, 7 (June 1996): 38–44. For another example, see John Boyd, "Computers: The Japanese Challenge," *The Journal of the American Chamber of Commerce in Japan*, 33 (October 1996): 30.

27. This point is made in both Normile (1996) and Boyd (1996).

28. Normile (1996): 40.

29. Normile (1996): 35.

30. Normile (1996): 43.

31. Lee Smith, "Hitachi Gliding Nowhere," *Fortune* (August 5, 1996): 83.

32. Normile (1996): 39–40.

33. Committee for Information, *Computer and Communications Policy, Information Infrastructure Convergence, and Pricing: The Internet* (Paris: OECD 1996).

34. Moschella (1997).

35. U.S. Department of Commerce, *U.S. Global Trade Outlook, 1995–2000* (Washington, D.C.: U.S. Government Printing Office, March 1995).

36. Kenneth L. Kraemer and Jason Dedrick, "From Nationalism to Pragmatism: IT Policy in China," *IEEE Computer*, 28 (1995): 64–73.

37. The authors would like to credit Peter Schavoir for helping to frame the following analysis of implications for the U.S. industry.

38. Consider the warnings from Prestowitz and Grove mentioned earlier, and numerous other doomsday predictions for the U.S. computer industry.

# References

Amsden, Alice H. 1989. *Asia's Next Giant: South Korea and Late Industrialization*. New York: Oxford University Press.

Anchordoguy, Marie. 1989. *Computers Inc.: Japan's Challenge to IBM*. Cambridge: Council East Asian Studies, Harvard University.

Arthur, W. Brian. 1994. *Increasing Returns and Path Dependence in the Economy*. Ann Arbor: University of Michigan Press.

Arthur, W. Brian. 1996. "Increasing Returns and the New World of Business," *Harvard Business Review* (July–August): 100–109.

Baba, Yasunori, Shinji Takai, and Yuji Mizuta. 1996. "The User-Driven Evolution of the Japanese Software Industry: The Case of Customized Software for Mainframes," in David Mowery (ed.), *The International Computer Software Industry: Structure and Evolution*. New York: Oxford University Press: 104–130.

Baily, Martin N. 1986. "What Has Happened to Productivity Growth?" *Science*, 234 (October): 443–451.

Bell, Daniel. 1973. *The Coming of Post-industrial Society; A Venture in Social Forecasting*. New York: Basic Books.

Bollier, David. 1997. *The Networked Society: How New Technologies Are Transforming Markets, Organizations, and Social Relationships*. Washington, D.C.: The Aspen Institute.

Bordenaro, Michael. 1996. "What does Seagate/Conner Hold for Asia's Factories?" *Electronic Business Asia*, 7 (April): 54–56.

Borrus, Michael. 1997. "Left for Dead: Asian Production Networks and the Revival of U.S. Electronics," in Barry Naughton (ed.), *The China Circle: Economics and Electronics in the PRC, Hong Kong, and Taiwan*. Washington, D.C.: Brookings Institution.

Boskin, Michael J., and Lawrence J. Lau. 1996. "Contributions of R&D to Economic Growth," in Bruce L. R. Smith and Claude E. Barfield (eds.), *Technology, R&D, and the Economy*. Washington, D.C.: Brookings Institution and American Enterprise Institute: 75–113.

Boyd, John. 1996. "Computers: The Japanese Challenge," *The Journal of the American Chamber of Commerce in Japan*, 33 (October): 30.

Branscomb, Lewis. 1989. "Policy for Science and Engineering in 1989: A Public Agenda for Economic Renewal," *Business in the Contemporary World*, 2.

Brynjolfsson, Eric, and Loren Hitt. 1996. "Paradox Lost? Firm-Level Evidence on the Returns to Information Systems Spending," *Management Science*, 42 (April): 541–558.

Buchannan, James, and Yoon J. Yong (eds.). 1994. *The Return to Increasing Returns*. Ann Arbor: University of Michigan Press.

Business Software Alliance. 1996. "1996 BSA/SPA Piracy Study Results" (www.bsa.org/piracy/96TABLES.HTM).

Callon, Scott. 1994. "Different Paths: The Rise of Taiwan and Singapore in the Global Personal Computer Industry." Japan Development Bank, JDB Discussion Paper Series, no. 9494.

Callon, Scott. 1996. *Divided Sun: MITI and the Breakdown of Japanese High-Tech Industrial Policy*. Stanford, Calif.: Stanford University Press.

"Chaebols Told to Behave Nicely." 1993. *Electronic Business Asia* 4 (June): 17–18.

Chong-Yah, Lim, and Associates. 1988. *Policy Options for the Singapore Economy*. Singapore: McGraw-Hill.

Choy, Jon. 1994. *Japan's Personal Computer Market: Awash in American Tsunami*. Japan Economic Institute (JEI) Report No. 6A. Washington, D.C.: JEI.

Chposky, James, and Ted Leonsis. 1988. *Blue Magic: The People, Power, and Politics Behind the IBM Personal Computer*. New York: Facts on File.

Climo, Dael. 1995. "Labor Crunch," *Electronic Business Asia*, 6, August: 32–38.

Climo, Dael. 1996. "Another Global Player Pulls Back," *Electronic Business Asia*, 7, April: 17.

Committee for Information, OECD. 1996. *Computer and Communications Policy, Information Infrastructure Convergence and Pricing: The Internet*. Paris: Organisation for Economic Cooperation and Development.

"Computer Makers Look Abroad For Parts." 1993. *The Nikkei Weekly*. Competition from U.S. Makes All-Japan PCs Too Costly for Market." September 20: 8.

"Computers: Japan Comes On Strong." 1989. *Business Week*, (October 23): 104–112.

"Contract Manufacturing Directory." 1995. *Electronic Business Asia* 6 (August): 54–55.

Coopers & Lybrand. 1995. "Information Technology Sector Development: A Workshop for MIMOS." Kuala Lumpur, Malaysia.

Cottrell, Tom. 1994. "Fragmented Standards and the Development of Japan's Microcomputer Software Industry," *Research Policy*, 23: 143–174.

Cusumano, Michael A. 1991. *Japan's Software Factories*. New York: Oxford University Press.

Darrow, Barbara. 1991. "Japan Inc.'s Rising Sun," *Infoworld*, 28 (January): 45.

"The Datamation 100." 1997. *Datamation*. July 14 (www.datamation.com/PlugIn/issues/1997/july/main100table.html).

Dataquest. 1996. "Worldwide PC Market Grew 24% in 1995," January 29,; press release on Dataquest web page (www.dataquest.com).

Dedrick, Jason, and Kenneth L. Kraemer. 1995. "National Technology Policy and Computer Production in Asia-Pacific Countries." *The Information Society*, 11: 29–58.

Dedrick, Jason, Seymour E. Goodman, and Kenneth L. Kraemer. 1995. "Little Engines that Could: Computing in Small Energetic Countries," *Communications of the ACM*, 38: 21–26.

Dedrick, Jason, Kenneth L. Kraemer, and Dae-Won Choi. 1995. "Korean Technology Policy at a Crossroads: The Case of Information Technology," *Journal of Asian Business*, 11: 1–34.

Economic Development Board (EDB). 1995. *Singapore: Film, Video, and Music Industries*. Singapore: EDB.

Electronics Industries Association of Korea (EIAK). 1989–1996. *Statistics of Electronics Industries* (annual yearbooks). Seoul: EIAK.

Ernst, Dieter. 1994. "Carriers of Regionalization: The East Asian Production Networks of Japanese Electronics Firms," Berkeley Roundtable on the International Economy (BRIE), Working Paper 73, Berkeley, Calif.: BRIE, University of California.

Ernst, Dieter. 1994. *What are the Limits to the Korean Model? The Korean Electronics Industry Under Pressure*. Berkeley, Calif.: Berkeley Roundtable on the International Economy.

Ferguson, Charles H., and Charles R. Morris. 1994. *Computer Wars: The Fall of IBM and the Future of Global Technology*. New York: Times Books.

Finan, William F., and Jeffrey Frey. 1995. *Understanding the Growth Crisis in Japan's Electronics Industry*. [English manuscript of book published in Japanese.] Tokyo: Nikkei.

Fisher, Franklin M., James W. McKie, and Richard B. Mancke. 1983. *IBM and the U.S. Data Processing Industry*. New York: Praeger.

Flamm, Kenneth. 1996. *Mismanaged Trade: Strategic Policy and the Semiconductor Industry*. Washington, D.C.: Brookings Institution Press.

Fransman, Martin. 1990. *The Market and Beyond: Cooperation and Competition in Information Technology in the Japanese System*. Cambridge: Cambridge University Press.

Fransman, Martin. 1995. *Japan's Computer and Communications Industry: The Evolution of Industrial Giants and Global Competitiveness*. New York: Oxford University Press.

"From Legend to Reality." 1996. *Business China*, (January 8): 4–6.

Galbraith, Mike. 1992. "NEC Taking No Part in Japan Price War," *Asia Computer Weekly*, 14: 1.

Costello, Maryellen C. and Benjamin Gomes-Casseres, "The Global Computer Industry, case no. 9-792-072. Boston: Harvard Business School, 1992.

Gomory, Ralph. 1989. "From the 'Ladder of Science' to the Product Development Cycle," *Harvard Business Review* (November–December): 99–105.

Gourevitch, Peter, Roger E. Bohn, and David McKendrick. 1997. "Who is Us? The Nationality of Production in the Hard Disk Industry." The Data Storage Industry Globalization Project. La Jolla, Calif.: Graduate School of International Relations and Pacific Studies, University of California, San Diego.

Greenfield, Colin C., and Eliza Lee. 1992. "Government Information Technology Policy in Hong Kong," *Informatization and the Public Sector*, 2: 125–132.

Grove, Andrew S. 1996. *Only the Paranoid Survive: How to Explain the Crisis Points that Challenge Every Company and Career*. New York: Doubleday.

Gurbaxani, Vijay, Kenneth L. Kraemer, John L. King, Sheryl Jarman, Jason Dedrick, K. S. Raman, and Chee-Sing Yap. 1991. "Government as Driving Force Toward the Information Society: National Computer Policy in Singapore," *Information Society*, 7: 155–185.

Hamilton, David P. 1996. "PC Makers Find China is a Chaotic Market," *The Wall Street Journal*, online edition, April 8.

Henderson, Jeffrey. 1989. "Hong Kong: The Making of a Regional Core," in Henderson (ed.), *The Globalisation of High Technology Production: Society, Space, and Semiconductors in the Restructuring of the Modern World*. London: Routledge: 77–117.

Heng, Toh Mun. 1993. "Partnership with Multinational Corporations," in Linda Low, Toh Mun Heng, Soon Teck Wong, Tan Kong Yan, and Helen Hughes (eds.), *Challenge and Response: Thirty Years of the Economic Development Board*. Singapore: Times Academic Press: 121–156.

Hiebert, Murray. 1996. "It's a Jungle Out There," *Far Eastern Economic Review*, (April 25): 58–61.

Hobday, Michael. 1995. *Innovation in East Asia: The Challenge to Japan*. Aldershot: Edward Elgar.

Holyoke, Larry. 1995. "How Toshiba's Laptops Retook the Heights," *Business Week* (January 16): 83.

Hong Kong Census and Statistics Department, *Annual Survey of Industrial Production* (1995).

Hong Kong Census and Statistics Department. 1995. Report prepared for authors.

Hong Kong Productivity Council (HKPC). 1995. *Consultancy Study on Hong Kong's Software Industry*. Hong Kong: Industry Department.

"Is It Time for the Information Appliance?" 1996. *Business Week*, (May 6): 42.

Ishihara, Shintaro. 1991. *The Japan That Can Say No: Why Japan Will Be First Among Equals*. New York: Simon and Schuster.

"Japan Computer Lead Seen." 1990. *New York Times* May 2.

Japan Electronics Industries Development Association (JEIDA). 1996. "Statistical Survey on Software Export/Import, 1995 Results." Tokyo: JEIDA.

Japan Information Processing Development Center (JIPDEC). 1993. *Informatization White Paper*. Tokyo: JIPDEC.

Japan Information Processing Development Center (JIPDEC). 1993. *Japan Computer Quarterly*, 93.

"Japanese Software: More Than Just Fun and Games?" 1993. *Electronic Business Asia* 4 (April): 30–41.

Jeong, Kuk Hwan. and John Leslie King. 1996. "Korea's National Information Infrastructure: Vision and Issues," in Brian Kahin and Ernest Wilson (eds.), *National Information Infrastructure Initiatives: Vision and Policy Design*. Cambridge: MIT Press: 112–149.

Johnson, Chalmers. 1982. *MITI and the Japanese Miracle*. Stanford, Calif.: Stanford University Press.

Johnson, Chalmers. 1989 "MITI, MPT, and the Telecom Wars," in Chalmers Johnson, Laura D'Andrea Tyson, and John Zysman (eds.), *Politics and Productivity: The Real Story of Why Japan Works*. Cambridge, Mass.: Ballinger: 177–240.

Jones, Capers. 1993. *Software Productivity and Quality Today—The Worldwide Perspective*. Carlsbad, Calif.: Information Systems Management Group. Data updated in 1995 in correspondence to authors.

Kahaner, David, and Julian Wu. 1995. "General Remarks About Hong Kong." Tokyo: Asian Technology Information Program.

Kahin, Brian. 1997. "The Internet Business and Policy Landscape," in *The Internet as Paradigm*. Queenstown, Md.: The Institute of Information and Studies: 47–69.

Kahin, Brian, and Ernest Wilson (eds.). 1997. *National Information Infrastructure Initiatives: Vision and Policy Design*. Cambridge: MIT Press.

Kajiwara, Hirokazu. 1993. "Taiwan's Electronics Industry: From an Import Substitution and Export Oriented Industry to a Highly Advanced Industry," in Ryuichiro Inoue, Hirohisa Kohama, and Shujiro Urata (eds.), *Industrial Policy in East Asia.* Tokyo: Japan External Trade Organization: 165–191.

Kim, Linsu. 1997. *Imitation to Innovation: The Dynamics of Korea's Technological Learning.* Boston: Harvard Business School Press.

Kim, Nak-Hieon. 1995. "MIC Unveils Ambitious National Software Policy," *Electronics,* 68, (February 27):3.

Kodama, Fumio. 1995. *Emerging Patterns of Innovation: Sources of Japan's Technological Edge.* Boston: Harvard Business School Press.

Kraar, Louis. 1995. "Acer's Edge: PC to Go," *Fortune* (October 30).

Kraemer, Kenneth L., and Jason Dedrick. 1994. "Payoffs from Investment in Information Technology: Lessons from the Asia-Pacific Region," *World Development,* 22: 1921–1931.

Kraemer, Kenneth L., and Jason Dedrick. 1995. "From Nationalism to Pragmatism: IT Policy In China," *IEEE Computer,* 28: 64–73.

Kraemer, Kenneth L., Jason Dedrick, and Sheryl Jarman. 1994. "Supporting the Free Market: Information Technology Policy in Hong Kong," *The Information Society,* 10: 223–246.

Kraemer, Kenneth L., Jason Dedrick, Chin-Yeong Hwang, Tze-Chen Tu, and Chee-Sing Yap. 1996. "Entrepreneurship, Flexibility, and Policy Coordination: Taiwan's Information Technology Industry," *The Information Society,* 12.

Krugman, Paul. 1994. "Competitiveness: A Dangerous Obsession," *Foreign Affairs,* 73 (March–April): 28–35.

Langlois, Richard N. 1992. "External Economies and Economic Progress: The Case of the Microcomputer Industry," *Business History Review,* 66 (spring): 1–50.

Levin, Mike. 1994. "VTech: Tough Lessons in Going Global," *Electronic Business Asia,* 5 (January): 38–42.

Levy, Brian, and Wen-Jeng Kuo. 1991. "The Strategic Orientation of Firms and the Performance of Korea and Taiwan in Frontier Industries: Lessons from Comparative Case Studies of Keyboard and Personal Computer Assembly," *World Development,* 19: 363–374.

Lichtenberg, Frank R. 1993. "The Output Contributions of Computer Equipment and Personnel: A Firm Level Analysis." Working Paper No. 4540, Cambridge, Mass.: National Bureau of Economic Research.

Magaziner, Ira C., and Mark Patinkin. 1989. "Fast Heat: How Korea Won the Microwave War," *Harvard Business Review* (January–February): 83–93.

Market Intelligence Center/Institute for the Information Industry (MIC/III). 1991. *Taiwan's Personal Computer Industry Report: Hardware/Software Strategies and Trends.* Taipei: MIC/III.

Market Intelligence Center/Institute for the Information Industry (MIC/III). 1995. "Upgrading Taiwan's IT Industry: New Challenges and the Role of International Competition." Taipei: MIC/III, presentation by T. C. Tu.

Market Intelligence Center/Institute for the Information Industry (MIC/III). 1996. "Taiwan's Information Services Industry and Market," *Asia IT Report* (April): 3–11.

Market Intelligence Center/Institute for the Information Industry (MIC/III). 1996. "Taiwan's IT Industry and Market in 1996," *Asia IT Report* (December): 3–11.

Market Intelligence Center/Institute for the Information Industry (MIC/III). 1997. "Taiwan's PC Sector: 1996 Report," *Asia IT Report* (January): 3–8.

Masuda, Yoneji. 1980. *The Information Society as Post-industrial Society*. Bethesda, Md.: World Futures Society.

McKinsey & Company. 1990–1996. *The Report on the Computer Industry* (annual reports). New York: McKinsey & Company.

McWilliams, Gary, Emily Thorton, and Paul M. Eng. 1997. "If at First You Falter, Reboot," *Business Week* (June 30): 81–82.

Meyer, Marc H., and Alvin P. Lehnerd. 1997. *The Power of Product Platforms: Building Value and Cost Leadership*. New York: Basic Books.

Meyer, Marc H., and Michael H. Zack. 1996. "The Design and Development of Information Products," *Sloan Management Review*, 37 (spring): 29–48.

Miller, Arnold. 1993. "Building a Modern Electronics Industry," in Bjorn Wellenius, Arnold Miller, and Carl J. Dahlman (eds.), *Developing the Electronics Industry*. Washington, D.C.: World Bank: 15–28.

Morris, Charles R., and Charles H. Ferguson. 1993. "How Architecture Wins Technology Wars," *Harvard Business Review*, 71 (March–April): 86–96.

Moschella, David C. 1997. *Waves of Power: Dynamics of Global Technology Leadership, 1964–2010*. New York: AMACOM.

Nakahara, Tetsushi. 1993. "The Industrial Organization and Information Structure of the Software Industry: A U.S.–Japan Comparison," Stanford, Calif.: Center for Economic Policy Research.

Nakarmi, Axmi, and Robert Neff. 1994. "Samsung's Radical Shakeup," *Business Week* (February 28): 74–76.

National Computer Board (NCB). 1994. *The Singapore IT Industry Survey Report*. Singapore: NCB.

"NEC Fends Off Foes with Cheap PC." 1995. *Japan Times Weekly International Edition* (January 30–February 5).

Nolan, Richard L., and David C. Croson. 1995. *Creative Destruction*, Cambridge: Harvard Business School Press.

Normile, Dennis. 1996. "Japan Hatches PC War Plan," *Electronic Business Asia*, 7 (June): 38–44.

Noyce, Robert N., and Marcian E. Hoff, Jr. 1981. "A History of Microprocessor Development at Intel," *IEEE Micro*, 1 (February):8–21.

National Science Foundation (NSF). 1993. *Human Resources for Science and Technology: The Asian Region*. Washington, D.C.: NSF.

National Science Foundation (NSF). 1996. *Science and Engineering Indicators, 1996*. Washington, D.C.:NSF.

Organization for Economic Cooperation and Development (OECD). 1994. *Information Technology Outlook: 1994*. Paris: OECD.

Overholt, William. 1995. *The Rise of China: How Economic Reform is Creating a New Superpower*. New York: W. W. Norton and Company.

Petska-Juliussen, Karen, and Egil Juliussen. 1996. *The 8th Annual Computer Industry Almanac*, Glenbrook, Nev: Computer Industry Almanac.

Petzinger, Jr., Thomas. 1997. "Analytical Graphics Waits for Windfall from a Freebie," *Wall Street Journal*, July 25: B1.

Poe, Robert. 1994. "Winds of Opportunity: Change in Japan Blows Business Asia's Way," *Electronic Business Asia*, 5 (April): 40–47.

Poe, Robert. 1993. "Can Fujitsu Reinvent Itself?" *Electronics Business Asia*, 4 (January): 34–41.

Pollack, Andrew. 1996. "Breaking Out of Japan's Orbit," *New York Times*, January 30.

Porter, Michael. 1990. *The Competitive Advantage of Nations*. New York: Free Press.

*Public Affairs Report.* 1995. January 3.

Rapkin, David P., and Jonathan R. Strand. 1996. "Is International Competitiveness a Meaningful Concept?" in C. Roe Goddard, John T. Passe-Smith, and John G. Conklin (eds.), *International Political Economy: State–Market Relations in the Changing Global Order.* Boulder, Colo.: Lynne Rienner: 109–129.

Rappaport, Andrew S., and Shmuel Halevi. 1991. "The Computerless Computer Company," *Harvard Business Review,* 69: 69–80.

Reed. 1991–1997. *Yearbook of World Electronics Data.* Oxford: Reed Electronics Research.

Reich, Robert B. 1991. "Who is Us?" *Harvard Business Review* (January–February): 53–59.

Republic of China. 1991. *Statistical Yearbook of the Republic of China.* Taiwan: Directorate-General of Budget, Accounting and Statistics, Executive Yuan.

Republic of China. 1995. *Taiwan Statistical Data Book, 1995.* Taipei: Council for Economic Planning and Development.

"Riding the Roller Coaster." 1997. *Electronic Business Asia* 8 (June): 37–45.

Roach, Steven S. 1988. *White Collar Productivity: A Glimmer of Hope?* New York: Morgan Stanley.

Robertson, Jack. 1997. "Japanese Share of U.S. Notebook Market Rising," *Electronic Buyers News,* March 14.

Rutkowski, Anthony M. 1997. "The Internet: An Abstraction in Chaos," in *The Internet as Paradigm,* Queenstown, Md: The Institute for Information Studies: 1–22.

Schein, Edgar H. 1996. *Strategic Pragmatism: The Culture of Singapore's Economic Development Board.* Cambridge: MIT Press.

Schware, Robert. 1992. "Software Industry Entry Strategies for Developing Countries: A 'Walking on Two Legs' Proposition," *World Development,* 20: 143–164.

Schware, Robert. 1996. *Prospects for Information Service Exports from the English-Speaking Caribbean.* Washington, D.C.: World Bank.

"Searching for a New Bullet." [Interview with Tadahiro Sekimoto], 1994. *Electronic Business Asia* 5 (August): 47–51.

Select Committee on Science and Technology. 1971. *The Prospects for the United Kingdom Computer Industry in the 1970s,* vol. 1–3. London: Her Majesty's Stationery Office.

"Shooting Stars, Comeback Kids & Also-rans." 1996. *Electronic Business Asia* 7 (July): 32–47.

Singapore Trade Development Board. 1995. *Singapore Electronics Trade Directory.* Singapore: Trade Development Board.

Skillings, Jon, and Rob Guth. 1997. "Asia-Pacific PC Market Leaps 32 Percent in 1996," *IDG China Market News Updates,* www.idgchina.com.

"Sliding Scales." 1996. *The Economist* November 2: 77.

Smith, Lee. 1996. "Hitachi Gliding Nowhere," *Fortune* (August 5): 83.

"Squeeze, Gently." 1996. *The Economist* November 30: 65–66.

Steinmueller, Edward W. 1996. "The U.S. Software Industry: An Analysis and Interpretive History," in David Mowery (ed.), *The International Computer Software Industry.* New York: Oxford University Press.

Stevenson, Mirek J. 1971. " '71 . . . The Year EDP Goes Multinational," *Datamation,* 7, (March 15): 32–36.

Tagliabue, John. 1996. "Why European Computer Makers Flop," *New York Times,* October 7.

Tang, Hung Kei. 1996. "The Ascent of Creative Technology: A Case Study of Technology Entrepreneurship," in Neo Boon Siong (ed.), *Exploiting Information Technology for Business Competitiveness: Cases and Insights from Singapore-Based Organizations*. Reading, Mass.: Addison Wesley.

Takezaki, Noriko. 1997. "Balancing Price With Quality: Japanese PC Makers Have Second Thoughts About Foreign Procurement," *Computing Japan* (March): 18.

Tang, Joy. 1995. "Tradelink Picks HP for EDI Network Project," *Asia Computer Weekly*, 16: 3.

Tyson, Laura D'Andrea. 1991. "They Are Not Us: Why American Ownership Still Matters," *American Prospect* (winter): 37–49.

Umeda, Mochio. 1994. "Failing to Change: The Plight of the Japanese Computer Industry," *Prism*, second quarter.

U.S. Department of Commerce. 1995. *U.S. Global Trade Outlook 1995–2000: Toward the 21st Century*. Washington D.C.: U.S. Department of Commerce, International Trade Administration.

Vogel, Steven. 1996. *Freer Markets, More Rules: The Paradoxical Politics of Regulatory Reform in the Advanced Industrial Countries*. Ithaca, N.Y.: Cornell University Press.

Wade, Robert. 1990. *Governing the Market: Economic Theory and the Role of Government in East Asian Industrialization*. Princeton, N.J.: Princeton University Press.

Wang, P. 1994. "Information Systems Management Issues in the Republic of China for the 1990s," *Information and Management*, 26: 341–352.

Watson, Jr., Thomas J. 1990. *Father, Son, and Co.: My Life at IBM and Beyond*. New York: Bantam.

West, Joel. 1995. "Software Rights and Japan's Shift to an Information Society: Evidence From the 1993–1994 Copyright Revision Process," *Asian Survey*, 35.

West, Joel. 1996. "Utopianism and National Competitiveness in Technology Rhetoric: The Case of Japan's Information Infrastructure," *The Information Society*, 12: 251–272.

West, Joel, and Jason Dedrick. 1997. "The Rise and Fall of the PC-98 Regime: How Architectural Revolution Toppled the Dominant PC Standard in Japan." Irvine, Calif.: University of California, Center for Research on Information Technology and Organizations (CRITO).

West, Joel, Jason Dedrick, and Kenneth L. Kraemer. 1996. "Back to the Future: Japan's NII Plans," in Brian Kahin and Ernest Wilson III (eds.), *National Information Infrastructure Initiatives: Vision and Policy Design*. Cambridge: MIT Press.

Wilson, Drew. 1997. "Locals Rule Home Market," *Electronic Business Asia*, 8 (May): 28.

Wong, Poh-Kam. 1995. "Competing in the Global Electronics Industry: A Comparative Analysis of the Strategy of Taiwan and Singapore." International Conference on the Experience of Industrial Development in Taiwan; Taiwan, National Central University, May 19.

Wong, Poh-Kam. 1997. "Implementing the NII Vision: Singapore," in Brian Kahin and Ernest Wilson (eds.), *National Information Infrastructure Initiatives: Vision and Policy Design*. Cambridge: MIT Press: 24–60.

World Bank. 1993. *The East Asian Miracle: Economic Growth and Public Policy*. New York: Oxford University Press.

Xinhua News Agency. 1996. "High-tech Industry Prospering in Shenzhen," June 11.

Yoffie, David B. 1994. *Strategic Management in Information Technology*. Englewood Cliffs, N.J.: Prentice Hall.

Yoffie, David B. (ed.). 1996. *Beyond Free Trade: Firms, Governments, and Global Competition*. Boston: Harvard Business School.

Yoffie, David B. 1996. "Competing in the Age of Digital Convergence," *California Management Review*, 38: 31–53.

Young, Lewis Y. 1995. "Betting on Chips to Prop Up Consumer Declines," *Electronic Business Asia*, 6 (March): 37–39.

# Index